Contemporary Issues of Economic Development in India

About the Editors

Professor Sebak Kumar Jana is currently Professor of Economics and Head in the Department of Economics with Rural Development, Vidyasagar University, West Bengal, India. Dr. Jana was graduated from Presidency College, Kolkata in 1989 and did his post-graduation in Economics from University of Calcutta in 1991. He obtained M.Phil. and Ph.D. degree in Economics from Jadavpur University, Kolkata. His major area of academic interest includes environmental and resource economics, agricultural economics, rural development and economics of education. He has about seventy publications in Journals and edited books. He has published six books as author or editor including *Tank Irrigation in the Dry Zones in India*, *Education in West Bengal – Looking Beyond Schools*, *Development in Development in Developing Economies (Edited)*. He, as a Principal Investigator, has completed a few research projects funded by ICSSR, UGC and NABARD and IWMI.

Professor Debasish Mondal has joined the Department of Economics, Vidyasagar University, West Bengal, India in 1987 and he is a Professor there since 2008. He is also the Coordinator of the UGC-SAP (DRS-I) Scheme currently run in the Department. His areas of work include economic and econometric analysis with focus on methodologies.

Contemporary Issues of Economic Development in India

Edited by
Sebak K. Jana
Professor of Economics and Head,
Department of Economics with Rural Development,
Vidyasagar University,
Midnapore, West Bengal

Debasish Mondal
Professor of Economics and Former Head,
Department of Economics with Rural Development,
Vidyasagar University,
Midnapore, West Bengal

CONCEPT PUBLISHING COMPANY PVT. LTD.
NEW DELHI-110059

ISBN-13: 978-93-5125-296-2

First Published 2017

Published and Printed by

Concept
Since 1974

Concept Publishing Company Pvt. Ltd.
Regd. Office:
A/15-16, Commercial Block, Mohan Garden,
New Delhi-110059 (INDIA)
T : 25351460, 25351794, *F* : 091-11-25357109
Email : publishing@conceptpub.com
Website: www.conceptpub.com

Cataloging in Publication Data--Courtesy: D.K. Agencies (P) Ltd. <docinfo@dkagencies.com>

Contemporary issues of economic development in India / edited by Sebak K. Jana, Debasish Mondal.

pages cm
Includes bibliographical references and index.
ISBN 9789351252962

1. Economic development—India. 2. India—Economic policy—1991- I. Jana, Sebak Kumar, editor. II. Mondal, Debasish, 1959- editor.

HC435.3.C66 2017 DDC 338.954 23

Preface

Economic development is a dynamic process and issues of development are the most important agenda for the present day society. A good number of issues are throwing up enormous challenges presently in the paths to development of developing countries like India. In this backdrop the Department of Economics with Rural Development, Vidyasagar University, Midnapore, West Bengal had organized a National Seminar on "Contemporary Issues of Economic Development in India" in 2012. The present book is an outcome of this seminar. The book consists of seventeen chapters. The chapters highlight some contemporary issues of economic development in India. The broad areas covered in this volume include impacts of globalization and liberalization and issues of development in social sector, agricultural sector and industrial sector in the context of Indian economy.

Indian economic reforms need to be analysed not literally but in terms of particular strategies employed in 1991 in the context of disintegration of USSR and introduction of liberalisation policies in India since mid-1980s. This epoch in Indian economic policies was the result of dictates by external agencies and not due to popular demand which resulted in a uni-polar world and near-termination of the second and third worlds. The First chapter "Needed Reforms of Indian Economic Reforms" by R.K. Sen has attempted to highlight the negative impacts of the current economic reforms in India during the last two decades and suggested the needed reforms of the ongoing process. Such negative impacts are well-known like neglect of agriculture and related problems like suicide by farmers and food insecurity problems, corporate-led industrialization and perverse forms of growth, growing income inequality and black money, plethora of scams and lack of good governance, negative impacts on environment, decline in Indian values and criminalization of politics, suffering by majority of the people, exposure of inherent contradiction of truncated globalization during the recent global meltdown etc. In this context, there is need to change the current process of economic reforms after the experience of two decades; till then substantial reform is required to the present strategies to impart a human face to the adopted policies even though this may go against the basic principles of market economy. A realistic redefinition of the role of state and its relationship with the market and creation of appropriate institutions to keep the market free to obtain the efficient and optimum allocation of resources for the interest of welfare maximization in economies like India.

The relevant questions that arise in the present context of elementary education in West Bengal are: What are the ways in which the elementary school education is modernized? What are their impacts on Sarva Shiksha Mission (SSM) objectives of 100 per cent access of children, equity, retention and quality education of children? Are the SSM objectives being realized and that to what extent in the era of globalization? What are the major constraints on fulfilment of the SSM objectives? The second chapter entitled "Globalization and Elementary School Education in West Bengal" by S.N. Sau seeks to address these and other relevant questions with reference to the State. It makes an attempt to explore the relationship between elementary school education under SSM and the globalization process in education with special reference to Paschim Medinipur and Purba Medinipur districts of the State.

India has been experiencing a decline in fertility compared to last two decades (*viz.* 1991 and 2001), but the pace of fertility decline does vary across the States. Some major States still has been remaining in the second stage of Demographic Transition; as a result future demographic dividend largely depends on these States. Children aged up to 18 years constitute nearly 45 per cent of India's population. It is obvious that their well-being which could and still can, secure national transformation. How this transformation is possible? The country's contribution to pre-health transition diseases affecting younger people is disproportionately high—23 per cent of world's under 5 mortality is found to exist in India. A similar kind of picture is found in respect of maternal death—20 per cent world's maternal death is occurred in India. Thus, the question of the formation of effective human capital does emerge, since health stock is an important component of endogenous growth model. Gargi Bhattacharya and Sushil Halder in their chapter "Demographic Outcome and Emerging Health Issues in India" discusse intensively all these issues. Keeping in mind the above perspective, first they try to understand the progress of health status in India over time. How far and to what extent the health outcomes do vary across the major states in India? In order to explore the answer to the former questions, different sources of data are used, viz. NFHS (I, II and III), SRS, NSSO, DLHS-RCH (I, II and III). Based on DLHS-RCH key parameters, a comparative inter-district study is carried out in West Bengal. Whether the districts of West Bengal are converging or diverging in respect of the key RCH parameters have been examined with a view to understand health inequality and regional imbalance in West Bengal.

The plight of a child labouring hard may bring forth a lot of pathos and sympathy to a person residing in the modern day First World countries. However, the problem of child labour is a complex phenomenon. It is a conglomeration of economic, social and cultural factors. It cannot be captured within a single model. In the standard rigorous models emphasis is placed on economic aspect of the problem. However, the child labour is not only a phenomenon. It reflects an attitude on the part of the society. It is not at all necessary that a child should be engaged in any gainful activity either partially or fully to bear the brunt of this negative assessment. A qualitative analysis is necessary to capture this attitudinal aspect. The fourth chapter entitled "Problems of Child Labour in India: A Qualitative Approach" by Atanu Sengupta and Manas Ghose addresses the qualitative aspect of this issue—the experiences that a child shares as a labour through selective case studies and qualitative analysis of the sample. These case studies demonstrate that child labour does not always rise from poverty. Also (mere) child schooling and child labour is not exclusive. A child dreams of a bright future, though the social strictures prevent her for achieving the goal.

Education, as the path to social and economic development, plays a prominent role in strengthening human capital. The most critical stage of this is the primary educational level of a child. The principal institutional mechanism for developing human skills and knowledge is the formal educational system. Most developing nations have been led to believe or have wanted to believe that it is the rapid quantitative expansion of educational opportunities which holds the basic key to national development. The more education, the more rapid is the anticipated development. Education is one of the most important services provided by governments in almost every country. This is something, which is very agreeable to most of us, and yet such a scenario seldom meets our eye when it comes to the state of education in India. The Constitution of India enshrines compulsory primary education to all her citizen in the directive principle of State policy. However, inadequate attention is paid to the delivery mechanism of the primary education. This remains a basic Achilles' wheel of the development process in India. In fact this inadequacy has added to injustice and inequality while stunting the prospect of development. In their chapter entitled "Delivery of the Primary Education System in India: A District Level Analysis" Atanu Sengupta and Naibedya Prasun Pal study the primary education system of India, using the district level DISE Statistics. They used several indicators to capture the multi-dimensional aspect of primary education system in India. But thier analysis reveals certain disturbing features. First, the provisional parameters (such as the proportion of schools without building and proportion of single teacher schools) are significantly and negatively correlated with the DEA efficiency score. The policy related parameter (proportion of schools received school development grant) is positively associated with DEA scores. However, two other variables (such as proportion of schools having common Toilet and proportion of schools without black board) are not significantly related though they are negatively correlated. As to the 'blackboard' factor a proportion of it is already explained away by the resource constraint in teachers. This has probably rendered it insignificant. Interestingly, the proportion of trained female to male teacher is positively related with the school performance as indexed by DEA efficiency. However, resource use efficiency (as measured by DEA) indicates wide inter-zonal differences.

The Sixth chapter on "The Interstate Variation of Technical Efficiency of Indian Pharmaceutical Industry: Stochastic Frontier Production Function Approach" by Chandrima Chakraborty and Arpita Ghose examines the extent of technical efficiency (TE) of Indian Pharmaceutical Industry using the Stochastic Frontier Production Function approach employing its State level data as unit of analysis for the period 1983-84 to 2007-08, analyses interstate variation of TE therefrom and also identifies the major determinants of TE for each of the 17 selected major states. The mean technical efficiency level turns out to be 0.1241 for All India and it ranges from 0.0118 to 0.2501 for the sample States. It is found that Maharashtra is the most technically efficient State whereas Bihar is the least. The major determinant of TE score are firm size for All India and also for most of the States like Andhra Pradesh, Assam, Himachal Pradesh, Jammu & Kashmir, Maharashtra, Madhya Pradesh, Orissa, Punjab, Rajasthan and West Bengal, capital-labour ratio for Bihar, Haryana, Karnataka, Kerala and Tamil Nadu and employee per production worker only in case of Gujarat and Uttar Pradesh.

Indian economy has experienced a growth of almost 225 per cent in real national income between 1991-92 and 2009-10, and the per capita real income increase by almost 170 per cent over the same period. Furthermore, annual GDP growth rates between 7 and 9 per cent during the last seven years have added more of a dynamism and buoyancy to the mood of optimism. There was also the evidence of quick and sharp recovery of GDP growth after the deceleration triggered by the global financial and economic crisis. The economy is transiting to a sustainable and higher growth trajectory accompanied by a number of important structural changes in the economy: a sharp rise savings and investment rates, a shift in the source of private savings in the economy away from the household to the corporate sector, the improvement of tax-to-GDP ratio and the dominance of services in growth. The Seventh chapter entitled "Economic Growth and Growth of Employment in India: An Analysis" by Pinaki Das deals with the impact of growth trajectory with these features on the labour market, especially the volume, pattern and nature of employment.

Today, the term 'globalization' has become a 'buzzword' in any economy all over the world. The growing integration of economies and societies all over the universe has been one of the most burning topics in international economics over the past few years. Globalization has many dimensions and has a variety of social, political and economic implications. The Eighth chapter entitled "Impact of Globalization on Economic Growth: Evidence from India" by Sarbapriya Ray, Mihir Kumar Pal and Ishita Aditya Ray attempts to enquire into the fact econometrically whether globalization is a cause of India's economic growth in the long run. More precisely, the chapter tries to find the causal relationship between globalization and economic growth in India. The regression results show that private investment, openness and human resource development have significant positive impact on economic growth *via* GDP growth. Financial integration variable (capital inflow+capital outflow) has negative impact, although not significant, on economic growth and public investment is also having insignificant positive impact on economic growth. Johansen's cointegration procedure showed that all the above-mentioned variables are cointegrated implying these macro-economic variables have long-run equilibrium relationship with economic growth *via* GDP growth. Error-correction model results also supported the cointegration results. They observe that the direction of causality between globalization and economic growth in India is generally bidirectional (causality runs in both directions) excepting a few where it is unidirectional.

The ninth chapter entitled "Impact of Foreign Capital Inflow in the Presence of Employment Subsidy: A Theoretical Analysis" by Anindita Basu (Chowdhury) has compared the domestic rate of return on capital with that of return on international capital. The chapter considers the impact of foreign capital inflow in the presence of employment subsidy in Heckscher-Ohlin-Samuelson type full employment framework. Within this framework, the impact of foreign capital inflow on the output of different sectors and on the level of welfare of the economy has been analyzed. This chapter shows that in the presence of employment subsidy to the manufacturing sector the production of the foreign enclave and agricultural goods sector increases and the production of manufacturing goods sectors decreases due to inflow of foreign capital. This chapter also shows that under some sufficient condition this foreign capital inflow is welfare improving.

In their chapter entitled "Effect of Per Capita Expenditure and Income on Student enrolment in Higher Education" by Jagabandhu Mondal, Ashit Baran Aich and Sanjib Basu examined gross enrolment ratio (GER) which is used as an index of higher education and mentioning some of its drawbacks. Enrollment in higher education is affected by the several factors. There are factors which will push this demand, some of these are: (a) Increased school enrolment, (b) Reduction in dropout rate after 12th grade, (c) Changed labour market arising from globalization, and (d) New inclusive growth through distance education etc. Another important factor that contributes to demand for higher education is the per capita net domestic product (NDP). It is seen that there is a high positive correlation between the gross enrollment ratio (GER) and NDP. Thus, the GER could be increased through an increase of net domestic product which is expected to rise substantially in the coming years.

Nepal is bordering by Republic of India in the South, East and West. India is the main foreign market of Nepalese agricultural products. Agriculture is the means of livelihood, main component of GDP and source of foreign exchange in Nepal. The agricultural products contribute the country's 80 per cent of the total foreign exchange and contribute 39 per cent in GDP approximately. The high value crop or cash crop like ginger is cultivated for local consumption and for earning foreign exchange. More than 60 per cent of the total produced ginger is exported to India as raw (fresh) or dry (*sutho*) form. It is cultivated for commercial purpose in more than two-third districts of the kingdom. This crop is easier to produce because, suitable for wide range of climate and be produced by labour intensive technique. The eleventh chapter entitled "High Value

Crop Production in Neighbouring Country of India: The Case Study of Nepalese Rural Village" by Dil Nath Fuel is based on the cross-sectional data collected through personal interview with the ginger farmers. A Nepalese rural village from the eastern hill was purposively selected for the study. The output of ginger is the endogenous variable and human labour, farmyard manure, bullock labour and seeds of ginger are the explanatory variables. The Cobb-Douglas production function and linear regression model are used to fit the seven models. This chapter analyzes the productivity, production function, responsiveness of inputs to the output, marginal physical productivity, economies of scale, isoquant and isocline of ginger for the study area.

Among the commercial flowers, both in terms of area under cultivation and quantity of production, marigold occupies the first position in West Bengal. The twelfth chapter entitled "Prospects of Marigold Flower Cultivation in East Midnapur District of West Bengal" by Joydev Bera and Sankar Majumdar is an attempt to understand the prospects of marigold flower cultivation by analyzing, (i) the economic feasibility of investment in marigold cultivation and its advantages over other major competing crops; and (ii) its employment generating prospects. The cultivation of marigold flower is very expensive. There is intensive use of human labour and especially family labour in marigold flower cultivation. Surpluses over different cost concepts are quite lucrative. Net return to management for his managerial function for one rupee of investment is significant. There are decreasing returns to scale for all types of cultivators of marigold flower. The prospects of marigold cultivation depend to a large extent on how the different aspects of managerial decisions are tackled by these flower farmers-*cum* entreprenuers. Marigold is a high income generating crop over other competing crops. Labour utilization in marigold cultivation and imputed value of family labour is highest in comparison to all other competing crops. Marigold being a common man's flower has high market demand and in a labour abundant and employment-scarce rural families in our rural areas this marigold cultivation is a good proposition.

Indian economy even after 70 years of Independence is still an agrarian economy. It is found that households with access to irrigation have much less incidence of poverty compared to the households without irrigated land. Rainfed areas in the country still accounts for about 60 per cent of the cultivated area with West Bengal being no exception. Repeated draughts and erratic rainfall have severely affected the livelihood of rural people in these areas. In this backdrop, there is an urgent need to explore the possibilities of sustainable forms of irrigation. Tank irrigation can play a vital role in this direction. Tank irrigation being based on surface water is an environmentally sustainable form of irrigation. The thirteenth chapter entitled "Tank Irrigation in the Dry Zones of West Bengal: A Regional Analysis" by Sebak K. Jana and Amit Das explores the different characteristics of tank irrigation in some dry zones of West Bengal based on primary survey data and attempts to find the factors affecting the productivity of the tank command area and the efficiency of the tanks. The results of the study suggest that different factors like depth of the tank, presence of the association affect the productivity of the tank command area.

Today, India has been facing two most vital problems which are directly related to agriculture, the first one is to meet the swelling demand for food and other agricultural products, and the second is enervating the widespread poverty in rural areas by the ever increasing population. The good performance in agriculture can diminish levels of rural poverty and meet increasing demand of agricultural products (Ahluwalia, 1978). Agricultural productivity is a measure of the efficiency with which inputs are used in agriculture to produce an output. This fourteenth chapter entitled "Agricultural Efficiency and Levels of Development: A Pathway of Food Security for Rural People" by Subrata Kundu deals with the estimation of technical efficiency for a group of cultivators using Stochastic Frontier Production Function approach. The present study is based mainly on cross-section data. The required information meant for the study was collected from the primary source. The primary data on various aspects relating to the inputs of production of the sample farms were collected through the personal interview method using suitably designed pre-tested schedule/questionnaire for the year 2009-10. These sample households were selected from four blocks located in Paschim Medinipore district in West Bengal, India. Blocks were purposively selected since it had varying socio-economic and geographical features. This study reveals that, most of the inputs influence the output and most of the farmers fail to exploit full potential of technology. This study also observed that quality of land influences the level of efficiency whereas increase in the farm size and ownership tends to reduce the efficiency level. However, the sociological factors (caste) have no influence on technical efficiency.

Own revenue of *panchayats* comes from tax and non-tax resources including voluntary contributions. Panchayats' tax receipt as well as voluntary contributions depend on rural people's willingness and capacity to pay, which in turn depends on people's saving and investment. The performances of panchayats in respect of own resource mobilization has, however, not been encouraging. Many government studies, e.g. Government of India (2001), Report of the Eleventh Finance Commission, reports of the State Finance Commission, Status Reports prepared by Department of Rural Development reveal that the performance of most of the States in India regarding own resources mobilization is poor. In this background a few questions that arise are: What is the trend and pattern of own resources mobilization in West Bengal and her districts during the recent years? Is their any significant variation of own resource mobilization across districts of West Bengal? What are the factors that accounted for the variation of own resource mobilization across districts of West Bengal? The fifteenth chapter entitled "Issuses of Own Resources Mobilization of Panchayats: A District Level Study in West Bengal" by Suman Chakraborty seeks to address these and allied questions.

The planned development strategy that Indian planners have been following since 1951 (with the inception of the First Five year Plan) put particular emphasis on rural development. It appears that constructive rural development strategy or initiative was almost absent in India during the pre-Independence period. However, this is not true altogether and this chapter is a modest attempt to show that the approach of Rabindranath Tagore towards rural development or more specifically, rural transformation, that evolved during late nineteenth century was appropriate for a complete transformation of a rural economy from its backward state in many less developed countries including India. His philosophy relating to rural upliftment was broad-based and multi-dimensional, and is still relevant for analyzing the problems of rural development in many less developed and developing countries of the world in the midst of economic globalization. Debashis Mazumdar and Santanu Bisai in their chapter "An Integrated Approach towards Rural Development: Tagore's Philosophy" discuss the ideas of Tagore.

Rabindra *sangeet* is the richest cultural capital of Bengal. Initially, the span of Rabindra *sangeet* was limited to a specific group of listeners, but today the world of music in Bengal witnessess typicallty specially in the spread effect in the sphere of Rabindra *sangeet*. This overwhelming factor gives a boost in the developmental scenario of Bengal music industry. Various factors play contributory role in this process. Role of technology, proliferation of technological equipments such as CD players, iPOD etc. along with intricate involvement of media in every sector of life act as impetus to this extraordinary happening. The 150th birthday celebration of Tagore is undoubtedly the catalytic force in this process of dispersion of Rabindra *sangeet*. Theoretically, social structural approach and Frankfurt school [with special reference to cultural industry] analyse the basic features of Rabindra *sangeet* industry of Bengal. Now, Rabindra *sangeet* has been manifested as an indispensable stuff of the innermost part of human life of the globe. Consequently and very naturally the global music–market cannot sit idle. It has considered Rabindra *sangeet* as one of the most essential cultural commodities and that is why Rabindra *sangeet* has been caught up as a super cultural product in commercial periphery of industry. Major impact of professional growth in the sector of Rabindra *sangeet* industry can be judged quantitatively as well as qualitatively. Consumerism is inseparably linked with mental makeup of modern listeners. Hence, Rabindra *sangeet*, the incomparable inner resource of Bengal, can be simultaneously treated as a part of specific cultural industry. In fine, we cannot ignore the fact that the eternal significance of Rabindra *sangeet* is always with us industrially as well as emotionally to the full brim of the core point of our heart. Susmita Bhattacharya in the final chapter "Development of Rabindrasangeet Industry: A Sociological Study" touches upon these issues.

We acknowledge the assistance of all the persons who have helped us at various levels in publishing this book. We are thankful to the UGC for the financial assistance. We extend our sincere thanks to Professor Ranjan Chakrabarti, Hon'ble Vice Chancellor, Vidyasagar University for his encouragement and kind support to publish this book. We are grateful to all the faculty members of the Department of Economics, Vidyasagar University, Professor Mihir K. Pal, Professor Joydeb Sasmal, Dr. Chandrima Chakraborty, Dr. Pinaki Das, Dr. Sudipta Jha for their valuable inputs and support in this endeavour. We are also thankful to Mr. A. K. Mittal of Concept Publishing Company (P) Ltd. for his suggestions in shaping the book.

Vidyasagar University
Midnapore

Sebak K. Jana
Debasish Mondal
Editors

Contents

Preface v

List of Contributors xvii

1. Needed Reforms of Indian Economic Reforms 1
   Raj Kumar Sen
2. Globalization and Elementary School Education in West Bengal 12
   Sachinandan Sau
3. Demographic Outcome, Utilization of Health Services and RCH Status in India: A State Level Analysis 60
   Gargi Bhattacharya and *Sushil K. Haldar*
4. Problems of Child Labour in India: A Qualitative Approach 101
   Atanu Sengupta and *Manas Ghose*
5. Delivery of the Primary Education System in India: A District Level Analysis 125
   Atanu Sengupta and *Naibedya Prasun Pal*
6. The Interstate Variation of Technical Efficiency of Indian Pharmaceutical Industry: Stochastic Frontier Production Function Approach 150
   Chandrima Chakraborty and *Arpita Ghose*
7. Economic Growth and Growth of Employment in India: An Analysis 164
   Pinaki Das
8. Impact of Globalization on Economic Growth: Evidence from India 184
   Sarbapriya Ray, Mihir Kumar Pal and *Ishita Aditya Ray*

9. Impact of Foreign Capital Inflow in the Presence of Employment Subsidy: A Theoretical Analysis — 201
   Anindita Basu (Chowdhury)
10. Effect of Per-capita Expenditure and Income on Student Enrolment in Higher Education — 217
   Jagabandhu Mandal, Ashit Baran Aich and *Sanjib Basu*
11. High Value Crop Production in Neighbouring Country of India: The Case Study of Nepalese Rural Village — 226
   Dil Nath Fuel
12. Prospects of Marigold Flower Cultivation in East Midnapur District of West Bengal — 251
   Joydeb Bera and *Sankar Majumdar*
13. Tank Irrigation in the Dry Zones of West Bengal: A Regional Analysis — 263
   Sebak K. Jana and *Amit Das*
14. Agricultural Efficiency and Levels of Development—A Pathway of Food Security for Rural People: A Study on Paschim Medinipore District — 282
   Subrata Kundu
15. Issuses of Own Resources Mobilization of Panchayats: A District Level Study in West Bengal — 299
   Suman Chakraborty
16. An Integrated Approach towards Rural Development: Tagore's Philosophy — 314
   Debashis Mazumdar and *Santanu Bisai*
17. Development of Rabindrasangeet Industry: A Sociological Study — 326
   Susmita Bhattacharyya

Index — 344

List of Contributors

Dr. Anindita Basu (Chowdhury), Department of Economics, Mahishadal Raj College, Mahishadal, Midnapore (East), West Bengal, India.

Amit Das, Research Scholar, Department of Economics, Vidyasagar, University, Midnapore.

Prof. Arpita Ghose, Professor, Department of Economics, Jadavpur University, Kolkata, West Bengal.

Prof. Ashit Baran Aich, Director, Professor, Study Centre, Netaji Subhas Open University.

Dr. Atanu Sengupta, Economics Department, Burdwan University, Burdwan, West Bengal.

Dr. Chandrima Chakraborty, Assistant Professor, Department of Economics with Rural Development Vidyasagar University, West Bengal.

Dr. Debashis Mazumdar, Associate Professor, Department of Economics, Bangabasi College.

Dr. Dil Nath Fuel, Senior Lecturer in Economics Education, Tribhuvan University, Nepal.

Gargi Bhattacharyya, Research Scholar, Department of Economics, Jadavpur University, Kolkata.

Ishita Aditya Ray, Bejoy Narayan Mahavidyalaya, Hooghly, West Bengal.

Jagabandhu Mandal, Research Assistant, Netaji Subhas Open University.

Joydev Bera, Research Scholar, Department of Economics, Vidyasagar University, Midnapore (West), West Bengal.

Dr. Manas Ghose, Raja N.L. Khan Women's College, Vidyasagar University, Midnapore (West), West Bengal.

Dr. Mihir Kumar Pal, Professor of Economics, Vidyasagar University, Paschim Medinipore, West Bengal.

Naibedya Prasun Pal, Research Scholar, Economics Department, Burdwan University, Burdwan, West Bengal.

Dr. Pinaki Das, Assistant Professor, Department of Economics with Rural Development, Vidyasagar University, Midnapore (West), West Bengal.

Prof. Raj Kumar Sen, Director, Tagore-Ikeda International Centre for Global Citizenship, and Former Professor and Head, Economics Department, Rabindra Bharati University, Kolkata.

Prof. Sachinandan Sau, Former Professor, Department of Economics, Vidyasagar University, Midnapore (West), West Bengal.

Dr. Sanjib Basu, Former Reader, Department of Economics, North Bengal University and Ex-Principal of K.K. Das College.

Prof. Sankar Majumdar, Professor in Economics, Palli Charcha Kendra, Visva-Bharati University, Santiniketan, West Bengal.

Dr. Santanu Bisai, Assistant Professor, Prasanta Chandra Mahalanobis Mahavidyalaya, Kolkata.

Dr. Sarbapriya Ray, Assistant Professor Shyampur Siddheswari Mahavidyalaya, Howrah, West Bengal,

Dr. Sebak Kumar Jana, Professor in Economics, Department of Economics with Rural Development, Vidyasagar University, Midnapore (West), West Bengal.

Dr. Subrata Kundu, Guest Teacher, Department of Economics, Vivekananda Satabarshiki Mahavidyalaya, Paschim Medinipur, West Bengal.

Dr. Suman Chakraborty, Lecturer, Department of Business Administration, Pailan College of Management and Technology, Kolkata and Research Scholar, Department of Economics with Rural Development, Vidyasagar University, Midnapore (West), West Bengal.

Dr. Sushil K. Haldar, Professor of Economics, Economics Department, Jadavpur University, Kolkata.

Dr. Susmita Bhattacharyya, Assistant Professor, Department of Sociology, Prasanta Chandra Mahalanobis Mahavidyalaya, Kolkata.

1
Needed Reforms of Indian Economic Reforms

Raj Kumar Sen

Indian economic reforms need to be analysed not literally but in terms of particular strategies employed in 1991 in the context of disintegration of USSR and introduction of liberalization policies in India since mid-1980s. This epoch in Indian economic policies was the result of dictates by external agencies and not due to popular demand which resulted in a uni-polar world and near-termination of the second and third worlds. This chapter has attempted to highlight the negative impacts of the current economic reforms in India during the last two decades and suggested the needed reforms of the ongoing process. Such negative impacts are well-known like neglect of agriculture and related problems like suicide by farmers and food insecurity problems, corporate-led industrialization and perverse forms of growth, growing income inequality and black money, plethora of scams and lack of good governance, negative impacts on environment, decline in Indian values and criminalization of policies, suffering by majority of the people, exposure of inherent contradictions of truncated globalization during the recent global meltdown etc. In this context, there is need to change the current process of economic reforms after the experience of two decades; till then substantial reform is required to the present strategies to impart a human face to the adopted policies even though this may go against the basic principles of market economy. A realistic redefinition of the role of state and its relationship with the market and creation of appropriate institutions to keep the market free to obtain the efficient and optimum allocation of resources for the interest of welfare maximization in economies like India.

This chapter is divided in the following sections: 1. Introduction and the perspective of Indian economic reforms; 2. Negative and anti-people impacts of the current reform policies; and 3. Suggested reforms of the reform process for benefit of developing countries like India.

Introduction and the Perspective of Indian Economic Reforms

Indian economic reforms need to be analysed not literally, but in terms of particular strategies employed in 1991 in the context of disintegration of the USSR and introduction of liberalization policy in India since mid-1980s. This epoch in Indian economic policies was the result of dictates by external agencies like the IMF and World Bank in the context of acute BOP and foreign exchange crises when India failed to secure internationally commercial loans due to her downgrading by international credit rating agencies and was compelled to pawn national gold to a foreign country.

This was done by a minority government without any national debate and also not due to popular demand which resulted in a unipolar world dominated by the USA and near termination of the second and third worlds. The neo-liberal capitalism suddenly got the unique opportunity to hold the sway almost throughout the world and India, the habitat of one-sixth of humanity and which was once the one of the leaders of non-aligned movement with Indonesia and Egypt was no exception to it. These economic reforms are also called the NEP—New Economic Policies and followed a U-turn from its declared policies of socialistic pattern of society and commanding heights for the public sector. Initially, it was declared that India is not deviating from the Gandhian path of self-reliance and Nehruwian model of socialism and the newly adopted economic policies will require not more than three years to tide over the then ongoing crisis. There was no change naturally in the preamble of the Constitution of India, which called the country since 1976, 42nd Constitution Amendment, a socialistic one, even though the NEP consisted in its core the LPG strategies (Liberalization, Privatization and Globalization) with structural adjustment. Later, this three-year time period was not only extended to five years, but also we are still continuing the process even after the lapse of two decades. The authorities are now saying that India is now entering into its second generation of economic reforms though nobody told about first generation of it at the beginning in 1991 and some others also talked about the second generation of reforms after the completion of first decade of reform in 2001. It is high time at the beginning of the third decade of this process to consider both positive and negative impacts of this policy because many are comparing the Indian situation now with that of 1991 following the recent decline in her GDP growth rate and downgrading her credit rank by international agencies. As India is not only an economic and demographic giant but also it is unfortunately the habitat of largest number of poor in the world, it is necessary to analyse their impacts on the people as in any economic development process the people are the most important to consider and the welfare of the people should be considered as the most important target of any economic policy. It should also be remembered that though Indian economy is now dominated by neo-liberal capitalism attempting to reach high rates of income growth, the new president of India has rightly pointed out in his inaugural address identifying mass poverty as a major problem and pointing to the failure of trickle down theory of benefits to reduce it at a time when the corporate sector is clamouring for stronger economic reform policies in new areas for improving rate of GDP growth from its current relatively low level. However, they are prescribing such policies like permission of foreign capital in the multi-brand retail trade, disinvestment of public sector enterprises at an accelerated rate, privatization of nationalized banks and entry of private capital in the banking and insurance sectors, adoption of forward trading and future trading in agriculture and other sectors, reform of pension bill, introduction of contract farming, steps to increase exports, reduction of subsidies specially in diesel and LPG cylinders beyond a certain limit and similar other steps. But we shall see later how far these steps, in the name of economic reform will be able to help GDP to grow at a higher rate or will harm the ordinary people further.

Negative and Anti-people Impacts of Current Economic Reforms Policies

As the corporate sector, government experts and mainstream media are constantly clamouring about the beneficial effects of reforms policies, it is necessary for us to investigate at this stage, some of the negative and anti-people impacts of current phase of economic reforms, be they of the second or third generation.

Since, the beginning of economic reforms policies in 1991 in particular and centralized planning strategies since Independence in general, agriculture in India has been neglected. In recent times we observed that though the share of agriculture in GDP has gone down sharply to less than 15 per cent approximately, share of workforce dependent on agriculture did not come down proportionately. Till now more than 60 per cent of the workforce are engaged in agricultural activity indicating that their welfare is gradually falling as they are to depend on a continuously decreasing pie of GDP. Now, the agriculture is becoming gradually corporatized and traditional agriculture has gradually changed in character being export oriented and adopting techniques like contract farming and other types. In the name of second green revolution based on gene technology, farmers are facing new difficulties which led to large number of farmer suicides due to the cultivation of Bt cotton based on terminator seeds. These and other events like production of bio-diesel have resulted into gradual shifting of land from cultivation of food crops to cash crops and this can ultimately lead to food insecurity in India in long-run. The new knowledge based technology under the second green revolution has also led to this changing type of Indian agriculture in a more accentuated manner.

Not only the nature of agriculture but also the pattern of industrialization has undergone sea changes since economic reforms. Our textbook knowledge of perfect competition consisting of large number of buyers and sellers with free entry and exit has changed into a different type of industrialization led by large corporate houses in place of the traditional entrepreneurs who had like any individual buyer no influence on the prevailing price level. The benefit of competitive market on which the prescribed neo-liberal policy depends are now completely lost in this new set-up which tends to control the market in a monopolistic form. In fact the corporate-led industrial policy has shifted its focus gradually from manufacturing into agriculture and mining. In this process they are concentrating their efforts in the mineral rich central India which is also the traditional habitat of different tribals of our country. The new strategies have led ousting the tribals from their habitat which led to the emergence of new paradoxical terminologies like development oustees. In fact our experiences since Independence have shown that as a consequence of the so-called development projects including big dams the tribals have suffered disproportionately and had to face the consequences of different adverse forms of economic growth like ruthless growth, voiceless growth and rootless growth. All these combine together with the situation of jobless growth which India had to experience in the first half of the present decade, has led to a situation which can be termed as hopeless or futureless growth specially for the tribals for whom development has become almost synonymous with displacement. This increase in menace of development oustees has led to the spread of extremism and terrorism in most of the mineral rich districts of India which are now called as the red-corridor. The lack of development of the tribals and their alienation from the government policy and consideration of the problems of extremism purely as law and order problem has created complacences and situation is gradually going out of control.

Our experience of two decades of economic reforms has gradually exposed the basic contradictions of the LPG strategies. For illustration let us consider the policy of liberalization and privatization which always try to argue that it is due to the government control and public sector units we observed a plethora of corruption. But with the decline of the public sector since 1991 we unfortunately observed a tsunami of scams to such an extent that the present Government of India has been termed as the most corrupted Government the country has seen so far. It was further argued that the state should withdraw itself from the economic affairs and Government has no business in business. But we observed that the withdrawal of State from the economic scene has led to more and more corrupt practices as listed under the sins of privatization by the HDR 1995 have come to the forefront.

We shall come to the other contradictions of economic reform strategies in the latter part of this chapter. It was expected that due to liberalization gradually the corruption will be reduced in India as it was believed widely that corruption arises due to excess control of the State and the source of corruption will go with the reduction of controls. But in reality the number of scams have increased under reforms to such an extent that the present Government has been mentioned sarcastically as the scam vending machine. Economic reform has opened with the share market scam by Harshad Mehta which was initially presumed to be the success of reforms policies in terms of rapid economic growth. The latest of the scams is also the greatest one which took place in the allocation of coal sector when the present Prime Minister was in charge of the Coal Ministry. The CAG, which is a Constitutional Authority of the Government of India has estimated the loss to the extent of Rs. 1,86,000 crore and the paradox of situation is that the Government itself is now challenging the calculation of the CAG. The situation has deteriorated to such an extent that the opposition demanded the resignation of the Prime Minister and the leader of the opposition has openly alleged that a huge amount of this loss has gone to the coffers of the ruling Congress Party and the Prime Minister was not allowed to place his address in the Parliament. In fact the lack of good governance has become so evident in our country that not the rich countries of the World like U.S.A. and Japan, but one of the poor countries like India has topped the list of black money holders in the Swiss Banks and similar other institutions in the foreign countries. In spite of repeated popular demand to bring back such money in our country the Government is reluctant to take any effective action in this matter and also not disclosing the list of the black money holders even when this is known to them. It has been also believed that India's level of GDP can go up considerably if this huge amount can be restored and utilized in proper manner.

Besides it has been further observed that during the last two decades of economic reforms, there has been unprecedented growth of wealth and inequality in the economy. This means that whatever growth of income took place in the economy during this period, was concentrated only in the hands of a few and did not spread in favour of the ordinary masses. On the one hand this signifies that there has been an utter failure of the trickle down theory of additional income to the bottom level and on the other hand also the neglect of distribution aspect in the economy which is one of the primary area of concern in a state which professes welfare to the people. Moreover, there has been no signal that this additional income as been ploughed back to the domestic economy as evident from the rapid increase in the black money to a Ministry group of people and transported to foreign banks following the advantage of ongoing globalization leading to free outflow of finance and capital. It is a really paradoxical situation that the Preamble of the Constitution of India describes our country still as a socialist one.

It is quite natural that current nature of partial or truncated globalization has led to disadvantage of Indian economy which is a labour surplus one and the present globalization does not allow free mobility of labour. Naturally, whatever benefit of globalization that took place in recent years are naturally concentrated in the capital intensive high income countries who could obtain the benefits of globalization process working in their favour.

We may mention here also a few non-economic aspects of the effects of economic reforms on the Indian economy during the last two decades. We can point out in this connection there has been a number of negative impacts on environment such as the harmful effects on environment due to degradation of environmental laws. India being a mega-biodiversity region, relaxation of environmental laws will harm through opening up of hither to restricted wildlife sanctuaries to industries and opening up of remote areas so far restricted to foreign tourists increasing the risk of bio-piracy and damaging the fragile environment.

While everybody attempts to highlight the fact that Indian economy has entered into high trajectory of growth, it cannot be forgotten at the same time that there has been immiserisation of majority of people also. This has been amply verified by the Arjun Sengupta Report that during 2001-2005 nearly 77 per cent of the Indian people could not spend a daily expenditure of more than Rs.20 only for their living. The controversy over the definition of poverty line in recent years also shows the casual official approach to the problem of poverty and also to conceal the depth and breadth of this problem as far as possible.

Some people are of the opinion that some of the non-economic effects of economic reforms are more serious than their economic counterparts. In this context we may refer to the decline of Indian values and rapid spread of the Western culture. In particular, the craze to present women as commodities has led to rapidly increasing violence against them in the society. Considering the Western practice of giving bribes as speed money to facilitate transactions has prompted some of the important authorities in India to suggest to take steps to regularize bribes in the society. While corruption is rampant in the Indian society since the ancient days, such statements usually lead to social acceptance of economic crimes beyond their tolerable limits. This is often expressed in terms of criminalization of politics on the one hand and politicization of economics in every sphere. This has been clearly pointed out how the number of MP and MLAs in the India's Parliament and legislatures with criminal charges is swelling at an accelerated rate.

While the economic reform started in 1991 it was said that there is no other alternative that this, popularly called in short as TINA. After two decades of observing the impacts now, we may say that this is also a TINA of a different type that is "this is no alternative". It is now high time we should go for the reforms of present economic reforms which we shall go for elaboration in the next section of the article.

Suggested Reforms of the Reforms Process for Developing Countries like India

It has been now clear that it is really a myth that the state has no role in the present system of market dominated growth process considering the adverse impacts of the reform process. The Government of India has declared many times that the reform process should possess a human face and specially during the Eleventh and Twelfth Five Year Plans the main focus of these plans have been to ensure that the growth process must be an inclusive one. Perhaps this has been declared to meet the criticism that during the reform process only a small portion of the population was benefited and the vast majority of the population could not enjoy any benefit. However, such objectives require the active intervention of the state and the market automatically cannot ensure such situation. In fact, it is well known from the point of view of radical humanists that a market cannot remain free if it is allowed to operate freely. On the other hand, if it is allowed to operate freely then there is every chance that a free market will be degenerated into oligopoly or even monopoly. Hence, the duty of the state will be to take necessary steps to keep the market free so that the benefits of competitive market can reach the people. Only in this manner a human face of the reform process can be ensured and also the benefits may percolate to everybody leading to an inclusive growth. Hence, the society should adopt to assign proper role to the state to monitor reform process in a continuous manner.

It is also necessary to create proper institutions to reduce corruption and to keep the market competitive as far as possible. It is true that just as perfect competition is an utopia, similarly, it is also not possible to reduce corruption to a zero level. In fact, in India corruption is an age old practice recognized by even Kautilya in the ancient days when it was admitted that it is impossible to prevent public officials to take bribes just as it is impossible to prevent the fish from drinking water. We have already noted that it is a false premise that corruption is due to mainly controls and a slackness of such controls instead of reducing corruption has led to a tsunami of scams in India since the origin of the reform process. The overall influence of corrupt practices is so severe and strong that the Government of India could not enact Lokpal Bill to overview public activities during the last three years and also has been unable to adopt positive steps to restore black money from foreign banks even when they have given the names of such account holders to the government for some time. It is quite clear that as an influence of widespread and massive corruption at every nook and corner of the economy sincere efforts of the Government get diluted and flagship programmes like MGNREGA could not deliver the benefits and achieve the target. If the market capitalism has to be successful then all attempts should be made very rigorously that a competitive market should be ensured as far as possible and benefits reach the people at large.

Since, the publication of the seminal article by Collin Clerk in 1940s, it is clear that world is divided mainly in two groups of countries, namely rich and poor. But the problem since then is that the rich countries are becoming richer and poor countries are poorer. The divergence between average standard of living and consumption has become so clear over time that the poor countries find it extremely difficult to reach the level of countries like UK and USA in the foreseeable future. Not only between the countries but also between the different income classes of the same country like India the divergence is increasing by leaps and bounds over time. We can get an empiricial idea of such growing inequalities from the statistics available from World Development Reports published by World Bank how the ratio between the countries with highest and lowest GDPs of the world has gone up substantially between 1990 and 2010. In fact it is necessary for every country to reduce income and wealth inequality within tolerable limits. Otherwise it is quite likely that high income group of countries or people will control the economy to their advantage and not to serve the interest of the common people.

Of course, it is quite difficult for politicians to get themselves free from the clutches of big capital but unless they are able to do so it is quite likely that things will go out of control of the authorities. A natural corollary of the increasing income and wealth inequalities in a country is the inability to reduce the poverty rapidly particularly in a country like India which has become the habitat of maximum member of poor in the world. It is also necessary to define poverty in a realistic manner and poverty should not mean an expenditure level just enough to get food to keep body and soul together. In this context we may mention the ridiculous level of poverty defined as Rs. 28 and Rs. 32 per day in rural and urban areas respectively necessary to cross the level of poverty line while spending lakhs of rupees to renovate the toilets in the Planning Commission or to serve in official parties plates at the rate of Rs. 7,000 only. It is also true that the most effective antidote to poverty is a creation of productive employment through agro-based industries so that people depending on agriculture may get a larger pie of the GDP to avoid the poverty trap. In India most of the poverty is an ecological poverty and therefore, its reduction through appropriate schemes like MGNREGA can also improve the environment and ecology of the country.

While discussing economic reforms we often forget that one of the most important component of it, namely, globalization is not a complete or full-fledged one. It is serving the interest of the rich countries by ensuring free flow of finance and capital, but working against the interest of the developing countries which are usually the labour surplus ones by not allowing the free movement of labour. Unfortunately, the developing countries are not at all vocal in claiming to convert the globalization process into a full-fledged one from its present truncated form and change or modifying the rules of WTO in an appropriate manner. The original target of globalization to enhance world trade in such a manner that this will ensure prosperity to every country of the world can be ensured only when the globalization process can operate in its full form.

It is also observed that for a number of reasons the developing countries are suffering from gradually increasing danger of food insecurity and also jobless growth. One basic reason behind such situation is the neglect of agriculture and slackening of investment in this sector specially to implement irrigation and lowering of the dependency on rainfall (till now much less than 50 per cent of the total arable area is irrigated) and in spite of its impressive growth rates over time, our economy is still dependent on the blessings of Lord Indra for a good rainfall (as mentioned in Union Budget 2011-12). It is a fact that in the name of irrigation India is tapping the wrong sources. By giving emphasis on big dams it is submerging huge areas of lands and forests and creating millions of development oustees mainly among the ST and SC people and on the other hand creating arsenic pollution through over dependence on ground water irrigation. We are simply neglecting small and tank irrigation including rain-water harvesting which was practised in different parts of our country not only since time immemorial but also in several areas (e.g., in Ralegaon Siddhi village demonstrated by Anna Hazare) even in present days. This may lead not only to food security but also to employment security for the ordinary people who are suffering from the paradox of high growth but falling employment.

One of the main reasons that why India is facing a situation in 2012 similar to 1991 is the falling share of industrialization over time. It is now well known that India's high growth story is mainly service-led and not dependent on the growth of real sectors, namely, agriculture and industry. But it is a known fact that a country's growth cannot be sustained for long without the growth of its real sectors. One of the main reasons of India's current situation is that its original process of entrepreneur based competitive industrialization is becoming substituted by corporate-led activities mostly concentrated not in industry, but in mining and agriculture (activities like contract farming) and activities in SEZ and similar other areas. It is also leading to non-economic effects like spread of terrorism and extremism in the red corridor districts in tribal dominated states of Eastern and Central India and large scale involuntary migration of tribals and untold atrocities by security forces on her own citizens in the name of law and order. It is extremely and urgently important that this nature of industrialization should be controlled for the sake of the country itself and to protect the people from the evil effects of various perverted forms of growth process being experienced at present (like jobless growth we are also experiencing ruthless and voiceless growth).

In this context it may be mentioned that the authorities in India are giving focus to income only approach for our development process. Hot debates are often heard above the changes of the rate of growth either in the overall GDP or in its sectors. As we have already noticed that the targeted policy of trickle down theory of growth has already failed miserably not only since the beginning of the planning process in the 1950s, but also more so during the period of economic reforms. Naturally, in this context simple acceleration of economic growth will not be sufficient, but it is necessary to complement with emphasis on proper distribution in a people friendly manner. India is a country with abundant natural resources and blessed with a large number of rivers and water bodies. She is also a land of mega bio-diversity with long coastal areas and lofty mountains. Her rich natural resources have drawn plunderers from time immemorial and it is necessary that Government of India should protect them by adopting people friendly strategy so that the contradiction of rich land with poor people can be removed for ever.

The chapter is based on the Key-note paper presented in the V.U. Departmental Seminar, 2012.

REFERENCES

Alternative Economic Survey, (2010), *Two Decades of Neo-Liberalism*, Daanish Books, Delhi.

Sen, Raj Kumar, (2012), "The Negative Impacts of Indian Economic Reforms", Parvesh K. Chopra (ed.) *Development Macroeconomics, Global Issues and Human Development*, Wisdom Publications, UK.

Sen, Raj Kumar, (2013), "Two Decades of Economic Reforms in India" A. Karmakar and S. Pan (eds.), *Two Decades of Economic Reforms in India*, Regal Publication, New Delhi.

2
Globalization and Elementary School Education in West Bengal

Sachinandan Sau

Introduction

The world is fast becoming a global village, a metaphor that is often invoked to depict global interdependence and the increasing interaction among and the integration of economic activities of human societies around the World (Ajayi, 2001). In concrete terms, globalization is the intensification of cross-border trade and increased financial and foreign direct investment flows as well as spread of cultural and educational ideas among nations, promoted by rapid advances in and liberalization of communication and information technology (Islam, 1999 and Aninat, 2002). Thus, globalization conjures the picture of a borderless world with greater economic and cultural integration that enhances the living standards and quality of living of people across the globe. Developing countries take recourse to external funding in order to meet its development challenges. Globalization increases the dependence of developing countries on foreign capital. It is more than the free interplay of market forces since economic questions like increasing inequality as consequent on globalization cannot be divorced from social issues like spread and quality of education. Access to credits is granted to developing countries for development under strict conditionalities. There is also anxiety that the sovereignty of states is at stake as globalization appears to question their rights to independent decision-making (Conwuka and Eguavoen, 2007).

It may be noted in this context that globalization, in contrast to internationalism as held and propounded by educationists and philosophers like Rabindranath Tagore, is a process to integrate a country including its economy and society with the global process, and that aims at maximization of global welfare. School elementary education as a social process is attempted to be integrated in the global process of education where private motives including profit maximization play supreme over social welfare maximization. Neo-liberalism becomes the dominant philosophy leading to the distortion of social values, value education and quality education in an underdeveloped country like India. The elementary school education in West Bengal, a constituent state of India, is also influenced in the globalization process of education in terms of both contents and methods of elementary education. The State Government has adopted a variety of initiatives including infrastructure development under the Sarva Shiksha Mission (SSM) being financed both internally and externally under the impact of globalization. Growth of private schools and private tuition has also accelerated while government-managed school elementary education has been modernized in tune with the globalization process. The quantitative expansion in elementary school education which is emphasized in the globalization era, however, has not been corresponded by qualitative improvement of education of children, rather the latter is seen to be deteriorating in recent years in many States of India including West Bengal in contrast to the general expectation that quantitative expansion would lead to quantitative improvement.

The relevant questions that arise in the present context are: What are the ways in which the elementary school education is modernized? What are their impacts on SSM objectives of 100 per cent access of children, equity, retention and quality education of children? Are the SSM objectives being realized and that to what extent in the era of globalization? What are the major constraints on fulfilment of the SSM objectives? The present note seeks to address these and other relevant questions with reference to West Bengal. It makes an attempt to explore the relationship between elementary school education under SSM and the globalization process in education with special reference to Paschim Medinipur and Purba Medinipur districts of the State.

The rest of this note is planned as follows: Section 2 discusses the issue of education for all. Section 3 discusses the initiatives and interventions as well as expenditure pattern under the SSM. Section 4 deals with the supply side facilities being developed as outcomes of state interventions in elementary education as a sequel to the globalization process. Section 5 analyses the learning achievement of children and Section 6 discusses the factors that explain the same. The last Section, i.e. Section 7 summarises the discussion made earlier and makes concluding observations.

Elementary Education for All

The United Nations Organization adopted Millennium Development Goals including 'Education for All' in 2000. India as a member of this international organization initiated in 2001 Sarva Shiksha Abhiyan (SSA), later known as Sarva Shiksha Mission (SSM) as a comprehensive and integrated national flagship programme for Universalization of Elementary Education (UEE) in a mission mode in the perspective that the country earlier adopted and experimented with Literacy Mission during the late twentieth century, but to little success. The SSM sets, four goals, namely improved access, equity and retention (Goals 1, 2 and 3) and also improved learning outcomes (Goal 4). SSA ensures that every child with special needs, irrespective of the kind, category and degree of disability, is provided meaningful and quality education. Hence, SSA has adopted a zero rejection policy. This means that no child having special needs should be deprived of the right to education. Under Integrated Education for Disabled Children special attention is to be given to education of children with special needs (CWSN) with an objective to integrate the handicapped with the general community at all levels as equal partners, to prepare them for normal growth and to enable them to face life with courage and confidence. Integrated Education for the CWSN proposed to provide educational opportunities for the disabled children in common schools, to facilitate their retention in the school system.

Bridging gender and social category gaps in elementary education is one of the main goals of SSA. We have already made significant headway in bridging gender and social category gaps in terms of numbers. Large numbers of girls and children from disadvantaged groups and weaker sections are enrolled in schools today. However, the different ways in which exclusion is manifested have not been sufficiently addressed across the components of children's participation, retention, achievement and completion of elementary education. This makes exclusion the single most important challenge in universalizing elementary education.

The Right of Children to Free and Compulsory Education (RTE) Act, 2009 in different sections makes reference to gender and social inclusion both explicitly and implicitly. Some of the relevant provisions are: no discrimination against children from disadvantaged groups and weaker sections on any grounds; inclusion of women in school monitoring committees; provision of good quality education that includes equity issues, curriculum development in conformity with Constitutional stipulations; training, enrolment in age appropriate classes (which will largely apply to girls, especially from the disadvantaged communities). There is a need to consider retention an equity issue, as SC, ST, Muslim Girls are vulnerable, and most likely to dropout. In the context of RTE the gender and social disadvantage must become integral to concerns of quality and equity. Gender and social inclusion, as a cross cutting issue, should be viewed as an integral and visible part of the quality agenda.

Many initiatives have been taken in West Bengal to achieve the SSA's four goals of 100 per cent enrolment, 100 per cent retention, equity and quality of education for all children. Paschim Banga Sarva Shiksha Mission (PBSSM) under the guidance of School Education Department, Government of West Bengal implements the SSM programme. Financing SSM is made from both internal and external sources including World Bank and DFID of the UK. The SSA Joint Review Missions (2010, 2011 and 2012) comprising the representatives of India, the UK, the World Bank reviewed the progress made by the State in implementing SSA and the results with respect to the overarching goals of SSA, including access, retention, equity and quality. They put quality in the forefront of the entire review of SSA. It is done on the belief that quality is now one of the most important factors leading not only to improved learning outcomes but also improved access, equity and retention.

The expansion of elementary education under Sarva Shiksha Mission in West Bengal has been spectacular. The districts of the State have achieved almost 100 per cent enrolment and about 100 per cent retention. The equity and quality aspects of elementary education under Sarva Shiksha Mission, however, do not progress satisfactorily. The Pratichi (India) Trust during the fieldwork for the study conducted by them and also in a parent-teacher workshop organized by it expressed major concerns as regards quality of education in the primary schooling system. Children tend to learn little in primary school and largely depend on private tuition which places a significant additional financial burden on parents even when the actual school education is ostensibly free.

The contribution of education to economic growth is, however, widely recognized. Innumerable research studies have quantified the contribution of education to the economic growth of nations of the world. The percentage share of education in the economic growth ranges between 0.8 per cent in Mexico and 15.6 per cent in Argentina. In India the contribution was estimated to be 6 per cent.[1]

Initiatives and Interventions under SSM

SSM is now considered a major government initiative to universalize quality elementary education in a mission mode through district-based, decentralized, context-specific planning and implementation strategies. The grants released in West Bengal under the SSM are utilized by the office of the Paschim Banga Sarva Shiksha Mission (PBSSM) and the offices of the Sarva Shiksha Mission of the districts.

Distribution of approved budget of Rs. 4,36,596.28 lakh under the PBSSM by head and activity during 2010-11 showed that teachers' salary constituted the largest component followed by civil works, interventions under CWSN, teaching learning equipment, maintenance management and MIS, Learning equipment programme and uniform. The percentage of utilization of funds was highest in school grants followed by free textbook, teachers' grant and uniform during 2010-11. Distribution of approved budget of Rs. 4,98,056.63 lakh under Paschim Banga Sarva Shiksha Mission (PBSSM) by head and activity during 2011-12 also shows that teachers' salary constituted the largest component followed by civil works, teachers' training, free textbook, maintenance management and MIS.

Teachers' salary payment constituted 45 per cent share during 2011-12 followed by civil works (33.54%), these two together accounting for 79 per cent of total SSM approved budget while the other 19 heads/activities comprised only the rest 21 per cent of the approved budget. These two heads of activities in terms of expenditure made out of approved budget accounted for over 80 per cent of the total expenditure. This shows how less important are the other SSM activities in terms of both approved budget and expenditure. Again, percentage of expenditure or utilization of funds/investment largely varied across the activities, which reflected the pattern of implementation of the SSM projects in financial terms. The percentage of utilization of funds was highest in school grants followed by maintenance teachers' grant and free textbook during 2011-12 while that was as low as 6 per cent in teaching learning equipment and 36.2 per cent in research and evaluation (*see* Table 2.1). This is quite evident while the frequency distribution of utilization of SSM approved funds is presented.

Frequency distribution of activities under SSM in West Bengal by percentage of expenditure achievement during 2011-12 shows that the lowest percentage of utilization of SSM funds (5 to 20%) was done in two activities, namely teaching learning equipment and block resource centre to be led by 5 activities, namely cluster resource centre, teachers' training, research and evaluation, learning enhancement programme and NPEGEL where the percentage of utilization of funds varied between 20 and 50. Other activities showed satisfactory and some activities excellent fund utilization.

Table 2.1: Percentage of Financial Achievement in West Bengal under PBSSM 2011-12

SSM Heads/Activities	Approved Budget (Rs. crore)	Percentage share	Expenditure (Rs. crore)	Percentage share	Percentage of utilization
Teachers Salary Payment	2250.81	45.19	1313.79	44.02	58.37
Teachers Grant	18.51	0.37	17.05	0.57	92.14
Block Resource Centre (BRC)/ UBRC	53.45	1.07	10.25	0.34	19.18
Cluster Resource Centres	62.57	1.26	26.25	0.88	41.97
Teachers Training	120.84	2.43	42.65	1.43	35.30
Free Text Books	121.47	2.44	107.38	3.60	88.41
Interventions for CWSN (IED)	81.02	1.63	58.64	1.96	72.39
Civil Works	1670.34	33.54	1144.68	38.36	68.53
Teaching Learning Equipment	46.15	0.93	2.66	0.09	5.77
Maintenance Grant	54.94	1.10	52.79	1.77	96.1
School Grant	42.31	0.85	42.02	1.41	99.3
Research and Evaluation	10.35	0.21	3.74	0.13	36.2
Management and MIS	113.81	2.29	59.54	2.00	52.32
Learning Enhancement Programme (LEP) (P & UP)	64.16	1.29	13.93	0.47	21.72
ECCE	2.00	0.04	1.54	0.05	77.28
Girls Education	3.00	0.06	2.74	0.09	91.41
SC/ST	2.00	0.04	1.64	0.05	82.33
Community Training	37.77	0.76	19.67	0.66	52.10
Total of SSA (Districts)	4886.38	98.11	2950.39	98.86	60.38
State Project Office	49.37	0.99	12.65	0.42	25.63
SSA Total (including SPO and RBRSSM)	4935.75	99.10	2962.92	99.28	60.03
NPEGEL	8.58	0.17	3.47	0.12	40.48
KGBV	36.25	0.73	18.27	0.61	50.41
TOTAL (SSA+NPEGEL+KGBV)	**4980.57**	**100.00**	**2984.35**	**100**	**59.92**

Source: Office of the Paschim Banga Sarva Shiksha Mission.

Supply Side Facilities and Outcomes of State Interventions

Paschim Banga Sarva Shiksha Mission has played a key role in the development of physical infrastructure at the school level, which is an important determinant of the progress in respect of school elementary education. We discuss here development of physical infrastructure by type in West Bengal. The physical infrastructure includes new set-up (NSB)—primary and upper primary schools, additional classrooms (ACRs), CLRC, CRC, toilets, drinking water facilities, NPEGEL and KGBV. Items of civil works under SSM in West Bengal expanded over years in order to expand multiple facilities for development of elementary education of the State. Major constraints identified include problems for land availability for new set-up schools, management problems at the school level, absence of any external agency and the inadequacy of the official staff to overview and monitor the progress of civil works.

Sarva Shiksha Mission inverventions have resulted in high enrolment ratio (GER and NER) of children at both primary and upper primary levels in both the districts under our study. The gross enrolment ratio of children was 99 or above for all blocks of Paschim Medinipur and Purba Medinipur districts at the primary level during 2009-10 while it was below 99 per cent for all blocks of Purba Medinipur district and 99 per cent or above for most of the blocks of Paschim Medinipur district (Table 2.2).

Table 2.2: Frequency Distribution of Blocks and Municipality by Gross Enrolment Ratio (%) of Primary and Upper Primary Children, 2009-10

GER (%)	*Primary*		*Upper Primary*	
	Paschim Medinipur	*Purba Medinipur*	*Paschim Medinipur*	*Purba Medinipur*
Below 99.00	0	0	11	25
99.00-99.99	29	27	18	0

Source: Office of the Sarva Shiksha Mission.

Net enrolment ratio was 80 per cent and above for most of the blocks and municipalities of Paschim Medinipur district at both primary and upper primary levels while it was 70 per cent and above for most of the blocks and municipalities of Purba Medinipur district (Table 2.3).

Majumdar and Rana (2012) also observed that significant progress has been made in near universalizing enrolment at the primary level.

The Gender Parity Index for both Paschim Medinipur and Purba Medinipur districts shows gender and social inclusion in respect of enrolment and retention. A general improvement in the Gender Parity Index (GPI) is observed at upper primary level (from 0.91 in 2008-09 to 0.92 in 2009-10), while at primary level it is 0.94.

Table 2.3: Frequency Distribution of Circles by NER (%) of Primary and Upper Primary Children

NER (%)	*Primary*		*Upper Primary*	
	Paschim Medinipur	*Purba Medinipur*	*Paschim Medinipur*	*Purba Medinipur*
60.00-69.00	2	9	10	4
70.00-79.99	8	13	7	22
80.00 and above	27	8	27	4
Total	**37**	**30**	**37**	**30**

Source: Office of the Sarva Shiksha Mission.

Around 17 per cent of Muslim children to total children in Purba Medinipur district and 11 per cent in Paschim Medinipur district at the primary level were enrolled during 2008-09 and 2009-10. The percentage of upper primary Muslim boys and girls children to total boys and girls children increased in both the districts and in West Bengal as a whole during 2008-09 to 2009-10. Percentage of newly set-up upper primary schools located in the minority concentrated blocks (MCBs) in Paschim Medinipur district was about 17 while it was about 5 in Purba Medinipur district as against 58 per cent in West Bengal as a whole. Percentage of ACRs in MCBs to total ACRs in Purba Medinipur district was 2.91 and in Paschim Medinipur 6.50 as against 60.54 in West Bengal as a whole. Percentages of enrolment of both SC and ST children to total children were higher than their respective shares in total population and the enrolment percentages recorded increase during 2009-10 to 2010-11 at primary school level. In upper primary schools also percentage of enrolment of SC children during 2009-10 was higher than the share of SCs in total population in both Purba Medinipur district and Paschim Medinipur district. But during 2010-11 while percentage of enrolment in Purba Medinipur district was higher that was lower in Paschim Medinipur district. Strikingly, percentage of enrolment of ST children in upper primary schools during 2009-10 was lower than the population percentage in both Purba Medinipur district and Paschim Medinipur district and West Bengal as a whole.

In order to make the teaching learning process attractive, delightful and scientific at the upper primary level computer aided learning has been introduced in districts. During 2010-11 in Purba Medinipur district 35 schools were covered under CAL programme while in Paschim Medinipur district the number was 23.

About 95 per cent of CSWN were enrolled in formal schools under Purba Medinipur and Paschim Medinipur districts in 2010-11 as against 81 per cent in West Bengal as a whole. In Paschim Medinipur district 62 per cent of schools were made barrier free while it was 81 per cent in Purba Medinipur district and 82 per cent in West Bengal as a whole. Above 95 per cent of the CWSN identified in blocks and municipalities in Paschim Medinipur district have been enrolled in schools. In all the municipal towns 100 per cent of CWSN identified have been enrolled in schools. In Paschim Medinipur district 45.82 per cent of teachers have been trained through annual inclusive education (IE) training while it was only 0.04 per cent for 90-day training.

There was commendable improvement in retention rate of children in primary schools of Purba Medinipur district from 65.89 per cent to 69.69 during 2007-08 to 2009-10, but there was deterioration of the same from 71.74 per cent to 70.39 per cent during this period in Paschim Medinipur district. There was, however, substantial disparity across blocks and municipalities in both Paschim Medinipur and Purba Medinipur districts. At the upper primary level there was also commendable improvement in retention rate of children in schools of both Paschim Medinipur and Purba Medinipur district (from 46.72% to 72.50% and 61.64% to 75.41% respectively) during 2007-08 to 2009-10. There was also substantial disparity across blocks and municipalities in both Paschim Medinipur and Purba Medinipur districts. Transition rate of 82.18 per cent was higher in Purba Medinipur district than that (66.82%) in Paschim Medinipur district.

Considerable improvement is evident in terms of new classrooms, toilets, and kitchen sheds that have been made; school meals are found to be regularly served in most of the schools surveyed, though there have been many complaints regarding the supply of provisions and systematic arrangements. The average rate of student attendance has improved form a little above 50 per cent in 2001 to around 68 per cent now—though a large spatial variation in this respect persists (Majumdar and Rana, 2012).

Learning Achievement of Children

Mean and Variance in Scores of Children

Our general observation for children of class IV as well as for those of classes I to III is that the average score of children in subjects like Bengali, English and Arithmetic under our study signifying their level of learning is low and variance high. As the children move to higher classes the average score of the children gradually diminishes on general basis. In other words, the average score of children of class IV is low compared to those in lower classes, that is, class I, class II and class III. The average score of girl children is observed to be low compared to that of boy children.

In Paschim Medinipur district the average score in English for girls is 21.60 per cent and that in Arithmetic is 19.86 per cent. Both scores are below the state-mandated passing grade of 34 per cent. The average scores of boys in these subjects are 36.66 per cent and 41.86 per cent respectively. Those in Bengali are 41.60 for girls and 51.31 for boys. The coefficient of variation in percentage of marks is found to be high–60 per cent in Bengali for girls, 78 per cent for boys and 105 per cent for girls in English, 65 per cent for boys and 116 per cent for girls in Arithmetic. For boys the coefficient of variation is, however, seen to be low in Bengali (40%) as compared with that of girls (60%) (Table 2.4).

Table 2.4: Mean and Variance of Learning Achievement of Class IV Sample Boys and Girls Children by Subject in Paschim Medinipur District

Indicators	*Bengali*		*Difference*	*English*		*Difference*	*Arithmetic*		*Difference*
	Boys	*Girls*		*Boys*	*Girls*		*Boys*	*Girls*	
Mean	51.31	41.8	9.51	36.66	21.6	15.06	41.86	19.86	22
S.D.	20.73	24.9	–4.17	28.53	22.61	5.92	27.29	23.18	4.11
C.V.	40.4	59.58	–19.18	77.51	104.68	–27.17	65.19	116.22	–51.03

Source: Field Survey.

In Purba Medinipur district the average score in English for girls is 20.97 per cent and that for boys is 22.15 per cent. Both scores are below the state-mandated passing grade of 34 per cent. The average scores of boys in Arithmetic is 42.53 per cent as against 38.45 per cent for girls. Those in Bengali are 41.55 per cent for girls and 44.08 per cent for boys. The coefficient of variation in percentage of marks is high in both English and Arithmetic—84 per cent for boys and 92 per cent for girls in English, 64 per cent for boys and 70 per cent for girls in Arithmetic. For boys the coefficient of variation is, however, seen to be comparatively low, i.e. below 50 per cent for both boys and girls. Difference in mean values of leaning achievement of boys children of class IV *vis-à-vis* girls children is positive but small (1 to 4 percentile point) in Arithmetic, English and

Bengali. Difference in values of coefficient of variation in leaning achievement of the former *vis-à-vis* the latter is also small (Table 2.5).

Table 2.5: Mean and Variance of Learning Achievement of Class IV Sample Boys and Girls Children by Subject in Purba Medinipur District

Indicators	*Bengali*		*Difference*	*English*		*Difference*	*Arithmetic*		*Difference*
	Boys	*Girls*		*Boys*	*Girls*		*Boys*	*Girls*	
Mean	44.08	41.55	2.53	22.15	20.97	1.18	42.53	38.45	4.08
S.D.	21.59	20.23	1.36	18.5	19.29	–0.79	27.12	26.96	0.16
C.V.	49	48.7	0.3	84	91.97	–7.97	64	70.11	–6.11

Notes: SD = Standard Deviation, CV = Coefficient of Variation.
Source: Field Survey

The West Bengal Board of Primary Education follows a five point scale as follows: 80-100 marks (Very Good), 65-79 marks (Good), 50-64 marks (Satisfactory), 35-49 marks (Average) and less than 35 marks (Unsatisfactory). We use this five-point scale to categorise students into five grades. In addition, for minute details at the lower end we include two grades—Very Poor (1 to 19 marks) and Poor (20 to 29 marks)—and thus we work with larger number of grades (total nine). We observe that in two districts of Paschim Medinipur and Purba Medinipur combined at least 11 per cent of children (222 in number out of total number of sample 1981 children studying in Class IV) were unable to score any points in taking our tests in English while this percentage was 7.43 in case of mathematics, In Bengali, the mother tongue of the sample children, some of them are seen to be too low performing to score any point. In English, above 50 per cent of children and in mathematics above 30 per cent children are seen to have not made the state-mandated passing grade of above 34 per cent marks. Most of the children belong to the low score categories of grades below satisfactory. Among those students who made the pass grade in our tests less than 6 per cent can be classified as very good (excellent) (Table 2.6).

Percentage distribution of boys and girls children by grade obtained in Paschim Medinipur and Purba Medinipur districts combined shows that at least 16 per cent of boys children and 12 of girls children studying in Class IV were unable to score any points in taking our tests in English while this percentage was 10 for boys and 11 for girls in Arithmetic. In English, above 70 per cent of both boys and girls children and in Arithmetic above 40 per cent of them are seen to have not made the state-mandated

Table 2.6: Distribution of Children Studying in Class IV in Paschim Medinipur and Purba Medinipur Districts Combined by Percentage of Marks Obtained in Subjects

	Grade	*Bengali*		*English*		*Arithmetic*	
		Number	*%*	*Number*	*%*	*Number*	*%*
0	Nil	9	0.51	222	11.21	147	7.43
	Very Poor	188	10.72	681	34.38	298	15.06
	Poor	183	10.44	284	14.34	198	10.01
1 to 34	Unsatisfactory	516	29.44	1089	54.96	619	31.286
35-49	Average	395	22.52	287	14.51	287	14.494
50-64	Satisfactory	370	21.092	170	8.574	454	22.952
65-79	Good	306	17.468	105	5.306	245	12.368
80-100	Very Good	157	8.97	108	5.44	232	11.67
Total		**1753**	**100**	**1981**	**100**	**1979**	**100**

Source: Field Survey.

passing grade of above 34 per cent marks. Among those students who made the pass grade in our tests less than 4 per cent can be classified as very good (excellent) (Table 2.7).

Table 2.7: Percentage Distribution of Boys and Girls Class IV Children by Percentage of Marks Obtained in Paschim Medinipur and Purba Medinipur Districts Combined

	Grade	*Bengali*		*English*		*Arithmetic*	
		Boys	*Girls*	*Boys*	*Girls*	*Boys*	*Girls*
0	Nil	0.4	0.7	16.7	12.6	9.9	10.9
1-19	Very Poor	12.7	10.2	39.6	45.3	17.0	19.6
20-29	Poor	10.2	11.1	15.7	13.1	11.2	9.8
1- 34	Unsatisfactory	31.8	31.2	60.3	64.2	34.62	35.88
35-49	Average	21.7	27.4	10.0	12.4	11.98	14.22
50-64	Satisfactory	23.2	18.9	7.3	6.3	24.44	23.52
65-79	Good	16.6	14.8	3.5	3.1	9.96	9.28
80-100	Very Good	6.7	7.0	2.2	1.4	9.1	6.2
Total	—	**100.0**	**100.0**	**100.0**	**100.0**	**100.0**	**100.0**

Source: Field Survey.

The average score of class VIII children of Paschim Medinipur district in English is 34.27 per cent for boys as against 40.31 per cent for girls. In Arithmetic the respective percentages were 41.49 and 42.92. In Bengali also girls' score (47.22%) was higher than that of boys (43.76%). The coefficient of variation is comparatively high in English and Arithmetic—above 50 per cent (Table 2.8).

Table 2.8: Mean and Variance of Learning Achievement of Class VIII Sample Boys and Girls Children by Subject in Paschim Medinipur District

Indicators	*Bengali*		*English*		*Arithmetic*	
	Boys	*Girls*	*Boys*	*Girls*	*Boys*	*Girls*
Mean	43.76	47.22	34.27	40.31	41.49	42.92
Standard Deviation	16.65	16.66	19.92	21.34	22.51	23.98
Coefficient of Variation (%)	38	35	58	53	54	56

Source: Field Survey.

In Purba Medinipur district the average score of class VIII children in English is 44.06 per cent for boys as against 44.23 per cent for girls. In Arithmetic the respective percentages were 40.30 and 35.34. In Bengali girls' score (45.93%) was marginally higher than that of boys (45.93%). The coefficient of variation is comparatively high in Arithmetic—above 60 per cent for both boys and girls (Table 2.9).

Table 2.9: Mean and Variance of Learning Achievement of Class VII Sample Boys and Girls Children by Subject in Purba Medinipur District

Indicators	*Bengali*		*English*		*Arithmetic*	
	Boys	*Girls*	*Boys*	*Girls*	*Boys*	*Girls*
Mean	45.38	45.93	44.05	44.23	40.30	35.34
Standard Deviation	17.54	15.10	21.86	21.06	25.13	23.15
Coefficient of Variation %	39	33	50	48	62	65

Source: Field Survey.

In Paschim Medinipur and Purba Medinipur districts combined at least 2 per cent of class VIII sample children were unable to score any points in taking our tests in English while this percentage was 0.8 in Arithmetic. In English, 30.37 per cent of sample children have not made the state-mandated passing grade of above 24 per cent marks. This percentage was 34.5 in Arithmetic and in Bengali this percentage was 12.65. Among those students who made the pass grade in our tests less than 4 per cent of children of class VIII in Bengali, English and Mathematics can be classified as excellent and extraordinary (Table 2.10).

In Purba Medinipur and Paschim Medinipur districts combined 2.2 per cent of sample boys of class VIII and 1.8 per cent of girls were unable to score any points in taking our tests in English while this percentage

Table 2.10: Distribution of Children Studying in Class VIII by Grade Obtained in Subjects in Paschim Medinipur and Purba Medinipur Districts Combined

Grade		Bengali		English		Mathematics	
		No.	%	No.	%	No.	%
Nil	0	5	0.23	50	2.28	41	1.8
Unsuccessful	Below 25	278	12.65	667	30.37	785	34.48
Marginal	25-34	286	13.03	363	16.53	303	13.32
Satisfactory	35-44	467	21.27	346	15.77	313	13.77
Good	45-59	639	29.07	379	17.26	349	15.33
Very Good	60-79	463	21.07	329	14.98	358	15.73
Excellent	80-89	64	2.91	112	5.09	168	7.37
Total		**2197**	**100**	**2196**	**100**	**2276**	**100**

Source: Field Survey.

was 1.3 for both boys and girls in Arithmetic. In English, 37.06 per cent of sample boys and 29.44 per cent of sample girls have not made the state-mandated passing grade of above 24 per cent marks. These percentages were 37.66 and 36.14 respectively for sample boys and girls in Arithmetic and in Bengali these percentages were 15.6 and 10.96 respectively for them. Among those students who made the pass grade in our tests less than 3 per cent of children of class VIII in Bengali, English and Mathematics can be classified as excellent and extraordinary (Table 2.11).

Table 2.11: Percentage Distribution of Boys and Girls Children Studying in Class VIII in Purba Medinipur and Paschim Medinipur Districts Combined by Percentage of Marks Obtained

Grade		Bengali		English		Mathematics	
		Boys	Girls	Boys	Girls	Boys	Girls
Nil	0	0.5	0.1	2.7	1.8	1.3	1.3
Unsuccessful	Below 25	15.6	10.96	37.06	29.44	37.66	36.14
Marginal	25-34	13.32	12.94	16.34	16.5	14.7	11.9
Satisfactory	35-44	20.28	22.12	13.96	14.98	13.78	13.54
Good	45-59	30.3	27.38	13.64	16.48	13.46	15.72
Very Good	60-79	18.4	23.2	13.7	17	12.8	15.3
Excellent and Extra ordinary	80-100	2.1	3.4	5.3	5.6	7.6	7.4
Total		**100**	**100**	**100**	**100**	**100**	**100**

Source: Field Survey.

Factors Explaining Learning Achievement

It is observed that infrastructural development which is associated with quality education is inadequate and unevenly spread across schools and education circles/blocks, and across SSM interventions/initiatives. Monitoring of SSM projects/plans implementation remains poor. Coordination in planning and implementation remains weak. Quantity of achievement of targets prevails over quality achievement resulting in huge wastage of resources. So, is in case of over-centralization of decision-making in respect of allocation of SSM funds across heads. There are certain heads of plan and budget like teachers' training and community training where large sums are centrally allocated without taking into consideration of the fact that impacts of such funds utilization/expenditure are imperceptible in relation to quality education. Principles of teaching subjects as embodied in National Curriculum Framework 2005 are hardly observed in teachers' training and classroom transactions at both primary and upper primary levels. Money (investment) in education matters in achievement of quantitative goals of SSM, but does not matter much in attainment of quality education. Various interest groups are involved in SSM planned investment projects. The expenditures there satisfy them differentially while there is discontent or dissatisfaction among teachers, children and the community, the formal pillars of the SSM and quality education.

In planning teaching method top-down approach/cascade method needs to be reviewed. It is observed that this method while suggested in the teachers' training camps and applied in actual classroom transactions a situation is created, where most of the children feel it foreign to their culture and are able to participate in the teaching learning process. In this method accent is made on process rather than on product of education. Children in their young age need to be familiar with 3R's in the classroom transactions. They and their guardians think that accent ought to be more on product than on process, on more relevant human ingredient for achievement of education quality, where the cascade method makes it complex through emphasis being on process of learning.

Joyful learning is suggested as an essential of lesson planning. The tools and techniques like materials, gestures and postures, drama used for doing so provide joyful learning for advanced children who knows and understands the theme. But for most of the children who are deficient in learning what is needed is understanding and reproducing the basics of education and understanding the theme or lesson that is imparted by the teacher following this method for joyful learning. Thus, these children appear to enjoy while he/she applies this method in classroom transaction, but the cruel fact is that they do not learn. Thus, human skill formation in children which is one of the goals of elementary education is missing or deficient. For the lagging children enjoyment in the classroom transactions turns out to be a luxury while for the advanced children enjoyment in the classroom transactions is a necessity because they know many things and know the theme that is imparted by the teachers in attractive ways by application of the new technique. The lagging children must learn necessarily skills in languages and arithmetic. Education must lead to the capability enhancement, which would contribute to human development.

In the whole of educational planning priority fixation in resource allocation across competing demands needs to be made in such a way that maximization of well-being of children is attained while teachers and guardians are also satisfied with it. In doing so the principle of 'last be put first' be observed so that the maximization of aggregate well-being of all children is attained. In designing curricula and syllabus accent need to be made on developing understanding capability of children so that they successfully face later the aptitude test which is presently emphasized in competitive examinations as are conducted by institutions like the UPSC in subjects including English.

Elementary education becomes non-sustainable while social constraints and cultural perspectives of children are ignored. Un-necessary experiments after experiments are made and those are attempted to be applied on children supposed to be ginny pig without considering the applicability of the same.

In planning pedagogy at the primary level it is observed that scientific teaching method through use of Listening Reading Writing and Speaking (LRWS) sequence method as is practiced in actual classroom transactions is useful rather than the suggested LSRW sequence method in the teachers' training modules. Teachers know what method of teaching suits best their children and they should be given freedom to apply it rather than otherwise imposed from above as method.

Children are now so taught that they gather much information but acquire little knowledge in government aided primary schools as compared to private schools. Productivity in classroom transactions in the former is relatively low. Teaching hours, contents and skills generated in children must be significant.

It is observed that large school in terms of number of children reflects the good quality of the school which attracts children and parents and enlists the attention and admiration of the society. Breaking up of these schools by spread of newly built schools results in quality deterioration in most cases though quantitively education spreads. Large schools need to be adequately equipped to impart quality education while students prefer enrolment in those schools to those in small schools. Relatively small schools are seen to be infrastructurally ill-equipped. For the sake of efficiency in activity small school concept needs be discouraged.

Teachers of primary and upper primary schools in West Bengal teach English in an environment where language learning mainly happens in language classroom. They teach in an acquisition poor environment.[2] A normal class in the English-speaking West is small. Classroom studies often get done with no more than 10-15 students; those with 20 to 25 seem to be the norm. For an EFL (English as a foreign language) teacher in South Asia including India a upper primary school class with 40+ pupils is no reason for complaining; a teacher normally works with much larger numbers in states of India including West Bengal as we have seen earlier.

Besides, there are established attitudes and expectations of not only the teachers and students of the school and those outside (parents, administrators and programme planners) whose priorities and preferences often influence the quality and character of what gets taught or learnt. This is one of the resons for conduction of and continuing with classroom transactions in a traditional way which is long tested and found to be effective in most of the schools while these are found to be appropriate to the existing socio-cultural environment where the children live, work and act.

The whole social and cultural and even institutional environment of today in general is not favourable for education of the children. Parents and the whole society do not look after their children in their education, practice and culture in education leaving the whole education of their children to private tuition. Besides, their present culture and religious practices detract the children from education. Institutions also come with all types of aid or help in all these. Personal interests of happiness disturb interests of education, research and civil practices. The whole administration functions to the cause of people's private gains and not to the social gains of education of children.

Teachers express concerns about gendered social norms of early marriage that render the educational right a "precarious right" for girl student, who keep dropping out under social pressure. A public institution like the government school allows such concerns to be aired, creating a possibility for it to be less gendered than the home. Also as schooling expands among the hitherto excluded, relatively better placed and better off teachers increasingly come into contact with the children of social underdogs in public classrooms.

Although such contact does not necessarily bridge the social distance between the teacher and the taught, and sadly may even reinforce it at times, there are real-life situations in which teachers acknowledge and empathise with the predicaments of poorer children who people their classrooms, and more crucially, revise their (mis) judgement influenced, in turn, by strong stereotypes about the "in-educability" of the so-called "first-generation learners" (Majumdar and Rana, 2012).

Productivity in classroom transactions of teachers at the primary level is low in government-managed schools as compared to private schools. Multi-faculty teachers are assets of the institution but these are few in number.

Do teachers make unbiased evaluation of children's progress, particularly in subjects of study? Does result of English subject evaluation prove so. In many primary schools 10 to 20 per cent of Class IV children are seen from their annual progress sheet to have secured 100 per cent marks in English while the My English Book for class IV is considered the heavy and tough book for children. While the concerned teacher awards 100 per cent mark in this subject a question arises as to the propriety and justice in his/her evaluation. Does it reflect wishful over-marking or rush/run for showing good quantitative performance of children at the expense of their enhancement of quality in era of neo-liberalism where the concept of society is denuded and quantitative performance of an individual or information mobilized by individual rather than acquisition of knowledge, physical infrastructure development rather than development of human infrastructure is shown to be important and emphasised. Ravitch (2012) observes, "when tests become too consequential for students, teachers and schools harmful consequences ensue, such as cheating, narrowing the curricula only to what is tested, or lowering standards to inflate scores."

In pure academic world this issue gets important while we observe the poor development of children's reading and writing skills which are downplayed in the modern methodology of teaching subjects including English. This kind of poverty is reflected in general while we observe festoons/hoarding where so many spelling errors are there in subjects of printing that shows sub-standard in the modern business world, which represents poor education and schooling in general. The roots of such poverty lie at the primary school level.

Are the guardians in close connection/involvement with their children or this is intervened through the private tuition/use of money power which does not make for quality development of children? Educated guardians even have little influence on children's education. Guardians ought to be cultured. They would play crucial role while they sit with children while studying at home and check what they are doing.

Education is a social process. But the dynamics of the society is that individuals that constitute the society are getting self-centric under the impact of neo-liberalism or radical liberalism of the present era. Foundations of the essence of the society are crumbling and at perils. The concept of "Individualization of education but socialization of man" is eroding. The social environment congenial for education is disturbed on account of excessive use of mechanical devices as ancillary to social functions like *pujas*/celebrities/celebrations. There is too much accent on individual rather than society. Head teacher with proper and adequate academic bent and culture be authorized to monitor classroom transactions and children's performance at class level.

Children achieve greater success if families and schools operate as overlapping sphere and working in an interacting way. In modern era the concept of parental involment has changed into family involvement which is a much broader term. Evidence shows a strong connection between parent and family involvement and children's academic achievement, attendance, attitude and continued education (Henderson and Beria, 1994; Hickman, 1996). However, academic culture and interest and involvement of educated parents with children, not their educational qualification alone can influence the children's upbringing in education. Besides, what is important parents and the society must be satisfied with the syllabus and curricula of the schools and with teachers' academic/teaching/pedagogic performance in classroom transactions and outside Teachers' sincerity, hours spent at schools, pedagogy plan, plan for children's physical and cultural, aesthetic and ethical development, and overall pivotal role of teachers is the key ingredients for children's learning achievement and quality education of children. Three Rs of children form the basic core of education of all children. Motivated (inspired) teachers and children are assets of the institution. Permanent rewards for improved services of teachers be part of the education system. Format for scientific assessment here be prepared.

Concept and system of education evolves with reference to the society and environment. So is the concept and role of teachers. These differ substantially between the East and West. Any attempt to uniform education throughout the world irrespective of the particular society, culture and environment leads to distortions, wastages and ineffectiveness, as are evident in India including West Bengal under the globalization impact on elementary education.

Foreign influences, be in the form of institutions or instructions or technology, are here to disrupt what India stands for, what she is glorified in the world. What they have rejected or do not practice at all are being transported and in fact emulated to make us suffer from the materialistic culture which becomes an issue all-over against the question of sustainable development. They have made themselves crippled and out of ego or non-sense they are out to make us crippled. We are to be alert and vigil against all these disturbances, intrusions and imperialism, so to speak fervently.

The whole educational and social system is disarrayed by the intervention/intersection of money/investment power in the government managed education system where quality is sacrificed for the sake of quantity which is much more emphasized by the policy-makers and administration at the expense of quality achievement.

Under the SSM interventions initiatives, originality and freedom of teachers are seen to be curtailed and public interests are injured while individual interests are promoted. This largely explains why the people's participation in guardians' meetings of schools is poor for many schools, where the dogma of modernism prevails and teachers' initiatives and guardians' views are lacking and dishonoured. There is a vicious circle of low participation of people and poor planning and development in government-aided school management where *status quo* is the rule and innovation is rare because this is tacitly discouraged. Fundamentalism prevails resulting in low productivity of schools and low participation of people in the educational process. People and society and their culture are excluded in the institutional process of textbook preparation and teaching methods in the name and honour of modern methodology.

While there is serious deficiency in language learning of children we discuss here some institutional constraints on children's learning English language. The notional-functional syllabus (NFS) was born in Europe in the 1970s. It was produced by the Council of Europe's expert group, for adults to enable them "to communicate non-professionally with foreign language speakers in everyday situations on topics of general interest". The outline syllabuses that they produced (e.g. *The Threshold Level*; van EK, 1975 and van EK and Trim, 1991) were meant for learners at various levels—from the most elementary to full proficiency in real-life language use.

Although the NFS began to take shape by about the middle of the 1970s, its theoretical framework had been laid earlier by linguists on both sides of the Atlantic. In the UK, J. R. Firth (1957) and M.A.K. Halliday (1973) had emphasized the need for descriptions of language to include information on the: what, by whom, for what purpose and in what modes it gets used. Around the same time the American sociolinguist Del Hymes (1971) had shown that true communicative competence manifests itself in not just grammatically correct and accurate use but importantly in language use that is appropriate for its purpose(s), as is also stated by Tickoo (2009: 245).

In a majority of today's language syllabuses and the course book based on them, the NFS now serves as an additional framework rather than as a replacement for the Structural Syllabus (SS). Such a syllabus combines the listing of a stated number of functions with an ordered list of sentence structures. In the best of such products one sees something like a structural ladder and a notional-functional spiral. Such an arrangement seeks to combine the advantages of teaching grammatical usage[3] with those using language for meaningful use (Tickoo, 2009: 249).

Long ago, Michael West (1962) coined the expression "*Mental Age of the Textbook*". He did so to highlight the importance of bringing textual materials into harmony with the ages, aptitudes and interests of their users (Tickoo, 2009: 259).

English Textbooks for primary school classes in recent years have been modernized through continuous experiments. But, it appears that in respect of the attainment of quality of the existing textbooks to be in conformity with the National Curriculum Framework 2005 still much is there to be achieved. Textbooks are scarcely prepared in consonance with child's nature and environment. It is noted that above 70 per cent children live in natural settings and the traditional socio-cultural environment. Children grow and acquire knowledge with nature and socio-cultural environment. But English learning hardly shifts away from rote learning. School and social ethos and value hardly develop in the children. Multi-lingual proficiency including proficiency in English is not much promoted in every child in absence of their learning being built on a sound language pedagogy in the mother tongue.[4]

English learning is now seen to be the weakest area at primary school level. It is recognized that understanding of English language and hence knowledge has much to do with appropriate approaches to text preparation, curriculum contents, plan and presentation of the texts. It is, however, found in West Bengal that the primary level English texts contain lessons which are not helpful for children's generating basic knowledge in English language at this primary level. The first requirement of English language learning is to get the children identified with letters, words and sentences. The major accent being on communicative English mars the process of basic English language learning, acquisition of language skills and thus education. In the English textbooks (*My English Book*) of Class I to Class IV sentences are presented but nowhere the process of construction of sentences is made known to the children. These textbooks present pictures that are drawn from cartoons and are not natural, rather these are artificial. The ordinary children are hardly familiar with these pictures. The themes presented in different lessons are also not familiar with most of the children and many of them appear to be unnatural to them. Hardly 10 per cent of the children find pleasure and joy in them being supported by their socio-cultural environment while 90 per cent of children suffer from the mechanical presentation of the themes and to the latter learning English language does not generate joyful learning. Besides, there is hardly any planning in preparation of the textbooks for fulfilling social objectives of education. There is no clearly stated approach to the text preparation and hence sequencing of studies in a text is not scientific. For example, for class II children sentences with inverted commas have been introduced (*My English Book, II Book* pp. 27, 54). Negative sentences have been introduced in this book in page number 32 of Lesson 11. There is a text on Mid-day meal in Lesson 12. Is this lesson intelligible to so young children most of whom live on Mid-day meals, particularly in rural areas while there is substantial proportion of the backward community children like Muslims, Scheduled Tribes and Scheduled Castes and even a large proportion of general caste children. All these act as impediments and constraints on the expansion as well as quality improvement of education in English. Moreover, the English texts also contain some errors in construction of sentences. This is particularly true in the textbooks of *My English Book, Book II* (for example, p. 27 where inverted commas are omitted). The heading of Lesson 12 of this book itself contains error (p. 41). Lesson 2 of *My English Book, Book IV* for Class IV children contains printing erros in page numbers 24 to 26 where commas have been omitted. Lessons 16 and 17 for class II are not understandable to children of age 6 to 7 years. The Textbooks of different classes contain large number of pages (54 pages for children of class II,

72 pages for class III and 110 pages for class IV). Are the lessons presented there joyful, interesting and meaningful to the children of the appropriate age? The sentences with the use of present continuous tense have been introduced in *My English Book, Book III* for class III children in Lessons 6,7 and 8, interrogative sentences in Lesson 7 and sentences with past tenses in Lessons 9 and 10 without any footnotes on simple English grammar. Lessons contain many stories in dialogue forms in *My English Book, Book IV* for class IV children. Many words and sentence construction are hardly understood by children and even by many teachers who are seniors. The textbooks appear to both children and many teachers difficult and tough to comprehend and also heavy to bear with. Do all these carry any sense and meaning to them? What is thus generated in the process of communicative English to develop "communicative competence" is actually no substantial education of children in English while much more accent is put on the memory organ of the children than their understanding and culture, more on cramming than creativity being generated and encouraged in students. Normal growth of students is aborted thereby while they cannot grow with nature and with their socio-cultural environment while studying and learning in the classrooms with the prescribed books in English. Neither in the classroom situation nor with the teachers nor at home they hardly find congenial atmosphere and culture to speak in and cultivate English.

It may be noted that textbook occupies an important place during primary education. In English teaching textbooks are all the more important. Trivedi rightly observes, "In the absence of any other instructional material the textbook becomes a potent tool in the hands of a teacher to teach the skill of a language and the more so of a foreign language." It is not merely a source of information but a course of study, a set of unit plans and a learning guide. It helps students in self study. But this is conspicuous by its absence in English textbooks for the primary school children in West Bengal.

The teaching method is another area where the children do not feel at all comfortable while they are taught a second language like English. Modern teaching method which puts emphasis on speaking and fluency, rather than sentence structure and correctness is experimented and propagated in teachers' training programme among the trainee teachers amidst their grievances without testing whether this modern procedural teaching method is effective in the classroom children's situation, and this is advised to be carried on in classroom transactions at the primary stage.

There are fewer accents on developing reading and writing skills throughout the primary classes. Deficiency in writing and understanding naturally crops up and that hinders the child's progress in curricular activities. Children and guardians are skeptical about the efficacy of this modern method and they are of the view that to make up their children's deficiencies in English they resort to private tuition which has become prevalent for over 90 per cent children. But, the children are hardly seen to be adept in English language. Rather they face contradictions in methodologies in teaching English. While modern methodology in the form of procedural language learning with accent on communication and fluency is prevalent in government run and aided schools private tutor has put accent on traditional method and rote learning.

West Bengal Board of Primary Education (2008) in their *Primary English Teachers Companion* noted that for the first two years of primary school they would try to improve the fluency of the children. Only after they have grounding in English they would introduce grammar teaching. But, the relevant questions are: How would the children acquire fluency? It is through repeated practice? Is that effective in the socio-cultural setting in which the children are brought up? Is the grammar teaching introduced with reasonable importance after two years of primary schooling of children?

The accent is still clearly on speaking. But speaking without understanding and knowledge of simple grammar does not generate language skills in children. Without adequate accent on children's reading letters and words and their proper understanding how would they speak and that fluently? Are the children treated as parrots and there is parrot cramming? Does parroting of children constitute teaching and learning process? Rabindranath Tagore cautioned us already against such parroting. Besides, does language learning constitute speaking only? What about other language skills like writing of letters, words and sentences? We must keep in mind that children in government-aided schools learn English as second language and they hail from a socio-economic and cultural background which does not offer environment for developing fluency in English and the limited time (hardly 40 minutes a class day) of English teaching-learning in the classroom situation is not sufficient for children to develop fluency in English. Most of them depend upon Mid-day meal which ensures their presence in the school, but they have hardly developed fluency in own language and also in the second language like English.

An analogy is drawn on how a child learns her mother tongue. By the age of 4 she can say her name, her mother's name, her father's name and so on in mother tongue. While she so answers her answer is grammatical and hence she already knows grammar, it is argued. In a similar way it is told that a child would learn a second language like English and its grammar. Is the analogy valid? The domestic and outside environment makes her up in learning mother tongue but where is that in case of the second language? It is told when we begin to teach grammar we should do so by making the child aware of the grammar she/he already has. Is it true in case of the child's early learning of English? Rather, we should be aware that the child has seldom learnt anything of English from the environment she/he lives in.

The Bilingual Method (BM) of teaching has received some attention from a number of practitioners of English Language Teaching (ELT) in the Non-English speaking world. In India a number of classroom experiments put the BM to work in Non-English Medium (NEM) classrooms (e.g. Sastri, 1967, 1970; Murthy, 1967-68; Nagarajan, 1969-70). In each case the experiment class (where the BM was used) showed better results. In Japan Ishii's (1979) and in Sri Lanka Walatara's (1973) experiments showed somewhat similar gains as did studies done in Germany and Denmark among other European countries (Butzkamm 1980; Caldwell, 1990).

The BM has not been part of the discussions on ELT methodology of the last three decades of the twentieth century. But given the fact that it demonstrates the value of the learner's language one (L1) as an untapped resource, there may be reason to consider its use as an alternative methodology for NEM classrooms (Tickoo, 2009:29:357).

Language Teaching Methods (LTMs) in use at any point of time form part of the educational thinking in a particular society. They generally remain tied to the socio-cultural contexts and the ecology of the classroom in which they exist. Transfer of methods from one linguistic and cultural context to another, therefore, almost always proves to be counterproductive. Studies done in different parts of the world, but especially in the Third World (e.g. Swales, 1980, Holliday, 1994) have been highlighting the fact that the transfer of LTMs made without a full view of the cultural load that the methods carry is capable of doing more harm than good (Tickoo, 2009:29:394-395). It is generally recognized that many of the concepts and skills which children have learnt in their first language transfer readily to their second language (Handscombe, 1994). The skills built in first language reading can help the leaner read his second language, the skills and strategies built in the former writing can come in handy in acquiring second language writing skills, and so on (Tickoo, 2009: 11).

Studies show that where reading abilities are well developed in one's first language, they can provide strong support for reading in the second language. The key lies in bringing about transfer of skills and abilities from the known language to the new (Tickoo, 2009:32).

The reading teacher can use first language literacy to the advantage of both reading in the second language and more mature reading in the first. A school based policy of additive bilingualism[5] that brings the two languages into a mutually supportive relationship, should help in this. Studies show that where reading abilities are well developed in one's first language, they can provide strong support for reading in the second language. The key lies in bringing about transfer of skills and abilities from the known language to the new (Tickoo, 2009: 29-32).

Translation as teaching method has been condemned. As a skill it has its importance. The translation skill involves a high level of understanding of one language and a good command of the other. Translation of ideas should be stressed. But, in West Bengal the communicative English method and functional English dominate the whole teaching learning process which does not help the Bengali-speaking children understand the meaning of English words and sentence, the simple grammar underneath the textual lessons and does not help develop in children creativity and promote independence and joy of both children and teachers in the teaching-learning process. In the absence of proper assimilation of the ideas as contained in the lessons studied adequate knowledge of English is hardly generated in the children and the language skills are hardly developed in them.

In the opinion of Sadler Commission, "a severe training in the mother tongue is not a rival, but the necessary preliminary to training in the use of English."

In bilingual classrooms ways need to be found to make the learners' creative abilities in their strong language, a valuable support to building their creativity in the second and subsequent languages. Learning how to write well may, in most cases, not end at the end of school but the foundations for it are best laid in school. The right type of feedback from the teacher and the right kind of cooperative learning environment may, for most learners, be of immense value in gaining their personal voices as writers (Tickoo, 2009: 87).

Tickoo (2009: 209) notes that translation can be a rich source of word knowledge which often saves teaching or leaning time. In some cases it may be the easiest available source of support. Where mother tounge equivalents for one or more meaning of a word (or a grammatical structure) exist, it may be part of good teaching to help learners build on them. Very often a teacher saves valuable time by pointing to the mother tongue equivalent of the word before helping the learner use it in context. What needs to be heeded is that the exclusion of the mother tongue from the class as a way of communicating meaning robs the teachers of one useful technique of encoding (or helping learners bring meaning of the word). It also leaves the learners to make their own uncontrolled and often incorrect translations (Nation, 1990:63).

Especially in the first few years of learning a foreign language, pupils find it natural to seek support in their mother tongue. A teacher who attempts to keep the class away from their learnt language often fights a loser's battle. Also as already pointed out, far from being just a source of errors and fossilized forms, the mother tongue is an abundantly rich source, especially where the teacher shares it with his pupils. Another use of the mother tongue is to check comprehension. This works by asking learners to suggest mother tongue equivalents (Tickoo, 2009:29, 209).

There is great confusion in the minds of the young teachers of English as to what should be the place of the mother tongue in teaching English. In the opinion of Champion (1957), "The Direct method does not insist that the mother tongue should be eliminated from the whole of the learning process. The teacher should aim at the complete exclusion of the mother tongue from the stage of interpretation as well as from the stage of use. But where he is satisfied that he is unable to explain the meaning of a new language form by the method of direct illustration or by verbal explanation in English, he should not hesitate to use the mother tongue." The teacher should have no bias against the use of the mother tongue. It must be remembered that sometimes giving the vernacular equivalent of an English word or phrase to the pupil is the more direct way of teaching that particular word or phrase than attempting any other device. To quote F.L. Billows (1961), "Laborious attempts to explain words without translation are very little better than translation, and if they are difficult to follow even worse." In the teaching of these two languages often the proper balance is not maintained and as a result, the mother tongue is neglected on one hand, on the other greater emphasis is placed on the teaching of English than it actually deserves as a second language. Champion (1957) observed, "The desire for knowledge and command of English, however, has led to a great neglect of Indian languages and the bilingual problem is the problem of Indian languages and the bilingual problem is the problem of restoring the proper balance between the two." Since, the efficiency in the mother tongue serves as a genuine basis to acquire efficiency in English, the neglect of the mother tongue in general nullifies a greater part of the effort made to improve the standard of efficiency in English. English is taught as a second language in our country. The fourfold aims of teaching this subject being to enable the pupil (i) to understand English when spoken; (ii) to understand English when written; (iii) to speak English; and (iv) to write English can be achieved by giving the pupils specific practice in the four types of language activities, viz. listening, speaking, reading and writing. English should be regarded only as skill subject and neither as a content subject nor as a subject for literary appreciation.

But in the teachers' training programme the use of mother tongue is forbidden and this practice is also advised to trainee teachers to be carried on in classroom situation to the result that most of the students lose interest in classroom transactions simply because they do not follow and understand what is going on in the classroom transactions led by the teachers. Most of them hardly speak out of their own as a means of participation and remain deficient in English as before and forever.

Champion (1957) holds that teaching process in English language be bi-lingual, which the National Curricula Framework 2005 also holds and the Expert Committee on Syllabus and Curricula as formed in recent months by the Government of West Bengal in their Draft Report also suggest the same. It is conspicuous by its absence in the teachers' training or orientation course in English language at the primary stage. It is quite contrasting that the mother tongue is used while it is felt necessary in the upper primary teachers' training process in the subject.

This results in uneasiness of teacher trainees and also even among many DRPs, which is later reflected in the deficiency of primary school children in skill of comprehension; they are not moved from their known domain to their unknown area as is done in the co-centric education model.

It is generally recognized that many of the concepts and skills which children have learnt in their first language transfer readily to their second (Handscombe, 1994). The skills built in first language reading can help the leaner read his second language, the skills and strategies built in the former writing can come in handy in acquiring second language writing skills, and so on (Tickoo, 2009: 11).

Here for example, is an excerpt from one English as a second language (ESP) practitioner's recorded experience in trying to put a communicative method to work in Sudan:

> The Sudanese language instructors for whom the ESP materials had been written generally found the communicative methodology implied by the materials culturally unfamiliar and often too difficult to use, as did the learners. Thus, even as I introduced these materials into the curriculum, instructors either avoided using them altogether or reinterpreted their methodological intent so as to be able to continue using more familiar methodologies (Murkee, 2000: 267).
> Murkee concludes that "the project failed in its use of modernizing the institution's educational capacity to deliver Western-style ESL instruction" (Murkee, 2000: 268).

Knowledge of grammar is important for using language competently in study and work contexts. Only some knowledge comes from the type of learning which excludes conscious attention to formal aspects (that is, the grammar) of the language. Also, especially where learners are mature and have already learnt a language, attention to the rules of target language grammar proves its value. However, it works even better when such rules are learnt in meaningful tasks that combine grammar and use (Tickoo, 2009:29:344). Logic of grammar and children's merit and their memory or imitation are both rich resources which contribute to language acquisition.

Ninety per cent of the teachers surveyed at the primary level are of the view that they themselves are deficient in English language. The relatively old teachers maintain that since the year the English was withdrawn from the curricula in primary schools they were not habituated in teaching English for over two decades and they have forgotten English language on account of lack of culture in it. The relatively young teachers are also not adept in English because they have also poor English learning, particularly of English grammar. There is no provision for remedial of deficiencies of teachers in English language in the teachers' training camps as are organized by the Office of the Sarva Shiksha Mission of the district for a short period of time, say 5 days.

Children at the primary stage of learning are found to be deficient not only in English but also in their own language. Deficiency in Bengali of the Bengalee rural children has an adverse impact on developing language skills in English and numeracy skill. This is important for our understanding why the children are deficient in English and even in arithmetic. Some children studying at primary and even at upper primary levels are seen to be incapable of reading the problems set in book on arithmetic and thus they fail to work out the same.

Children suffer in subjects including English largely because their pre-schooling learning is almost nothing. They hardly learn English letters in the ICDS centres which are supposed to be pre-school institutions. Thus, most of the children feel uncomfortable while the teachers start teaching with *My English Book*, Book I. everything and every lesson of the textbook appears to most of them to be Greek letters.

The districts of West Bengal including Purba Medinipur and Paschim Medinipur witness recently rapid growth of Bengali Medium Private Schools and English Medium Schools which attract and enroll the children who belong to the educated and even the ordinary peasant community. The large trend of relatively affluent and meritorious children being admitted in those educational institutions leads to a situation where only children of economically lagging families whose children mainly depend on Mid-day Meal programme are admitted largely in government-aided and government schools. This obviously poses constraint on the experimentation with modern English books and the modern teaching method in these primary schools.

In both Paschim Medinipur and Purba Medinipur districts as in the rest of West Bengal there is sizeable percentage of fathers of children having no schooling or having schooling of low standard. Their education level has much to do with their children's achievement in subjects including English. The ASER study throws light on the phenomenon.

Quantitative factors that promote quality education are essential but more important is the quality academic ambience. To encourage creativity among children (as per NCF 2005) and teachers what is vital is the setting of more descriptive and quality questions and lessening the importance of objective type questions which largely depends upon children's rote learning which ought to be discouraged. Syllabi and curricula ought to be designed in such a way as to encourage children's creativity and proficiency in subjects. Money being invested under SSM is necessary and important as money matters. But money is an aid and not the supreme. What is of more consideration is the use of money in the pursuit of quality education which demands quality performance under the SSM initiatives and interventions, which is often neglected and even ignored in the rush for the quantitative achievement. School elementary education provides the foundation of individual and social progress, which ought to be developed quantitatively and more substantially and significantly qualitatively.

Also, schools in low income neighbourhoods are relatively more starved of teachers. In North Bengal 41 per cent of schools are found to have more teachers than required; in 31 per cent of schools it is just the reverse. Only in 28 per cent of schools there seems to be a balance between the requirement and availability [as per the right to education (RTE) norm].

In Paschim Medinipur district 13.4 per cent of the sample schools has less number of teachers than required as per RTE Act, 2009 while 59.3 per cent has just the reverse. Only in 27 per cent of the sample schools there seems to be a balance between the requirement and availability [as per the right to education (RTE) norm].

The average rate of school attendance among the children in north Bengal is found be 60 per cent, much lower than the corresponding figure of 75 per cent in the district of southern Bengal. The variation is palpably correlated with inadequate provision of school facilities in North Bengal (the expansion of which has begun only recently). Even among schools within the districts of North Bengal, wide variations in pupil attendance exist, ranging between 30 per cent and 90 per cent having strong connections with the remoteness of school, the number of teachers in position, the frequency of school inspection, and the social accessibility of pupils to their teachers. The issue of erratic school attendance of the teacher and the taught cannot be adequately and independently addressed without paying heed to the issue of "fair" financing of public education in the "neglected areas" spread over vast tracts of the State—form tea gardens in north Bengal to the plateau of Paschim Medinipur, Bankura and Purulia.

In Paschim Medinipur district the average attendance at the primary level for class IV sample children was 81.05 per cent, ranging between 97.6 per cent for the developed block and general caste-dominated region and 75.9 per cent in the relatively backward block and Muslim-dominated area. The coefficient of variation was 15.2 per cent which is low. In Purba Medinipur relatively developed district the average attendance at the primary level for class IV sample children was higher, i.e. 87.1 per cent, ranging between 95.0 per cent for the developed block and general caste-dominated region and 85.3 per cent in the relatively backward block and SC-dominated area. The coefficient of variation was 8.8 per cent which is even lower than that of Paschim Medinipur district.

Thirtynine per cent of surveyed schools were found to have had no inspection in last six months, and 27 per cent with no inspection in the last one year (Pratichi Trust, 2009). What is more, Inspectors have traditionally been expected to perform the role of policing; they have not been oriented or trained to work as academic supervisors, facilitating and improving teachers' academic and instructional tasks and skills (also *see*, IIM Kolkata, 2011). Hence, if and then they have managed to visit schools, they have remained faithful to their job description, i.e., inspection, that has resulted in a situation in which schools are both controlled and neglected, controlled under a hierarchical regime of top down inspection that neglected in terms of much needed academic supervision and assistance.

The in-service teachers training tended to have taken a conventional line, and more disappointingly, the impact of the training imparted, in many cases dried out before reaching the classroom (Pratichi Institute, 2012b).

There is a growing tendency to quality of schooling solely in terms of test scores of students and to hold teachers primarily culpable for students' achievement deficits, without paying adequate heed to the problem of curriculum overload.

Testing may certainly give information with respect to making teaching and learning useful for both teachers and students; but harmful consequences ensue, as Ravitch convincingly claims (2012), "when tests become too consequential for students, teachers and schools, such as cheating, narrowing the curricula only to what is tested, or lowering standards to inflate scores." Also so much focus on test scores, and not on making curriculum less onerous, or on how *via* professional development of teachers a school can deliver improved opportunity for learning to children runs the risk of de-emphasizing the need for improving teachers' subject matter knowledge and pedagogic skills, which are crucial to improve teaching. And without improved teaching, it is hard to improve students' academic achievement.

Research has to engage with the public at large to generate and influence a collective understanding of good education, of the failings of public education, and of how educational institutions can be designed better. This is, of course, a political question (Dreze and Sen, 1995). This is so because the socio-political and policy environments in which teaching learning takes place in school are as important as goals and strategies of individual families in affecting how much students learn and whether in an equitable manner (Carnoy, 2004).

Conclusions

Elementary school education under SSM in West Bengal has witnessed a sea change in the globalization era in terms of development of capita-intensive physical infrastructures including school building, kitchen sheds, toilets, teaching learning materials. But this phenomenal quantitative achievement has not translated itself into the improvement of quality education of children in terms of their learning achievement in subjects like English, Mathematics and Bengali, in children's own cultural progress including co-curricular activities and in their decent behavioural pattern. Various researches including our own conducted on both primary and upper primary school children reveal that a significant proportion of children studying in Classes III and IV and even beyond cannot read small letters in English, cannot read simple words and easy sentences and cannot understand the meaning of words and sentences. Even the percentage of children who cannot write correctly the names of their parents, relatives etc. in English and Bengali is substantial. In Mathematics also deficiencies of many children are glaring in case of subtraction, division, ratios, percentages and decimals, and in understanding the logic of Mathematics. Thanks to the prevalence of objective type questions in the recent syllabus and curricula of subjects percentage of marks secured by children is high enough but this does not signify the good quality of their education.

Reasons for multiple deficiencies of children in subjects of their study are not far to seek and not too difficult to understand. Both contents of subjects and the teaching methods in them are largely influenced by the globalization process where major accent is on information-based learning. Assimilation of ideas based on information and experiences takes the back seat or ignored and hence knowledge which is power is hardly generated in children. Wisdom which is generated through application of knowledge to solve problems is hardly developed in children. Modern teaching methodology in English and Mathematics involves round-about teaching and learning process which is too lengthy and complex to follow correctly by children. Logical senses in subjects, particularly in English are hardly developed in them since accent on learning structure of sentences through English grammar and the correct use of words and sentences are scarcely emphasized and developed in children, particularly at the primary stage. There is little the children are learning. As per National Curriculum Framework 2005 that is approved by the NCERT learning of subjects ought to be child-centric and multi-lingual but in English at the primary stage both teachers' training and classroom transactions are largely conducted uni-lingually, i.e. in English for the dubious achievement of speaking skill and oral fluency of children.

In the modern era new technology is seen to be the growth elevator of an underdeveloped economy. But whether the modern technology that is being applied in the elementary school education ensures quality education is still to be tested. Without knowing the results of this crucial test the application of the new methodology only runs the risk of deterioration in school education of children. There is lack of integration and coordination in the planning process under the SSM as well as gap in the implementation stage. There are so many wastages and inefficiencies that are generated and galore in the process. Guardians, community, children, even the teachers are not satisfied with what is going on in the process and the era of privatization in the form of growth of private schools and private tuition strengthens. The equity objective in the SSM-sponsored school education system is disturbed, and in fact the inequity in quality education across different categories of children enhances.

Thus, a critical problem develops in both primary and upper primary levels of elementary education under SSM in West Bengal. While quantitative achievement under the SSM being financed in the globalization process is commendable quality of elementary school education is seen to be deteriorating and at stake leading to a very important crisis on quality education of children which the State now confronts for the children who would constitute its future.

The teachers' training is generally associated with quality education. Five days' teachers' training programme in English on Class IV Book is hardly conducted on a good plan and programme schedule basis. In many orientation centres no printed copy of the programme prepared by the District Resource Persons (DRPs) and approved by the Circle Project Coordinator (CPC)/Sub-Inspector of Schools (SIs) is available. Again, wherever it is available it is not strictly followed. Lack of adherence to the programme schedule is a feature. Many of the Lessons of *My English Book, Book IV* are not discussed. Teacher trainees derive benefits and inputs little. Lack of completeness and pursuit for attainment of perfection and integration in planning is evident.

DRPs are found to feel uneasy to carry on the training programme soundly because they have not much to contribute to the stock of knowledge of the teacher-trainees and methodology in English language teaching. To spend five days fruitfully in the orientation programme seems difficult for the DRPs because they are not sufficiently equipped. A substantial time is lost in matters which are not related to the teachers' training, to speak frankly.

Learners' diary and report are prepared by the teacher trainees but these contain so many errors which are hardly examined and corrected and the loopholes there are scarcely brought out to the notice of the teacher-trainees and remedies are suggested and done.

In the teacher training process majority of teacher-trainees and also many District Resource Persons and even some Master Resource Persons are seen to speak in incorrect English while Thompson (1957) and National Curriculum Framework (NCF) 2005 hold that use of English be correct and idiomatic. This should be for the sake of beauty while it is all appreciated that beauty is truth and truth is beauty. Quality education of children demands quality teachers, their academic culture, sincerity, devotion, dedication, inner urge or motivation, earnestness, creativity, innovation and commitment to the services of education which are either lacking or deficient or stifled. Teachers' training and community training remain largely ineffective in actual classs room transactions.

The strength of many primary schools lies in their accent being placed on children's writing. This is justified on the ground that about 90 per cent of marks in examination is allotted on writing tests and the children and teachers are found to be busy in tasks/writing tests on the themes/lessons the children study in classroom situations. Teachers are also busy with preparing the children for scholarship test of children (Class IV) even beyond class hours. Children's success at this test make the schools prominent and scholastic and eminent, which is reflected in their being large school accommodating above 200 children being admitted and learned these schools obviating the distance barrier of schools being located from children's residence, i.e., no matter for the schools whether located within 1 km/2 km distance from residence of children. Teachers live close to schools in teachers hostel/quarters there available.

Our research study on problems of deficiency among primary school children in English reveals that this deficiency is formidable among most of the children, particularly among the relatively backward community like ST, Muslim and SC. There are nstitutional, demographic, social and cultural constraints on children's English language learning.

At the stages of Class II to Class IV large amount of vocabulary in English could be developed in children as part of English language learning. But that is hardly done in the actual classroom transactions as well as in the teachers' training programme. Much of the valuable and limited time is spent on rhymes, chanting which are mainly performed by the resource persons as well as by the teacher trainees. The lacuna develop in teachers as well as among children because their first language is Bengali and they have not developed sufficient language skills in English, their second language. Rhymes, chanting miming, drama etc. are joyful, while children are well-developed in English learning.

In the modern methodology at the primary level the teaching process is made joyful and attractive through noisy classroom by means of miming and dramatization process without making any effort for children's understanding of the theme. It does not make the children learned in English language because basic skills of the language like reading, writing, speaking and comprehension or understanding are not adequately generated in them, which are very important as per language experts like Thompson and Watt (1959).

Champion (1957) and other language experts hold that teaching process in English language be bi-lingual, which the NCF 2005 also holds and the Expert Committee on Syllabus and Curricula as formed by the Government of West Bengal in their Draft Report suggest. It is conspicuous by its absence in teachers' training or orientation course in English at the primary stage while in contrast it is widely prevalent in the upper primary teachers' training process in the subject. This generates in primary school children deficiency in skill of comprehension; they are not moved from their known domain to their unknown area.

Community participation in school management has much to do with the quality of teaching-learning process of children for schools where the guardians of children are conscious and attentive of children's education, their attendance in VEC and MTA meetings is high and teachers take care of and are also attentive to children's education.

Quality of education remains to be an important issue at the upper primary level also. The major bottlenecks in this respect are reported to be the large classroom size of children at the upper primary level and inadequate number of classrooms and secondary teachers, which need to be improved. There is also disparity across blocks and municipalities on account of unscientific process of distribution of qualified teachers and classrooms across both primary and upper primary schools, which needs to be corrected so that there is rational distribution of teachers and classrooms for the sake of equity and quality of education.

Group learning method is suggested in the new methodology. Nowhere in the schools we visited so far this method is found to be in practice. It assumes for its success children well advanced in language skills, small size classrooms and holisticism to prevail in the minds of children, particularly among the much advanced children. In a class and caste divided society this hardly is found. Nowhere in the schools we visited so far this method is found to be in practice.

No home task is suggested to reduce the burden of education on children. Information puts up burden on them but that is not education which is generated in children through the process of assimilation of ideas as Swami Vivekananda, other educationists and the National Curriculum Framework 2005 hold. Thus, the concept of burden of education appears to be absurd. This is because real education gives joy and delight, which does not put up any real burden on them. The attempt to reduce the so-called burden of education renders education light, which tends to be no meaningful education. This dissuades children and their guardians from entering government-aided educational institutions, which rather paves the way for expansion of private schools.

In foreign developed countries there is no necessity for children doing home task because there everything in classroom transactions is organised in such a way that children do and complete their tasks in schools. This cannot be followed in India where the first generation learners are massive in number and schools are not well-equipped in both physical and human infrastructures. There is vicious circle of underdevelopment in education of most of the children, particularly of the backward community children.

Syllabi and curricula including examination pattern also influence quality education. These are so framed as to make quantity/information load of children prevail over their absorption/assimilation of ideas and thus improvement of quality/creativity (as per NCF 2005 which upholds constructivism) in children is aborted.

There is a lot of experimentation of foreign models in Indian soil on elementary education. We adopt so many things without going through the outcome of experimentation. Thus, what ought to be essentially done for the elementary school children is not done while what is not essential is done with profligacy. Wastage is rampant, which makes the children and the society still poorer.

Too much accent is made in teachers' training at the primary and upper primary levels on theory and experiments in education without examining its outcome in the classroom transactions and children's real learning achievement. Quality of education in them is at stake.

Children's achievement in extra-curricular activities is hardly considered while their evaluation is made. Thus, one important aspect of quality education is ignored. Quality education implies not only learning achievement of children but also their participation, performance and proficiency in extra-curricular activities like games and sports, recitation, debates, music and dance and in other artistic fields and also in decent behavioural pattern including discipline that is developed in them. Since, education makes for a complete man of body, mind and soul evaluation of children's attainment in education should also encompass extra-curricular activities and behavioural pattern of children, not alone quantitative evaluation of the learning achievement of children.

Infrastructural development which is also associated with quality education is still inadequate and unevenly spread/distributed across schools and education circles/blocks, and across SSM interventions/initiatives. Monitoring of SSM projects/plans implementation remains poor. Coordination in planning and implementation remains weak. Quantity of achievement of targets under different heads prevails over quality achievement of children in education resulting in huge wastage of resources. Principles as embodied in National Curriculum Framework 2005 are hardly observed and executed at both primary and upper primary levels while syllabus and curricula are framed and classroom transactions are conducted.

We may make the following policy recommendations based on our discussion made so far:

1. Teachers have to play a vital role in the achievement of quality education. They ought to be cultured, innovative and creative. They should be allowed to exercise their freedom in classroom transactions in the way that best suits the different strata of children whose competency levels the teachers know best by following the best possible and appropriate practices known to them. Not the cascade method of teaching a subject which has been introduced recently by the West Bengal Board of Primary Education and the West Bengal Board of Secondary Education, but the best democratically established and appropriate method of the same has to be explored and adopted. Teachers' freedom in respect of academic pursuits including teaching methods has to be honoured and thus the risk of wastage is minimized.

2. Teachers should conduct the baseline survey of each child which enables them to apply themselves as regards where and what to start with, how to conduct the process of teaching and where to end while they conduct classroom transactions.

3. Academic culture among not only children but also teachers and guardians has to be developed so that many abberations are avoided and an interactive process of education works so that real positive culture develops and India's strong conventional academic culture and tradition

as are being practiced in many prominent schools (so far visited) even today are maintained and flourished in all schools, and not forgotten.

4. The National Curriculum Framework 2005 (NCF 2005) suggests active children where teacher would be facilitator. While children are active, teacher has to be not only facilitator/friend, but also philosopher and guide in the existing socio-cultural context of India.

5. Teaching and contact hours of teachers with children have to be lengthened in schools so that schools become their second homes for their education (upbinging).

6. Teachers have to plan academic lessons, to make TLM use plans, and also to have some sound commanding authority in the subjects they teach and thus impart education in the classroom in the way that is most effective on children. For each class the teacher must have a lesson plan as prepared by him/her and this must be submitted to the Head Teacher and circulated/shown among the students in the classroom according to which he/she would conduct the classroom transactions.

7. Teachers must ensure the minimum level of learning (MLL) of all children. He/she shall start his/her teaching in the classroom in the way which would facilitate learning of the lowest merit students and gradually move up to serve the learning needs of the relatively high merit students so that every student is given the scope of participation in the teaching-learning process. At least 40 per cent of the time allotted for a class be devoted to serve the learning process of the less meritorious students so that at least basic knowledge of the subject is imparted to each student. At least 20 per cent of the time allotted for class teaching be utilized as question answer time and for interaction among students and between the teacher and the students. Accent here also shall be on relatively low merit students and first generation learners. A teacher shall take class tests as many as possible/desirable and at least 10 per cent marks of any subject be allotted for the class test as part of the comprehensive and continuous evaluation (CCE). Sufficient accent ought to be made on developing in children appreciable writing skill because writing tests constitute 90 per cent of the marks allotted under the examination system.

8. Quality and accountability of teachers of schools have to be promoted through enforcement of rules and regulations and monitoring by the appropriate euthority, through teachers' training on Motivation at the upper primary level and through the community participation for the same.

9. Learning of children should be linked with activities/works from the primary stage upwards and it should generate important personal and social values such as self-reliance, creativity and cooperation.

10. Number of pupils in a class shall never exceed 30 for primary schools and 40 in upper primary schools. For each class there shall be a teacher irrespective of the size of the class or number of children. If necessary, nearby low enrolment schools may be merged in the interest of efficiency in the process of teaching. Low enrolment schools (both primary and upper primary) have to be intensively studied so that adequate measures for their development are adopted. Accent ought to be made not so much on proximate schools with inadequate facilities being set-up but on quality school development with standard infrastructures so that (social) quality exclusion of children is avoided.

11. Monitoring of teachers' training programme needs to be strictly done. Such programme must provide scope for practice teaching where children of varied strata would remain present and selected teacher trainees would impart practice teaching so that effectiveness of the teacher training programme is assessed and enhanced.

12. Only the subject teachers at the upper primary levels should be invited to participate in the teachers' training programme for longer days than at present, where deficiencies of children as well as teachers would also be discussed so that remedial measures are adopted in the interest of improvement of quality of education.

13. Report of the teacher trainees of each subject should be academic covering the features of the methodology they are trained with and also the problems that are associated with it with an eye to the academic status of children across their different socio-cultural and economic strata. A teacher may be a researcher to analyse the problems of quality education and to throw light on them for their possible solution.

14. Feedbacks from teachers undergoing teachers' training/orientation programme have to be obtained and analysed. Such formats containing multiple choice questions on the subject of training shall be devised for all subjects of training, be served to the teachers to be filled in and then checked, which would reveal the level as well as type of quality of teachers which needs to be improved in the interest of quality improvement of children. Purba Medinipur district has made a unique experiment with preparation of the Feedback Format that has been filled in by the primary and upper primary teacher-trainees. While many of these filled in formats are not checked so far measures ought to be adopted for checking all formats. This process has to be replicated in other districts, which will help the appropriate authority adopt such plan and programme as would facilitate and ensure the process of development of quality teachers and thus the process of much coveted quality education of children.

15. Learners' diary has to be introduced at the upper primary teachers' training programme as is there at the primary level and that has to be checked thoroughly by experts so that quality improvement of teachers could be achieved along with that of their children of schools.

16. Not only development of speaking skill but also development of reading skill, proper pronunciation, writing skill and adequate understanding of the theme be emphasized so that these contribute to the child's progress in curricular areas. Findings from action research on these areas will shed lignt on developing appropriate skills in children.

17. The major problem of both children and teachers at both primary and upper primary levels lies in writing correct English, which needs to be improved through teachers' training programme being conducted on English. Since, while speaking both the teacher trainees and even the DRPs are seen to use sentences that contain errors which are structural in nature it is suggested the teachers' training should be having accent on discussing the structural features of the Lessons of English books so that quality teachers develop, which would help develop quality education in children. It is recalled and worthnoting that as per NCF 2005 teachers should use simple and correct English for the creation of beauty since beauty is truth and truth beauty.

18. In the light of NCF 2005 English language teaching-learning process has to be bi-lingual, which would help understanding, assimilation of ideas and enhancement of knowledge of children. It should put sufficient accent on vocabulary enhancement and on simple English grammar learning as is done in Sanskrit language learning. It is essential considering the level of English language knowledge of the existing teachers (who feel uneasy even to teach Class V English Book), the low learning base of children in the absence or insufficiency of exposure/conversation at home and environment and also to avoid cumulative poverty of English language base of children. The teacher of English in the classroom would start teaching a subject in a class in Bengali, the children's mother tongue and then gradually proceed to use bi-lingual and multi-disciplinary process of teaching with focus on the particular subject he/she teaches. It would make children participative, responsive and really delightful while they learn and enjoy the subject. The new methodology of teaching unfortunately takes the round about process with accent on the process rather than on outcome/product in which the children feel shaky and confused.

19. Communicative and Functional English hardly does work in absence of suitable environment and leads to poor English language learning base of children. Every language learning be made bi-lingual at

the primary stage and multi-lingual at the upper primary stage with due accent on vocabulary and grammar.

20. Specialization of teachers in subjects of teaching even at the primary school level be introduced, as is there in some renowned schools of Purba Medinipur district. This is essential in view of the recent developments in syllabi and curricula which are being modernized, which would minimize the wastages of teaching hours and save time for the sake of the efficient teaching learning process. In the teachers' training/orientation programme only subject teachers be invited to avail of the training facilities. In this way also sufficient economy in respect of costs of the programme as well as its efficiency could be achieved. Subject teacher at the primary and upper primary classes ought to be fixed.

21. The new methodology which has got its merits and the traditional methodology which is long tested and found to be effective and sound ought to be blended or combined in a useful way to remedy the glaring deficiencies of children in subjects, particularly in English, Bengali and Mathematics which appear to them to be still fearful. In English both the new methodology with accent on oral fluency and the traditional methodologies with accent on accuracy based on grammar ought to be blended or combined in a useful way. Complex and round-about methods of teaching as being propagated through the modern methods of teaching subjects at the primary level have to be reviewed and their faults and limitations if any in classroom transactions should be avoided. Teaching method in subjects in real classroom transactions ought to be as simple and straight as possible as the National Curriculum Framework 2005 suggests.

22. In the new methodology as in NCF 2005 teachers are to facilitate the children who are supposed to be active. Better effective would be if as in our traditional methodology advanced children are invited to take over classroom transactions after the teachers' brief and simple presentation on a lesson is over. They would use TLMs etc. and make presentation of the theme which the teachers have already made. In this way these children develop gradually into teachers while the other children closely follow theme and teaching process of the advanced children. No fear of teachers, if any is there, because they accept their class-mate and advanced children to be their own and may think if their advanced children or class-mates can do they can also do. Shadow of fear is gone, a congenial environment prevails and in this way a busy, though not noisy classroom, is created, which is highly coveted. Participatory teaching-learning/group learning/scholar learning have to be followed and enforced.

23. In respect of teachers' training in Arithmetic at the primary level the problem is that in the new methodology the process of solving a mathematical problem is made lengthy and complex, over which many DRPs, some State Respurce Persons and teacher trainees are seen to be confused between the traditional methodology and the new one. But this confusion is hardly addressed. Quality teaching demands that the teaching method be as easy as possible so that each teacher trainee and also each child comprehend it easily. The traditional easy method of solving a problem may be used along with a relatively complex modern method so that the teacher trainees as well as the children feel happy, get adjusted and improved in terms of learning the methodologies for the solution of a mathematical problem.

24. Teachers' training in Natural Science training courses are seen to be commendable. It is suggested here that TLMs used and scientific explanations of a theme or an event may be developed based on experimentation and secular culture on the same.

25. Teachers' training in Motivation is important in the present era of neo-liberalism which puts accent on individualism and consumerism against the resource constraint of the globe/globe much more than attainment of social goals as emphasized in SSM. But here the lacuna is that hardly any resource person on Motivation is developed. One module on Motivation has been printed, which is circulated to the teacher trainees, but that is not seen to be sufficient. This module is based on foreign culture hardly presents the culture and tradition India has developed through the works and achievements of great educationists like Vidyasagar, Rabindranath Tagore, Swami Vivekananda, S. Radhakrishnan and the great teachers and scientists like Acharya Prafulla Chandra Roy, Satyen Bose. Materialist culture is important, which is upheld in the module/book on Motivation but that is not all. "Lives of great men all remind us"—it should be emphasized so that individualization of education but socialization of man is realized.

26. Since, use of teaching learning materials (TLMs) is found to be insufficient, particularly at the SSK, MSK and Upper Primary level training camps and classroom transactions it is suggested that those be prepared by using locally available resources in a collaborative way between the teachers and the children. Along with Lesson Plan the TLM use plan ought to be prepared so that the training process as well as the teaching learning process in classroom situations is made really attractive, joyful and delightful. Unit-wise TLM will have to be prepared by the teacher and must be used in classroom transactions. To facilitate the

process TLM grants shall be released against each teacher. The Head Teacher/Head Master at the first instance would monitor the use of TLM in the classroom and report to the VEC/Managing Committee and higher authorities on this matter for their information and possible reaction.

27. Training modules in subjects have been prepared by experts drawn from the higher education and also from secondary schools. It is suggested that those modules be prepared by drawing experiences of teaching of reputed teachers. After these modules are tested among children and these are found sound and succeessful on testing, these modules be circulated to each school and kept in school libraries (both primary and upper primary and secondary) for consultation of teachers and children. These modules shall be printed after they are finalized in a workshop attended by reputed teachers of schools, colleges and universities.

28. While percentage of attendance of upper primary teacher-trainees is high in subjects like Bengali, English and Mathematics, that in Geography, History, Physical Science and Biological Science is not so, which needs to be improved. Percentage of absentees in some centres exceeds 10. Necessary measures ought to be adopted so that all the teachers attend the orientation courses and that for the whole period. For this purpose the attendance sheet should contain both arrival time and departure time of teachers. The time period of presence of teachers as per schedule should be strictly enforced.

29. At both primary and upper primary levels of Teachers' Training College, University and reputed school teachers of subjects be made SRPs/KRPs and DRPs so that the essences of the training modules prepared by them are explained to the teacher trainees adequately. Valuable suggestions of these experts ought to be made available for the qualitative improvement of the teachers' training process and also of the whole school elementary education. Suggestions made by the trainee teachers of/on different subjects are also valuable and these be highlighted and consulted while making teacher training plans as follow-up democratic measures.

30. The teachers' training programme needs to be oriented in a manner that would develop in teachers such capabilities as would facilitate the process of creativity and overall quality education of children.

31. Not only run/rush for quantity achievement but also due accent on quality assurance has to be made. Accent should be made, particularly by teachers, on children's quality search/exploration and its development.

32. Syllabi and curricula have to be reformed with an eye to the prevalent socio-economic-cultural milieu and with due regard for quality and value education. In the interest of quality education and for attaining effectiveness

of teachers' training syllabi and curricula need to be reformed in the light of NCF 2005, which suggests curriculum development with an eye to social and cultural and natural environment in which children are born and grown.

33. Not only financial but also physical and human resource planning under Sarva Shiksha Mission ought to be done at the decentralized levels. To fulfil this objective adequate database has to be prepared and printed at the grassroots school level. Social mobilization on elementary education needs to be effectively done to help develop adequate database for planning so that wastages in education are minimized. The data management system needs to be oriented under SSM to the school level and not the State level alone, which means that the data be processed and used at the school level and only relevant information be passed up. If this needs to be computerized—this too should be done at the school and cluster level rather than the block level. To this end computers be provided for data management at a decentralized level. Schools may be furnished with computers so that their sound database is developed, which may be compiled at Circle, district and state levels.

34. Social welfare and well-being maximization through elementary education should be the goal of SSM planning so that social exclusion in elementary school education is avoided through developing at least minimum level of learning (MLL) for all children and thus they see and feel that the opportunity cost of education in terms of child labour is negligible and they derive net gains from continuing their education. In this way quality education for 100 per cent children would be ensured.

35. Provision of additional teachers in schools, both primary and upper primary, be corresponded by provision of additional classrooms in the schools so that effective utilization of human resources could be done to the improvement of quality education among children. Class section arrangement ought to be made on scentific basis.

36. There is disparate level of educational attainment of children across social and economic classes. The disadvantaged groups of children including the poorly performing children need to be specially educated. The teacher trainees report that the remedial teaching hardly takes place and the deficiencies accumulate in them, leading to their dropout of the educational system. Appropriate planning and necessary measures need to be formulated and adopted to remedy the language deficiencies of children through appropriate reforms of the system so that great improvement can be achieved in respect of children's teaching learning process. Residential hostels in schools not only for backward community children but also for other lagging/

retarded children have to be set-up and properly managed so that schools become the favourite second home of children for their education and developing culture and thus their cumulative errors over years are corrected. Teachers hostels/quarters have to be developed so that children and teachers study/work in cooperation and all the children, whether deficient or advanced grow into prominence and eminence. This is in conscience with India's culture and tradition of the Vedic and post-Vedic Age.

37. Model schools based on their quality achievements ought to be identified, awarded and the principles followed there and the system developed in the schools be replicated.

38. Model management of schools has to be explored, developed and propagated.

39. Monitoring mechanisms for schools needs to be improved so that serious discrepancies in respect of utilization of ACR grants are adequately addressed. DISE data as regards ACRs, toilets and other physical infrastructures also need to be checked and verified so that their relevance and authencity are established.

40. Pervasiveness of private tuition at both primary and upper primary levels be checked through improvement of learning achievement of all categories of children. Emphasis should be made upon minimum level of learning of all categories of children with provision/proviso of higher graded learning for the advanced children. Private tuition has to be regulated in such a way that it does not take place during the school hours of teaching. Private tuition has got important bearing with attendance of children.

41. Evaluative research on SSM interventions and that on elementary school education have to be conducted by external agencies including colleges, universities, researchers and even schools and that be grass-roots-based.

42. For the time being, the graded assessment tools designed by ASER can be used to assess levels of children and flexible materials put together for graded teaching within each classroom.

43. Over and above this, children from marginalized sections and first generation learners who are getting mainstreamed require support within the schools. For this the models being run outside government schools can also be mainstreamed into schools and with the help of these organizations also expanded through the school system.

44. Teacher education, both pre-service and in-service, as well as the academic support system needs a major reform and needs to be well aligned with the main curricular and learning pedagogy frame.

45. The academic support system also requires academic strengthening, as do the SCERT, Boards and DIETs. A plan for this should also be worked out.

46. In a perfectly competitive exchange and market economy both buyers and sellers gain to the maximum. Such competitiveness has also to be introduced in government and government-managed education sector which is funded by the government through introducing reward and punishment provisions and regulations. The issues of commitment, dedication and devotion, sincerity etc. of teachers to the cause of adequate and improved services of education to children are addressed in this way.

NOTES

1. *See* Bowman (1980), Psacharopoulos (1983 and 1984) and Schielfelbein (1982).
2. An acquisition poor environment is one where language is used only inside the classroom (e.g. 35 minutes a day for six working days) by a teacher who may not always be highly proficient in its use. Very often the classroom is large and may lack the facilities that make it possible to learn a living language for use.
3. The useful between 'usage' and 'use' comes from Professor Henry Widdowson (1978). Here 'usage' denotes language used to show knowledge of grammar; 'use' denotes language use made for communicative purposes. Usage is a customary manner in which a language or a form of a language is spoken and written.
4. *National Curriculam Framework*, 2005.
5. Additiuve bilingualism refers to a system where two (or more) languages work together. They add to or strengthen each other. The dominant language does not stand against or weaken the small or local or minority language(s).

REFERENCES

Billows, F. L. (1961), *The Techniques of Language Teaching*, Longman.

Champion, H.C., (1957), *Lectures on Teaching of English in India*, Oxford University Press.

Conwuka, E. and E. Eguavoen, (2007), "Globalization and Economic Development: The Nigrian Experience", *Journal of Social Science*, 14 (1): 44-51.

Cummings, T.C.P., (1916), *How to Learn a Language*, Kegan Paul.

Government of India, (2007), *Study of Student Attendance*, Document presented to the Sixth Review Mission of Sarva Shiksha Abhiyan, Ministry of Human Resource Development.

Government of West Bengal, (2004), *West Bengal Human Development Report*, Development and Planning Department, Kolkata.

Halliday, M.A.K., (1973), *Explorations in the Functions of Language*, London: Edward Arnold.

Haq, M. and K. Haq, (1998), *Human Development in South Asia*, Oxford University Press, Karachi.

Holliday, A., (1994), *Appropriate Methodology and Social Context*, Cambridge: Cambridge University Press.

Hymes, D. (1971), "On communicative competence", in Pride, J. and L. Holmes (eds.), *Sociolinguistics*, Middlesex: Penguin.

India Sarva Shiksha Abhiyan (SSA) Eleventh Joint Review Mission, (2010), *State Report: West Bengal,* January 17-22.

Long, M.H. and P. Robinson, (1998), "Focus on Form: Theory, Research and Practice" in Doughty, C. and J. Williams (eds.), *Focus on Form in Classroom Second Language Acquisition*, Cambridge: Cambridge University Press.

National Council of Educational Research and Training, (2003), Learning Achievement of Students at the End of Class V, NCERT, New Delhi.

National Curriculum Framework 2005.

Paschim Banga Sarva Shiksha Mission, (2010), *Status Report of SSA,* West Bengal.

————, Analytical Report on DISE 2010.

————, Annual Report, 2010-11.

Pratham Resource Centre, (2005 onwards), *Annual Status of Education Report*, Mumbai, Pratham.

PROBE, (1999), *Public Report on Basic Education in India*, Oxford University Press, New Delhi.

Rana, *et al.*, (2002), *The Delivery of Primary Education: A Study in West Bengal* (with an Introduction by Amartya Sen), TLM Books in Association with Pratichi (India) Trust, New Delhi.

Ravitch, Diana (2012), "Schools we can envy", *The Newyork Review of Books*, 8 March.

_______, (2003), "State of Primary Education in West Bengal", *Economic and Political Weekly,* Vol. XXXVIII, No. 22, May 31.

_______, (2006), *Public Private Interface in the Primary Schooling System: A Study in West Bengal,* Pratichi (India) Trust, Delhi.

Schultz, T.W., (1961), "Investment in Human Capital", *American Economic Review*, 51/1 (March)

The Pratichi Education Report II, (2009), *Primary Education in West Bengal: Change and Challenges*, Pratichi Trust (India), New Delhi.

Thompson, M.S. and H.G. Wyat, (1959), *The Teaching of English in India.*

Tilak, J.B.G., (1987), *The Economics of Inequality in Education*, Sage Publications, New Delhi.

West, M., (1962), *Teaching English in Difficult Circumstances*, London: Longman.

World Bank, (1997), *Primary Education in India*, Washington DC, USA.

3

Demographic Outcome, Utilization of Health Services and RCH Status in India

A State Level Analysis

Gargi Bhattacharya and *Sushil K. Haldar*

Introduction

The exogeneity of technological progress in the neo-classical model and the difficulty of explaining long-term economic growth because of diminishing returns to capital have limited the analytical capacity of the neo-classical model and its empirical verification. The ever widening gap between rich and poor economies has thus led researchers to look for new theories that they feel might explain this dynamic. For a long time economists have tended to ignore health as both a relevant factor of production and important determinant of economic growth Adrean Van Zon and Joan Muysken (2005). Fogel (1994), Barrow (1996), Barro and Sala-i-Martin (2004) were among the first in examining the relationship between economic growth and health, and their research has subsequently given rise to a substantial store of work focusing on the link between wealth and health. Gradually, more and more economists have come to recognize that the relationship between health and economic growth is not only demand driven, but that health itself is an important determinant of economic growth. Sustained economic growth depends on levels of human capital (comprising health, education and skill) whose stocks increase as a result of higher levels of health status, better education and new learning and training procedures. Without a labour force with some minimum levels of education and health status a country is incapable of maintaining a state of continuous growth (Lopez-Casasnovas *et al.*, 2005). Better health will lead to a better growth outcomes. The greatest challenge of twenty first century is to provide every human being on the planet with a long, healthy and fulfilling life, to participate in the activities of their community. The Millennium Development Goals—signed by 189 countries in 2000 set clear targets for reducing poverty and other causes of human deprivation and for promoting sustainable development. But how far is India from meeting those goals? Is there any progress of the health status in India over the last fifty years? What is the over-all public health scenario in this developing nation? And what are the resources needed to help the country, not on track? How far and to what extent the health status (measured by different indicators) does vary across the states in India?

Health is not only the absence of illness, it is also the ability of people to develop to their potential during their entire lives. In that sense health is an asset which individual possesses, and which has intrinsic as well as instrumental value. Intrinsic value is in the sense that being healthy is very important source of well being. In instrumental terms, health impacts economic growth in a number of ways. It reduces production losses due to worker illness, raises the productivity of adult as a result of better nutrition, and it lowers absenteeism rates and improves learning among school children. Health affects economic growth directly through labour productivity and the economic burden of illness, for example. Health also indirectly impacts economic growth since aspects such as child health affects the future income of people through the impact health has on education. This indirect impact is easier to understand if it is observed on a family level. When a family is healthy, both the mother and the father can hold a job, earn money which allows them to feed, protect and send their children to school. Healthy and well nourished children will perform better in school and better performance in school will positively impact their future income. If parents ensure that their children have a high probability of reaching adulthood, in general, they will have fewer children and they will be able to invest more in health and education for each of them. This is followed from the household economic theory of fertility developed by Chicago-Columbia School.

Declining fertility rates have changed the age structure of India's population, resulting in a "bulge" in the working age-group. This "demographic dividend" leads to the hypothesis that the bulge in working population will lead to acceleration in growth (Chandrasekhar, Ghosh and Roychoudhury, 2006). India is and for some time will remain one of the youngest countries in the world. In 2020, the average Indian will be only 29 years old, compared with the average age of 37 years in China and US,

45 in West Europe and 48 in Japan (Dyson, 2008). This implies that the demographic process would create a large and growing labour force, which is expected to deliver spin-offs in terms of growth and prosperity through a number of routes. However, recent employment figures indicate that absorption of the Indian youth into the labour force is not as high as one would expect. This is due to the poor employability of the workforce, which is severely affected by attainment in good health. Although India accounts for 16.5 per cent of the world's population, it contributes to one fifth of the world's share of diseases (WHO, 2000). A major health challenge posed by the specific phase of the demographic transition that India is going through is related to infant mortality and reproductive health. This is inevitable given the fact that the proportion of women in the reproductive age-group is projected to rise to a peak of nearly 55 per cent in 2016 and remain around that level for the next decade. But the increase in this proportion requires increased efforts to reduce not only maternal mortality, but also the number of infant and child deaths. Moreover, if we do not combat malnourishment of the children then we cannot expect the benefits of Demographic Dividend properly. This needs to be remedied in order to take advantage of the opportunity for growth that the demographic dividend is supposed to give to India.

Objective of the Study and Associated Research Questions

Keeping in mind the importance of health in general and reproductive and child health in particular in social development paradigm, the following are the research objectives:

A. The first objective of the study is to know about the progress of health status in India over time. The mortality and morbidity situation of different states of our country have also been discussed in this context.
B. The second objective is to determine the positions of the sixteen major states of India in respect of achievement indices of the key Reproductive and Child Health (RCH) parametres estimated by Relative Distance Methodology for two points of time (viz. 1998-99 and 2005-06). The progress of achievement indices over time (viz. 1998-99 to 2005-06) is also measured.
C. The deprivation indices are estimated from the key RCH parametres of the states using the Power Mean formula developed by Sen and Anand (1997).

D. Whether the sixteen major states are converging or diverging in respect of achievement (as well as deprivation indices) indices over time are examined using various inequality measures like Generalized Entropy (with different values of weights of the distribution viz. (α) and social welfare based measure viz. Atkinson measure of inequality (with different values of inequality aversion parametre viz. (Σ). Additionally, we examine the inequality of all the selected RCH parametres in two different time points. This helps to explore in which RCH parametre, the inequality is found to be maximum and minimum over time across the states of India. Such a study is expected to have some importance in understanding heath in general and RCH in particular across the major states in India. Regional variation in respect of different heath parametres is studied with a view to understand the debate over health convergence across the major states in India.

Data and Methodology

Data

The present study has been carried out using different data set from various sources. Over-all health scenario of India has been depicted with the time series data set of Infant Mortality Rate available from 1951 to 2006. This has been collected from the SRS, Registrar General, Government of India. The data set of life expectancy at Birth at five years interval from 1971 to 1997 has been drawn from Ministry of Health and Family Welfare and Sample Registration System (SRS). Morbidity related data was available from NSSO different rounds. NFHS-I, NFHS-II and NFHS-III published by International Institute of Population Science (IIPS) have also been used for the study of prevalence of different types of diseases across the major states in India.

For the construction of two types of indices (viz. achievement and deprivation indices) from the selected key RCH parametres, the present chapter uses the dataset of National Family Health Survey (NFHS) under the Reproductive and Child Health (RCH) Project (Round-II: 1998-99; Round-III: 2005-06). We have taken sixteen major states (comprising 95 per cent of India's population) for our analysis. For carrying out the study of this part, information has been collected on various indicators pertaining to reproductive and child health (RCH). Eleven RCH key indicators have been chosen from NFHS-II and NFHS-III.

Different indicators with their corresponding notations are given as follows:

1. Percentage of women age 20-24 married by age 18 (X_1)
2. Percentage of married women with 2 living children wanting no more children (X_2)
3. Percentage of women using any family planning method (X_3)
4. Percentage of mothers who had at least 3 antenatal care visits for their last birth (X_4)
5. Percentage of institutional deliveries (X_5)
6. Percentage of children 12-23 months completely immunized (X_6)
7. Percentage of children with diarrhoea in the last two weeks prior to survey taken to health facility (X_7)
8. Percentage of children under 3 years who are under weight (X_8)
9. Percentage of women whose body mass index is below normal (X_9)
10. Percentage of children age 6-35 months who are anaemic (X_{10})
11. Percentage of women having knowledge of AIDS (X_{11})

Methodology

Construction of Different Indices

Different indices are computed to study the pattern of reproductive and child health status in the sixteen major states of India. All the states are ranked according to the absolute values of these indices.

State Level RCH Achievement Index (AI)

In this present chapter, for the construction of RCH Achievement Index (AI), Range Equalization Method or the Relative Distance Methodology developed by UNDP (1990) has been followed.

Here it is worth mentioning that from the available dataset relative position of each state in two different time points can be obtained in respect of any particular indicator of RCH. But what is the overall position of a state in respect of all the RCH parametres? In order to answer this question, we construct an index that certainly reflects overall achievement of each and every state of India in terms of all the eleven RCH parametres.

So, these chosen eleven different parametres of RCH are incorporated to construct RCH Achievement Index (AI).

The steps of constructing AI using range equalization are as follows:

(1) Since the index is related to 'development', it needs to make all the indicators uniformly positive. The indicators have been made scale free. For this purpose the range of each indicator has been computed. The range R_{ij} would be $(X_{ij max} - X_{ij min})$, where they are the maximum and minimum values respectively for ith indicator across the states. Then $(X_{ij} - X_{ij min})$ has been computed and each value is divided by the range. We thus obtain the scale free values of the *i*-th indicators as
$(X_{ij} - X_{ij min})/R_{ij}$ for all *j*, where *j* = 1,2,......, N. N is the total number of the states, which is 16 in our present study and *i* = 1, 2...11.
So, $Y_{ij} = (X_{ij} - X_{ij min})/R_{ij}$, where Y_{ij} is the normalized value of i-th indicator for *j*-th state.

(2) The aggregate achievement index (AI) for the *j*-th state would be $\Sigma Y_{ij}/M$ where M is the total number of indicators, which in the present study is eleven.

How, do we measure the progress of a particular state in respect of AI? The AI ranks states relative to each other for a particular year. The maximum and the minimum values that define the maximum distance to be travelled for each variable (parametre) are specific to that year. Now, over time the actual achieved values of the parametres change, consequently, the maximum and the minimum values also change over time as well as across the states in India.

Now, improvement in the component of AI in any state over time may be reflected as a decline in its AI value, if over time, its relative position is deteriorated. If the maximum and the minimum values were to change over time, this might lead to an anomaly in which a state's actual indicators (parametres) of RCH could go up while its score goes down. This may happen because the minimum has gone up or the range has widened over time or both. Thus, moving the goal posts makes comparing the AI over time more difficult. Therefore, in order to measure the progress of AI of a state over time and across the states in India, we should modify the Relative Distance Methodology.

Without changing the logic of the AI, the maximum and the minimum should be defined, not for each point of time but over a period of time, using fixed goal posts. Thus, if we are interested to measure the progress of a state in AI between 1998-99 and 2005-06, the minimum would be the minimum of all values for each RCH parametres for all states over the 7 years, similarly, for the maximum. The distance to be travelled is thus stretched out as the maximum over the 7 years period. With this logic the RCH- AI becomes comparable over time as well as across states. The difference in the value of AI over time can be shown to be a weighted sum of the growth rates in the seven variables (parametres): the weights are given by the ratio of the initial values of a variable (parametre) to the maximum range.

To express this Algebraic way:

$$Z_{ijt} = [X_{ijt} - \underset{j,t}{\text{Min}}\, X_{ijt}]*[\underset{j,t}{\text{Max}}\, X_{ijt} - \underset{j,t}{\text{Min}}\, X_{ijt}]^{-1} \quad \text{...(1)}$$

Where

j = states, t = time, i = indicators. The denominator will remain unchanged for all states and for all time periods.

$$\text{Thus; Modified RCH} - \text{AI} [= \text{MAI}_{jt}] = \Sigma Z_{ijt}/11 \quad \text{...(2)}$$

Therefore, the difference between the two values of MAI_{jt} corresponding to initial and terminal time points gives us relative progress of a particular state in respect of achievement of RCH parametres.

State level RCH Deprivation Index (DI)

In order to know how far and to what extent each state in absolute terms has been suffering from vulnerability in respect of the above key RCH parametres, we use the power mean function developed by Sen and Anand (1997). It is to be mentioned here that a state with higher achievement (AI) generally manifests lower deprivation but it may always not hold good because of the power of the average. Thus, in order to find out the Deprivation Index in respect of the RCH parametre, we subtract each parametre from 100, since all are given in percentage terms.

Thus, following Sen and Anand (1997), we consider the following function:

$$DI(\alpha) = [\Sigma\omega_i.P_{iD}{}^{\alpha}/\Sigma\omega_i]^{1/\alpha} \quad \text{...(3)}$$

where, $P_{iD} = (100–X_i)$, α stands for the order of the average, ω_i be the weights attached to $(100–X_i)$ parametre, $i = 1,2\ldots11$. We consider $\alpha = 3$ and $\omega_1 = \omega_2 = \ldots. = \omega_7 = 1$ for our estimation. Equation (3) does follow the following properties:

1. $\text{Min}\{P_{1D}, P_{2D}, \ldots.P_{11D}\} \leq DI(\alpha) \leq \text{Max}\{P_{1D}, P_{2D},\ldots. P_{11D}\}$
2. As $\alpha \to \infty$, $DI(\alpha) \to \text{Max}\{P_{1D}, P_{2D},\ldots. P_{11D}\}$
3. DI (α) is homogeneous of degree 1 in $\{P_{1D}, P_{2D},\ldots P_{11D}\}$
4. For each i = 1, 2,....11more $\partial DI(\alpha)/\partial P_{iD} > 0$
5. DI (α) is convex with respect to P_{iD}. For each i = 1, 2,...11 $\partial^2 P(\alpha)/\partial P_{iD}^2 > 0$
6. For any *i*, $\partial P(\alpha)/\partial\omega_i \geq 0$ as $P_{iD} \geq DI(\alpha)$, similarly, $\partial DI(\alpha)/\partial\, \omega_i \leq 0$ as $P_{iD} \leq DI(\alpha)$
7. For given $P_{1D}, P_{2D} \ldots.P_{11D}$ that are not equal, if $\alpha > \gamma > 0$, then $DP(\alpha) > DP(\gamma)$
8. For $\alpha \geq 1$, $\sum_{J=1}^{m} nj / n.DPj(\alpha) \geq DP(\alpha)$
9. The elasticity of substitution (σ) between any two deprivation sub-indices of DI(α), that is, between any two of P_{1D}, P_{2D} ......P_{11D}, is constant and equal to $1/(\alpha - 1)$.

Cluster Analysis

It is our interest to know what are the states are found to be closed to each other based on the observed values of the RCH parametres drawn from NFHS-II and NFHS-III findings. That is why we have employed the cluster analysis.

Cluster analysis groups individuals or objects or respondents into cluster so that objects in the same cluster are more similar to one another than they are to objects in other clusters. The attempt is to maximize the homogeneity of objects within the clusters while also maximizing the heterogeneity between the clusters. The following are the steps in the agglomerative hierarchical clustering algorithm for grouping N objects (Johnson and Wichern, 2002):

1. Start with N clusters, each containing with single entity and N X N symmetric Matrix of distances (or similarities) $D = \{d_{ik}\}$. The Euclidean (straight line) distance between two p-dimensional observations (i.e. items) $X = [x_1, x_2, x_3 \ldots x_p]$ and $Y = [y_1, y_2,$

$y_3 \ldots y_p]$ is measured by: $d(X, Y) = [(x_1-y_1)^2 + (x_2-y_2)^2 + \ldots (x_p-y_p)^2]^{1/2}$

2. Search the distance matrix for the nearest (most similar) pair of clusters. Let the distance between 'most similar' clusters U and V be d_{UV}.
3. Merge clusters U and V; label the newly formed clusters (UV). Update the entries in the distance matrix by (a) deleting the rows and columns corresponding to clusters U and V, and (b) adding a row and column giving the distances between cluster (UV) and the remaining clusters.
4. Repeat steps 2 and 3 a total of (N –1) times. All objects will be in a single cluster after the algorithm terminates. Record the identity of clusters that are merged and the levels (distances or similarities) at which the mergers take place.

It is to be mentioned here that the inputs to a single linkage algorithm can be distances or similarities between pairs of objects. Groups are formed from the individual entities by merging nearest neighbour, where the nearest neighbour connotes the smallest distance or largest similarity. We have used Dendrogram which is a graphical representation (tree graph) of the results of a hierarchical procedure in which each object is arrayed on one axis and the other axis portrays the steps in the hierarchical procedure. Starting with each object represented as a separate cluster, the Dendrogram shows graphically how the clusters are combined at each step of the procedure until all are contained in a single cluster.

Methods to study the Inequality of the Indices (both Achievement and Deprivation) and the selected RCH parametres:

The inequalities are analyzed using two different inequality measures. These are:

1. Generalized Entropy Class of Measure (GE)
2. Atkinson Class of Measures

The Lorenz Class like Gini Coefficient is not applied here because of non-monetary values of the RCH parametre. The GEM and Atkinson inequality measures give different implications for the distribution to be analyzed. The General Entropy class of measures, for example, GE(0) or mean log deviation is more sensitive to the changes in the lower tail of the distribution. GE(1) or Theil index applies equal weights to entire distribution. GE(2) is ½ of the squared coefficient of variation (CV).

This index is more sensitive to the upper tail of the distribution (Litchfield 1999).

The Atkinson measure (AT) is originated from the social welfare point of view. Inequality aversion parametre (ε) ranges from zero to infinity, with 0 representing no preference for equality. This index is a measurement of inequality that explicitly incorporates normative judgement about social welfare (Atkinson, 1970).

$$\text{GE}(0) = \text{Theil }(0) = \frac{1}{n}\left[\sum_{i=1}^{n} \log \frac{\bar{y}}{y_i}\right] \quad \ldots(4)$$

$$\text{GE }(1) = \text{Theil }(1) = \frac{1}{n}\sum_{i=1}^{n}\left(\frac{y_i}{\bar{y}}.\log \frac{y_i}{\bar{y}}\right) \quad \ldots(5)$$

$$\text{GE }(2) = (½)*\text{CV}^2 \quad \ldots(6)$$

$$\text{AT} = 1-\left[\frac{1}{n}\sum_{i=1}^{n}\left(\frac{y_i}{\bar{y}}\right)^{1-\epsilon}\right]^{\frac{1}{1-\epsilon}} \quad \ldots(7)$$

Here, n = number of states = 16, y_i = RCH parametre/indicator, ε = inequality aversion parametre. In our analysis, we have used $\alpha = 2$ for calculation of GEM; while the Atkinson Index is estimated for the value 2 of the inequality aversion parametre ($\in$).

Results and Discussion

Progress of Health in India Since Independence

In the years since independence there have been significant gains in health status in India, but they do not compare favourably with those in many similarly placed developing countries. In isolation Indian figures represent an impressive record. Life expectancy has gone up from 36 years in 1951 to 62 years in 1995 (MHFW, 1999-2000). Infant mortality rate is down from 146 in 1951 to 71 in 1997 though there has been a worrying levelling of in the IMR since 1993. Crude birth rate has been reduced from 36.9 in 1970 to 26.1 in 1998 and crude death rate from 14.9 to 8.7 during the same period. These gains have been made possible by the growth and development of health infrastructure and efforts to control communicable diseases such as immunization and improvements in water supply and sanitation.

For our present analysis, data of life expectancy at birth for all India from the period 1971 to 2000 at five years interval has been collected from SRS, RGI (2000) which is presented in Table 3.1.

Table 3.1: Life Expectancy at Birth from 1971 to 1997 at five years interval

Period	*Life expectancy at birth (years)*	
	Male	*Female*
1971-75	50.5	49.0
1976-80	52.5	52.1
1981-85	55.4	55.7
1986-90	57.7	58.1
1991-95	59.7	60.9
1996	60.1	61.4
1997	60.4	61.8

Source: Ministry of Health and Family Welfare and Sample Registration System (SRS), Registrar General, Government of India.

Plotting this life expectancy value over time, as shown in Fig. 3.1, we get a joint graph for male and female from where we can see the trend of the health status (considering LE as an indicator) of overall India during the above mentioned period.

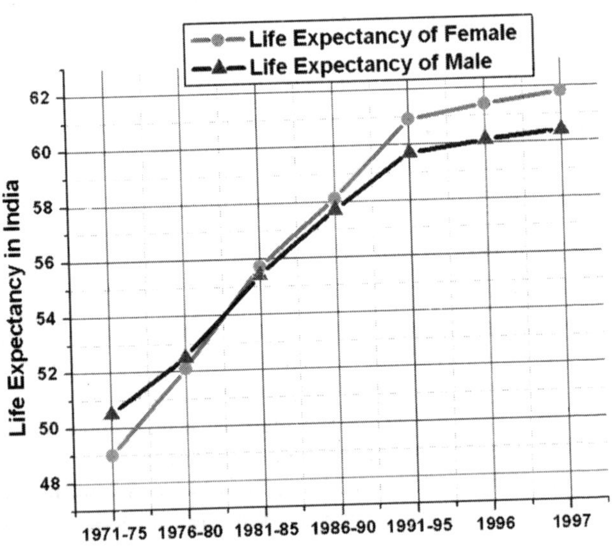

Fig. 3.1: Life Expectancy graph for male and female

From the above Graph (Fig. 3.1), we see that initially life expectancy of birth of female was lower than the male in period 1972 to 1975, during 1981 to 1985 both of them was almost equal at 55. But from then onwards increase in life expectancy of female was found to be higher than the increase in life expectancy of male up to 1997. Can we say about the gender discrimination from the above Fig. 3.1? It is observed from the OECD countries that the female life expectancy is found to be higher by 5-8 years compared to male, if there is no discrimination against female and it is physiologically true that female survival rate is higher than that of male; and females are less susceptible to infectious diseases compared to males. Therefore, we can say that gender discrimination is found to exist in India and over time, it was more pronounced before 1981-85 but it starts declining thereafter.

We have collected data on Infant Mortality Rate from Sample Registration System—Registrar General, Government of India. The data is available from 1961 to 2006. From this data set, we take Infant Survival Rate (1000 - IMR) as a good indicator of health status. Treating ISR as the good indicator of health status, it is shown graphically (in Fig. 3.2) the trend of the overall health status of India over the period from 1961 to 2006.

There has been a phenomenal improvement in the health status of India, as measured by ISR after independence. From the graph (Fig.3.2) of Infant Survival Rate, we notice the improvements of the health status. Although there was a sudden fall of ISR from 874 in 1974 to 860 in 1975, but it was for a very short span. From 1977 onwards it increased moderately and reaches its peak level in 2006 with the value, 946.

The Current Health Scenario of India and her Major States

India has its endless diversity of population, climate, topography, religious beliefs, languages, socio-economic and cultural settings. The health scenario also reflects this diversity in ample measure. Among the demographic and health indicators of sixteen major states in India, Kerala compares favourably with most middle income countries and even some high income countries on West Asia [Low-Income ($ 760 and less), middle income ($ 761-$ 9360) and high income countries ($ 9361 and above) are defined on the basis of per capita incomes in 1998 in World Development Report (WDR), 2000]. But Madhya Pradesh, Orissa, Rajasthan and Uttar Pradesh are well below the average of low income countries and just above the levels of sub-Saharan Africa. Together the

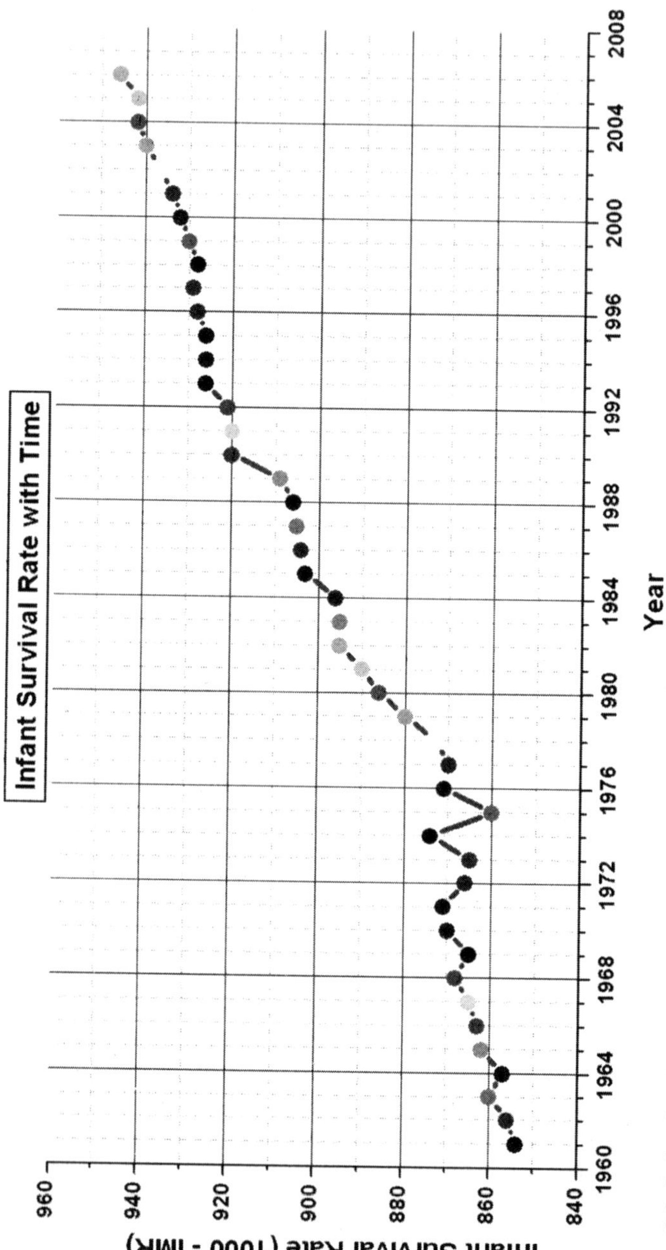

Fig. 3.2: Infant Survival rate with time

different states represent the whole range of health outcomes within these two extremes.

India's health indicators are almost at the same level as the average of low income countries (UNDP, 2000). But with per capita income as the benchmark, India is at the level of Sub-Saharan Africa. A comparison with China, Brazil, Indonesia and Thailand for under-5 mortality and crude birth rates indicates a lower rate of progress despite initial advantages. India compares unfavourably even with low income countries in terms of availability of health infrastructure and its utilization, as well as the overall disease burden. The combined factors of population and unsatisfactory health make India account for a fifth of the global disease burden with a 17 per cent share of the world's population, India accounts for 23 per cent of the child deaths, 20 per cent maternal deaths, 30 per cent TB cases, 68 per cent leprosy cases, and 14 per cent of persons infected with HIV the same trends are apparent in poverty reduction, sanitation, access to safe drinking water and literacy—all important determinants of heath status (WHO, 2000). Though the proportion of the population below the poverty line has declined from 36 per cent in 1993 to 26.10 per cent in 1999-2000 (*Economic Survey*, 2000-01), but the overall picture indicates that social infrastructure in India has remained relatively neglected.

Among the Indian states, the remarkable success of Kerala has been attributed to historical factors contributing to high literacy and women's empowerment. But recent experiences in Tamil Nadu, Andhra Pradesh and West Bengal suggest that significant improvement is possible without accompanying progress in literacy and gender equality. Despite the disparities among the states, however, there are strong common features as well. All the states have followed more or less the same development and administrative model and thus their health systems exhibit, in varying degrees, the same strengths and weaknesses. This common thread facilitates generalizations, though the extent of their application varies from state to state.

From the Annual Report of Ministry of Health and Family Welfare (1999-2000) some data on demographic and health indicators of India and its states have been presented in Table 3.2. On the basis of this data set, a number of graphs and pie charts have been drawn to show the state-wise variation in health status of India.

If we look into the Life Expectancy at Birth of male and female, West Bengal and Punjab show the best possible ratio, whereas Uttar Pradesh, Madhya Pradesh and Orissa are comparatively in worse situation.

Table 3.2: Demographic and Health Indicators—India and her Major States

Major States	*MMR 1997*	*Life Expectancy (1991-96)*		*IMR 1998*	*Under 35 mortality rate (1993-98)*
		Male	*Female*		
Andhra Pradesh	154	61.4	64.5	66	85.5
Assam	401	58.7	58.5	78	89.5
Bihar	451	60.8	60.1	67	15.1
Gujarat	29	60.9	62.7	64	85.1
Haryana	105	65.2	64.2	69	76.8
Himachal Pradesh	—	—	—	68	42.4
Karnataka	195	64.2	65.3	58	69.8
Kerala	195	68.6	75	16	18.8
Madhya Pradesh	498	59.2	58	97	137.6
Maharashtra	135	64	65.9	49	58.1
Orissa	361	60.1	58.4	98	14.4
Punjab	196	66.6	66.5	54	72.1
Rajasthan	677	60.5	61.3	83	114.9
Tamil Nadu	76	62.3	63.1	53	63.3
Uttar Pradesh	707	57.1	52.8	85	122.5
West Bengal	264	61.9	61.9	53	67.7
India	**408**	**60.6**	**61.7**	**70**	**94.9**

Source: Annual Report, 1999-2000, MHFW, GoI.

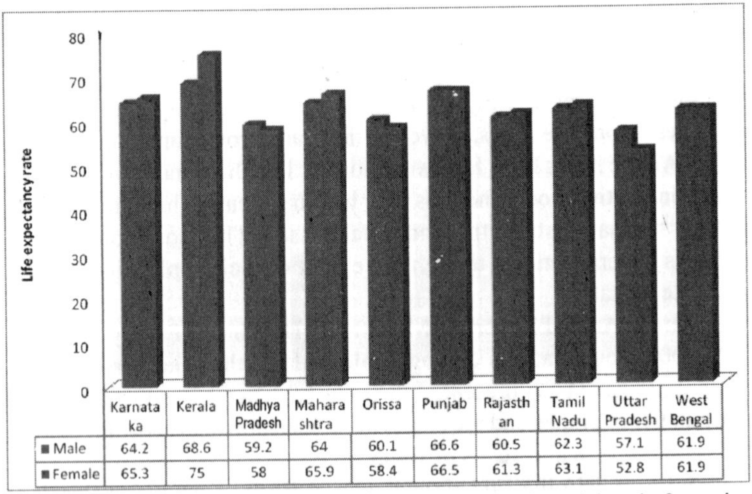

Fig. 3.3: Comparison of life expectancy at birth of male and female for major states of India (1991-96)

Rest of the states shows better Life Expectancy of females compared to males. During the period from 1991 to 1996, the Life Expectancy at birth is found to be the maximum in Kerala with 68.6 years for male and 75 years for female.

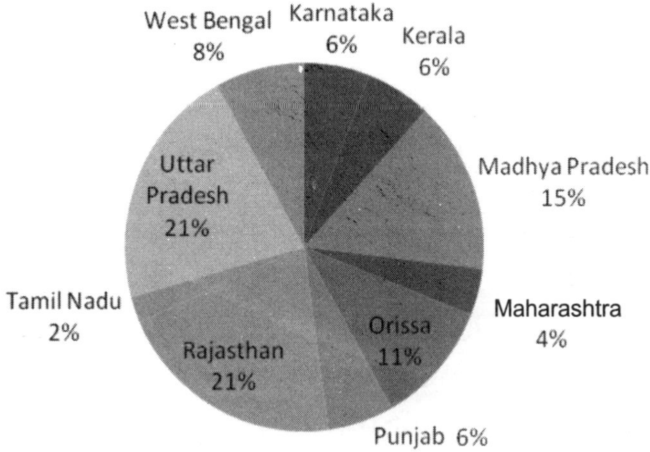

Source: SRS, RGI (1997).

Fig. 3.4: Maternal Mortality Rate (MMR) in Major States of India (1997)

Maternal Mortality Rate is found to be highest in Uttar Pradesh followed by Madhya Pradesh, whereas in Tamil Nadu, MMR is only 2 per cent of the total share of MMR.

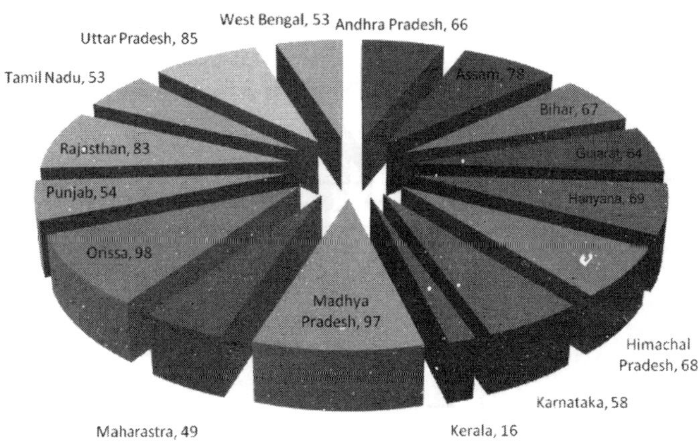

Source: SRS, RGI (1998).

Fig. 3.5: Infant Mortality Rate (IMR) in 16 major states in 1998

In terms of Infant Mortality Rate, the scenario is found in Orissa followed by Madhya Pradesh. From the above pie chart, it is clear that IMR continues to remain at its maximum (98) in Orissa in 1998 and the least figure for IMR is found in Kerala (16) which is attributable to massive social development in Kerala.

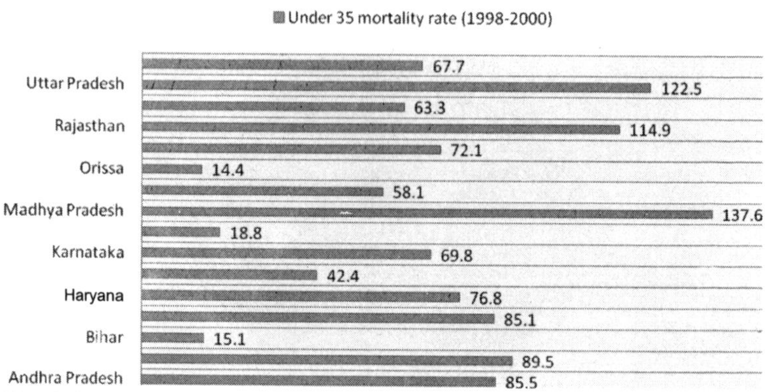

Fig. 3.6: Under 35 mortality rate (1998-2000)

Under 35 mortality rate is found to be the highest in Madhya Pradesh during the time period from 1993 to 1998, but it is surprising to note that it is minimum in Orissa. So, we can see some anomalies here. Orissa is found to be the worst in terms of child health, but comparatively in better status in terms of death under 35, whereas Uttar Pradesh and Madhya Pradesh are always found to be worse off among the major states.

The BOD estimates of five states, as shown in Table 3.3 present a similar kind of picture as outlined earlier. Uttar Pradesh is happened to be almost at the same level as sub Saharan Africa in epidemiological

Table 3.3: Burden of Disease—India and her States

	Category	*India*	*Andhra Pradesh*	*Karnataka*	*Punjab*	*West Bengal*	*Uttar Pradesh*
% of DALYs lost	Communicable disease	50.3	54.0	56.5	53.5	56.0	62.0
	Non-communicable disease	33.0	30.0	28.0	29.0	28.0	26.0
	Injuries	16.7	16.0	15.5	17.5	16.0	12.0

Source: India: New Directions in Health Sector Development at the State Level and Operational Perspective, World Bank, 11 February, 1997.

transition. Communicable disease account for 62 per cent of burden in Uttar Pradesh compared to 65.9 per cent for Sub-Saharan Africa (*Ad Hoc* Committee on Health Research, WHO 1997).

The combined factors of population and unsatisfactory health status make India account for a fifth of the global disease burden. With a 17 per cent share of world's populations, India accounts for 23 per cent of child's deaths, 20 per cent of maternal deaths, 30 per cent of TB cases, 64 per cent leprosy cases and 14 per cent of persons infected with HIV (WHO, 2000).

Table 3.4: HIV Prevalence in India, 1998

India/State	*Total number of HIV infected persons (in thousands)*
Andhra Pradesh	567.078
Assam	29.153
Bihar	114.012
Gujarat	81.873
Haryana	34.287
Himachal Pradesh	3.318
Karnataka	309.772
Kerala	169.34
Madhya Pradesh	137.814
Maharashtra	747.049
Orissa	44.775
Punjab	43.734
Rajasthan	50.47
Tamil Nadu	307.994
Uttar Pradesh	108.631
West Bengal	117.081
India	**2933.736**

Source: Annual Report, 1999-2000, MHFW, GoI.

The threat presented by the rapidly growing HIV/AIDS epidemic has not received the attention it deserves. On the basis of state-wise HIV prevalence in 1998, as shown in Table 3.4, the total estimated population infected in the year 1999 is 3.09 million, with a range of 2.47 to 3.71 million (*Annual Report*, 2000-01, MFHW). The epidemic is spreading in metropolitan as well as in rural areas in India. If India is to avoid the kind of catastrophe that has fallen Africa, for greater efforts will have to be made to keep the epidemic in check.

On the basis of some data available from India Health Report (2003), this study attempts to summarize the present health structure of India in terms of various diseases and deaths. Among large variety of diseases,

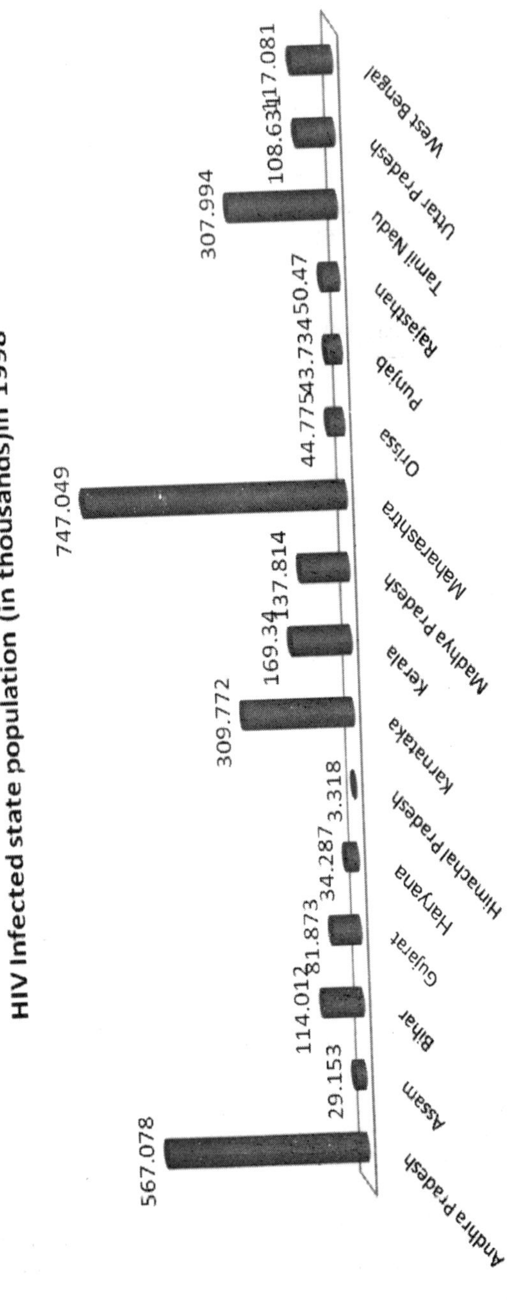

Source: Health Report, GoI (2003).

Fig. 3.7: HIV Prevalence in India, 1998.

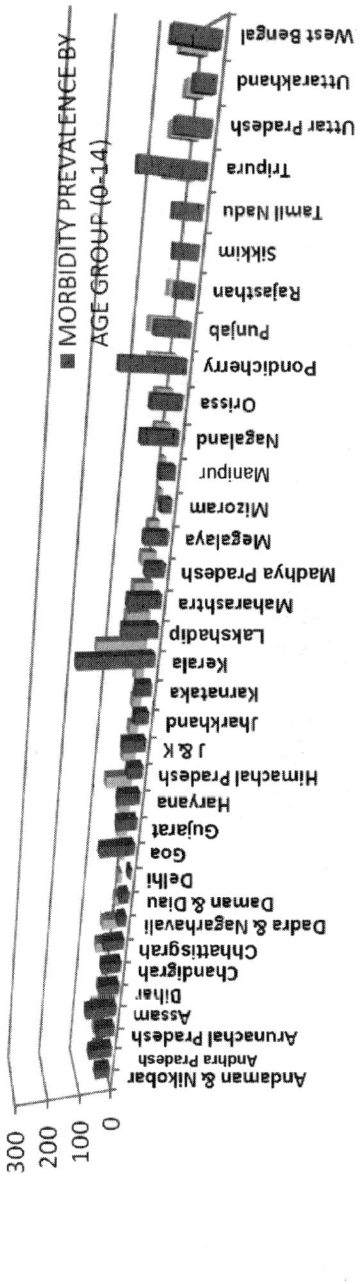

Source: NSSO, Department of Statistics, GoI (2004).

Fig. 3.8: Morbidity Prevalence by Age Group (0-14) and (15-29)-2004

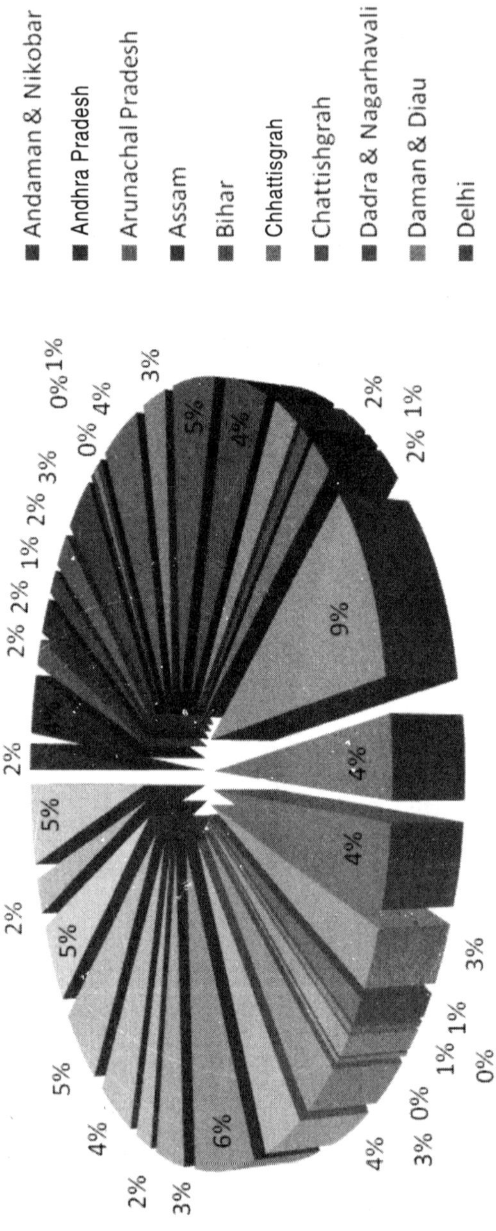

Source: NSSO, Department of Statistics, GoI (2004).

Fig. 3.9: Morbidity Prevalence Rate across states and UT by age group (30-44)–2004

Source: NSSO, Department of Statistics, GoI (2004).

Fig. 3.10: Morbidity Prevalence by Age Group (45-59) and (60 and above)—2004

leprosy cases are found as the most dominant. The child death of 23 per cent is really a very alarming for the developing country like India.

From the above Figure 3.7, we find that Maharashtra is the most infected state with HIV in 1998 whereas HIV prevalence is found to be minimum in Assam during the same period.

Morbidity prevalence (Fig. 3.8) is found to be the maximum in Kerala followed by Tripura and West Bengal whereas it was least in Delhi followed by Mizoram. It is again providing a conflicting result, because Kerala's life expectancy is found to be maximum—thus it proves that higher life expectancy does not necessarily imply better heath outcome.

Morbidity Prevalence Rate across States and UT by age group (30-44) shows that (as shown in Fig. 3.9), it is found minimum in Gujarat whereas it is lowest in Delhi.

The same trend is noticed in the middle and upper age cohort of the population as shown in Fig. 3.10. Therefore, an interesting fact is revealed from the NSSO data that that states which exhibit higher life expectancy does not necessarily imply lower MIR or MPR. Diabetes has been considered as silent killer; persons suffering from diabetes (per thousand population) is shown in Rader Fig. 3.11. The same picture is noticed in

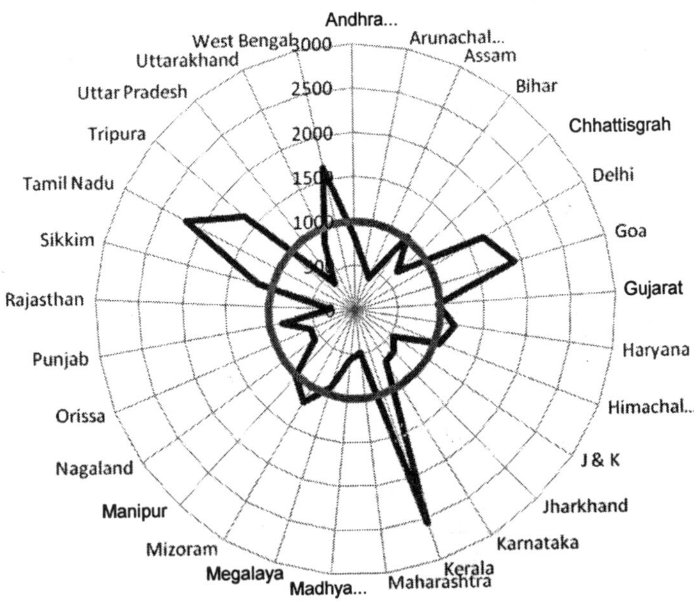

Source: NSSO, Department of Statistics, GoI (2004).

Fig. 3.11: Men per 1,00,000 affected in Diabetes in Different States (2004)

case of the prevalence of diabetes; Kerala is the worst state followed by Tamil Nadu; whereas Rajasthan (followed by J&K) is found to be better off in this case.

Nine out of twenty nine states and UT do lie outside the mean value. Those states which are socio-economically backward generally show lower incidence of diabetes. What are the plausible explanations of such contrasting results? It may happen that persons living in the socio-economically well-off states are aware of diabetes; as result they report such incidence. On the other hand, persons living in comparatively backward states are not well aware of the incidence of diabetes.

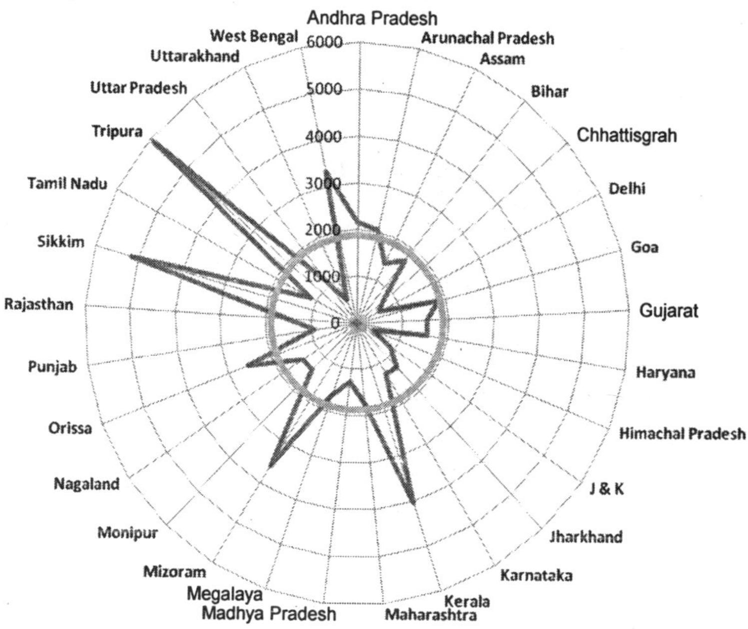

Source: NSSO, Department of Statistics, GoI (2004).

Fig. 3.12: Men per 1,00,000 affected in Asthma in Different States (2004)

Persons suffering from *asthma* do vary across the states; it is to be mentioned here that persons suffering from *asthma* is found to be present with a higher proportion in those states where rainfall is found to be higher compared to the national average. The incidence of *asthma* is found to be the maximum in Tripura followed by Sikkim and Kerala whereas the least number is found in Himachal Pradesh followed by Uttarakhand.

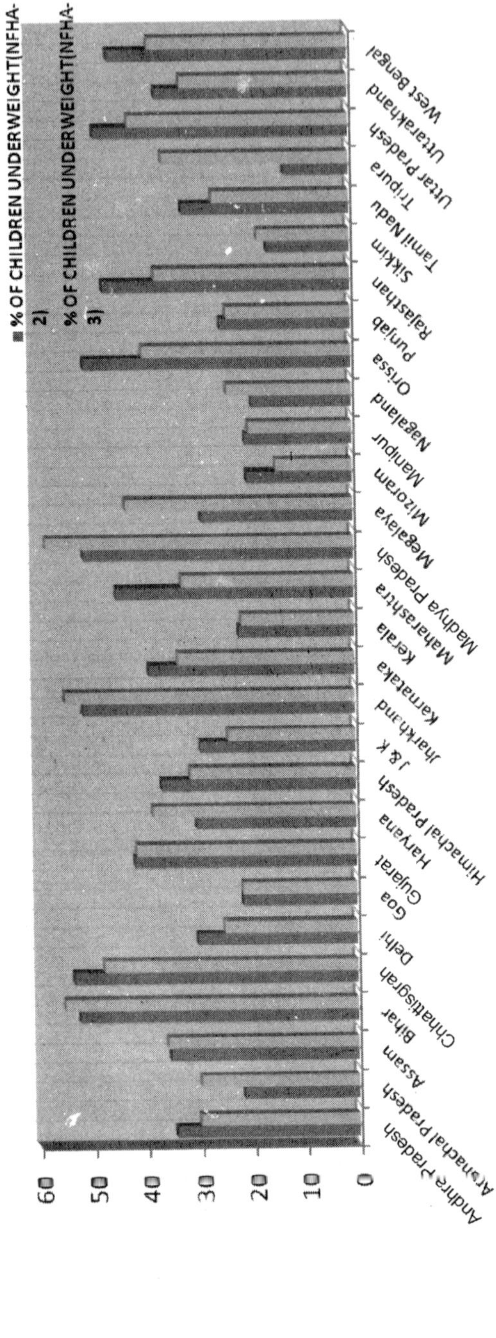

Source: NFHS-I (1998-99), II (2005-06), MHFW, GoI.

Fig. 3.3: Percentage of Underweight Children in Different States (in 1998-99 and 2005-06)

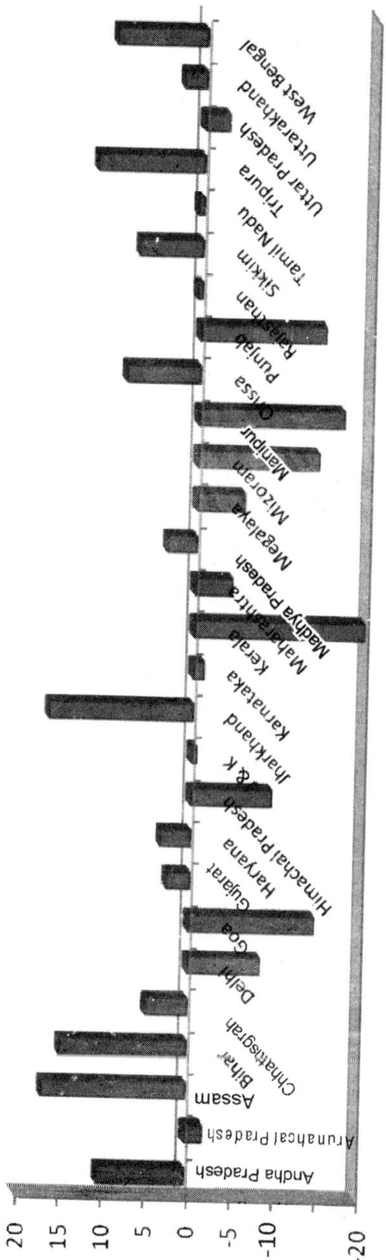

Source: NFHS-II, MHFW, GoI.

Fig. 3.14: Percentage of Women affected from Anaemia in 2005-06

Let us now have a look of the status of health of the states in respect of NFHS-II and NFHS-III findings. The percentage of underweight children under 5 years of age has been an important component of human poverty index. It is noticed that the percentage of under-weight children is found maximum in Madhya Pradesh in both the two surveys followed by Bihar; while it was least in Mizoram, as shown in Fig. 3.13. It is observed that the smaller states generally manifest lower incidence of under-weight children.

Dispersion of the percentage of women suffering from anaemia is shown in Fig. 3.14 which is drawn from NFHS-III findings. It is observed that the least percentage of women suffering from anaemia is found in Kerala followed by Manipur whereas the maximum is found in Assam followed by Jharkhand.

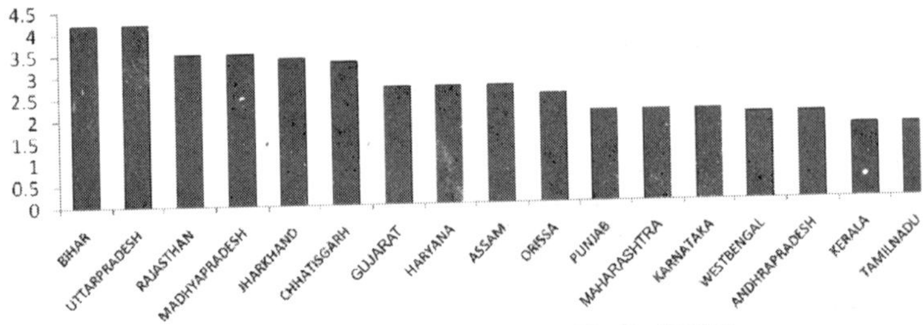

Source: SRS, Registrar General, Government of India (2007).

Fig. 3.15: Total Fertility Rate of Seventeen States in India in the Year 2007

The least IMR is observed in Kerala followed by Maharashtra whereas the maximum IMR is found in Madhya Pradesh followed by Orissa. Life expectancy is generally taken as a good measure of health status already incorporated in UNDP's HDR. Kerala has managed the first position followed by Punjab whereas the least value is found in Assam followed by Madhya Pradesh (as shown in Fig. 3.17). There exists a wide range of difference of LE_0 across the states.

The overall health scenario across the states in India gives us an alarming picture of regional diversity. Here, we did not analyze the causes of such differential in health status. However, there are some states which are found to be lagging far behind from the States like Kerala, Tamil Nadu, Punjab and Maharashtra. The low base of health indicators combined with and overwhelming burden on available morbidity and mortality accounted for by pre-transition diseases makes possible dramatic improvements in health status on a relatively short time span. These

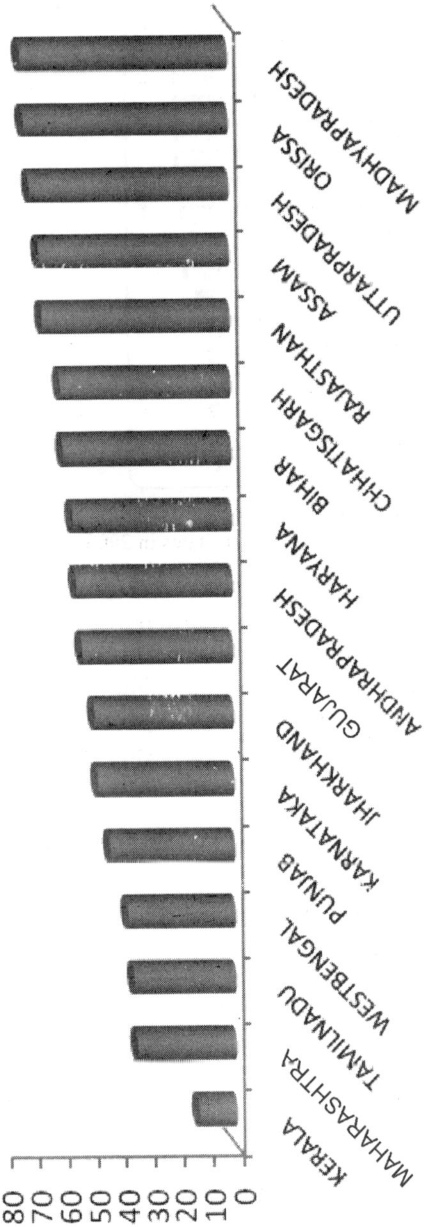

Source: SRS, Registrar General, Government of India (2007).

Fig. 3.16: Infant Mortality Rate of Seventeen States in India in the Year 2007

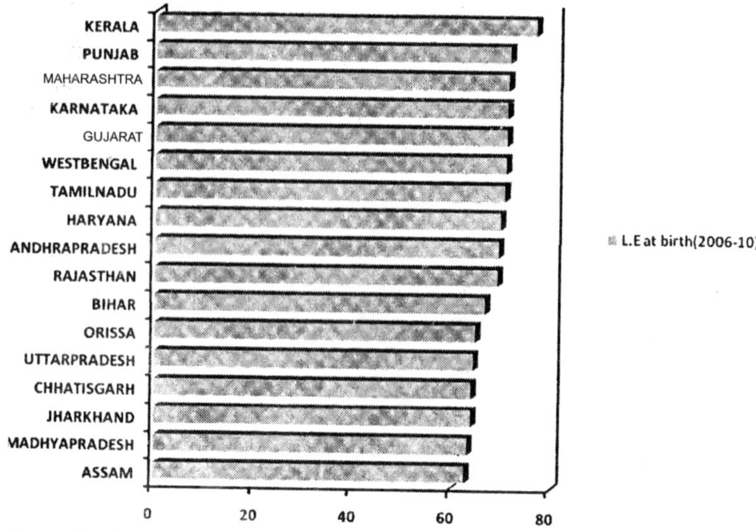

Fig. 3.17: Expectation of Life at Birth of Major States in 2006-2010.
Source: SRS, Registrar General, Government of India (2007)

present a rare opportunity to the policy-makers to rescue millions from the vicious cycle of poverty caused by low level health status. Certainly, these would demand significantly enhanced public investments in healthcare, which by itself requires wide ranging systematic reforms to ensure the efficient utilizations of public resources to benefit the really needy and the poor.

Maternal and Child Health in India: An Inter-state Analysis

Government of India has launched several programmes related to maternal and child health from time to time and updates its strategies in order to improve health status of women and children and fulfil the unmet need of the MCH care throughout the country. Since, the introduction of family welfare programmes in First Five Year Plan (1951-1956), Government has taken various steps to strengthen the maternal and child health. Maternal and child health and nutrition were integrated with family planning programme during Fifth Five Year Plan (1974-1979). In the year 1992-1993, programme was renamed as child survival and safe motherhood programme (CSSM) with a view to improve quality and utilization of MCH services. In the year 1997, the programme was again renovated and renamed as Reproductive and Child Health (RCH) which incorporates all components of CSSM along with reproductive tract infections and sexually transmitted diseases. Broadly, the programme aims at to universalize immunization, antenatal care, skilled attendance during delivery as well as for common childhood elements. A step further of new endeavour of Government of India, National Rural Health Mission (NRHM, 2005) outlines its objectives to promote "equity, efficiency, quality and accountability of public health services through community driven approaches, decentralization and improving local governance to rural population, particularly among poor, underserved women and children."

Despite of all the programmes and efforts taken by the Government, some studies have revealed that reproductive and child health situation in India is quite alarming, especially in Northern states in India. According to recent estimates, nearly 28 per cent of Indian population lived below the poverty line with large inter-state variations (Planning Commission, 2007). The poverty is largely concentrated in Uttar Pradesh, Madhya Pradesh, Chhattisgarh, Bihar, Jharkhand and Orissa where poverty is significantly higher than the national average and accounts for 55 per cent of poor Indian population. Importantly, majority of these states also contributes to nearly half of maternal deaths in India during 2004-06 (SRS 2009). In the Northern states (*viz.* Uttar Pradesh, Madhya Pradesh, Bihar and Rajasthan), the utilization of Government health facilities for delivery was poor that is only 5 to 16 per cent, whereas home deliveries were widely prevalent and largely attended by untrained birth attendants that is 80 to 92 per cent with greater probability of high risk of maternal morbidity and mortality (Raju, 2002). The variation in RCH outcome indicators is also notified among different districts within a region of the state (Raju, 2002).

With this overall scenario, an urge is felt to explore the inter-state variation in RCH indicators of India. This study is thus aimed at to examine the variation in the reproductive and child health status among the sixteen major states of India in two points of time *viz.* 1998-99 and 2005-06. The RCH achievement index is estimated using the methodology as outlined earlier. This is presented in Table 3.5. Kerala has been a distinct outlier—remains top in both the two time points—1998-99 and 2005-06. Similarly, Bihar has been remaining in bottom in both the time points. Assam, Gujarat and Punjab could not retain their position in 2005-06 whereas Maharashtra, Orissa, Rajasthan and West Bengal were capable to raise their relative positions in 2005-06. Andhra Pradesh, Haryana, Himachal Pradesh, Karnataka, Madhya Pradesh, Tamil Nadu and Uttar Pradesh did retain their former position in 2005-06.

Table 3.5: RCH Achievement Index (AI) of the sixteen states of India in 2 points of time

States	*AI in 1998-99*	*Rank*	*AI in 2005-06*	*Rank*
Andhra Pradesh	0.605815291	5	0.650328143	5
Assam	0.309826115	11	0.276057641	14
Bihar	0.150627141	16	0.149021386	16
Gujarat	0.448549373	9	0.455849532	10
Haryana	0.530233729	8	0.560785273	8
Himachal Pradesh	0.658445999	3	0.676525328	3
Karnataka	0.547241872	7	0.582487516	7
Kerala	0.836373677	1	0.823778582	1
Madhya Pradesh	0.309076236	12	0.339447633	12
Maharashtra	0.569303601	6	0.655073692	4
Orissa	0.278319256	13	0.433721656	11
Punjab	0.612748917	4	0.644727334	6
Rajasthan	0.261985382	14	0.338581274	13
Tamil Nadu	0.681970552	2	0.750322468	2
Uttar Pradesh	0.19952598	15	0.225141686	15
West Bengal	0.382718658	10	0.516667593	9

Source: Estimated by the authors following the above cited methodology using the NFHS-I and NFHS-II.

Table 3.6: Progress of Reproductive Health Status of the States in India over the Period of 1998-99 and 2005-06

States	*Progress of AI in RCH*
Orissa	0.147366104(1)
West Bengal	0.12031965(2)
Rajasthan	0.097808218(3)
Maharashtra	0.076235591(4)
Uttar Pradesh	0.059534743(5)
Madhya Pradesh	0.053317515(6)
Tamil Nadu	0.046534003(7)
Haryana	0.046438086(8)
Punjab	0.043683964(9)
Karnataka	0.039867053(10)
Bihar	0.039794682(11)
Andhra Pradesh	0.03894049(12)
Gujarat	0.026883153(13)
Himachal Pradesh	0.017933728(14)
Assam	–0.010283171(15)
Kerala	–0.02378802(16)

Note: Achievement Index of RCH are calculated for the two time points (1998-99 and 2005-06) across the 16 States using equation (2). The difference of the values of two periods gives us the progress of achievement index over the specified period. Number within parentheses represents rank.

Source: Author's estimation.

In Table 3.6, we find that Orissa's progress is found to be the highest among the sixteen states in terms of reproductive and health achievement status, while that is the lowest in Kerala. West Bengal has witnessed the second highest progress during this period followed by Rajasthan; whereas second least progress is found in Assam followed by Himachal Pradesh.

To what extent the states of India are vulnerable to all the eleven key RCH parametres has been captured by constructing the deprivation index across the sixteen states of India for the two points of time. It is to be mentioned here that in measuring DI, we consider the same variables but all are negative in respect of development parametres *viz.* all are deprivation RCH parametres. States having higher AI, should theoretically manifest lower DI. Does it hold good across the states? Or in other words, the rank correlation coefficient between AI and DI should be (–1). But, in reality, we did not find such one to one correspondence. The DI for the two points of time (viz. 1998-99 and 2005-06) is estimated using the formula given by equation-3, this is the α-order average which means that as α increases, DI will approach to the maximum value of deprivation parametres as outlined in the properties of DI.

Table 3.7: RCH Deprivation Index (DI) of the sixteen states of India in 2 points of time

States	*DI in 1998-99*	*Rank*	*DI in 2005-06*	*Rank*
Andhra Pradesh	43.84104	15	44.47155	14
Assam	63.82011	4	64.27639	2
Bihar	72.22855	1	66.23558	1
Gujarat	52.51977	11	51.81354	6
Haryana	56.56658	8	49.73211	9
Himachal Pradesh	52.88122	10	48.32726	10
Karnataka	45.68237	13	46.99096	12
Kerala	41.5086	16	43.89858	15
Madhya Pradesh	62.51315	5	57.24445	5
Maharashtra	45.89897	12	43.20274	16
Orissa	59.2986	6	51.71828	7
Punjab	54.32029	9	50.03288	8
Rajasthan	65.84832	3	58.32332	4
Tamil Nadu	44.95788	14	45.70585	13
Uttar Pradesh	69.09194	2	64.11987	3
West Bengal	56.17842	7	47.92934	11

Note: Order of the power mean viz. $\alpha = 3$

Source: Authors estimation using Equation-5.

RCH-DI is found to be maximum in Bihar (72.228) and minimum in Kerala (41.508) in the year 1998-99. Uttar Pradesh is found to be the second highest deprived state in terms of RCH status, value of the RCH DI being 69.091. A very worsening situation is observed in Rajasthan (65.84832) and Assam (63.82011) whereas Andhra Pradesh (43.84104), Tamil Nadu (44.95788) and Karnataka (45.68237) are found to be comparatively less deprived in respect of reproductive and child health status.

Results of 2005-06 shows that RCH-DI is maximum in Bihar (66.23) followed by Assam (64.27). Maharashtra (43.20), Kerala (43.89) and Andhra Pradesh (44.47) are comparatively less vulnerable as revealed from Table 3.7.

Rank correlation coefficient between AI and DI is estimated for the two time points; this is given as:

> Rank correlation coefficient between AI and DI in 1998-99 is: –0.897
>
> Rank correlation coefficient between AI and DI in 2005-06 is: –0.912

The above rank correlation coefficient does imply that states with higher values of AI, generally manifest lower value of DI, but it is not one to one correspondence. This is because the power mean formula is applied towards estimation of DI while simple relative distance method is applied in case of AI.

How far the states are clubbed together based on various values of RCH achievement parametres for the two time points is represented by the Dendrogram (viz. Tree Graph) as shown by the Figs. 3.18 and 3.19. Cluster analysis helps us to know about the homogeneous groups of the states.

The following groups are formed in 1998-99 as shown in Fig. 3.18:

Cluster-I: Madhya Pradesh and Rajasthan are found to be very close to each other; similar pattern is noticed between Bihar and Uttar Pradesh. Assam has joined with these four states and forms a 5 states cluster.

Cluster-II: Kerala and Tamil Nadu are found to be very nearest; Himachal Pradesh and Punjab are also close to each other, Haryana joins with them. Consequently, we have 5 states cluster.

Cluster-III: Andhra Pradesh, Karnataka and Maharashtra make a Cluster.

Cluster-IV: Gujarat, West Bengal and Orissa are found to be very close and they form a cluster.

The following groups are formed in 2005-06 as shown in Fig. 3.19:

Cluster-I: Andhra Pradesh, Karnataka and Maharashtra make a Cluster.

Cluster-II: Gujarat, West Bengal and Orissa are found to be very close and they form a cluster. Kerala and Tamil Nadu forms a new sub-cluster and at last they merge with the former cluster formed by Gujarat, West Bengal and Orissa.

Cluster-III: Haryana and Punjab forms a sub-cluster; Himachal Pradesh joins with them.

Cluster-IV: Madhya Pradesh and Rajasthan are found to be very close to each other; similar pattern is noticed between Bihar and Uttar Pradesh. Assam has joined with these four states and forms a 5-state cluster.

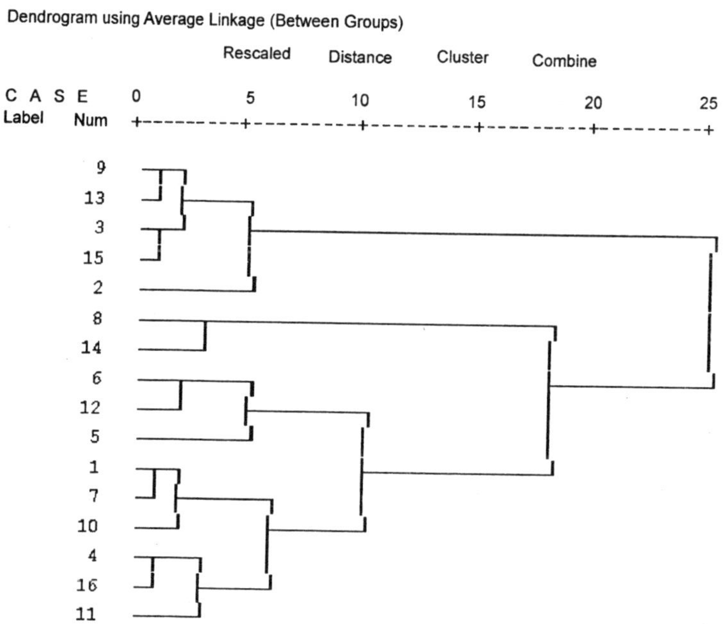

Fig. 3.18: Cluster Analysis for the year: 1998-99

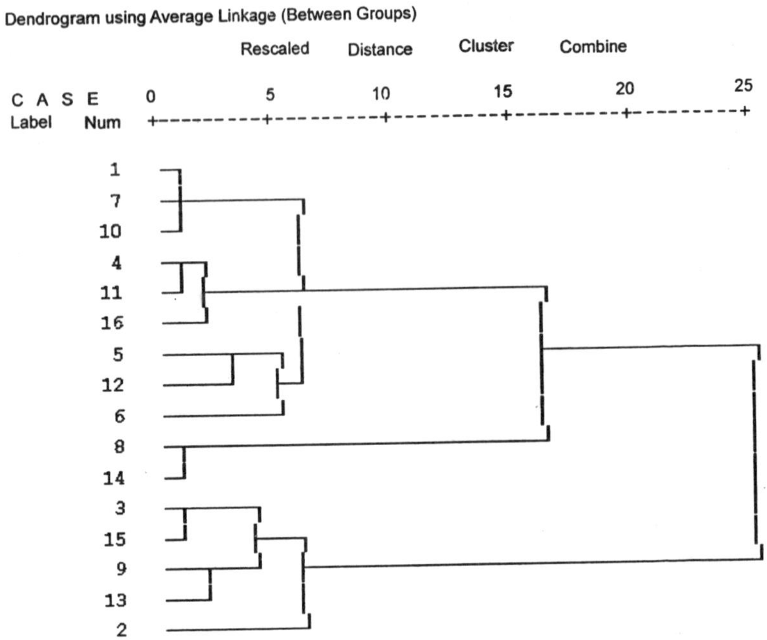

Fig. 3.19: Cluster Analysis for the year: 2005-06.

Study of Inequality of RCH Achievement and Deprivation Index and all seven Key RCH Parametres across the states in India for two points of time:

The extent of inequality of achievement and deprivation indices (AI and DI) is given in Table 3.8. The results show that the overall inequality of the Achievement Index as well as of the Deprivation Index falls over time. This means that all the states are converging in respect of achievement and deprivation in aggregate—since index is composed of all the seven key RCH parametres.

Table 3.8: Inequality Measurement of the Two Indices (AI, DI) Over Time

Variable	*Year*	*GE(2)*	*AT(2)*
Achievement Index (AI)	1998-99	0.091833	0.199172
	2005-06	0.076321	0.192614
Deprivation Index (DI)	1998-99	0.014706	0.027341
	2005-06	0.010686	0.018478

Source: Authors Estimation. Note: GE(2) = (1/2)*cv^2; AT = Atkinson Index

Are all the states converging in respect of all the RCH parametres in India? In order to answer this question, we estimate the inequality of all the RCH parametres for two points of time across all the major states in India, which is shown in Table 3.9. Using the same logic, we examine the inequality of the deprivation parametre across states for two points of time as shown in Table 3.10.

It is observed that inequality of all the achievement parametres is reduced from 1998-99 to 2005-06 except parametre-10 (*viz.* Percentage of children age 6-35 months who are anemic). Parametre-7 (*viz.* Percentage of children with diarrhoea in the last two weeks prior to survey taken to health facility) gives us an inconclusive results because it is reduced in case of GE(2) while it goes up in AT(2).

An interesting findings is observed in case of deprivation parametres, half of the deprivation parametres show a convergent outcome, half of the parametres show a divergent outcome and only one parametre (*viz.* P_{4D} = 100 – percentage of mothers who had not received at least 3 antenatal care visits for their last birth) show a mixed result as evidenced from Table 3.10.

Inequality is reduced across the states for the following deprivation parametres:

P_{1D} = 100 – Percentage of women age 20-24 married by age 18

P_{6D} = 100 – Percentage of children 12-23 months completely immunized

P_{7D} = 100 – Percentage of children who are not affected with diarrhoea in the last two weeks prior to survey taken to health facility

P_{8D} = 100 – Percentage of children under 3 years who are not under weight

P_{10D} =100 – Percentage of children age 6-35 months who are not anaemic

Inequality is found to be increased for the following parametres:

P_{2D} = 100 – Percentage of women not using any family planning method

P_{3D} = 100 – Percentage of mothers who had not at least 3 antenatal care visits for their last birth

P_{5D} = 100 – Percentage of children 12-23 months not completely immunized

P_{9D} = 100 – Percentage of children age 6-35 months who are not anaemic

P_{11D} = 100 – Percentage of women having no knowledge of AIDS

Therefore, we have obtained some kind of inconclusive results about the convergence outcome of the states if measured in respect of deprivation parametres. What is the meaning of rising inequality in respect of deprivation parametres? Actually, this means that the pace of decline of the deprivation parametres does vary across the states.

Table 3.9: Inequality Measurement of the Achievement Parametres

Parameters	*Year*	*GE(2)*	*AT(2)*
Parameter 1	1998-99	0.104419	0.291984
	2005-06	0.078595	0.2034
Parameter 2	1998-99	0.022791	0.054661
	2005-06	0.007366	0.016401
Parameter 3	1998-99	0.041851	0.111507
	2005-06	0.035014	0.085395
Parameter 4	1998-99	0.120816	0.278294
	2005-06	0.074184	0.196349
Parameter 5	1998-99	0.178024	0.257352
	2005-06	0.113109	0.192264
Parameter 6	1998-99	0.135342	0.334628
	2005-06	0.059516	0.128052
Parameter 7	1998-99	0.023764	0.042606
	2005-06	0.020576	0.048942
Parameter 8	1998-99	0.018672	0.031999
	2005-06	0.012032	0.025273
Parameter 9	1998-99	0.008228	0.014837
	2005-06	0.008184	0.014181
Parameter 10	1998-99	0.059536	0.083332
	2005-06	0.06971	0.105917
Parameter 11	1998-99	0.135805	0.275095
	2005-06	0.048844	0.093047

Source: Authors estimation.

Table 3.10: Inequality Measurement of the Deprivation Parametres

Parameters	*Year*	*GE(2)*	*AT(2)*
Parameter 1d	1998-99	0.06256	0.119672
	2005-06	0.032739	0.058864
Parameter 2d	1998-99	0.178049	0.264
	2005-06	0.205296	0.305131
Parameter 3d	1998-99	0.031033	0.050032
	2005-06	0.040847	0.068807
Parameter 4d	1998-99	0.151488	0.702519
	2005-06	0.17959	0.520544
Parameter 5d	1998-99	0.069253	0.355407
	2005-06	0.103436	0.866317
Parameter 6d	1998-99	0.144433	0.314733
	2005-06	0.069465	0.146643
Parameter 7d	1998-99	0.109999	0.333039
	2005-06	0.072122	0.12085
Parameter 8d	1998-99	0.036087	0.093435
	2005-06	0.023217	0.042981
Parameter 9d	1998-99	0.031917	0.07533
	2005-06	0.040973	0.115414
Parameter 10d	1998-99	0.008438	0.021422
	2005-06	0.006829	0.01486
Parameter 11d	1998-99	0.087131	0.281698
	2005-06	0.125893	0.437288

Source: Authors estimation.

Concluding Observations

The strategy "of Health for All" emphasizes that there will be an even distribution among the population of whatever resources for health are available. Union and different State Governments of India have taken various necessary actions to trim down high level of maternal and child mortality. But despite of the fact there exists a large scale of disparity across the states of our country in respect of reproductive and child health status and utilization of RCH services. This study has elicited different RCH status indices for all the sixteen major states of. Different indices show different results, but by and large states like Kerala, Tamil Nadu, Himachal Pradesh, Maharashtra are found to be better off, while states like Bihar, Assam, Uttar Pradesh, Rajasthan, Madhya Pradesh are comparatively worse off. The broad idea of present chapter has also been to capture the inequality in access to and utilization of various RCH services *viz*. ante-natal care, safe delivery for maternal care and complete child immunization under childcare. The results of inequality measurement of various deprivation parametres are suggestive enough to the clear pattern of unequal utilization of RCH services emerging from this analysis. Inequality in utilization of maternal health-care services is more pronounced in the case of service provided by ANM/health worker. Inequality is pronounced in the case of complete child immunization, usage of any kind of family planning method, suffering of the children from anaemia. Important predictors like women's literacy and employment, extent of urbanization, economic development might have significant impact on the RCH status. Women's education and employment help towards fertility reduction, higher contraceptive usage, higher utilization of reproductive health-care and child immunization. Incidence of poverty might also play a major role in non-accessibility of some major RCH services. There might be so many economic, social and cultural barriers which lead to widen the gap of both the RCH status and utilization of RCH services across the states.

Nevertheless, it is an accepted view that for preventive services, that too for maternal and child healthcare, there is enormous dependence on public sector. The international conference on primary healthcare, held in Alma-Ata in 1978, issued the declaration of Alma-Ata which stated that primary healthcare is the key to attaining 'Health for All'. The National Health Policy (2002) for rural area is based on a combination of preventive, promotive and curative services. The rural healthcare structure is vertical in nature comprising three tiers: community health centre (CHC), primary health centre (PHC), and sub-centres (SC). In almost all the states of India, there exists a wide gap between the national norms laid down for the primary health-care structure and the actual position. All the states are suffering from inadequate rural health facilities in all the three categories (i.e. CHC, PHC and Sub-Centres). The performance of the health workers/ANM at sub-centres is very poor. In India additional 10,793 number of health workers are required to mitigate the prevailing health infrastructural gap between national norm and its actual position. This requirement is highest in Uttar Pradesh (3276) [Rural Health Statistics in India, 2010]. Given this inadequate and uneven provision of health facilities, "Health for All" has been a distant dream in rural India. It is expected that states which have higher utilization of RCH services, better public provision of services will have better RCH status. So, Government should focus on the mostly deprived states and try to improve the availability and the quality of the service in order to reduce the reproductive and maternal morbidities and to curb down the high level of infant and child mortalities in overall India. In this context ranking of the states according to the absolute value of different RCH indices provide clues to policy implementers at the disaggregated level about the areas to be focused upon with budgetary support in the initial phases that will bring about the significant result to ensure the inclusive growth and social justice of our country.

REFERENCES

Anand, S. and A.K. Sen, (1997), "Concepts of Human Development and Poverty: A Multidimensional Perspective", Background Papers for Human Development Report.

Annual Health Report, (1999-2000), *India Health Report*, Ministry of Health and Family Welfare, Government of India.

_______, (2000-01), *India Health Report*, Ministry of Health and Family Welfare, Government of India.

_______, (2002-03), *India Health Report*, Ministry of Health and Family Welfare, Government of India.

Atkinson, A.B., (1970), "On the Measurement of Inequality", *Journal of Economic Theory*, 2(3): 244-63.

Barro, R., (1996), *Health and Economic Growth*. Unpublished Paper.

Barro, R. and X. Sala-i-Martin, (1995), *Economic Growth*. New York: McGraw-Hill.

Casanovas, Lopez and Bereta Rivera, (2005), *Health and Economic Growth: Findings and Policy Implications*, The MIT Press, Cambridge.

Chandrasekhar, C.P., J. Ghosh, and A. Roychowdhury, (2006), The Demographic Dividend and Young India's Economic Future. *Economic and Political Weekly*, December 9, 5055-5064.

Dyson, T., (2008), *India's Demographic Transition and its Consequences for Development*, Golden Jubilee Lecture Series of the Institute of Economic Growth, IEG on 24 March, 2008.

Economic Survey, (2001), Government of India, New Delhi.

Fogel, R.W., (1997), New Findings on Secular Trends in Nutrition and Mortality: Some Implications for Population Theory. In *The Handbook of Population and Family Economics*, Vol.1A, edited by M. Rosenzweig and O. Stark. Amsterdam: North Holland.

Johnson, Richard A. and D.W. Wichern, (2002), *Applied Multivariate Statistical Analysis*, Pearson Education, New Delhi.

Litchifield, J.A., (1999), *Inequality: Methods and Tools*. World Bank, March.

National Family and Health Survey, (1998-99), Ministry of Health and Family Welfare, Government of India.

_______, (2003-04), Ministry of Health and Family Welfare, Government of India.

_______, (2004-05), Ministry of Health and Family Welfare, Government of India.

National Health Policy, (2002), Ministry of Health and Family Welfare, Government of India.

National Population Policy, (2000), Ministry of Health and Family Welfare, Government of India.

National Sample Survey Organization, (2004), Department of Statistics, Government of India.

NRHM, (2005), MIS Report, Ministry of Health and Family Welfare, Government of India.

Planning Commission, (2007), Report of the Human Development, Government of India, New Delhi.

Raju, S., (2002), *Health Status of the Urban Elderly: A Medico-Social Study*, B.R. Publishing Corporation, New Delhi.

Sala-i-Martin, X., (2005), "On the Health Poverty Trap": In G. Lopez-Casanovaz *et al.*, (Eds.) *Health and Economic Growth: Findings and Policy Implications*: 95-113; The MIT Press.

Sample Registration System, (1999-2000), Report on Vital Statistics in India, Registrar General, Government of India, New Delhi.

_______, (2000-01), *Report on Vital Statistics in India*, Registrar General, Government of India, New Delhi.

_______, (2009), *Report on Vital Statistics in India*, Registrar General, Government of India, New Delhi.

United Nations Development Programme, (1990), *Human Development Report*, Technical Appendices, Oxford University Press, New York.

Van Zon Adrian and Joan Muysken, (2005), "Health as a Principal Determinant of Economic Growth", In *Health and Economic Growth: Findings and Policy Implications*, edited by Guillem Lopez-Casanovas and Berta Rivera, The MIT Press, Cambridge.

World Development Report, (2000), *World Healh Report*, World Bank.

World Health Organization, (1997), *World Health Report*, World Health Organization, Geneva.

World Health Organization, (1998), *World Health Report*, World Health Organization, Monograph, Geneva.

World Health Organization, (2000), *World Health Report*, World Health Organization, Monograph, Geneva.

4

Problems of Child Labour in India

A Qualitative Approach

Atanu Sengupta and *Manas Ghose*

Introduction

Any analysis of child labour should start with its definition. "Child labour" is, generally speaking, work for children that harms them or exploits them in some way (physically, mentally, morally, or blocking access to education). There is no universally accepted definition of "child labour". Varying definitions of the term are used by the international organizations, non-governmental organizations, trade unions and other interest groups. Writers and speakers do not always specify what definition they are using, and that often leads to confusion.

Not all work is bad for children. Some social scientists point out that some kinds of work may be completely unobjectionable—except for one thing about the work that makes it exploitative. For instance, a child who delivers news papers before school might actually benefit from learning how to work, gaining responsibility, and a bit of money. But, what if the child is not paid? Then he/she is being exploited. As UNICEF'S 1997 State of the World's Children Report puts it, "Children's work needs to be seen as happening along a continuum, with destructive or exploitative work at one end and beneficial work-promoting or enhancing children's development without interfering with their schooling, recreation and rest-at the other. And between these two poles are vast areas of work that need not negatively affect a child's development." Other social scientists have slightly different ways of drawing the line between acceptable and unacceptable work.

International conventions also define "child labour" as activities such as soldering and prostitution. Not everyone agrees with this definition.

Some child workers themselves think that illegal work (such as prostitution) should not be considered in the definition of "child labour". The reason: These child workers would like to be respected for their legal work, because they feel they have no other choice but to work.

To avoid confusion, when writing or speaking about "child labour," it is best to explain exactly what you mean by child labour. This chapter defines: "Child labour" is work for children under age 14 that in some way harms or exploits them (physically, mentally, morally, or by blocking children from education).[1]

According to an estimate by the International Labour Organization (ILO), for the years 1999-2006, substantial of the world's children (aged 5-14) in the poor countries, are engaged in strenuous labouring activities. The proportion varied across the regions. In the Latin America, it was below 10 per cent while it was above 30 per cent in the Sub-Saharan Africa. In India, the figure was between 10-29 per cent. However, the data was incomplete since there was no data for China, arguably a country with some amount of child labour. However, the picture is quite alarming.

However, this mere number does not all reveal all the harsh realities of child labour. Child labour is often associated with lack of proper education, exploitative wages, early physical decay, early marriage and a low quality of life.

The picture is succinctly put forward by Dasgupta (2008). There he considered the story of two girls—one Becky in a suburban town of American Midwest and a Desta in rural Ethiopia. He argued that the lives of these two girls [who are "intrinsically very similar" Dasgupta (2008)] are so distinct from each other that they could be imagined to inhabitate different worlds. He describes Desta's world as follows: "Desta knows well that she will be married (in all likelihood to a farmer, like her father) when she reaches eighteen and will then live on her husband's land in a neighbouring village. She expects her life to be similar to that of her mother." In the terminology of mobility analysis, Desta finds herself in a perfectly immobile position. In contrast, Becky's world is depicted as a dynamic changing world. "Becky's parents also remark that her generation will be more prosperous than they." In conclusion, Dasgupta (2008) asserts, "In this article, I have used Becky's and Desta's experiences to show how it can be that the lives of essentially very similar people can become so different."

In the case of India there are some disturbing features of child labour as noted by ILO. First, there is a high incidence of children below the working age engaged with direct "economic" activities. In fact India earns an ignoble position of being second only to Sub-Saharan Africa in this regard. Secondly, there are huge undocumented records of child labour in India. Children working in the family enterprises, children use in agricultural activities are often not regarded in the official documents. Also there are cases where a child helps his/her father/mother in their workplace. Thirdly, a huge number of children are engaged in family works. According to Friedrich Huebler (2008), in India 70 per cent of the female children and 47 per cent of the male children are doing household chores. This roughly amounts to 13.3 hours per week for female and 9.5 hours per week for the male children. All these are reflected in the child health outcomes. According to Dreze and Sen (2012) in terms of under five mortality and infant mortality, India ranks fifth among the six SAARC countries just above Pakistan.

In India thus child labour is a 'harsh reality' and one can only mitigate some of the harshness of the exploitative aspects of child labour. The 'harsh reality' of child labour arises out of the fact that in the present state of development in the country many parents, on account of poverty, have to send their children to work in order to supplement their income and the income derived from the child labour, however meagre, is essential to sustain the family. This is the poverty argument of the child labour.[2]

A number of policy initiatives and programmes have been undertaken in this country over the last decade with the basic objective of dealing with the problem of the rapidly increasing number of child workers. The formulation of a National Child Labour Policy, the enactment of the Child Labour (Prohibition and Regulation) Act, 1986, the setting up of a Task Force on child labour, the adoption of the Convention on the Rights of the Child and so on have all formed a part of this process. Corresponding initiatives were taken in the related area of education where a New Education Policy was formulated which incorporated a separate component for working children. Even after all the efforts have been taken into consideration children remain economically active in virtually all economic sectors: in industry, agriculture, the informal sector and in the household as well as uneconomic sector also. The term "economic activity" refers to the broad nature of children's work. It includes all productive activities, household or market-oriented, undertaken by a child in a paid or unpaid capacity. The term uneconomic sector refers to the occupation such as prostitution, begging etc.

Economic and Non-Economic Factors

The problem of child labour is severe in the underdeveloped economy like India. To solve this problem researchers have to find out the determinants of it and the way of relationship between child labour and its determinants.

Economists seek various structures for understanding the prevalence of child labour. Theoretically, there may be four different approaches to study child labour:

- *"Selfish" parents*—Poor parents tend to be selfish. They care little about the child's welfare and send them to labour market to augment their income (Gupta, 2000).
- *Poverty argument* (Basu and Van, 1998; Priya Ranjan, 1999, 2001; Baland and Robinson, 2000; Ravallion and Quentin Wodon, 2000; Hazan and Berdugo, 2002; Emerson and Souza, 2002; Jafarey and Lahiri, 2002; Chakraborty and Das, 2005; Emerson and Knabb, 2006).
- *Poor quality of schooling* (Skinner, 1998; PROBE, 1999; Banerji, 2000; Ramchandran, 2000; Ramchandran *et al.*, 2003; Swaminathan and Rawal, 2000).
- *Social factors*—such as parent's alcoholism, caste ostracism, sex of the household head, cultural values etc. (Basu and Van, 1998; Dreze and Goyal, 2003; Mahajan, 2008).

However, several authors have opined about the limitations of the quantitative analysis and the need to incorporate the qualitative analysis in the context of child labour (Hoot *et al.*, 2006; Sandra, 2006). Their main argument is simple. A child is not only deprived of their rights and capability formation when forced to enter into the labour market. They also undergo certain unpleasant experiences that shape their view of the world. Many a times such views are so derogatory as to hamper their full blossoming into human being.[3]

For this we use the technique of qualitative data analysis by giving different case studies. In social sciences, quantitative data analysis may not always reveal the picture in totality that a case study can. On the contrary, qualitative analysis is interesting, fun and seemed to yield insight into problems and considered as important to solve, socially and morally (Piore, J. Micael, 2004; Dunlop, 1958; Dunlop, 1957; Livernash, 1957). So, we choose to use a qualitative approach to understand the problem.

This is in no way a challenge to the mainstream economics or any reshuffling of the existing wisdom. We merely try to unravel some of the realities that are approximated away by the rigourists in their bid to build nice mathematical models. However, in the process the boundary is so often transgressed that the massage of the rigorous models may be refined, elaborated or even altered in some cases. The result may be an outcome of the expanded arena of analysis rather any questioning of received wisdoms.

This chapter is divided into four parts. Section 2 gives a brief introduction to the literature of qualitative analysis and it is rational for the analysis of child labour. In Section 3 we have given quantitative and qualitative data analysis with some case studies and Section 4 contains our conclusion.

Rationale of Qualitative Data Analysis

There is a long history of qualitative analysis in economics. Economists always combined qualitative analysis with quantitative rigour. It was the famous pin factory example that was behind the labour efficacy model of Adam Smith. Similarly, the basic theory of market and exchange was explained by the famous deer-beaver example by Samuelson. Robinson Crusoe for example is used as a convenient tool for introducing general equilibrium theory by many of the standard economics textbooks. However, modern economists tend to be sceptical about the use of qualitative analysis to arrive at some major premise. Qualitative analyses were best use only for illustrative purpose.

However, a group of economists (Piore, J. Michael, 2004; Dunlop, 1958; Dunlop, 1957; Livernash, 1957) vigorously argued in favour of qualitative analysis. The arguments of Piore (2004) are most succinct. He starts from the methodological issues raised by Thomas Kuhn (Kuhn, 1970). Kuhn argues that science has to be understood first as social practice and only afterwards as an intellectual endeavour. A scientific discipline is a social community, and people enter it through a process of initiation and imitation (Kuhn, 1970). What we learn in the university is not scientific theory and certainly not a theory of how to do science. We are exposed to practices: the practices of our teachers in the classroom and laboratory, and the practices they admire, which we read about in the articles they assign us. The theory of how science should be done is almost never taught. And even the theory that explains the practices and articles to which we are exposed and that gives the discipline some coherence is constructed after the fact. It is not always taught directly, is always incomplete, and is often internally contradictory.

Certainly, then alternative practices should have its scope within the framework of Kuhn. Hence, there is a need to move towards the qualitative approach. Qualitative approach is often described as a case study approach. But case studies as practiced in the social sciences tend to be viewed as essentially offering empirical results. The use of open-ended interviews as a research technique depends on the ability to draw out of the interview material something that is interesting and meaningful. It depends, in other words, on the ability to "read" the interviews, to *interpret* the interviews and honesty of the researchers.

One of the advantages of open-ended interviews is that the respondents often answer questions you would not have thought to ask. Yield of the open-ended interviews is stories the respondents tell. The story is the "observation". The stories are basically narratives. The question is thus what to do with the stories. Typically stories are not analyzed as statistical data; stories are "interpreted". We have used the stories not as data points but to suggest particular revisions in theory.

Among the mainstream economists, Bardhan (1989) made an early attempt to initiate a conversation between the quantitative generalized theorists (termed by him as "economists") and specific case centric (mainly) qualitative analysts (termed as "anthropologists"). Recently, there has been a lot of debate regarding integrating the quantitative and the qualitative analysis (in the context of poverty dynamics)—the so-called Q^2 approach (Addison, Hulme and Kanbur, 2009). While some of the authors opine in favour of this integration (Kanbur, 2003; Kanbur and Shaffer, 2007), others strongly oppose this view (Harriss, 2009; du Toit, 2009). While the former the mainstream quantitative theorists believe that an integration of the qualitative analysis will increase their depth and variety, the opponents are sceptical of such attitudes.

We provide an example from micro-economics in order to understand the interaction between qualitative and quantitative analysis. The typical exercise deals with the preference pattern at the low level of survival (Sen, 1973; Karalis, 2007). Karalis (2007) argues that the standard theory of preference facts in situation where the people have to choose between alternative survival outcomes. Karalis (2007) argues the utility have two meanings—pain redresser and pleasure. The quantitative economists have equated utility to pleasure principle. However, for a poor, utility is more of pain redresser than pleasure maximization. In this case it is difficult to maintain the assumption of substitutability over different pairs. The classic story is that of "Sophie's Choice". According to the story, Sophie was a polish Christian in the Nazi occupied Poland. She was arrested with her two children—a boy of age 8 and a girl of age 6, because her husband was a Communist. Not being a Jew, a Nazi official at Auswitch had given her a "choice". She will be allowed to live with one of her children.

A similar situation happens to a poor, when he has to choose between either "less food" or "less cloth" both at the bare survival level (figure 4.1). As a consequence a "no substitutability zone" generate where the traditional indifference curve cannot exist. As Karalis (2007) argues the radically transforms the entire foundation of contemporary micro-economics and the resulting thinking procedure.

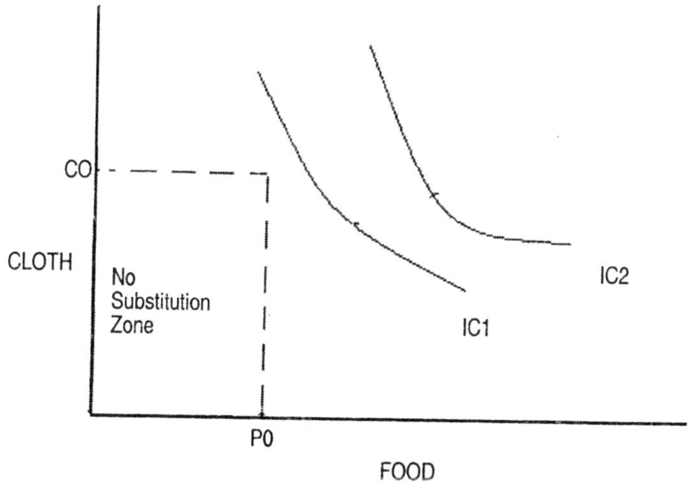

Fig. 4.1: Survival Level

As recently commented by the economist Robert Solow (2011) about the approach "..........are allergic to grand generalization about the secret of economic development. Instead they appeal to many local observations and experiments to explore how poor people in poor countries actually cope with their poverty, what they know, what they seem (or do not seem) to want, what they expect of themselves and others, and how they make the choices that they can make. I was fascinated and convinced."

As noted earlier, the rigorous economic analysis of child labour is only a part of the larger issues involved in the problem (Basu and Van, 1998). Non-economic factors—that may not be easily (if not impossible) quantified—do play an important role in case of child labour. The pangs and atrocities that a child has to face cannot be reduced to simple quantity. These may work as a deterrent to their work effort and reduce the work efficiency. Hence, it is necessary to hear their voice—the stories they have to tell to us. It is only in this way can we hope to grapple the issue.

There has been some attempt in recording the child's voice in matters that involve them (Middleton, Ashworth, and Walker, 1994; Kempson, 1996; Hindle, 1998; Balen, 2000; Smith *et al.*, 2001; Fortier, 2006). In all these studies children describe their experiences under conditions of poverty and deprivation. The hardships that these kids face, their social exclusion and shattering of dream world is well pictured. In many of these studies the acute feeling of child is hunger—the incentive towards eating expired food or stealing food. Moreover, they have to use shabby and unclean clothes, tight boots etc. Also having to cope up with inefficient medical care is a painful activity of the child.

However, these studies are based on developed parts of the world. Hoot, Tadesse and Abdella (2006) deals with the problem of child prostitutes in Africa. Poverty's most egregious outcome is child prostitution (Hoot *et al.*, 2006). They have shown how the children come into such deadly profession-voices seldom heard. Generally, work opportunity of the girls is lower than boys. However, feelings about parental poverty are same for both—boy and girl. These feelings bring them into such deadly profession. Sometimes, poverty driven parents also forced their children into prostitution to earn income as a means of family support.

In this chapter we deal with child labour—another offshoot of children in poverty in the context of a developing economy.

Qualitative Data Analysis with Case Studies

Structure of the Study and the Respondents

In order to understand the problems of child labour the authors undertook a field survey regarding some projects under the government programme of Primary Education for All (*Sarva Shiksha Abhiyan—SSA*). In this survey we have surveyed 357 girl children spread over the entire district of Burdwan, West Bengal, India. The district of Burdwan is unique. Western part of it is highly urbanized with industrial activity—one of the oldest industrial zone of the country. On the other hand, Eastern side is largely rural with one of the most fertile soils of India. Our investigators have travelled the length and breadth of the district to collect information. They have collected data covering almost every agent that are important in the child's world. This includes the child herself, her parents, the teachers of the school[4] where she studies and also local political representatives. Care was taken to elicit independent views from each of them.

The collection of data involved open ended interviews about their day-to-day activities and family stories and some structured quantitative questions. Six different types of question sets were prepared. As for the qualitative information, it is gathered from the open ended questions. The participants were allowed to express their views without trying them to hook them into some common blanket. However, they were being helped if they found difficult to answer any question. Roughly 45 minutes were given to interview the participants. The monotonous nature of the standard questionnaire method could be avoided by resorting to story-telling and emotional revelation that made the interactive process very interesting. The diversity of personal experiences is breath-taking, but they have some very common features that render some generalizations. We, however, present only a few of these diverse experiences that we had.[5] They speak of the children's voices regarding the child labour and how they feel about it.

Quantitative Data Features

We have surveyed 357 students from 117 schools, purposively, from the entire district. Out of them we found 311 (87%) child labourers. Sex-ratio among the sampled children is 1366, high enough. Not only child sex-ratio, but also adult sex-ratio is also high enough that is 1060. This reflects unbiased attitude of the adults towards new born child. Adult literacy rate is 74 per cent . However, most of the families are large family. Average number of children in the family is 3.

The following diagrams (Figs. 4.2 and 4.3) depict some of the important features of the sampled children.

Figure 4.2 shows that about 95 per cent students want to continue their study. This percentage figure is relatively higher in the rural areas compare to the urban areas.

In figure 4.3, we have shown the percentage distribution of the sampled students who enjoy play in the school. In the aggregate level about 96 per cent students enjoy play in the school. A rural urban difference is very low in this respect.

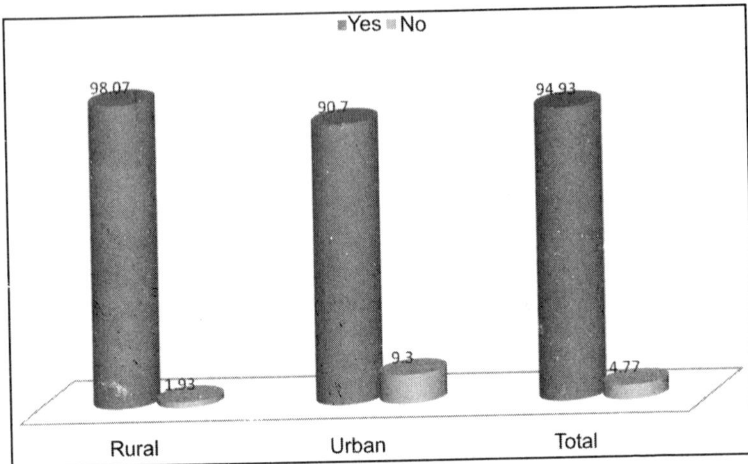

Fig. 4.2: Percentage of students wish to continue study

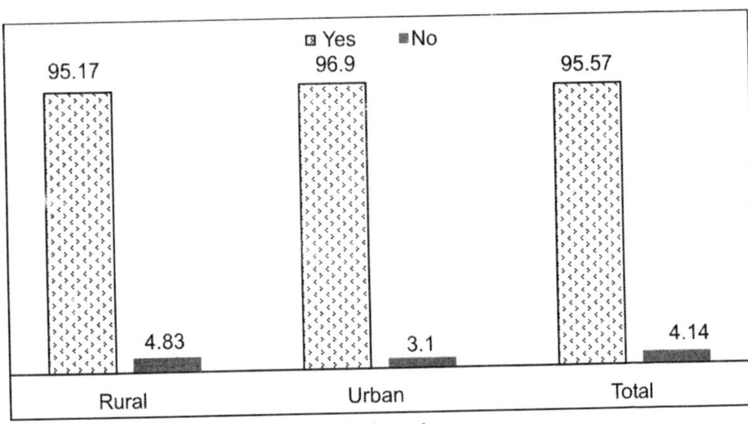

Fig. 4.3: Percentage of students enjoying play

From figure 4.4, it is seen that about 96.5 per cent students enjoy education. In this respect, also, rural urban difference is very low.

From figure 4.5, it is seen that 80 per cent students have aim in life. Their aims are doctor, teacher, lawyer, officer, engineer, politician, social worker etc.

From figure 4.6, it is seen that about 86 per cent students have private tuition. Most of them take private tuition to acquire more knowledge so that they can achieve their aim in life.

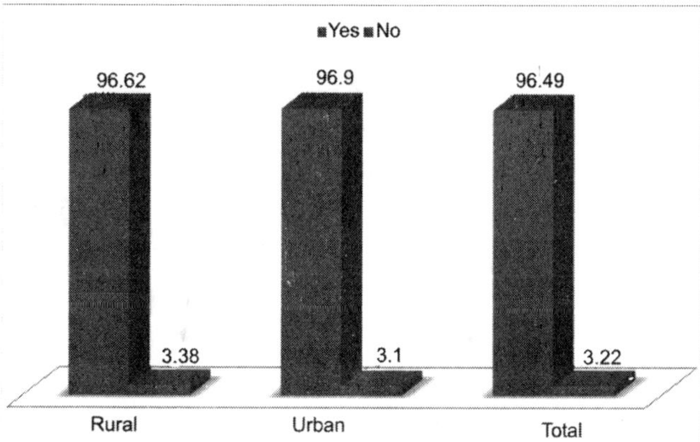

Fig. 4.4: Percentage of students enjoying education

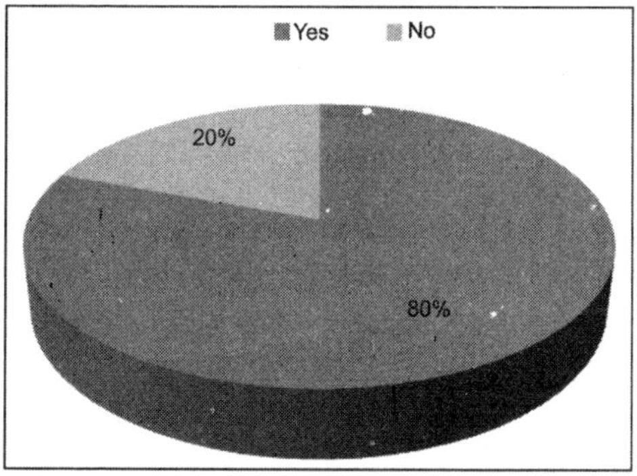

Fig. 4.5: Percentage of students having aim in life

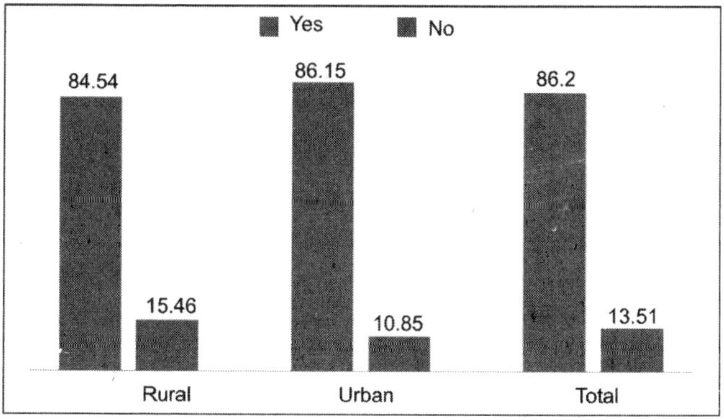

Fig. 4.6: Percentage of students having private tuition

From figure 4.7, we have seen that almost all the students have favourite subjects.

From figure 4.8, it is seen that about 87 per cent students do some work that may be in the household chores or wage work.

Figure 4.9 shows the distribution of working children according to the types of work. From the figure it is seen that 31 per cent working

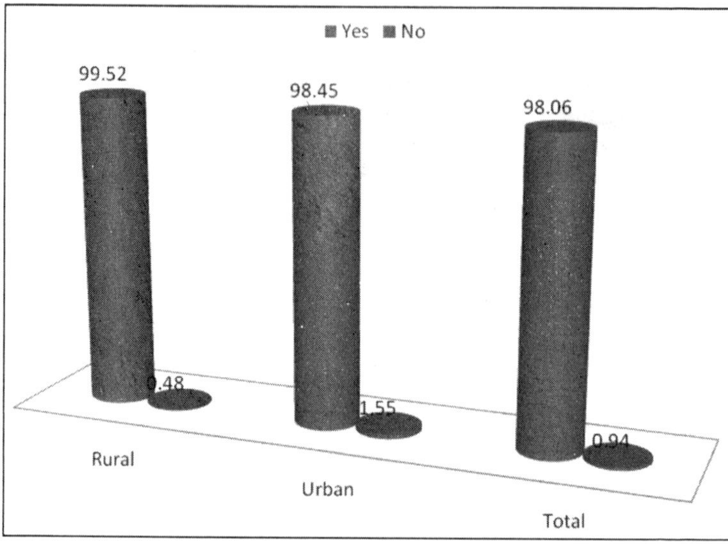

Fig. 4.7: Percentage of students having favourite subject

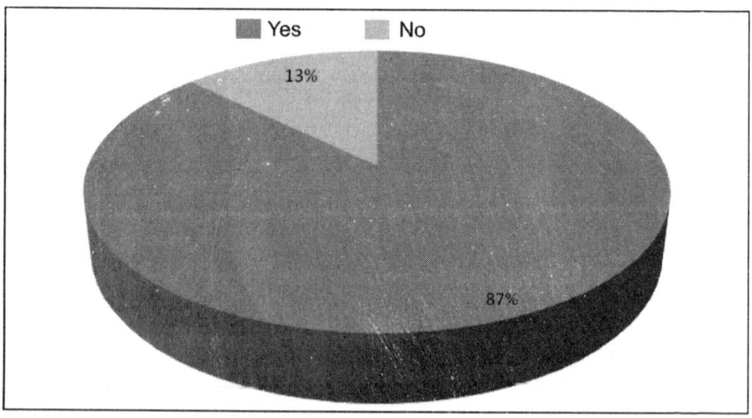

Fig. 4.8: Percentage of students doing different types of work

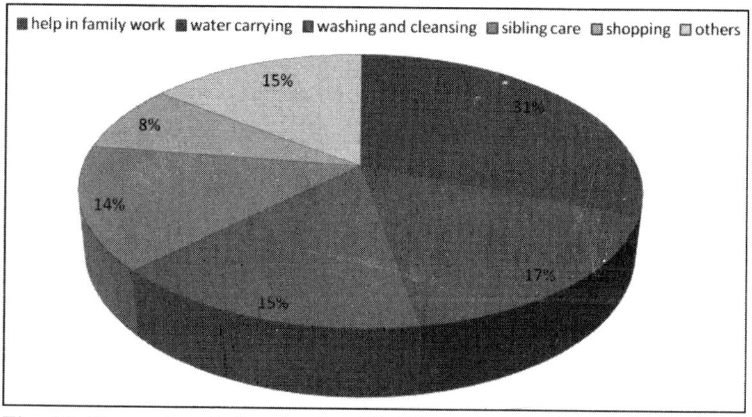

Fig. 4.9: Types of work done by the child labour

children are helping in the family work. 17 per cent are carrying water for their family and 15 per cent are engaged with washing and cleansing.

These quantitative data features points out to a very different picture of the reality than pictured by standard rigorous approach. Child labour is not a mere phenomenon—it is an attitude that permits other aspects of child. All of our children are so called school goers. Apparently they can coexist with the labouring activities of the child. However, the families have a very pathetic view of these children. Their studies are neglected and often deemed non-important by the parents. However, the quantitative tools fail miserably, if we try to probe more deeply into these attitudinal issues. Hence, we turn to some case studies[6] hoping to capture the qualitative issues in child labour.

Stories of the Labouring Children

In our sample we have found N = 311 (87% of 357) child labourers. They became child labourers due to different reasons. Not all child labourers are caused by poverty. There are some other reasons also. Now, we will discuss the case studies translating in English. However since our subjects express themselves in the local language, its symbols, meaning and structure are not always easily translatable to English. In fact, some of these local vocabularies are kept intact in order to enable us to peep into their world. We would however try to convey their feelings and observations beyond this linguistic barrier, as far as possible.

***Case-I**: Female Child Labour at the Cost of Better School for the Male Child*

Consider this story as told by Sumita Mallo in the Sadhumoti School of Burdwan Municipality, age 10:

> *"My mother works as a maid servant in a house. So, my mother cannot do all the familial duties and I perform remaining familial duties before going to school. After the school I help my father in selling foochkas (one type of junk food) but my little brother (he is a student of class three) is relieved from such activities. My little brother is studying in a "better" school."*

Likewise, Aisa Khatun, age 8, of Maharani Adhirani Balika Vidyalaya stated:

> *"My elder brother has no familial duties at all. However, my mother assigned me so many familial duties such as washing and cleansing, drinking water collection and help in cooking etc."*

Musferi Khatun, age 10, of Haji Qadam F. P. School from Asansol block also added:

> *"My brother, he is a student of class two, have a private tuition and do not do any work. However, I have no private tuition and I have to do so many familial duties side-by-side I have to care my little sister. As my father is a truck driver most of the time he stays out of the home. If I do not care my little sister my mother cannot do the familial work. However, I am performing better in the examination than my brother."*

From the above case studies, [50% of cases (N = 156)], it is clear that there exist a gender deprivation within the siblings of the family. Parents think that as she is a girl. So, human capital formation in her no way give any utility to them because after her marriage (in this case it is likely to be at a tender age), then she will go to another house (*paraaya ghar*) with her husband. So, parents take care on their male child as he is the successor of the family. Parents enjoy utility in their older age from their male child but not from a girl child. A male child is a most valuable asset and a great insurance of the parents. Primary objective of the parents is to form human capital in their male child. If parental income is sufficiently above what is necessary to perform the primary objectives then only they try to form human capital in their girl child. Therefore, human capital formation in the girl child is a secondary objective of the parents. If parental income is not sufficient to achieve their primary objectives then a girl child act, as supplement of the family. This fact partially challenges the luxury axiom popularized by Basu and Van (1998). Not all children are asset to the family—some are liabilities.

The above case study clearly contrasts with the evidences that are put forward by Basu and Van (1998). Consider the following quotation: "A different kind of evidence comes from David Vincent's (1981) study of working class autobiographies. The study showed that children who worked rarely blamed their parents, believing instead that it was poverty that drove the parents into making the children labour (*see* also Michael Anderson, 1971)" (Basu and Van, 1998). The only exception to this is alcoholism (Basu and Van, 1998).

The child in our study does not complain of parents' alcoholism. Yet her eyes and expressions clearly indicate that she is complaining against her parents—about their insensitivity towards her studies. From the above case study we have seen that she is willing to study but cannot do so.

Case-II: *A Child With "No Play"— A Sad Truth from a Village*

Now, we will consider another story told by Siuli Khatun, age 10, in the Moregram Uttarpara F.P. School of Ketugram block.

To collect our relevant data we talked with her more than half an hour but sad experience was that when we asked her that how you pass the time at afternoon. After our question she burst into tears. On further enquiry, the weeping child said that—

> *"I have no leisure time of my own. My father is a bus driver—most of the time he stays outside the home. My mother is a maid servant and she binds bidi (a local smoking product of tobacco—a substitute for cigarette) for merchants. So, being an elder child, I have to perform most of the domestic duties. In my "pass time" I have to bind bidi that would help my mother in enhancing family income. So, I have no pass time of my own."*

Another girl child Asima Khatun, age 10, of Kulgaria High Madrasa of Galsi 2 block told similar type of story.

> *"My mother is a maid servant and father is a casual farm labour. My mother come back to home from the workplace between 10 to 11 a.m. So, I have to do all the familial duties including cooking. So, I cannot attend school everyday."*

We have found 14 per cent (N = 44) of such type of case. This fact (her cry) clears some ideas, we explain one-by-one. Firstly, the idea that the children have no separate utility function from the family head is falsified. Here, parent does not give much value to the children's leisure. In this case her utility is positive function of amount of pass time, but utility function of her family head is negative function of her pass time. Therefore, when her family head maximizes his utility then she is exploited and she feels it clearly. But she cannot go against her parents as she is not adult and has no alternative. She gives more value to the exploitation than love and affection of her parents. Secondly, exploitative child labour exists even within the family. Most of the social scientists say that some extent domestic child labour is good for the society. Reason for such argument is that if children do some domestic duties then that increase their responsibility and efficiency on that works. However, even such domestic duties can become quite a burden for a child if overburdened.

Case-III: *Uncertain Schooling: A Child who Does Not Know How Far She Can Study*

Jamila Khatun, age 10, of Sanko Girls F.P. School of Galsi 2 block, told us her story about her future study. She is a student of class four.

When we asked whether she want to continue study or what is your aim etc. The girl answered that— "I cannot say anything" then we asked why. She told us—

> *"My parents married my elder sister at 13 years of age and after that she did not continue school. She has to do so many familial duties in her in-law's home. Though my elder sister was a good student and stood first in all her exams including her last examination. Still the janguru (religious priest) insisted that a girl need not study (Meyeder parashuna korte hoy na)."*

A similar story told by Nasrin Khatun, age 9, of Joaupur Surabala

F.P. School of Memary block. She is a student of class three.

> *"I want to be a teacher. If my parents do not marry me like my elder sister (whose marry has just done at 12 years age)."*

Another story told by Jesmine Sultana, age 13, of Sirrai A.M. High School of Galsi 1 block. She is a student of class six.

> *"My parents search my bridegroom since six months ago. So, I cannot continue my study."*

The facts (18%, N = 56) imply that the girl has been suffering from an uncertainty whether she can continue her study or it will stop in near future. Burden of all the domestic duties of in-law's family and burden of bearing a child will fall on her. Here, free education is uncertain due to tradition, customs and lack of education of the parents. Most of the researchers concluded that the determinants of child labour are lack of free and quality education, low parental income, adult unemployment, adoption and implementation of proper laws to restrict child labour and limited opportunity for girls. But in these cases we have found that child labour, especially for girls, is also determined by tradition and customs.

Case-IV: *The "virtue" of Private Tuition—A Child with Bruised Hand*

In Madhabdihi F.P. School of Raina block, we found a student (Rizia Khatun, age 7) from this school which was an exploitative domestic child labour. When we asked about her daily routine then she told us—

> *"Except school and tuition time most of the time of the day she works as stitching worker (showing her bruised hands she give its proof). My father only brings the order of the work and my mother only supply the order, I alone does the work. I wake up from the sleep at early morning and after brushing her teeth I take my breakfast (panta vath-rice cooked long ago mixed with water) and goes to private tuition before going to school. After the school I start to work that ends at night. I work about four hours (one Azan to another)."*

Another story of the same type is told by Samima Khatun, age 10, of Madhpur F.P. School of Khandoghosh 1 block.

> *"I am a maid servant. My mother is also a maid servant. However, my father does not go to work everyday (he is a casual farm worker). If he wish to go to work and find work then only he go to work. I go to my workplace at 6.30 a.m. and back from there at 9.30 a.m. Mainly cleansing home, washing clothes and utensils, help in cook are my duties there. I cannot go to school, in some days, if there is more work pressure. However, I go to private tuition at night. Because my parents are illiterate so without my private tutor I cannot complete the task of the school."*

We have found 16 per cent (N = 50) cases of such type. In almost all the studies on this topic, researchers assume that parents are altruistic. Here, parents are selfish. They do not work as much as necessary to sustain the family rather they forced their child to work. Therefore, this case study challenges the mainstream belief. This case also argues in favour of private tuition. The private tuition is not a result of teachers' inefficiency but to complement her formal education. Answering our question she told that she is well satisfied about the school teachers, but as school is for limited time so she needs private tuition. Without private tuition, she has no time to study except at school. At last when we asked her that why your parent do not work much more rather than you then she feels shy and try to avoid the story told just before. Though the child is feeling shy speaking about her parents' selfishness, her parents do not feel ashamed at such selfishness.

Case-V: *A Middle-Class Child Labour: The Child as a Labour in Her Own House*

We have some child labour in the middle class (from several enquiries about the family assets and consumption it appears that their families are quite well-off) families also. Now, we consider few stories of such child labour. Story told by Hena Parvin, age 9, of Rahmania F.P. School of Asansol Municipality.

> *"My father is an army personnel and mother is a housewife. However, my father has to stay out of the home-town due to official duties. My mother does domestic duties. So, my mother does not get enough time to care my little sister and brother. So, I have to care my little brother and sister and other familial duties (shopping, storing drinking water etc.). I am a budding*

> *athlete and want to pursue my career in that field. I feels bore to do her familial duties but I have no choice."*

Another story of this type is told by Ramisha Farhan, age 10, of Manimala Girls Primary School of Raniganj-Hirapur block.

> *"My father is a businessman (retail business of stationary goods) and my mother is a housewife. However, I have a little brother and a little sister. So, I have to care them in most of the time of the day, except school time. Otherwise, my mother cannot do the familial duties. Sometimes, I have to do some familial duties, as helper, when my mother busy with my little brother and sister. I cannot play with my friends."*

The above stories, found 39 per cent (N = 121), reveals the fact that child labour is caused by sibling rivalry or sibling care and their bore feel indicates that she is exploited. As their family income is sufficiently above the subsistence level so we may call them a middle class child labour.

The above case challenges the poverty argument for child labour popular in the dominant economic thinking. According to this argument, child labour exists only if adults' income is insufficient to maintain the family. But in this case family income of the child's family is sufficient to maintain the family till she becomes a child labour.

Case-VI: *Exchange Labour and Study: A Child Buys her Private Tuition*

Lastly, we have found another type of child labour. We will discuss here two such types of stories. The first is told by Sabinu Khatun, age 8, of Ganguli Danga F.P. School of Katwa block.

> *"I am a maid servant. My mother also a maid servant and father is a rickshaw puller. I go to work only in the morning session (about 6 a.m. to 8.30 a.m.). Then I go to school. After returning from the school I go to my aunt's home (near my home). As my father and mother are illiterate and I have no private tuition so to manage my home assignment given by the school teachers. I take care of my cousin brother and sisters when my aunt is busy doing household activity, in exchange, my aunt teaches me."*

This type of another story is told by Abira Sultana, age 9, of Ratapur

F.P. School of Ketugram block.

> *"My mother is a housewife and my father is small farmer. I have not to do any work in the family. I go to private tuition to my neighbouring aunt as my parents are illiterate. She does not take any money from me. However, I have to do their different types of familial duties and also work as helper in the farm work at the busy session when the need."*

These (10%, N = 31) are a peculiar type of child labour. The child directly enters into the labour market for not adding to her family basket. Instead she pays for her own educational expenditure. According to the sociologists, a child not always earn for her parents. She sometimes earn for her "own needs"—paying for some junk foods she likes (ice cream, foochkas, chicken items etc.), visiting the place she desires (amusement parks, joy rides, fair etc.) and so on and so forth. Here, the child pays for her own human capital formation.

From the deliberations of the above cases and a detailed discussion regarding our sample reveals some interesting features about the female child labour emanates out of our study:

- Child labour is not always a detriment to child education. Most of our sampled children attend schools despite being a child labour. In other words, access to education did not help to reduce the burden of child labour as is usually thought.
- In some cases, they act as a complement. Almost all our child actually pays for their education. In some cases (such as Case VI above), she directly pays for it through exchange labour. In some cases, she contributes (about 4.23%) financially to the family's earning.
- However, the chief help come through domestic labour. The girls are heavily burdened with familial duties (about 87%). Such duties include works that strain heavy physical strength such as water carrying (17%) and washing and cleansing (15%).
- However, there are some so-called less heavy duties—such as sibling care (14%) and shopping (8%).

From our field survey, we have felt that the teaching authorities at the local level (both the head teachers and assistant teachers) almost unanimously supportive of the potentialities of the girl students. Very few of them felt any deficiency of the girls especially in their talent or diligence. In fact, they argued that girls are more attentive than the boys.

The girls for their part are eager to carry on studies. Most of the students have a strong inclination towards learning. They can point out their favourite subject and answer some elementary questions related to it. It is clear that the new method has at least made learning a joyful process. This is no mean achievement considering that most of the rural children are from backward section of the society. Some of them are first generation learners while most others are of second generation. Some of them have aim in life while others do not. They love to come to school and study. They also love to play with their friends, mix and communicate with the outside work.

Unfortunately, most of them are burdened with heavy familial duties (such as carrying water, cleansing, washing, sibling care etc.). Some have to stay home if their mother becomes ill. Even at their tender age they are burdened with heavy family burden. This is in sharp contrast to the minority boys who often do not have such heavy duties. Some are spared when they have an elder sister to take on their duty. Some of them are engaged with income earning job (such as *bidi* binding, stitching etc.). Strange enough they all take private tuitions. In fact for them, private tuition is the only time they have time to study for their own. Some of these girls are not sure when their study will be discontinued though they themselves want to continue study. Uncertain future seems to close down the glitter we saw in their tiny eyes.

Conclusion

The above case studies widened before us the entire canvas of child labour. It put forward a number of provocative questions that the standard theory could hardly answer. Is the child labour merely an economic phenomenon with low income constraint as its chief determinant? The answer is clearly negative. Not only do decisions regarding child labour are influenced by social factors, they shape its very arena. Child labour is not only found in poor families, it is sometimes found in a rather well to do family. Contrary to popular belief, domestic child labour is in no way good for the society—some of them are exploitative. In the low income families parents do not give much value to leisure of their children. However, the children do value their pastime greatly. Therefore, utility function of the children is different from that of the house head. When forced by the parents, decision to work, they might respond with reduced efficiency. Thus, the parents' *gain in utilizing* child labour may be reduced. This may be a good explanation of the so-called luxury axiom proposed by Basu and Van (1998).

NOTES

1. See Karelis (2007) for similar discussion on definitional issues regarding the concept of poverty.
2. This is the so-called luxury axiom popularized by Basu and Van (1998). This axiom tries to refute some earlier arguments that harp on the morality of the parents of child labour. The parents of child labour are not exceptionally cruel than normal parents. They are forced by their material conditions to take such a decision.
3. Hoot (2006), for example, discusses the mental trauma that a child encounters when she is forced into prostitution.
4. According to the recent government estimates (based on DISE) in 2006-2007, the Gross Enrolment Ratio is 111 per cent in the primary education system. In the same source, the drop-out rate is only 9.08 per cent in total (9.63% for the girls) at the primary stage.
5. We have purposefully subdued their name for the sake of anonymity.
6. It is terribly miserable to defend that these case studies are truly "representational". However, we may loosely argue that they cover the major prototypes found in our sample.

REFERENCES

Addison, T., D. Hulme, and R. Kanbur (eds.)., (2009), "*Poverty Dynamics: Measurement and Understanding from an Intradiciplinary Perspectives*", Oxford University Press.

Anderson, Michael, (1971), Family Structure in Nineteenth Century Lancashire. Cambridge: Cambridge University Press.

Baland, J.M., J. Robinson, (2000), "Is Child labour Inefficient?" *Journal of Political Economy*, 108, 663-679.

Banerjee, A.V. and E. Duflo, (2011), "Poor Economics: A Radical Rethinking of the Way to Fight Global Poverty", Random House, India.

Banerji, R., (2000), "Poverty and Primary Schooling: Field Studies from Mumbai and Delhi". *Economic and Political Weekly*, March 4, 2000, pp. 795-802.

Bardhan, Pranab (ed.), (1989), "*Conversations between Economists and Anthropologists: Methodological Issues in Measuring Economic Change in Rural India*", New Delhi: Oxford University Press.

Basu, K., P.H. Van, (1998), "The Economics of Child Labour", *American Economic Review,* 88, 412-427.

Chakraborty, S., M. Das, (2005), "Mortality, Fertility, and Child Labour" *Economics Letters,* 86, 273-278.

Dre'ze, J., G. Gandhi-Kingdon, (2001), "School Participation in Rural India", *Review of Development Economics* 5, 1-24.

Dunlop, John T., (1957), "Wage Contours," in *New Concepts of Wage Determination,* George W. Taylor and Frank C. Pierson, (eds.) New York: McGraw-Hill, 127-39.

Dunlop, John T., (1958), *Industrial Relations Systems*. New York: Holt.

Emerson, P. and S. Knabb, (2006), "Fiscal Policy, Expectation Trap and Child Labour", *Economic Inquiry* forthcoming.

Emerson, Patrick and André Portela Souza, (2003), "Is There a Child Labour Trap? Inter-Generational Persistence of Child Labour in Brazil," *Economic Development and Cultural Change,* 51(2): 375-98.

Fortier, M.S., (2006), "On being a Poor Child in America", *Journal of Children and Poverty*, 12: 2, 113-128.

Friedrich Huebler, (2007), www.friedrichhueblerblogspot.com

Gupta, M., (2000), "Wage Determination of Child Worker: A Theoretical Analysis", *Journal of Development Economics*, 4 (2), 219-228.

Harriss, J., (2009), "Bringing Politics Back into Poverty Analysis", *Poverty Dynamics,* edited by T. Addison, D. Hulme and R. Kanbur.

Hazan, M. and B. Berdugo, (2002), "Child Labour, Fertility, and Economic Growth", *Economic Journal*, 112(482): 810-28.

Hindle, D., (1998), "Loss, Recovery, and Adoption: A Child's Perspective", *Journal of Social Work Practice* 12 (1): 17-26.

Hoot, James, Tadesse Selamawit and Abdella Rahmet, (2006), "Voices Seldom Heard", *Journal of Children and Poverty*, 12: 2, 129-139.

International Labour Organization, (1996), "Child Labour Surveys: Results of Methodological Experiments in Four Countries, 1992-93". International Programme on the Elimination of Child Labour, IPEC. ILO, Geneva.

Jafarey, S. and S. Lahiri, (2002), "Will Trade Sanctions Reduce Child Labour? The Role of Credit Markets", *Journal of Development Economics*, 68(1), 137-56.

Kanbur, R. and Shaffer Paul, (2007), "Epistemology, Normative Theory and Poverty Analysis: Implications for Q-Squared in Practice" *mimeo.*

Kanbur, R., (2003), Q-squared? A Commentary on Qualitative and Quantitative Poverty Appraisal. In *Q-squared: Qualitative and Quantitative Poverty Appraisal,* (ed.) R. Kanbur, pp. 1-21. Permanent Black, Delhi.

Karelis, C., (2007), *The Persistence of Poverty: Why the Economics of the well-off cannot help the Poor*, Yale University Press.

Kempson, E., (1996), "Life on a Low Income". York: Joseph Rowntree Foundation. LITTLECHILD, B. 2000. Children's rights to be heard in child protection processes: Law, Policy and Practice in England and Wales. *Child Abuse Review*, 9 (6):403-15, England, 1987, pp. 120-121.

Livernash, Robert E., (1957), "Job Clusters," in *New Concepts of Wage Determination*, George W. Taylor and Frank C. Pierson, (eds.) New York: McGraw-Hill, 140-160.

Mahajan, S., (2008), "*Education for Social Change: MVF and Child Labour*", National Book Trust, New Delhi, India.

Middleton, S., K. Ashworth, and R. Walker, (1994), "*Family Fortunes: Pressures on Parents and Children in the 1990s*". London: CPAG.

Piore, Michael J., (2004), "*Qualitative Research: Does it fit in Economics?*" Massachusetts Institute of Technology.

Ramchandran, (2003), "Backward and Forward Linkages that Strengthen Primary Education", *Economic and Political Weekly*, March 8, pp. 959-968.

Ramchandran *et al.*, (2003), "Through the Life Cycle of Children: Factors that Facilitate/Impede Successful Primary School Completion", *Economic and Political Weekly*, November 22, pp. 4994-5000.

Ranjan, P., (1999), "An Economic Analysis of Child Labour", *Economic Letters*, 64, 99-105.

Ranjan, P., (2001), "Credit Constraints and the Phenomenon of Child Labour", *Journal of Development Economics*, 64, 81-102.

Ravallion, M., Q. Wodon, (2000), "Does cheaper schooling means less child labour? Evidence from behavioural responses to an enrolment subsidy", *Economic Journal*, Vol. 110, pp. 158-175.

Ray, D., "*Development Economics*", Princetone University Press.

Sandra, M. Fortier, (2006), "On Being a Poor Child in America, Views of poverty from 7-12 years old", *Journal of Children and Poverty*, 12(2), 123-128.

Sengupta, A., K. Nath and M. Ghose, (2009), *Status of Girls Students of Minority Communities,* Impact assessment under Sarva Shiksha Abhiyan, India.

Skinner, (1998), "Basic Education as a Political Issue", *Conferrence Report*, Common Security Forum, King's College, Cambridge.

Smith, J.R., J. Brooks-Gunn, C. McCarton and D. Kohen, (2001), "Transitions on and off AFDC: Implications for parenting and children's cognitive development", *Child Development*, 72, pp. 1512-1533.

Solow, R., (2011), Comments on A.V. Banerjee and E. Duflo, "Poor Economics": A Radical Rethinking to the Way to Fight Global Poverty, Random House Publications, India.

Swaminathan and Rawal, (2000), Primary Education for All, *India Development Report,* 1999-2000, (eds.) Indira Gandhi Development Research: Oxford University Press.

Toit du A., (2009), "Poverty Measurement Blues: 'Q-Squared' Approaches to Understanding Chronic Poverty in South Africa", *Poverty Dynamics* edited by Addison, T. Hulme, D. and Kanbur R.

UNICEF global database-2007.

Vincent, David Bread, (1981), "Knowledge and Freedom: A study of nineteenth-century working class autobiography". London: Europa Publications.

5

Delivery of the Primary Education System in India

A District Level Analysis

Atanu Sengupta and *Naibedya Prasun Pal*

Introduction

Education is a complex network of learners, learning materials, teachers, administrators, guardians and all most all who are interested in these very vital aspect of human life. It involves a number of factors—some material, some man-made and some behaviour. Without grappling this complex network, nobody can aspire to capture the working of our education system and its delivery mechanism. As noted by Sen (2006), Japan had emphasized on education as the basic building block of economic development, at the onset of Meiji restoration in the mid-nineteenth century.

In the human development paradigm, education is considered as one of the basic pillars of human endowment. A man can achieve his/her full potential only if he/she can attain proper education. Vidyasagar stressed the importance of primary education in enhancing national consciousness. The emphasis is obviously more on primary education because it is the base on which the large superstructure of learning is erected. As a faulty base weakness the structure show a defect in the primary education system can jolt the further progress to the frontiers of knowledge. Thus, human development emphasizes primary enrolment together with literacy rate as one of the basic component of Human Development Index, constructed by UNDP. The above link now brings forth the importance of primary education in the larger matrix of man and his society.

It is universally acclaimed that primary education is always the basic pillar in human capital formation. India has also suffered due to a faulty education system. The Constitution of India enshrines compulsory primary education to all her citizens in the Directive Principle of State Policy. After Independence the Right to Education was included in our Directive Principle. Recently, the Education Bill 2010, introduces education as a basic right of all the children in India.

However, inadequate attention is paid to the delivery mechanism of the primary education. This remains a basic Achilles' wheel of the development process in India. In fact, this inadequacy has added to injustice and inequality while stunting the prospect of development.

Mere assurance of physical access to education cannot guarantee quality education (Ramchandran, 2004; Sengupta, Sengupta and Ghosh, 2004). Although several attempts have been made in the past to assess the accessibility, enrolment and learners' achievement, little information is available on the internal efficiency of primary schools in the country. Very few studies have attempted to look into all the indicators of internal efficiency of primary education system from a comparative perspective covering all States and UTs. Recently, Arun C. Mehta (Mehta, 2005) has constructed the internal efficiency indicator of primary education system in his chapter "Student Flow at Primary Level—An Analysis based on DISE Data". The indicator emphasized on the completion of at least two years in the primary school by a child. However, this indicator is inadequate because its inability to capture social and gender issue.

Again Sengupta and Pal (2009, 2010) used the DISE data set to generate a host of indicators that are directly related with educational performance.

The main limitation of the analysis is its dependence of a set of derived indices. Notwithstanding their logic, an analysis directed towards the more immediate data would be more useful.

In this chapter our aim is to provide a region-wise panoramic view of the primary education system in India at the district level with its frailties and inequalities that require immediate policy action. The publications of all India DISE data for three consecutive years have facilitated this type of analysis. However, consistent district level analysis is available only for the year 2005-06.

Our chapter is divided as follows. In section 2 we discuss the data and methodology used. The next section and sub-sections discuss these aspects of the delivery system in primary education viz. the lack of resources, policy indicators, social stigma and efficiency (DEA) of the system. In section 4 we try to find out some relation between these four aspects and the effect they have on the broader social phenomenon. Section 5 concludes the study.

In the Appendix, we have presented zone-wise name of the districts (589 districts we have covered in our study).

Data and Methodology

Data Description and Variables Used

In this study we have used data from secondary sources. It has been collected from "DISE Statistics (Elementary Education) for the year 2005-06, which is based on DISE District raw data. The DISE data gives various district-specific key indicators (pupil-teacher ratio), student-classroom ratio, GER, NER, school with boy's toilet, school with girl's toilet' proportion of female teachers, drop-out rate, retention rate etc.) for good quality primary education.

The purpose of this study is manifold:

- To understand primary education as a multifaceted phenomenon not captured by the one-dimensional outcome variables (such as literacy rate or enrolment).
- To identify and quantify these various dimensions of achievements and constraints in the functioning of the primary schools at the district level.
- To define and evaluate efficiency of primary schools incorporating the social aspect of primary education at the district level.
- To relate these district level parametres to the efficiency indicators.
- In short, we have tried to understand the functioning of the primary schools within a comprehensive framework.

In this chapter we use three types of methodologies. First, we use simple proportion technique to derive the school level indicators of various aspects (resource constraints, impact of government policy etc.). Next, we use the mathematical programming technique of Data Envelopment Approach (DEA) to estimate efficiency at the school levels. Lastly, we used various regression techniques (White's regression, Tobit and Jacknife regression) to relate the school level parametres to their performance as captured by the efficiency scores.

However, the concept of economic efficiency cannot be totally neglected. Though economic efficiency has both a technical and cost component, we have to disregard the cost (or allocative component) due to the lack of reliable price data on various educational inputs. In the education sector, we have to deal with a multi-input; multi-output decision making units which attempt to maximize their outputs for given inputs and technology. This is output-oriented approach. Here, we measure decision-making unit's technical efficiency, that is, how well a decision-making unit's converts its inputs to outputs, based on its available technology. For measuring technical efficiency we use Data Envelopment Analysis (DEA) in which only factors under a decision-making unit's control are included as inputs in computing efficiency scores.

In this exercise, we use non-parametric DEA to estimate efficiency. Data Envelopment Analysis is a generalization of the non-parametric technique developed by the same Farrell (1957) to measure efficiency. Charnes, Cooper and Rhodes (1978, 1979, 1981) generalized the DEA framework to a multiple-output-multiple-input framework using the mathematical programming approach which is referred to as the Charnes, Cooper and Rhodes (CCR) model. The essential idea of the CCR model is to minimize the weighted input output ratio subject to certain restrictions on the production technology. These are *constant returns to scale, strong disposability* and *convexity*. Convexity and returns to scale are obvious. Disposability generally refers "to the ability to stockpile or dispose of unwanted commodities" (Färe *et al.,* 1994). With some algebraic manipulation this boils down to:

$$\max_{E_f \lambda} E_f$$

$$\text{subject to: } y_f \leq Y\lambda,$$
$$X\lambda \leq E_f x_f,$$
$$\lambda \geq 0$$

The matrices X and Y are assumed to satisfy Karlin conditions that require strictly positive row and column sums. In the DEA, we judge the performance of a firm on the basis of its ability to increase output given the restrictions placed by the best-practised firms. From this point of view, E_f denotes the Debreu-Farrell output efficiency measure.

The imposition of constraint on the intensity vector λ guarantees that Ei lies between zero and one. The above problem assumes Constant Returns to Scale (CRS).

Zonal Classification

India is a large country with wide variations in the socio-economic culture across its length and breadth. It is well known that education and its determinants are shaped by the socio-political culture of the respective communities. A casual look at our country will reveal various differences among the Northern and Southern, Western and Eastern parts of the country. The North-East with its largely tribal population has some unique features of its own. We wish to capture the effects through zonal dummies.

In order to facilitate our analysis, we have segregated the districts into five zones: Northern districts, North-Eastern districts, Eastern districts, Western districts, Southern districts respectively. This zone-wise district segregation is incorporated into five state zones respectively. We describe the Zonal classifications of the state in the following table (Table 5.1). Here, we consider only eighteen major State, and UTs. Again seven North-eastern States considered as North-east State as a whole. We compare and contrast the zone-wise indicators in the following sections.

Table 5.1: Zonal classification of the States/UTs

Zone	*Name of the States/UTs*
Northern	DL, HR, HP, J&K, PNB & CN, RJ, UP & UK
North-Eastern	ACP, MZR, MGL, NGL, MN, TR, SK
Eastern	AS, WB, OR, BR & JH
Western	MP & CG, GR, MHR
Southern	KN, KRL, AP, TN

Note: CN: Chandigarh, DL: Delhi, HR: Haryana, HP: Himachal Pradesh, J&K: Jammu & Kashmir, PNB: Punjab, RJ: Rajasthan, UP: Uttar Pradesh, UK: Uttarakhand, ACP: Arunachal Pradesh, MZR: Mizoram, MGL: Meghalaya, NGL: Nagaland, MN: Manipur, TR: Tripura, SK: Sikkim, AS: Assam, WB: West Bengal, OR: Orissa, JH: Jharkhand, BR: Bihar, CG: Chhattisgarh, MP: Madhya Pradesh, GR: Gujarat, MHR: Maharashtra, KN: Karnataka, KRL: Kerala, AP: Andhra Pradesh, and TN: Tamil Nadu.

Aspects of Resource Constraint in Education

If we pay attention to the scenario of primary education in India there are many ills plaguing educational scenario in India at primary level.

The DISE data gives various district-specific key indicators (pupil-teacher ratio), student-classroom ratio, GER (Gross Enrolment Ratio), NER (Net Enrolment Ratio), school with common toilet, school with girl's toilet, proportion of female teachers, per cent distribution of schools having no *'pucca'* building, drop-out rate, retention rate etc. for good quality primary education.

Following this spirit, we have visualized education as a multi-dimensional entity. It is possible to identify four basic aspects of any educational institution:

- Deprivation aspects (dearth in some basic provision),
- Social aspects (indicators of social equity),
- Policy aspects (micro impact of government policies), and
- Farrell's non-parametric efficiency scores.

In our analysis we have considered mainly indicators that are quantifiable in a definite form (such as proportion of schools without building, proportion schools having no '*pucca*' building etc.). Based on some of these factors we can identify the degree of deprivation that a school faces. Specifically, we note the factors as follows: per cent of Schools without building, per cent distribution of Schools having no '*pucca*' building, per cent distribution of Schools without classrooms, per cent of single teacher schools, per cent of Schools having no Drinking Water Facility, per cent of Schools having no Common Toilet, and per cent of Schools without Blackboard. These are the Deprivation aspect. First we compare across different basic provision. This is shown in Table5.2.

Deprivation Aspects

Table 5.2: Zonal Differentiation in the Value of Basic Resource

Zone districts	*Proportion of School without building*	*Proportion of School having no 'pucca' building*	*Proportion of distribution of School without classrooms*	*Proportion of single teacher schools*	*Proportion of School having no Drinking Water Facility*	*Proportion of School having no Common Toilet*	*Proportion of School without Blackboard*
Northern District (N = 187)	0.05 (0.07)	0.11 (0.15)	0.66 (0.20)	0.15 (0.16)	0.14 (0.15)	0.26 (0.25)	0.08 (0.10)
North-Eastern District (N = 55)	0.10 (0.15)	0.75 (0.21)	0.69 (0.16)	0.26 (0.26)	0.32 (0.23)	0.58 (0.33)	0.19 (0.21)
Eastern District (N = 132)	0.11 (0.15)	0.44 (0.22)	0.47 (0.18)	0.17 (0.13)	0.20 (0.14)	0.67 (0.25)	0.12 (0.16)
Western District (N = 127)	0.12 (0.15)	0.21 (0.19)	0.56 (0.18)	0.20 (0.14)	0.16 (0.13)	0.57 (0.24)	0.11 (0.14)
Southern District (N = 103)	0.04 (0.08)	0.15 (0.14)	0.67 (0.22)	0.10 (0.10)	0.16 (0.11)	0.29 (0.21)	0.11 (0.10)

Note: Figures in parentheses represent standard deviation and N-Number of districts.

From Table 5.2, we find a clear zonal differentiation in the value of basic resource. It is seen from Table 5.2 that proportion of without building is highest in Western district (0.12) and lowest in Southern districts (0.04). In adequacy of '*pucca*' building is highest in North-eastern districts (more than 75%) and lowest in Northern districts (11%). Maximum number of 'Without classroom schools' is present in Southern districts (67%) and lowest in Eastern districts (47%). Maximum number of Single teacher schools' is present in North-eastern districts (26%) and lowest in Southern districts (10%). Drinking water facility is worst in North-eastern districts (32%) and Northern districts acquired comparatively better position (i.e. 14%). In case of common toilet facility, maximum number of schools in Eastern districts (i.e. 67%) are suffering in this ill. And 19 per cent schools in North-easterrn districts have no blackboard. In other words, this indicates that inadequacy in infrastructure network is the most serious bottleneck of our educational system. Hence, their efficiency is seriously constrained by the availability of adequate support system.

Intra-State Disparity

Now, we have an attempt to analyze inter-district variation of various basic resources. However, the results are given in Table 5.3. Here, we use co-efficient of variation (C.V.) to compare the variability of the various poverty indicators through the inter-district variation for different states.

Thus, we see that there is a cleavage between the incidence of basic resources and the spread of inter-district variation. Consider Andhra Pradesh. It has a very low mean 'without building' of about .01, but the inter-district variation is very high (479.58). Consider now Orissa. Its mean of 'no *pucca* building' is 0.61, but the co-efficient of inter-district variation is only 14.30. In case of Maharashtra, co-efficient of inter-district variation is 163.42 its mean is 0.11. This means in Orissa, all the districts are equally 'poor' in terms of building inadequacy, but in Maharashtra there is wide variation. For example, in 'Aurangabad' this proportion is as high as 0.15 while it is zero in 'Gadchiroli' and 'Mumbai suburban'. It is this wide variation that is reflected in the C.V.

In case of mean of without classroom 'Assam' has highest C.V. (32.57) and Delhi scored lowest C.V. (3.61). Even in Kerala, where mean of 'single teacher schools' is very low, the C.V. is 250.37. Himachal Pradesh is a better state with mean of 0.13 and C.V. of 23.10. In Orissa, mean of 'inadequacy of drinking water facility' is 0.15 but the C.V. is low (36.52). In Rajasthan, mean of 'inadequacy of blackboard' is 0.09, but

Table 5.3: Intra-state variations of various resources

States		Proportion of Schools without Building	Proportion of Schools having no Pucca Building	Proportion of Schools without Classrooms	Proportion of Single Teacher Schools	Proportion of Schools having no Drinking Water Facility	Proportion of Schools having no Common Toilet	Proportion of Schools Without Black-board
Jammu &	Mean	0.08	0.39	0.59	0.10	0.41	0.77	0.07
Kashmir	CV	79.02	59.11	13.84	51.32	56.85	23.63	65.92
Himachal	Mean	0.01	0.29	0.69	0.13	0.10	0.57	0.07
Pradesh	CV	102.21	52.55	7.71	23.10	87.82	33.40	97.07
Punjab	Mean	0.06	0.06	0.72	0.20	0.08	0.17	0.10
	CV	139.37	91.87	12.24	45.40	75.02	50.13	100.22
Haryana	Mean	0.04	0.06	0.68	0.21	0.11	0.23	0.04
	CV	110.02	108.95	10.47	62.10	70.11	58.98	91.74
Delhi	Mean	0.01	0.01	0.77	0.05	0.05	0.26	0.02
	CV	100.45	72.58	3.61	64.18	73.27	16.68	98.51
Rajasthan	Mean	0.11	0.16	0.68	0.27	0.22	0.31	0.09
	CV	105.91	101.67	27.48	83.73	69.14	65.58	155.76
Uttar	Mean	0.03	0.08	0.72	0.12	0.12	0.18	0.09
Pradesh and Uttarakhand	CV	185.80	96.89	9.52	125.60	94.21	107.53	103.07
North-east	Mean	0.10	0.75	0.69	0.26	0.32	0.58	0.19
	CV	146.10	28.07	23.68	99.74	70.76	56.67	106.11
Assam	Mean	0.03	0.51	0.37	0.23	0.29	0.71	0.04
	CV	191.40	36.71	32.57	43.18	64.21	29.24	127.73
West Bengal	Mean	0.01	0.41	0.64	0.06	0.20	0.34	0.03
	CV	84.20	51.25	9.60	105.91	63.06	53.76	154.18
Jharkhand	Mean	0.22	0.37	0.43	0.20	0.21	0.79	0.22
and Bihar	CV	78.76	53.76	31.81	81.53	63.61	15.06	89.45
Orissa	Mean	0.06	0.61	0.62	0.16	0.15	0.74	0.07
	CV	66.23	14.30	9.91	43.00	36.52	19.51	86.68
Chhattisgarh	Mean	0.19	0.28	0.52	0.29	0.12	0.71	0.11
and MP	CV	92.70	64.89	28.10	46.37	47.56	23.91	129.96
Gujarat	Mean	0.13	0.18	0.65	0.11	0.21	0.43	0.07
	CV	93.84	74.32	14.76	60.32	63.38	39.82	65.48
Maharashtra	Mean	0.02	0.11	0.63	0.15	0.21	0.49	0.15
	CV	124.61	163.42	27.39	72.51	82.67	40.36	116.02
Andhra	Mean	0.01	0.08	0.64	0.11	0.19	0.40	0.12
Pradesh	CV	479.58	86.07	16.66	58.15	57.73	41.74	112.51
Karnataka	Mean	0.11	0.11	0.62	0.17	0.21	0.39	0.12
	CV	102.09	102.51	18.78	47.55	49.67	53.41	86.64
Kerala	Mean	0.02	0.18	0.82	0.07	0.09	0.18	0.11
	CV	88.04	70.55	12.23	250.37	64.38	101.77	72.66
Tamil Nadu	Mean	0.01	0.27	0.83	0.06	0.15	0.21	0.12
	CV	102.06	68.07	6.01	07.32	64.38	70.40	57.41

Source: Authors' calculation from DISE.

the C.V. is 155.76. In all there are states where most of the districts are 'poor'. However, in our 'advanced states' there are pockets of extreme 'poverty' in educational infrastructure. So, the bleak picture of our primary education system becomes very clear by these results.

Social Indicators

There are two sides of social aspects of education-backward group and gender. Under 'backward' group we include the 'SC' and 'ST' representation while 'gender' indicates the male-female divide in representation. Under social indicators we include, proportion Distribution of SC Teachers to Total Teachers, proportion of ST Teachers to Total Teachers, proportion SC Enrolment, proportion ST Enrolment at Primary level, proportion of girl's enrolment to proportion of boy's enrolment, proportion of trained Female Teachers to proportion of trained male teachers, proportion of 'SC' and 'ST' teachers. We compute mean and standard deviation of these factors zone-wise for the year 2005-06. This is shown in the following table.

Table 5.4: Mean of social indicators

Zone Districts	*'SC' enrl/ Tot enrl*	*'ST' enrl/ Tot enrl*	*Girl enrl/ Boys enrl*	*Trained fml tcr/Trained male tcr*	*Proportion of SC and ST teacher to total teachers*
Northern Districts (N = 187)	0.39 (0.20)	0.12 (0.33)	1.36 (0.79)	0.84 (1.07)	0.22 (0.15)
North-Eastern Districts (N = 55)	0.05 (0.07)	0.98 (0.81)	1.54 (1.25)	0.57 (0.57)	1.03 (0.79)
Eastern Districts (N = 132)	0.14 (0.06)	0.15 (0.18)	0.94 (0.12)	0.41 (0.24)	0.29 (0.16)
Western Districts (N = 124)	0.16 (0.05)	0.21 (0.18)	1.61 (1.62)	0.59 (0.91)	0.36 (0.15)
Southern Districts (N = 91)	0.19 (0.08)	0.08 (0.10)	4.96 (11.07)	2.15 (2.63)	0.26 (0.11)

Note: Figures in parentheses represent standard deviation and N-Number of districts, Enrl: Eenrolment, and tcr: Teacher.

From Table 5.4, we find a clear zonal dichotomy in the changes of social equity. Proportion of 'SC' enrolment is highest in Northern districts and lowest in North-eastern districts. Proportion of 'ST' enrolment is highest in North-eastern districts and lowest in Southern districts. Girls' enrolment is highest in Southern districts with respect to boys' enrolment and lowest in Eastern districts. Trained female teacher is highest in Southern districts with respect to trained male teachers and lowest in Eastern districts. Proportion of 'SC' and 'ST' teacher is highest in North-eastern district and lowest in Northern districts.

Intra-state Disparity

Now, we have an attempt to analyze inter-district variation of various social indicators. However, the results are given in Table 5.5. Here, we use co-efficient of variation (C.V.) to compare the variability of the various social indicators through the inter-district variation for different states.

From Table 5.5, it is clear that the picture is some what mixed. Consider Jammu & Kashmir. It has a very low mean "SC' enrolment' of about .25, but the inter-district variation is very high (189.90). In case of Haryana C.V. is very low (18.87). Consider now Uttar Pradesh (including Uttarakhand). Its mean of "ST' enrolment' is 0.10, but the co-efficient of inter-district variation is only 250.54. In case of Orissa, co-efficient of inter-district variation is 56.90 its mean is 0.16. In case of mean of 'girls' enrolment' Andhra Pradesh has highest C.V. (270.14) and West Bengal scored lowest C.V. (3.65). Even in Rajasthan, where mean of "trained female teacher with respect to trained male teacher" is low, the C.V. is 195.89. In Himachal Pradesh, C.V. is 35.46. In Jammu & Kashmir, mean of "proportion of 'SC' and 'ST' teacher with respect to total teacher" is 0.28, but the C.V. is (123.18). In Haryana, C.V. is 19.49. Thus, as before not only are there backward states in social representation even advanced states have pockets of gross under representation.

Policy Indicators

In our analysis, Government policy include proportion of schools that received school development grant, proportion of student getting free textbook, proportion of girls receiving free textbook to proportion of boys receiving free textbook, proportion of student getting free stationary. We compute mean and standard deviation of these policies zone-wise for the year 2005-06. This is shown in table 5.6.

Table 5.5: Intra-state variations of various social indicators

States		*'SC' enrolment/ Total enrolment*	*'ST' enrolment/ Total enrolment*	*Girl enrolment/ Boys enrolment*	*Trained female teacher/ Trained male teacher*	*Proportion of 'SC' and 'ST' teacher to total teachers*
Jammu & Kashmir	Mean	0.25	0.69	1.40	0.57	0.28
	CV	189.90	120.63	31.75	58.48	123.18
Himachal Pradesh	Mean	0.35	0.16	1.07	0.79	0.34
	CV	24.41	172.68	6.90	35.46	82.35
Punjab	Mean	0.67	0.01	0.97	1.76	0.24
	CV	20.88	94.02	10.02	42.21	29.79
Haryana	Mean	0.37	0.03	1.33	1.36	0.14
	CV	18.87	193.06	24.05	62.98	19.49
Delhi	Mean	0.35	0.00	0.92	0.95	0.14
	CV	42.63	153.66	28.88	78.84	27.46
Rajasthan	Mean	0.41	0.09	1.19	1.11	0.23
	CV	50.24	159.03	36.76	195.89	48.26
Uttar Pradesh and Uttarakhand	Mean	0.36	0.10	1.60	0.47	0.22
	CV	30.88	250.54	66.79	44.20	43.19
North-east	Mean	0.05	0.98	1.54	0.57	1.03
	CV	145.76	82.75	81.14	100.47	77.59
Assam	Mean	0.06	0.23	1.03	0.54	0.29
	CV	46.74	100.20	13.40	44.90	72.21
West Bengal	Mean	0.20	0.06	0.99	0.38	0.26
	CV	34.92	99.89	3.65	76.91	30.20
Jharkhand and Bihar	Mean	0.14	0.14	0.86	0.34	0.28
	CV	33.55	143.79	12.47	46.51	66.08
Orissa	Mean	0.16	0.16	1.00	0.50	0.32
	CV	22.53	56.90	5.67	54.03	33.29
Chhattisgarh and MP	Mean	0.16	0.26	1.15	0.32	0.42
	CV	32.89	68.16	16.84	38.91	32.90
Gujarat	Mean	0.13	0.23	1.36	1.05	0.36
	CV	33.51	98.18	45.08	147.71	55.19
Maharashtra	Mean	0.16	0.12	2.62	0.76	0.27
	CV	36.86	102.04	105.88	129.09	36.19
Andhra Pradesh	Mean	0.19	0.12	7.07	0.77	0.32
	CV	25.37	71.81	270.14	107.00	29.48
Karnataka	Mean	0.18	0.07	1.71	1.59	0.25
	CV	22.49	95.77	59.16	94.01	24.28
Kerala	Mean	0.12	0.15	2.33	2.55	0.21
	CV	83.89	117.63	53.80	78.21	38.30
Tamil Nadu	Mean	0.22	0.04	7.78	3.69	0.29
	CV	44.76	114.81	119.71	103.15	27.25

Source: Authors' calculation from DISE.

Table 5.6: Mean of policy indicators

Zone Districts	*Proportion of schools received school development grant*	*Proportion of student getting free textbook*	*Proportion of student getting free stationary*
Northern Districts (N = 187)	0.76 (0.26)	0.71 (0.23)	0.11 (0.21)
North-Eastern Districts (N = 55)	0.72 (0.57)	0.44 (0.35)	0.06 (0.19)
Eastern Districts (N = 132)	0.63 (0.36)	.0.69 (0.29)	0.01 (0.03)
Western Districts (N = 124)	0.81 (0.26)	0.80 (0.22)	0.06 (0.09)
Southern Districts (N = 91)	1.09 (0.73)	0.80 (0.26)	0.31 (0.39)

Note: Figures in parentheses represent standard deviation; and N-Number of districts.

From Table 5.6, it is clear that impact of Government policies is asymmetry as expected. Southern districts have received maximum amount of development grant with respect to other zone districts where as Eastern districts are getting looser than other districts. Western and Southern districts are getting maximum amount of free textbook compare to other zone districts. North-eastern districts are comparatively looser. Student of Southern districts are getting maximum amount of free stationary items. Eastern districts are deprived.

Intra-state Disparity

Now, we have an attempt to analyze inter-district variation of various policy indicators. However, the results are given in Table 5.7. Here, we use co-efficient of variation (C.V.) to compare the variability of the various policy aspects through the inter-district variation for different states.

Here, various policy indicators is again asymmetry as expected. First we consider Orissa. It has a very low mean 'receiving development grant' of about .19, but the inter-district variation is very high (191.54). In case of Himachal Pradesh C.V. is very low (1.59). Consider now North-eastern districts. Its mean of 'receiving free textbook' is 0.45, but the co-efficient of inter-district variation is only 78.32. In case of Assam, co-efficient of inter-district variation is 6.30 its mean is 0.93. Now, we consider mean of 'receiving free stationary'. Here, North-eastern districts have high C.V. (i.e. 300.38). Its mean value is only 0.06. But the picture is opposite in Delhi. Here C.V. is 23.22. Its mean is 0.46.

Table 5.7: Intra-state variations of various policy indicators

States		*Proportion of school received school development grant*	*Proportion of student getting free textbook*	*Proportion of student getting free stationary*
Jammu & Kashmir	Mean	0.56	0.77	0.01
	CV	32.19	22.64	77.00
Himachal Pradesh	Mean	0.98	0.84	0.57
	CV	1.59	14.45	40.47
Punjab	Mean	0.86	0.70	0.01
	CV	23.43	27.46	167.46
Haryana	Mean	0.92	0.84	0.15
	CV	7.44	12.50	148.12
Delhi	Mean	0.97	0.75	0.46
	CV	2.18	22.21	23.22
Rajasthan	Mean	0.75	0.81	0.13
	CV	27.15	19.86	134.15
Uttar Pradesh and Uttarakhand	Mean	0.81	0.72	0.04
	CV	17.50	18.53	344.37
North-East	Mean	0.72	0.45	0.06
	CV	79.68	78.32	300.38
Assam	Mean	0.79	0.93	0.01
	CV	20.38	6.30	244.96
West Bengal	Mean	0.89	0.94	0.02
	CV	12.11	17.65	177.13
Jharkhand and Bihar	Mean	0.76	0.48	0.02
	CV	24.22	32.80	189.90
Orissa	Mean	0.19	0.91	0.02
	CV	191.54	8.66	142.13
Chhattisgarh and MP	Mean	0.73	0.86	0.04
	CV	19.72	18.81	105.91
Gujarat	Mean	0.88	0.89	0.04
	CV	10.96	14.43	59.00
Maharashtra	Mean	0.99	0.71	0.13
	CV	29.51	22.02	112.57
Andhra Pradesh	Mean	0.91	0.88	0.09
	CV	11.93	16.66	130.71
Karnataka	Mean	0.83	0.91	0.86
	CV	16.01	14.12	33.38
Kerala	Mean	1.95	0.61	0.10
	CV	70.49	23.02	225.20
Tamil Nadu	Mean	1.30	0.89	0.13
	CV	34.02	13.74	59.49

Source: Authors' calculation from DISE.

In case of policy indicators, the variability is considerably lower then that under other parametres of deprivation. This is expected. Since, this is a conscious decision. Yet, the range of variability is not satisfactory.

DEA Efficiency Scores

We also present the DEA technical efficiency scores. Efficiency indicators mainly point out to the performance of teaching institutions while DEA scores measure the degree of utilization of the available resources. Here, we have attempted to restrict the total number of input and output variables in the analysis to ensure some degree of discretionary power remained. The model hence involved only four inputs—

(i) proportion of schools having drinking water facility in school;
(ii) proportion of schools having girl's toilet in school;
(iii) classroom-student ratio;
(iv) teacher-pupil ratio; and
(v) one output-gross enrolment ratio.

It may be argued that net enrolment ratio is more appropriate. However, the relevant data is not forthcoming for all the districts. The specification of output is a challenging task. Schooling of children is a factor determined by demand side as well as supply side variables. There are many situations where children have access to schooling and homogeneous supply side factors. In spite of that we come across many children remain out of school. Children's participation in schools is the outcome of household's decision-making process in the absence of any compulsory education law of the state. So, we have decided to include Gross enrolment ratio as our output variable.

Now, we present DEA efficiency scores in Table 5.8.

Table 5.8: Mean of DEA Efficiency scores

Zone Districts	*DEA Technical Efficiency indicators*
Northern Districts (N = 187)	0.63 (0.17)
North-Eastern Districts (N = 55)	0.60 (0.22)
Eastern Districts (N = 132)	0.67 (0.17)
Western Districts (N = 124)	0.72 (0.18)
Southern Districts (N = 91)	0.53 (0.16)

Note: Figures in parentheses represent standard deviation.

From this table, we see that for all the years, technical efficiency is much higher in Western districts than rest of the zone districts. In case of Southern districts, technical efficiency is lowest. But in case of North-eastern and Eastern districts, technical efficiency has middling in position. This discrepancy may be a reflection of the fact that these zones are seriously constrained by the dearth of resources. However, whatever resources are available has been efficiently utilized.

Table 5.9: Intra-state variations of DEA efficiency scores

States		*DEA efficiency scores*
Jammu & Kashmir	Mean	0.61
	CV	32.54
Himachal Pradesh	Mean	0.44
	CV	20.08
Punjab	Mean	0.43
	CV	26.75
Haryana	Mean	0.63
	CV	19.40
Delhi	Mean	0.81
	CV	21.38
Rajasthan	Mean	0.63
	CV	18.46
Uttar Pradesh and Uttarakhand	Mean	0.68
	CV	21.62
North-East	Mean	0.60
	CV	36.07
Assam	Mean	0.67
	CV	33.85
West Bengal	Mean	0.64
	CV	17.56
Jharkhand and Bihar	Mean	0.76
	CV	19.98
Orissa	Mean	0.61
	CV	11.70
Chhattisgarh and MP	Mean	0.74
	CV	28.94
Gujarat	Mean	0.67
	CV	15.86
Maharashtra	Mean	0.72
	CV	18.66
Andhra Pradesh	Mean	0.56
	CV	19.03
Karnataka	Mean	0.60
	CV	31.02
Kerala	Mean	0.45
	CV	40.83
Tamil Nadu	Mean	0.51
	CV	23.64

Source: Authors' calculation from DISE.

Intra-State Disparity

Now, we have an attempt to analyze inter-district variation of DEA efficiency scores. However, the results are given in Table 5.9. Here, we use co-efficient of variation (C.V.) to compare the variability of the various policy aspects through the inter-district variation for different states.

From Table 5.9, we see that the asymmetry of input and output is reflected in efficiency. First we consider Kerala. It has a very low mean (0.45), but the inter-district variation is very high (40.83). North-eastern districts are in second position. Its C.V. is 36.07. In case of Orissa, mean is 0.51 and its co-efficient of inter-district variation is only 11.70.

Determinants of Efficiency

Having traced down the various indicators associated with the primary education system, it is now necessary to link them up. For this we argue that our ultimate aim is to explain the incidence of efficiency (DEA scores). For this we link up all the other factors with this factor through regression analysis. However, a standard problem of such estimation lies in the fact that efficiency indicators are truncated variables (lying between zero and one). As such Ordinary Least Squares (OLS) might not be very suitable for this purpose (Maddala, 1983). It would be better to consider certain other forms of truncated estimation procedure. However, we have considered three types of estimation. The first is OLS with White's correction [OLS (HETCOV)]. Next we considered the Jackknife re-sampling technique that tests the sensitivity of the OLS parametres. Finally, we measured a Tobit regression. All these regression results are shown in Table 5.10.

In our regression equation we have considered several factors that may influence the efficiency of the educational institutions. Out of fit as shown by the various alternative models is very good. Out of the eleven variables considered by us, six are significant. All of them have the expected sign. For example, the provisional parametres (such as the proportion of schools without building and proportion of single teacher schools) are significantly and negatively correlated with the DEA efficiency score. The policy related parametre (proportion of schools received school development grant) is positively associated with DEA scores. However, two other variables (such as proportion of schools having common Toilet and proportion of schools without blackboard) are not significantly related though they are negatively correlated. Interestingly,

Table 5.10: Determinants of DEA efficiency scores

Dependent variable: DEA Technical efficiency			
Variables	*OLS (HETCOV) N = 589*	*Jackknife N = 589*	*Tobit N = 589*
Proportion of School without building	−12.890 (−1.997)**	−13.243 (−1.986)**	−12.670 (−1.9078)Δ
Proportion of single teacher schools	−0.41671 (−4.961)*	−0.41915 (−7.630)*	−0.43170 (−7.3422)*
Proportion of School having Common Toilet	−2.5744 (−0.6175)	−3.2512 (−0.3948)	−1.7443 (−0.26280)
School without Blackboard	−0.0105 (−0.4783)	−0.0117 (−0.3151)	−0.0027 (−0.0788)
Trained female teacher/Trained male teacher	0.3596 (4.944)*	0.34241 (5.449)*	0.35470 (5.1485)*
Proportion of schools received school development grant	0.0611 (1.918)Δ	0.0559 (1.773)Δ	0.0659 (1.8695)Δ
Northern District Dummy	1.2531 (0.2613)	1.1937 (0.2142)	1.7981 (0.30102)
North-Eastern District Dummy	−9.7304 (−3.510)*	−9.9571 (−2.393)*	−8.6844 (−2.0821)*
Eastern District Dummy	−2.1911 (−1.125)*	−2.3198 (−0.7422)	−1.0367 (−0.3422)
Western District Dummy	−0.0130 (−1.484)	−0.0142 (−0.9352)	−0.0133 (−0.9375)
Constant	46.773 (6.762)*	47.878 (5.709)*	46.429 (5.4138)*
Log-likelihood	−1144.83	−1144.83	−1114.71

Notes: Figures in parentheses represent asymptotic *t* ratio.
* indicates level of significance at 1 per cent.
** indicates level of significance at 5 per cent.
Δ indicates level of significance at 10 per cent.

the proportion of trained female to male teacher is positively related with the school performance as indexed by DEA efficiency. This seems to support the view that induction of more female teacher is likely to boost the educational standard. Among the dummy, North-eastern dummy is significant though with a negative relation.

Conclusion

Our analysis of the primary education system in rural India reveals certain disturbing features. First, the system is seriously jolted by the lack of adequate resources that are necessary to boost up a decent standard. There appear wide zonal discrepancies in this regard. Second, discrepancies with regard to social and policy factors are more or less uniformly distributed. However, resource use efficiency (as measured by DEA) indicates wide inter-zonal differences. Basic resources infringes upon efficiency in a negative way sufficiently. Social resources are significantly related to efficiency improvement. Among the districts, Northern districts show the best picture. Policy factors have any significant effect on the level of efficiency. In all, the picture is alarming and requires immediate policy action.

REFERENCES

Charnes, A., W.W. Cooper, A.Y. Lewin and L.M. Seiford, (1995), *"Data Envelopment Analysis: Theory, Methodology and Applications"*, Kluwer.

"Elementary Education in India, Progress towards UEE", *DISE 2005-06: Flash statistics (District level):* National University of Educational Planning and Administration, New Delhi.

Gujarati, Damodar N., *Basic Econometrics*, Third Edition, McGraw-Hill, Inc.

Hanushek, Eric A., (1995), "Interpreting recent research on schooling in developing countries". *The World Bank Research Observer,* Vol. 12, No. 2, pp. 227-246.

Kumar, Niraj, (2005), "Primary Education in India Initiatives and Prospects", *Kurukshetra,* Vol. 53, No. 9, pp. 9-14.

Mehta, Arun C. (April 2007), *"Student Flow at Primary Level an Analysis Based on DISE Data"*. National University of Educational Planning and Administration, New Delhi.

Maddala, G.S., (1983), *Limited Dependent and Qualitative Variables in Econometrics*, Cambridge University Press, New York.

NIEPA and Government of India, (2005), Elementary Education in India: Where Do We Stand, *Analytical Report* 2004, New Delhi.

Rao, D.S. Prasad, Battese George E., Coelli, Tim, Kluwer, (1998), "*An Introduction to Efficiency and Productivity Analysis*", pp. 133-160. Academic Publishers, London.

Ramachandran, Vimala, (2004), "Backward and Forward Linkages that Strengthen Primary Education", *Kurukshetra,* Vol. 52, No.11, pp. 17-21.

Swaminathan, Madhura and Vikas Rawal, "Primary Education for All". *India Development Report 1999-2000*. Oxford University Press.

Sen, A., (2006), *"Identity and Violence: The Illusion of Destiny"*, Penguin Books, New Delhi.

Sengupta, Atanu, Madhumita Sengupta, (2004), "Economics of learning: A village level study based on Midnapore (West) district, West Bengal". Paper has been presented at National Seminar in Vidyasagar University, West Bengal, March 30-31, 2004.

Sengupta, A. and N.P. Pal, (2009), "Poverty and Efficiency in the Primary Education System of India: An analysis is based on DISE Data", *Journal of Educational Planning and Administration*, Vol. XXIII, No. 1, pp. 33-47.

Sengupta, A. and N.P. Pal, (2010), "Primary education in India: Delivery and outcome—A district level analysis based on DISE Data", *Journal of Educational Planning and Administration*, Vol. 24, No. 1, pp. 5-21, January.

APPENDIX

List of Districts of India

Northern Region

State: Jammu & Kashmir
Districts of Jammu & Kashmir

Kupwara, Baramula, Srinagar, Badgam, Pulwama, Anantnag, Kargil, Doda, Udhampur, Punchh, Rajauri, Jammu, Kathua, Leh (Ladakh).

State: Himachal Pradesh
Districts of Himachal Pradesh

Chamba, Kangra, Lahul and Spiti, Kullu, Hamirpur, Una, Bilaspur, Solan, Sirmaur, Shimla, Kinnaur, Mandi.

State: Punjab
Districts of Punjab

Gurdaspur, Amritsar, Kapurthala, Jalandhar, Nawanshahr, Ropar, Fatehgarh Sahib, Ludhiana, Moga, Ferozepur, Muktsar, Faridkot, Bathinda, Mansa, Patiala, Hoshiarpur, Sangrur, Chandigarh (U.T.).

State: Uttarakhand
Districts of Uttarakhand

Uttarkashi, Chamoli, Rudraprayag, Tehri Garhwal, Dehradun, Garhwal, Pithoragarh, Bageshwar, Almora, Champawat, Udham Singh Nagar, Haridwar, Nainital.

State: Haryana
Districts of Haryana

Panchkula, Ambala, Yamunanagar, Kaithal, Karnal, Panipat, Sonipat, Jind, Fatehabad, Sirsa, Hisar, Bhiwani, Rohtak, Jhajjar, Mahendragarh, Rewari, Gurgaon, Faridabad, Kurukshetra.

State: Delhi
Districts of Delhi

North, West Delhi, North Delhi, North-East Delhi, East Delhi,

New Delhi, Central Delhi, West Delhi, South Delhi, South-West Delhi.

State: Rajasthan

Districts of Rajasthan

Ganganagar, Hanumangarh, Bikaner, Churu, Jhunjhunun Alwar, Bharatpur, Dhaulpur, Karauli, Sawai Madhopur, Sikar, Nagaur, Jodhpur, Jaisalmer, Barmer, Jalor, Sirohi, Pali, Ajmer, Tonk, Rajsamand, Udaipur, Dungarpur, Banswara, Chittaurgarh, Kota, Jaipur, Bundi, Baran, Dausa, Bhilwara, Jhalawar.

State: Uttar Pradesh

Districts of Uttar Pradesh

Saharanpur, Muzaffarnagar, Bijnor, Moradabad, Rampur, Jyotiba Phule Nagar, Meerut, Baghpat, Ghaziabad, Gautam Buddha Nagar, Bulandshahr, Aligarh, Agra, Firozabad, Etah, Mainpuri, Budaun, Bareilly, Pilibhit, Shahjahanpur, Kheri, Sitapur, Hardoi, Unnao, Lucknow, Rae Bareli, Farrukhabad, Kannauj, Etawah, Kanpur Dehat, Kanpur Nagar, Jalaun, Jhansi, Hamirpur, Mahoba, Banda, Chitrakoot, Fatehpur, Pratapgarh, Kaushambi, Barabanki, Faizabad, Sultanpur, Bahraich, Shrawasti, Balrampur, Gonda, Basti, Sant Kabir Nagar, Maharajganj, Gorakhpur, Deoria, Mau, Ballia, Jaunpur, Ghazipur, Chandauli, Varanasi, Sonbhadra, Bhadohi, Mathura, Auraiya, Allahabad, Siddharthnagar, Mirzapur, Lalitpur, Kushinagar, Hathras, Ambedkar Nagar.

North-Eastern Region

State: Sikkim

Districts of Sikkim

North Sikkim, West Sikkim, South Sikkim, East Sikkim.

State: Arunachal Pradesh

District of Arunachal Pradesh

Tawang, West Kameng, East Kameng, Papum Pare, Lower Subansiri, Upper Subansiri, West Siang, East Siang, Upper Siang, Dibang Valley, Lohit, Changlang, Tirap, Kurung Kumey, Lower Dibang Valley.

State: Nagaland
Districts of Nagaland

Mon, Tuensang, Mokokchung, Zunheboto, Wokha, Dimapur, Kohima, Phek.

State: Manipur
Districts of Manipur

Senapati, Tamenglong, Churachandpur, Bishnupur, Thoubal, Imphal West, Imphal East, Ukhrul, Chandel.

State: Mizoram
Districts of Mizoram

Mamit, Kolasib, Aizawl, Champhai, Serchhip, Lunglei, Lawngtlai, Saiha.

State: Tripura
Districts of Tripura

West, South, Dhalai, North.

State: Meghalaya
Districts of Meghalaya

East Garo Hills, South Garo Hills, West Khasi Hills, Ri Bhoi, East Khasi Hills, Jaintia Hills, West Garo Hills.

Eastern Region

State: Assam
Districts of Assam

Kokrajhar, Goalpara, Bongaigaon, Barpeta, Kamrup, Nalbari, Darrang, Marigaon, Nagaon, Sonitpur, Lakhimpur, Tinsukia, Dibrugarh, Sibsagar, Jorhat, Golaghat, Karbi Anglong, North Cachar Hills, Cachar, Karimganj, Hailakandi, Dhubri, Dhemaji.

State: West Bengal
Districts of West Bengal

Darjiling, Jalpaiguri, Koch Bihar, Uttar Dinajpur, Dakshin Dinajpur, Maldah, Murshidabad, Birbhum, Bardhaman, Nadia, North Twenty Four Parganas, Hugli, Bankura, Puruliya, Haora, Kolkata, South Twenty Four Parganas, Purba Medinipur, Paschim Medinipur, Siliguri.

State: Jharkhand
Districts of Jharkhand

Garhwa, Palamu, Chatra, Hazaribag, Kodarma, Giridih, Deoghar, Sahibganj, Pakaur, Dumka, Dhanbad, Bokaro, Ranchi, Lohardaga, Gumla, Pashchimi Singhbhum, Jamtara, Saraikela-Kharsawan, Simdega, Latehar, Godda, Purbi Singhbhum.

State: Bihar
Districts of Bihar

Pashchim Champaran, Purba Champaran, Sheohar, Sitamarhi, Madhubani, Supaul, Araria, Katihar, Kishanganj, Madhepura, Saharsa, Darbhanga, Muzaffarpur, Gopalganj, Siwan, Saran, Samastipur, Jhanja, Khagaria, Bhagalpur, Banka, Munger, Lakhisarai, Sheikhpura, Nalanda, Patna, Bhojpur, Buxar, Kaimur (Bhabua), Rohtas, Aurangabad (Bihar), Gaya, Nawada, Jamui, Jehanabad, Purnia, Vaishali.

State: Orissa
Districts of Orissa

Bargarh, Jharsuguda, Sambalpur, Deogarh, Sundargarh, Mayurbhanj, Balasore, Bhadrak, Kendrapara, Jagatsinghpur, Cuttack, Jajpur, Dhenkanal, Nayagarh, Khordha, Puri, Ganjam, Gajapati, Kandhamal, Boudh, Sonepur, Bolangir, Nuapada, Kalahandi, Nawarangapur, Koraput, Malkangiri, Keonjhar, Angul, Rayagada.

Western Region

State: Chhattisgarh
Districts of Chhattisgarh

Koriya, Surguja, Jashpur, Raigarh, Korba, Janjgir-Champa, Bilaspur, Kawardha, Rajnandgaon, Durg, Mahasamund, Dhamtari, Kanker, Baster, Dantewada, Raipur.

State: Madhya Pradesh
Districts of Madhya Pradesh

Sheopur, Morena, Bhind, Gwalior, Datia, Shivpuri, Guna, Tikamgarh, Chhattarpur, Panna, Damoh, Satna, Rewa, Umaria, Shahdol, Sidhi, Neemuch, Mandsaur, Ratlam, Ujjain, Shajapur, Dewas, Jhabua, Dhar, Indore, Khargone, Barwani, Khandwa,

Rajgarh, Vidisha, Bhopal, Sehore, Harda, Hoshangabad, Katni, Jabalpur, Narsinghpur, Dindori, Mandla, Chhindwara, Seoni, Balaghat, Ashok Nagar, Anup Pur, Burhanpur, Betul, Sagar, Raisen.

State: Gujarat
Districts of Gujarat

Kachchh, Banas Kantha, Patan, Mehsana, Sabarkantha, Gandhinagar, Ahmedabad, Surendranagar, Rajkot, Jamnagar, Junagadh, Amreli, Bhavnagar, Anand, Kheda, Panch Mahals, Dohad, Vadodara, Narmada, Bharuch, Surat, Navsari, Valsad, Porbandar, The Dangs.

State: Maharashtra
Districts of Maharashtra

Nandurbar, Jalgaon, Buldana, Akola, Washim, Amravati, Wardha, Nagpur, Bhandara, Gondiya, Gadchiroli, Chandrapur, Nanded, Parbhani, Jalna, Aurangabad, Nashik, Thane, Mumbai (Suburban), Mumbai, Raigarh, Pune, Ahmadnagar, Bid, Solapur, Satara, Ratnagiri, Sindhudurg, Kolhapur, Sangli, Hingoli, Latur, Dhule, Osmanabad, Yavatmal.

Southern Region

State: Andhra Pradesh
Districts of Andhra Pradesh

Adilabad, Nizamabad, Karimnagar, Medak, Hyderabad, Rangareddi, Mahbubnagar, Nalgonda, Warangal, Srikakulam, Vizianagaram, Visakhapatnam, East Godavari, West Godavari, Krishna, Guntur, Prakasam, Nellore, Cuddapah, Anantapur, Chittoor, Khammam, Kurnool.

State: Karnataka
Districts of Karnataka

Belgaum, Bagalkot, Bijapur, Gulbarga, Bidar, Raichur, Koppal, Gadag, Dharwad, Uttara Kannada, Haveri, Bellary, Davangere, Shimoga, Udupi, Chikmagalur, Tumkur, Kolar, Bangalore, Bangalore Rural, Mandya, Hassan, Kodagu, Mysore, Chamrajnagar, Chitradurga, Dakshina Kannada.

State: Kerala

Districts of Kerala

Kasaragod, Kannur, Kozhikode, Malappuram, Palakkad, Ernakulam, Idukki, Kottayam, Alappuzha, Pathanamthitta, Kollam, Thiruvananthapuram, Thrissur, Wayanad.

State: Tamil Nadu

Districts of Tamil Nadu

Chennai, Kancheepuram, Vellore, Dharmapuri, Tiruvannamalai, Viluppuram, Salem, Namakkal, Erode, The Nilgiris, Coimbatore, Dindigul, Karur, Perambalur, Cuddalore, Nagapattinam, Thiruvarur, Thanjavur, Pudukkottai, Madurai, Theni, Virudhunagar, Ramanathapuram, Thoothukkudi, Tirunelveli, Kanniyakumari, Krishanagiri, Thiruvallur, Tiruchirappalli, Sivaganga.

6

The Interstate Variation of Technical Efficiency of Indian Pharmaceutical Industry

Stochastic Frontier Production Function Approach

Chandrima Chakraborty and *Arpita Ghose*

Introduction

Indian pharmaceutical industry (IPI) has been growing at record levels in recent years but still has unprecedented opportunities to expand.

The Government started to encourage the growth of drug manufacturing by Indian companies in the early 1960s, and with the Patent Act in 1970. With the change in the patent law from product to process patent in 1972 which were shortened to a period of five to seven years, large scale production of bulk drugs was started by the indigenous sector in 1980s. However, economic liberalization in 1990s enabled the industry to become what it is today. In 1990s significant changes occurred in this sector like (a) signing of TRIPS agreement; (b) ammendment of FERA and MRTP Acts; and (c) de-licensing of the drugs in two stages reserved for production by the public sector. As a result uneven growth had taken place in this industry.

Since, 2005, full-fledged product patent regime in pharmaceuticals started in India and so can develop new drugs themselves or can collaborate for the new drugs developed by the MNCs as manufacturing or marketing partners (Chaudhuri, 2005). The January draft publication of the Government's National Pharmaceuticals Policy for 2006, aimed at boosting the domestic industry's global competitiveness as well as improving the population's access to medicines.

Given the changed scenario of IPI after 1994, the estimation of efficiency is essential as since 1991 Government adopted the economic reform policies which became less friendly to the less efficient industries. Also the study of the interstate variation of efficiency of IPI will be interesting. Side-by-side the choice of the suitable functional form of production and identification of major determinants of technical efficiency of each of the 17 major selected states of India as well as All India are needed.

There are only few studies in the literature regarding estimation of TE of IPI. In this connection mention should be made of the following names:

Majumder (1994), Majumdar and Rajeev (2009) and Majumdar, Rajeev and Ray (2009), Pannu, Kumar and Farooquie (2010) had examined TE using firm level data and employing DEA approach whereas Chaudhuri and Das (2006) used the SFPF approach to measure the output efficiency.

Majumder (1994) found that the private firms are more efficient than the public sector firms while studying the capabilities and resource utilization on nine large firms using the data from 1987 to 1990. Majumdar and Rajeev (2009) found that vertically integrated firms exhibit higher efficiency while examining TE of Indian Pharmaceutical firms for the years 1991-2005. According to Majumdar, Rajeev and Ray (2009) there is a negative trend for the output efficiency levels of firms, but there is evidence of efficient use of labour and raw-material and they also inferred that research and development (R&D), export expenditure and imported technology played a negative role in improving the Technical Efficiency of Indian Pharmaceutical firms for the period 1991 to 2005. Pannu, Kumar and Farooquie (2010) found a positive impact of R&D investment and patents on productivity (sales), market share, exports and ability to attract contract manufacturing among Indian pharmaceutical companies during the period 1998 and 2007 in Indian Pharmaceutical Industry (IPI). According to Chaudhuri and Das (2006) the mean efficiency scores of the firms in the industry which are large in size and exporting more of their product in the international market had improved over the sub-period 1999 to 2001 against the sub-period 1990-1998.

The literature review, therefore, reveals that most of the above studies had done their analysis using the CMIE data. Also there is dearth in the study regarding the exploration of the linkages between some of the important industry characteristic variables like composition of the workforce among others on technical efficiency and also in the study relating to the estimation of Technical efficiency score of IPI for different states of India.

The present chapter adds the literature in this direction by

- Measuring TE of IPI for All India level as well as for different states of India, using it's state level data of 17 selected major states and considering each state as a producing unit, for the period 1983-84 to 2007-08;
- Measuring interstate variation of TE by calculating mean TE values for all the different states for the sample period considered;
- Selecting the suitable functional form of production, which can act as a better representative of the production frontier; and
- Identifying the major determinants of TE of each of the 17 selected major states of India as well as All India, in terms of its industrial characteristics.

The chapter unfolds as follows: Section 2 describes the econometric methodology and data sources. The results of estimation are presented in Section 3. Section 4 concludes.

Methodology and Data Sources

Methodology

Measurement of Efficiency Score

Farrell (1957) started the effective measurement of TE and distinguished between Technical Efficiency (TE) and Allocative Efficiency (AE). TE can be 'output-oriented' or 'input-oriented'. The present chapter uses the idea of TE and output oriented measure in particular. The stochastic frontier production function (SFPF) approach is used.

Generalized Likelihood Ratio (LR) Test is conducted to test whether Cobb-Douglas (CD) production function or translog production function is a proper representation of production frontier for IPI.

The stochastic frontier production function (SFPF) is represented by equation (1) denoting the maximum producible output for the ith producing unit under the time index t given the non-negative input vector X_i, and the technology parametre vector B.

$$Yi = f(X_i, t; \beta) \exp(v_i) \qquad \ldots(1)$$

Y_i denotes the actual output of the ith producing unit.

v_i is the error term of the model and is independently and identically distributed normal variable with zero mean and uniform variance.

The difference between the frontier output $f(X_i, t; \beta)$ and the observed output (Y_i) of the *i*th producing unit is taken as the measure of TE.

As the actual output is less than or equal to the frontier output, equation (1) can be written as

$$Yi = f(X_i, t; \beta) \exp(v_i) \exp(-u_i) \quad \ldots(2)$$

with $u_i \geq 0$ implying that $\exp(-u_i) \leq 1$

u_i is the Index of Technical inefficiency of the *i*th producing unit and is distributed independently and normally with mean = μ_i and variance = σ^2_u, truncated at zero, i.e. $u_i \sim idN^+ (\mu_i, \sigma^2_u)$.

The correlation between the error term and the inefficiency term is assumed to be zero.

The time-varying output-oriented TE measure of Farrell of the *i*th producing unit is as follows:

$$TE_i = \frac{Y_i}{f(X_i, t; \beta)\exp(v_i)} = \exp(-u_i) \quad \ldots(3)$$

with $\exp(-u_i) \cong 1 - u_i$, the measure of TE ranges between 0 and 1 and varies inversely with u_i.

In the present chapter the methodology of Battese and Coelli (1993) and Lundvall and Battese (2000) is applied for estimating the time-varying Technical inefficiency across different states taking each selected major states of India as a producing unit in IPI.

For identification of the determinants of TE, a two-stage procedure was suggested by some empirical studies. In the first stage, firm-specific TE scores are estimated applying SFPF and in the second stage, the estimated TE scores are regressed on a number of explanatory variables. But the problem is that in many cases, this two-stage procedure although gave satisfactory results but suffers from an inconsistency problem due to the assumption of constant exp (u_i) in the first stage, which may contradict the assumption in the second stage that the predicted efficiencies vary with the firm-specific explanatory variables [Coelli *et al.* (1998, pp. 207-209); Kumbhakar and Lovell (2000, pp. 262-264)].

An alternative approach was put forward by Battese and Coelli (1993) which is a single stage procedure and is followed in this chapter. In this procedure the estimation of TE scores and the reason behind the variation of TE are done simultaneously.

Hence, Single-stage Maximum Likelihood Estimation (MLE) method is adopted.

Equation (4) represents the mean Technical Inefficiency which is as follows:

$$\mu_i = \delta' Z_i \qquad \ldots(4)$$

μ_i = mean before truncation for u_i.

Equation (4) along with equation (2) represents the model for the present chapter.

Z_i = represents the vector of exogenous and endogenous variables in explaining the inefficiency effect of the *i*th producing unit.

δ = parametres of Z_i to be estimated and δ' is the transpose of δ.

The above assumption is consistent with the assumption that u_i is a non-negative truncation of $N(\delta' Z_i, \sigma_u^2)$. The specification of u_i is considered in such a way that the density function of u_i can be easily obtained conditional on $\varepsilon_i = v_i - u_i$ as well as the expected value of TE_i, given ε_i.[1]

Equation (4) along with equation (2) also gives the TE values for all the 17 different states for the sample period considered and the mean TE values are calculated for each of the selected states and hence interstate variation of TE is done.

Determinants of Technical Efficiency

The variables considered in this present study as the major determinants of TE are as under:

Output per factory (*Y/F*): One of the major reasons for the variation of TE of the firms may be the difference in their relative size. There is debate in the literature regarding the relationship between firm size and efficiency of the firm. There is a variation both with respect to the measure of firm size as well as its conclusions. In this connection mention may be made of studies, linking TE and firm size, like Bhandari and Roy (2010), Baduneko (2010), Yasar and Paul (2009), Truett and Truett (2009), Tran, Graften and Kompas (2008), Bhandari and Maity (2006), Berghall (2006), Cheng and Lo (2004), Mengistae (1998), Ramaswamy (1994), etc. Few studies found a positive relation between firm size and efficiency and others postulated a negative relation. Also different measures of firm size are available like number of workers [Mukherjee (1963)], log value of sales [Majumder, S.K. (1997)], asset of firms [Urata and Kawai (2002), Biesebroeck (2005), Palangkaraya, Stierwald and Yong (2005)], amount of intermediate inputs [Lundvall and Battese (2000)], capital stock per factory [Ahluwalia (1991)].

Output per factory (Y/F) is used to measure firm-size in the present chapter and is concerned with testing whether firm-size hinders efficiency in IPI or not.

Capital-labour ratio (*K/L*): To understand the relative degree of mechanization of IPI the variable K/L is used. By incorporating advanced and sophisticated technology into the production process higher degree of mechanization can help to enhance TE. But poor management of more capitalistic and sophisticated technology can hinder TE score (Jeanneney and Hua, 2003). As a result, a rise in K/L can imply decline in TE score over the years.

Employees per production worker (*E/L*): To capture the composition of work-force this variable is used. A negative relation between E/L and TE signifies a higher degree of bureaucratic control within the firm resulting inefficiency in the production unit. On the other hand, a positive relation can be obtained between E/L and TE if the combination of work-force is just right to operate the production process efficiently.

Data Sources

The chapter uses the data on gross value added (Y), number of workers (L), fixed capital (K), fuel consumption (Fu), material consumption (M), number of factories (F) and number of employees (E) for the 17 selected major states of India for the period 1983-84 to 2007-08 obtained from various issues of "Annual Survey of Industries, Summary Results for the Factory Sector" published by Central Statistical Organization, Government of India.

The 17 selected major states considered in the present chapter are as follows—

Andhra Pradesh (AP), Assam (AS), Bihar (BI), Gujarat (GU), Haryana (HA), Himachal Pradesh (HP), Jammu & Kashmir (JK), Karnataka (KA), Kerala (KE), Mahasashtra (MA), Madhya Pradesh (MP), Orissa (OR), Punjab (PU), Rajasthan (RA), Tamil Nadu (TN), Uttar Pradesh (UP) and West Bengal (WB).

The Perpetual Inventory Accumulation Method is used to obtain data on capital stock which is as follows:

The real fixed investment series is $I_t = \left(\frac{B_t - B_{t-1} + D_t}{P_t}\right)$

where

B_t is the book value of fixed assets at the end of year t,
D_t is the depreciation allowances made in that year, and
P_t is the capital goods price index, i.e. machinery and equipment index for that year.

Hence, the capital stock series (K_t) can be derived by using the following relationship:

$$K_t = K_{t-1} + I_t \quad \ldots(a)$$

or

$$K_t = K_0 + \Sigma I_t \quad \ldots(b)$$

where K_0 is an estimate of real capital stock for a benchmark year.

This chapter had used expression (b) to generate the capital stock series.

Data on gross value added is deflated by the price index of the Pharmaceutical industry output whereas material consumption and fuel consumption are deflated by the price indices of industrial raw material and fuel, power and lubricants respectively.

One problem is that there is multicollinearity among the explanatory variables and it is observed that all the explanatory variables are correlated with the other. So, while running MLE, various regressions are tried out taking into account different combinations of explanatory variables and the results with the best fit is reported.

The translog form of the SFPF used to explain technical inefficiency in terms of the firm specific variables is written as follows:

$$\ln Y_i = \left[\beta_0 + \sum_{j=1}^{4} \beta_j x_{ji} + \sum_{j \le k=1}^{4} \sum^{4} \beta_{jk} x_{ji} x_{ki}\right] + (v_i - u_i) \ldots(5)$$

Here, the subscript i refers to the ith firm, $i = 1, 2, 3\ldots n$, where n is the number of firms in the industry.

X_{ji} = the amount of jth input used by the ith firm, and
x_{ji} = the natural logarithm of X_{ji}, $j = 1, 2, 3, 4$

The inefficiency sub-model in which μ_i, the mean of u_i, is postulated to be determined is as follows:

$$\mu_i = \left[\delta_0 + \sum_{m=1}^{r} \delta_j z_{mi} + \sum_{m \le p=1}^{r} \sum^{r} \delta_{mp} z_{mi} z_{pi} \right] \quad \ldots(6)$$

Here also 'i' refers to the ith firm ranging from 1 to n where n is *the* total number of firms in the industry.

Z_{mi} = the firm-specific variable considered to explain the variations in TE scores, and
z_{mi} = the natural logarithm of Z_{mi}, the subscript m refers to the number of firm-specific factors included in the Z_i vector and $m = 1, 2, 3\ldots r$.

Results of Analysis

Results of Estimation of Efficiency Score

If one consider Pharmaceutical industry of different states of India as a whole, it can be presumed that such products are of similar type and share same frontier operating under similar kind of technology. The frontier is generated in the present chapter for IPI using the state level data considering each state as a producing unit and a measure of TE is obtained for all the 17 states considered as well as for aggregate Pharmaceutical industry at all India level.

Generalized Likelihood Ratio (LR) Test is conducted to test whether Cobb-Douglas (CD) production function is a proper representation of production frontier for IPI over translog form. Results of such tests are presented in Table 6.1.

The estimated value of the test statistic presented in Table 6.1 suggests that the hypothesis that Cobb-Douglas fit is better approximation over translog specification is rejected at 1 per cent level. Hence, translog specification is used.

Table 6.1: Generalized Likelihood Ratio Tests in the Estimated Stochastic Frontier [To test whether the estimated Translog or the Cobb-Douglas (CD) specification is better approximation]

Null Hypothesis	*Industry*	*Estimated Generalized Likelihood Ratio Statistics*
$\beta_{jk} = 0$ for $j, k = 1, 2, 3, 4$ (Cobb-Douglas Function)	IPI	36.77
Critical Values 1%		23.209

By employing the computer programme Frontier (Version 4.1) developed by Tim Coelli (1994) the mean value of the TE score of IPI and also the maximum-likelihood estimates of the parametres of the SFPF along with inefficiency sub-model defined by equations (5) and (6) are obtained. The estimated results of TE of 17 major selected states as well as AI are presented in Table 6.2.

The estimated values of TE score of IPI for the different states of India along with the rank of each state with respect to the TE score is presented in Table 6.2. The mean TE turned out to be 0.124 for IPI and only 1 per cent of the variation in industry output can be explained by the variation in technical inefficiency which can be said from the value of $\gamma = \sigma_u^2 / \sigma^2$.

The result of estimation supports the existence of high interstate variation of TE of IPI. For the 17 sample states mean TE ranges from 0.0118 to 0.2501. The value is maximum for MA and minimum for BI. For the states like HP, KA, GU and MP the TE scores differed by 1 per cent. The TE score of PU and AS are almost same. Again AP, WB, TN and UP differed by 1 per cent. For RA and KE the TE score is 7 per cent. Hence, it can be said that MA is the most technically efficient state and BI is the least among the sample states considered. Comparing the performance of 17 different states individually with All India as a whole, All India occupies 9th position.

Determinants of TE

The result of the analysis of the determinants of TE can be seen from Table 6.2 which suggests the following:

The relation between Y/F and TE is found to be positive and statistically significant for all the states as well as for All India except

Table 6.2: Estimated results of TE and its major determinants

Place	*TE*	*Constant*	*Y/F*	*K/L*	*E/L*	*Adj. R^2*	*D.W.*	*Rank of States*
AP	0.137	0.053	0.189	–0.254	0.033	0.963	1.464	8
		(4.19)***	(16.77)***	(–1.67)	(2.55)**			
AS	0.163	0.186	0.859	–2.261	0.211	0.545	1.600	7
		(1.87)*	(2.93)***	(–2.37)**	(1.11)			
BI	0.011	–0.005	0.347	0.854	0.005	0.982	1.798	18
		(–3.26)***	(31.82)***	(7.63)***	(1.62)			
GU	0.201	0.120	0.081	–0.352	0.133	0.421	1.318	4
		(1.43)	(1.28)	(–1.27)	(2.17)**			
HA	0.089	0.012	0.247	0.257	0.018	0.911	1.799	13
		(0.94)	(11.42)***	(1.44)	(1.73)*			
HP	0.223	0.022	0.169	–1.668	0.126	0.980	2.344	2
		(1.45)	(32.05)***	(–1.67)	(3.24)***			
JK	0.066	–0.018	0.154	0.0241	0.075	0.912	1.236	16
		(–1.48)	(15.38)***	(0.32)	(3.73)***			
KA	0.213	0.035	0.190	0.388	0.024	0.988	1.441	3
		(2.23)**	(44.87)***	(3.55)***	(1.34)			
KE	0.075	–0.013	0.235	0.295	0.068	0.988	1.657	15
		(–2.31)**	(44.21)***	(5.55)***	(6.86)***			
MA	0.251	0.084	0.172	–0.017	0.041	0.972	1.573	1
		(6.80)***	(27.28)***	(–2.56)**	(4.06)***			
MP	0.196	0.029	0.159	–0.057	0.140	0.990	1.349	5
		(2.80)**	(33.94)***	(–5.35)***	(8.38)***			
OR	0.044	0.001	0.240	0.056	0.041	0.801	1.350	17
		(0.02)	(9.22)***	(1.75)*	(4.44)***			
PU	0.165	0.024	0.225	–0.215	0.038	0.971	1.784	6
		(1.87)*	(19.23)***	(–1.26)	(3.82)***			
RA	0.078	–0.016	0.251	0.206	0.056	0.987	1.775	14
		(–2.89)***	(38.12)***	(10.22)***	(5.55)***			
TN	0.112	–0.023	0.269	0.523	0.049	0.972	2.168	11
		(3.67)***	(22.30)***	(5.07)***	(4.47)***			
UP	0.105	0.059	0.044	–0.487	0.097	0.204	0.713	12
		(2.45)**	(2.59)**	(–2.071)*	(2.58)**			
WB	0.122	0.034	0.191	0.086	0.020	0.990	1.467	10
		(3.91)***	(39.74)***	(0.32)	(0.97)			
AI	**0.124**	**1.126**	**0.441**	**0.015**	**0.238**	$\gamma = \sigma_u^2 / \sigma^2$	**Log-Likelihood**	**9**
		(1.489)	**(2.31)****	**(0.17)***	**(1.16)**	**= 0.014**	**Value**	
						(.031)	**= 163.71**	

Note: Absolute *t* values are in parenthesis

***,**,* implies significant at 1 per cent, 5 per cent and 10 per cent respectively.

GU for which the coefficient is statistically insignificant. This implies that an increase in firm size measured by Y/F will improve TE for all the sample states excepting GU and also for All India perhaps due to easier access of quality inputs.

The variable K/L has positive relation with TE and statistically significant in case of states like BI, KA, KE, OR, RA, TN and at All India level. Hence, an increase in K/L induces TE for those states and at All India level and so more capitalistic and advanced sophisticated technology improves the efficiency level of the industry for these places. For the states like AS, MA, MP and UP the coefficient is statistically significant but negative. Hence, an increase in K/L hinders TE for those states. But the coefficients of K/L are statistically insignificant for the states like AP, GU, HP, PU, HA, J&K and WB.

The determinant E/L, i.e., the employees per production worker captures the composition of work-force. For the present sample in the chapter an increase in E/L may lead to right combination of workforce and hence will improve TE for all the states considered as the coefficient of E/L is positive and statistically significant excepting AS, BI, KA, WB and at All India level.

Conclusion

This study analyses TE of IPI, using the SFPF Model, employing its state level data of the 17 selected major states of India for the period 1983-84 to 2007-08 considering each selected state as a producing unit. The mean TE values are also calculated for each states as well as for All India level and major determinants of TE are identified for each of the cases.

The main results of the study could be summarized as follows:

- The level of TE in IPI is poor. The mean TE turned out to be 0.124 for IPI.
- The estimated value of TE score supports the existence of inter-state variation. For the 17 selected major states mean TE ranges from 0.0118 to 0.2501. The value is maximum for MA and minimum for BI.
- All the determinants of TE considered in this chapter are statistically significant for the states KE, OR, RA, TN, MA, MP and UP. For KE, OR, RA and TA all of them have a positive influence on TE whereas for MA, MP and UP the determinants Y/F and E/L have a positive influence but K/L have a negative influence on TE. But all the determinants considered in the chapter are not together significant for all the states. For example in case of AP, HA, HP, J&K and PU excepting K/L all other determinants are positive and statistically significant whereas

for the states BI, KA and for All India level, all the other determinants are positive and statistically significant excepting E/L. Similar is the case for AS, i.e. E/L is insignificant, but the coefficient is positive for Y/F but negative for K/L. For GU only E/L is positive and statistically significant and for WB only the determinant Y/F is positive and statistically significant.

The present analysis thus supports the existence of inter-state variation of the extent of TE score as well as its determinants for IPI. It is worthwhile to mention that although the level of TE of IPI is low, only 1 per cent of the variation in industry output can be explained by the variation in technical inefficiency. Thus, the level of TE will not have too much impact on output level.

NOTE

1. According to Battese and Coelli (1988, 1993), the expected value of TEi, given ε_i is $E[\exp(-u_i) | \varepsilon_i$.

REFERENCES

Ahluwalia, I.J., (1991), *"Productivity Growth in Indian Manufacturing Industry"*, Oxford University Press.

Badunenko, O., (2010), "Downsizing in the German chemical manufacturing industry during the 1990s. Why is small beautiful?" *Small. Bus. Econ.* 34:413-431.

Battese, G.E. and T.J. Coelli, (1988), "Prediction of Firm-Level Technical Efficiencies with a Generalized Frontier Production Function and Panel Data", *Journal of Econometrics* 38(3), pp. 387-399.

Battese, G.E. and T.J. Coelli, (1993), "A Stochastic Frontier Production Function Incorporating a Model for Technical Inefficiency Effects", *Working Paper No. 69. Department of Econometrics,* University of New England, Australia.

Berghall, E., (2006), "Technical Change, Efficiency, Firm Size and Age in R&D Intensive Sector", Working paper no. 390, *Government Institute for Economic Research*, Helsinki, Finland.

Biesebroeck, J.V., (2005), "Firm Size Matters: Growth and Productivity Growth in African Manufacturing", *Economic Development and Cultural Change,* Vol. 53, No. 3, pp. 545-583.

Central Statistical Organization, Government of India, *Annual Survey of Industries, Summary Results for the Factory Sector*, various issues.

Chaudhuri, S., (2005), "*The WTO and India's Pharmaceutical Industry*", Oxford University Press.

Chaudhuri and Das, (2006), "WTO, the TRIPS and Indian Pharmaceutical Industry", *Journal of Quantitative Economics*, Vol. 4 (1), pp. 97-110.

Cheng, Yuk-Shing, Lo, Dic, (2004), "Firm Size, Technical Efficiency and Productivity Growth in Chemical Industry", *Working Paper.*

Coelli, T.J., (1994), A Guide to FRONTIER Version 4.1: A Computer Programme for Stochastic Frontier Production and Cost Function Estimation, *mimeo.*

Farrell, M.J., (1957), "The Measurement of Productive Efficiency", *Journal of the Royal Statistical Society*. Series A, General 120(3), 253-281.

Jeanneney, S.G. and P. Hua, (2003), "Real Exchange Rate and Productivity in China", Working Papers no. 200328, *CERD,* France, 37 pages.

Kodde, D.A. and F.C. Palm, (1986), "Wald Criteria for Jointly Testing Equality and Inequality Restrictions", *Econometrica* 54(5), 1243-1248.

Kumbhakar, S.C. and C.A.K. Lovell, (2000), "*Stochastic Frontier Analysis*", Cambridge, Cambridge University Press.

Lundvall, K. and G.E. Battese, (2000), "Firm Size, Age and Efficiency: Evidence from Kenyan Manufacturing Firms", *Journal of Development Studies,* 36(3), 146-163.

Majumdar, M. and M. Rajeev, (2009), "Comparing the Efficiency and Productivity of Indian Pharmaceutical Firms: A Malmquist-Meta-Frontier Approach", *International Journal of Business and Economics*, Vol. 8, No. 2, 159-181.

Majumdar, M., M. Rajeev and S.C. Ray, (2009), "Output and Input Efficiency of Manufacturing Firms in India: A Case of the Indian Pharmaceutical Sector", *Institute for Social and Economic Change*, Bangalore, *Working Paper*, 219.

Majumdar, (1994), "Assessing Firms Capabilities—Theory and Measurement —A Study of Indian Pharmaceutical—Industry", *Economic and Political Weekly*, Vol. 29(22), pp. M 83-M 89.

Majumder, S.K., (1997), "The Impact of Size and Age on Firm—Level Performance: Some Evidence from India", *Review of Industrial Organization*, Vol.12, pp. 231-241.

Mukherjee, G.P., (1963), "On Size-productivity Relationship in Indian Industries", *The Journal of Industrial Economics*, Vol. II, No. 2, pp. 141-159.

Mengistae, M., (1998), "Age-Size Effects in Firm Growth and Productive Efficiency: The Case of Manufacturing Establishments in Ethopia", *Working Paper*.

Palangkaraya, A., A. Stierwald and J. Yong, (2005), "Is Firm Productivity Releted to Firm Size and Age? The Case of Large Australian Firms", *The Melbourne Institute of Applied Economics and Social Research*, The University of Melbourne, Revised Version.

Pannu, H.S., U.D. Kumar and A. Farooquie Jamal, (2010), "Impact of Innovation on the Performance of Indian Pharmaceutical Industry using Data Envelopment Analysis", Indian Institute of Management, Bangalore *Working Paper* no. 2010-02-302.

Ramaswamy, V.K., (1994), "Technical Efficiency in Modern Small-scale Firms in Indian Industry: Applications of Stochastic Production Frontier", *Journal of Quantitative Economics*, 10(2), 309-324.

Tran, T.B., R.Q. Grafton and T. Kompas, (2008), "Firm Efficiency in a Transitional Economy: Evidence from Vietnam", *Asian Economic Journal,* 2008, Vol. 22, No. 1, 47-66.

Truett, D.B. and L.J. Truett, (2009), "Firm-Size and Efficiency in the South African Motor Vehicle Industry", *Australian Economic Papers*, 333- 341.

Urata, S. and H. Kawai, (2002), "Technological Progress by Small and Medium Enterprises in Japan", *Small Business Economics*, Vol. 18, pp. 53-67.

Yasar, M. and C.J.M. Paul, (2009), "Size and Foreign Ownership Effects on Productivity and Efficiency: An Analysis of Turkish Motor Vehicle and Parts Plants", *Review of Development Economics,* 13(4), 576-591.

7

Economic Growth and Growth of Employment in India

An Analysis

Pinaki Das

Introduction

An alternative and equally, if not more, meaningful way of looking at economic growth is to view it as function of employment and productivity. Aggregate growth of output in this approach is the outcome of increase in employment and that in productivity. It is derived either by employing more people, or improving output per worker or both. This linkage between employment and growth is often forgotten and the two are treated as independent of each other. Such an approach sends misleading signals to policy-makers who then treat growth as productive process and employment as a welfare measure (Papola, 2011).

In an economy like India with large surplus labour, importance of an employment oriented growth is obvious. 'Jobless' growth is not by for the most desirable form of growth. At the same time, an over-emphasis on employment generation without any regard to productivity and incomes of workers is also not desirable, particularly in an economy where productivity and income levels are generally low. Emphasis has to be on 'productive' and 'remunerative' employment: the new employment that is generated has to be at increasing levels of productivity in order that it does not assume poverty-perpetuating or poverty generating nature. In other words, economic growth should result from a suitable combination of employment growth and productivity growth. It implies that employment-oriented growth in a country like India would have, of necessity, to be at a high rate.

The high rate of growth during the last few years was accompanied by a number of important structural changes in the economy. *First*, to a large extent, the 'miracle' of India's economic growth performance has hinged on the tertiary sector. Since, the mid-1990s, the rate of growth of services GDP has been significantly higher than the rate of growth of overall GDP (Fig. 7.1). The share of the tertiary sector in the economy has gone up from 36 per cent in 1977-78 to 45 per cent in 1993-94 and to 57 per cent in 2009-10. In fact, well over 60 per cent of the incremental growth in GDP since mid-1990s is accounted for by the rate of growth of the services sector.

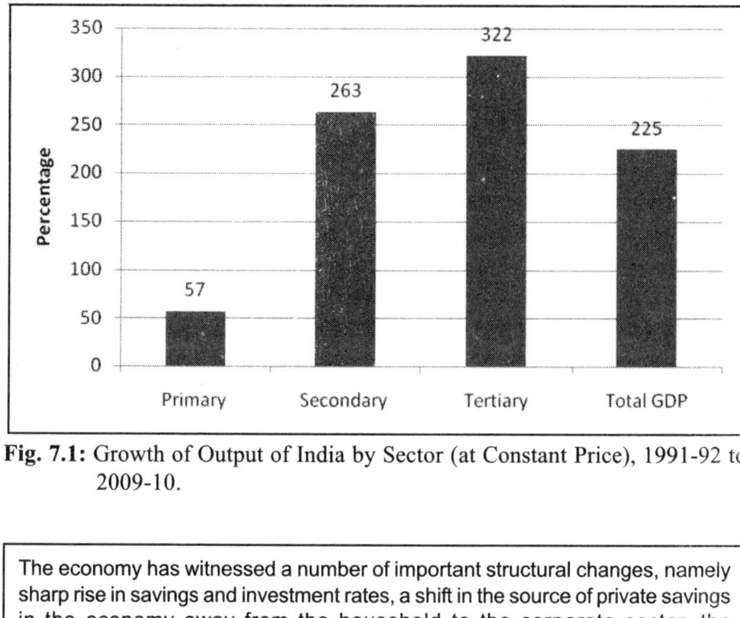

Fig. 7.1: Growth of Output of India by Sector (at Constant Price), 1991-92 to 2009-10.

> The economy has witnessed a number of important structural changes, namely sharp rise in savings and investment rates, a shift in the source of private savings in the economy away from the household to the corporate sector, the improvement of tax-to-GDP ratio and the dominance of services in growth.

Second, the performance of the commodity producing sectors has been relatively poor. While the share of primary sector has shown a drastic decline leaving from 40 per cent in 1977-78 to 30 per cent in 1993-94 and further to 15 per cent in 2009-10. The share of industrial sector remained almost stagnant up to 1999-2000; it has marginally increased to 28 per cent during in 2009-10 (Fig. 7.2).[1]

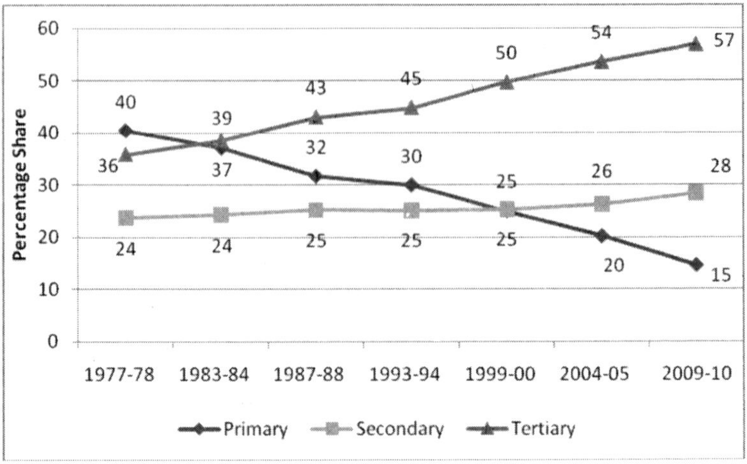

Fig. 7.2: Structural Change in India: Contribution of Different Sectors in GDP

Third, much of the spurt in the service sector is accounted for the impressive growth in information technology (IT), in particular the export of software and IT-enabled business services. The ratio of the IT sector output to the country's GDP increased from 0.38 per cent in 1991-92 to 4.5 per cent in 2004-05 and over the same period, IT services exports grew at a phenomenal 47.5 per cent per annum.

Along with the above structural changes there have been other phenomenal changes in Indian economy. The *first* of these was a sharp rise savings and investment rates. The gross savings rate rose from 32.2 per cent in 2004-05 to 36.4 per cent in 2007-08 and further to 38.2 per cent in 2009-10. The rise in the savings rate coincided with an increase in the rate of investment, which explains the higher rate of growth over the last few years, suggesting that the economy is transiting to a sustainable, higher growth trajectory, financed by domestic resources.

The *second* structural change was a shift in the source of private savings in the economy away from the household to the corporate sector. The share of the corporate sector in the gross domestic savings rose from 20.4 per cent in 2004-05 to 26 per cent in 2009-10, while that of household sector fell from 72.3 per cent to 60.0 per cent.

The *third* was a turnaround in the tax-to-GDP ratio. During the last decade (2001-10) the tax-to-GDP ratio at the Centre rose from 5.8 per cent to 9.5 per cent. The tax-to-GDP ratio of the Centre and States rose even more sharply from 13.8 per cent to 20.1 per cent. The improvement of tax-to-GDP ratio was not just the result of higher growth, but was due to the fact that high growth was accompanied by significantly increased inequalities (in the organized sector).

Against this brief backdrop the present chapter deals with the impact of growth trajectory with its implications for the volume, pattern and nature of employment in India.

In the present study, National Sample Survey (NSS) data are used for seven points of time—38th round (1983), 43rd round (1987-88), 50th round (1993-94), 55th round (1999-2000), 61st round (2004-05) and the latest being the 66th round survey conducted in 2009-10. All are the quinquennial round of National Sample Survey Organization (NSSO). Our analysis uses the usual status employment and unemployment data of NSSO. In the case of usually employed, the information was collected for both principal status (ps) and subsidiary status (ss) workers. It is to be mentioned here that in NSS 38th and 43rd rounds the industry classification followed (National Industrial Classification) NIC 1970 while NSS 50th round used NIC 1987. In the 55th and 61st round survey, the industry classification followed NIC 1998. In latest round, i.e. in 66th round it followed NIC 2004. The inter-rounds 38th to 66th data are comparable by making adjustment into eight industry division: (i) agriculture, (ii) mining and quarrying, (iii) manufacturing, (iv) electricity, gas and water, (v) construction, (vi) trade and commerce, (vii) transport, storage and communications and (viii) 'other services'. It is noted that the categories (ii) to (viii) are treated as non-farm sector and the corresponding employment are non-farm employment.[2] The labour force indicators derived from the different NSS employment and unemployment surveys are generally presented as ratios. Absolute number of workers was estimated by using Census segment-wise population (male, female, rural and urban) projections and NSS segment-wise workers population ratio. Accordingly, we computed afresh the absolute number of workers for 1983, 1987-88, 1993-94 and 1999-2000. In 66th round NSSO itself estimated the absolute number of workers for the year 2004-05 and 2009-10 by using the same methodology.[3] To see through pre- and post-reform contrasts in employment growth and structure, we use the NSS data for the years 1983, 1993-94, 2004-05 and 2009-10. The period 1983 to 1993-94 stand in pre-reform years while the period 1993-94 to 2004-05 captures the impact of economic reforms. The global slowdown 2008 has its adverse implications on the domestic economy especially on the employment sphere. Therefore, the period 2004-05 to 2009-10 is expected to captures the changes brought about by economic slowdown and treated as the period of economic slow-down. That is, the entire post-reform period is divided into two sub-periods, 1993-94 to 2004-05 for first and 2004-05 to 2009-10 for second.[4] The present study also used CSO data for GDP. Output data are clubbed into eight sectors (as specified above).

The rest of the chapter is divided into four sections. Section 2 analyses the trends of GDP, labour productivity and employment as well as the trends of their growths and employment elasticities of output in India. Section 3 discusses the phenomenal change in the labour market in India. The dynamics of growth of employment for male as well as female in rural *vis-à-vis* urban India across activities are dealt with in Section 4. Finally, section 5 gives some concluding observations.

Theoretical Relationship between Growth and Employment

Growth theory looks exclusively at a capitalist economy existing in splendid isolation and uses the assumption of perfect augmentability of all inputs other than one primary input which is normally taken to be labour.[5] Within the paradigm where everything other than labour is produced, the relationship between output and employment growth is fairly straightforward. If we assume fixed coefficients (FC) which change over time through technological progress, and no deficiency of aggregate demand (ND) (with capacity rather than labour availability being the constraining factor for output), then the rate of growth of employment is determined as the difference between the rate of growth of output (which depends upon the savings and capital-output ratios) and the rate of growth of labour productivity (which depends on the pace of technical progress) (Patnaik, 2011). Here, a rise in the rate of growth (G), unless accompanied by a still greater rise in the rate of growth of labour productivity (G_{lp}), will necessarily raise the rate of growth of employment (G_e). That is,

$$G_e = f(G - G_{lp}) f' > 0,$$

Here, $G = \dfrac{Y_t - Y_{t-1}}{Y_{t-1}} = S/C$, ($S$ = propensity to save and C = capital-output ratio)

G_{lp} = Growth of Labour Productivity = f_l (Technological progress), and $f_l' > 0$

$$G_e \geq 0, \qquad \text{if } G \geq G_{lp},$$

If we take the Kaldor-Verdoorn formulation (Kaldor, 1966) of the rate of growth of labour productivity being a function of the rate of growth of output, say

$$G_{lp} = a + bG$$

Then the rate of growth of employment Ge which simply equals $G\text{-}G_{lp}$, becomes an exclusive function of the rate of growth of output, i.e.,

$$G_e\,(= G - G_{lp}) = -\,a + (1 - b)\,G$$

And with $b < 1$, any rise in growth rate of output (G) raises the rate of growth of employment (G_e).

When this perception is put together with another, quite plausible, perception, namely that in a situation where the unemployment rate is very high [$(UR)_h$], real wages remain tied to a certain subsistence level [$(W/P)_S$], so that all gains in labour productivity (LP) accrue to the capitalists, the share of surplus in output (π/Y) rises, and with it the savings ratio (S/Y) in the economy. The rise in the savings ratio, since the capital-output ratio (C/Y) can be taken to be a constant, raises the growth rate (G = S/C). This, in turn, as we have just seen, raises the rate of growth of employment (G_e). If the rate of growth of the workforce is given, this must eventually lower the unemployment rate (UR). The typical relationship is depicted in Fig. 7.3.

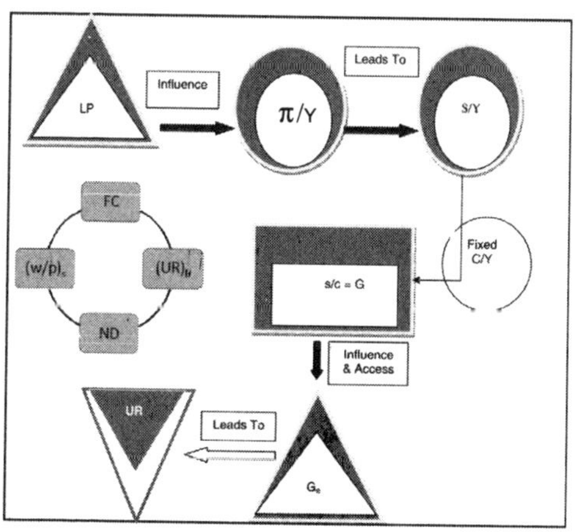

Fig. 7.3: A Typical Relation among Labour Productivity, Economic Growth and Growth of Employment

But this entire reasoning has been shown to be untenable in practice. In India, for example, despite high growth being maintained for years there is no sign of any tightness in the labour market. One obvious argument would be that even though the labour market has remained slack till now, further acceleration in the growth rate, which will necessarily ensue because of the rising share of surplus, will eventually make it tight. The theory outlined above in other words is right but its validation will be visible only after a lapse of time. But India's rapid growth rate has been going on for almost a decade now, and if it still has made no impact on the labour market then there is no reason to believe that it will do so in the years to come, or that it will do so by becoming even more rapid in the coming years. What we find in other words is a lack of conformity between the theory given above and the real-world Indian experience (Patnaik, 2011).

Growths of Output and Employment in India: Empirical Evidence

Trend of Per capita GDP, Labour Productivity and Employment Rate

The differences and changes in per capita GDP and employment can be investigated by distinguishing the level of per capita GDP in the following components:

$$GDP/P = GDP/E \times E/P$$

where, GDP/P = GDP/population = per capita GDP
GDP/E = GDP/Employment = labour productivity
E/P = employment/Population = employment rate

Per capita GDP of India was Rs. 10,458 in 1983-84 which became double in 2004-05 and triple in 2009-10. The raise of per capita income was considerably higher during 2004-05 to 2009-10 as compared with the previous periods. Labour productivity was also increased from Rs. 24,800 in 1983-84 to Rs. 52,168 in 2004-05 and further to Rs. 78,166 in 2009-10 (Table 7.1). Labour productivity has also similar trend as the trend witnessed for per capita GDP, both have upward trend (Fig. 7.3). But rate of employment, i.e., the ratio of employment to population, seemed to be constant during 1983-84 to 2004-05, but declined thereafter and for the whole period the trend is downward (Fig. 7.4). As population increased more or less a constant rate, the fall of employment ratio during 2004-05 and 2009-10 indicated an alarming situation in the employment sphere.

Table 7.1: GDP, Per Capita GDP, Labour Productivity and Employment Rate in India, 1983-84 to 2009-10

	1983-84	*1987-88*	*1993-94*	*1999-00*	*2004-05*	*2009-10*
GDP	752670	880267	1223817	1786527	2388768	3587806
GDP/P	10458	11127	13693	17802	21859	30500
GDP/E	24800	27093	32705	44899	52168	78166
E/P	0.42	0.41	0.42	0.40	0.42	0.39

Note: Output Value (in Rs. Crores) at Constant Price.

Source: 1. Central Statistical Organization, Government of India, www.mospi.nic.in.

2. *NSSO, Employment and Unemployment (Situation) in India; NSS* 38th Round (1983), *NSS* 43rd Round (1987-88), *NSS* 50th Round (1993-94), *NSS* 55th Round (1999-2000), *NSS* 61st Round (2004-05), *NSS* 66th Round (2009-10).

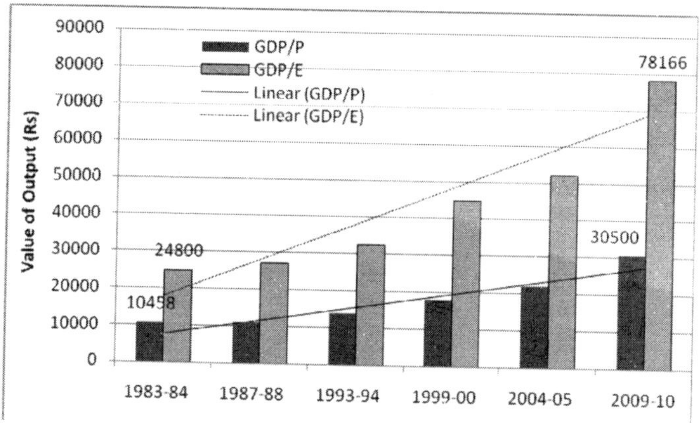

Fig. 7.4: Trends of Per Capita GDP and Labour Productivity

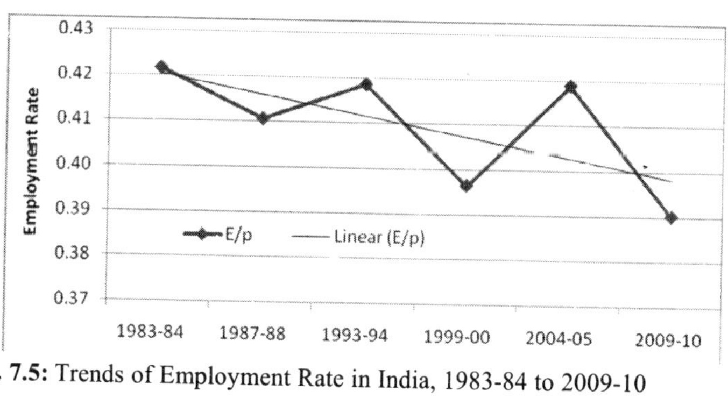

Fig. 7.5: Trends of Employment Rate in India, 1983-84 to 2009-10

Trend of Growths of Output, Labour Productivity and Employment

Output, Labour Productivity and Employment are related as follows:

$GDP = GDP/E \times E$

i.e., Output = Labour Productivity×Employment

In terms of growth the relationship becomes

Growth of Output = Growth of Labour Productivity + Growth of Employment

The relationship is quite same as it is explained in section 2. Average annual growth rate of output, productivity and employment in India are shown in Table 7.2 at five years interval spreading from 1983-84 to 2009-10. The growth rate of GDP rose from 3.39 per cent per annum during 1983-84 and 1987-88 to double digits figure 10.04 per cent during 2004-05 and 2009-10. The corresponding growth of labour productivity also rose from as low as 1.79 per cent to 10.01 per cent. But the trend of growth of employment was misleading. The period 1999-2000 to 2004-05 was distinct because the growths of both output and productivity were relatively low and consequently high growth of employment. After that the growth of labour productivity increased significantly and thus high growth of output. As a result Indian economy has experienced a very low growth of employment (0.03% per annum) during 2004-05 to 2009-10. For the entire period the trends of growth of GDP and growth of labour productivity seemed to be upward which was in contrast with the downward trend of growth of employment (Fig. 7.5).

Table 7.2: Average Annual Growth Rate of Output, Productivity and Employment in India, 1983-84 to 2009-10

	1983-84 to 1987-88	*1987-88 to 1993-94*	*1993-94 to 1999-2000*	*1999-2000 to 2004-05*	*2004-05 to 2009-10*
Output (GDP)	3.39	7.81	9.20	6.74	10.04
Labour Productivity	1.79	4.95	7.89	3.68	10.01
Employment	1.60	2.86	1.31	3.06	0.03

Note: Point to point simple growth rate has been calculated.
Source: Author's Calculation based on Table 7.1.

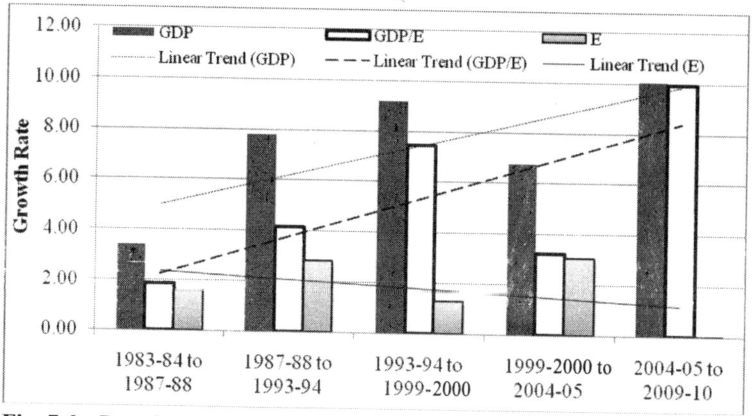

Fig. 7.6: Growth Rate of Output, Productivity and Employment and their Trend in India, 1983-84 to 2009-10.

Phenomenal Change in the Labour Market in India

It is to be expected that a growth trajectory with these features would have adversely impacted the labour market, influencing the volume, pattern and nature of employment. The period between 2004-05 and 2009-10 was the period when India moved to the much higher growth rate, most of the sectors except agriculture and electricity-gas-water supply have witnessed double digits growth rate (Table 7.3). A slower rate of employment expansion during this period points to a significant fall in the elasticity of employment with respect to output. Almost jobless growth seems to be prominent features of India's recent economic performance. The sector like agriculture and manufacturing has experienced the job-loss growth where the employment elasticity during 2004-05 to 2009-10 was –1.0 and –0.1 respectively. Other sectors have also experienced the fall of employment elasticity as compared with the earlier period (1999-2000 to 2004-05). The construction sector is the exceptional where employment elasticity of output was relatively high (0.9) (Table 7.4). The trend of overall employment elasticity during 1983 to 2009-10 has downward (Fig. 7.6).

It is to be expected that a growth trajectory with these features would have adversely impacted the labour market, influencing the volume, pattern and nature of employment. *First*, number of workers gradually increased during 1983-84 to 2004-05 for all segments in India, across region as well

Table 7.3: Growth Rates of Output and Employment and their Trend in India, 1983-84 to 2009-10

Sector	*Growth Rate of Output*					*Growth Rate of Employment*				
	1983-84 to 1987-88	1987-88 to 1993-94	1993-94 to 1999-2000	1999-2000 to 2004-05	2004-05 to 2009-10	1983 to 1987-88	1987-88 to 1993-94	1993-94 to 1999-2000	1999-2000 to 2004-05	2004-05 to 2009-10
1. Agriculture and allied activities (Primary)	0.3	5.8	4.3	1.6	1.7	0.3	2.7	0.1	1.5	-1.6
2. Mining and Quarrying	4.9	9.2	7.1	5.3	13.4	3.5	3.0	-3.1	2.5	3.0
3. Manufacturing	4.0	7.0	9.8	7.3	12.0	1.8	2.1	2.0	5.5	-1.3
4. Electricity, Gas and Water Supply	8.4	12.4	10.0	4.6	5.6	7.4	5.8	-6.1	3.3	0.7
5. Construction	3.7	7.2	9.0	11.0	16.0	11.9	-0.2	9.0	9.7	13.9
Secondary (2-5)	4.3	7.7	9.4	7.7	12.6	3.7	1.7	3.0	6.5	3.5
6. Trade, Hotel, Transport and Communications	5.3	7.7	13.7	11.8	10.9	3.6	4.6	8.3	4.6	1.1
7. Other Services	6.8	10.0	11.4	6.5	12.9	2.4	5.6	-0.4	3.8	1.5
Tertiary	6.1	9.0	12.4	8.8	11.9	3.7	5.2	3.7	4.3	1.3
Total	**3.4**	**7.8**	**9.2**	**6.7**	**10.0**	**1.4**	**3.0**	**1.3**	**3.0**	**0.05**

Note: Point to point simple growth rate has been calculated.

Source: As in Table 7.1.

Table 7.4: Employment Elasticity of Output by Sectors in India

Sector	1983-84 to 1987-88	1987-88 to 1993-94	1993-94 to 1999-2000	1999-2000 to 2004-05	2004-05 to 2009-10
Primary (Agriculture and Allied)	0.9	0.4	0.0	0.9	–1.0
1. Mining and Quarrying	0.7	0.3	–0.4	0.5	0.2
2. Manufacturing	0.4	0.3	0.2	0.8	–0.1
3. Electricity-Gas-Water Supply	0.9	0.5	–0.6	0.7	0.1
4. Construction	3.3	0.0	1.0	0.9	0.9
Secondary (1-4)	0.9	0.2	0.3	0.8	0.3
5. Trade, Hotel, Transport and Commerce	0.7	0.6	0.6	0.4	0.1
6. Other Services	0.4	0.6	0.0	0.6	0.1
Tertiary (5-6)	0.6	0.6	0.3	0.5	0.1
Total	**0.4**	**0.4**	**0.1**	**0.4**	**0.0**

Source: Author's Calculation based on Table 7.3.

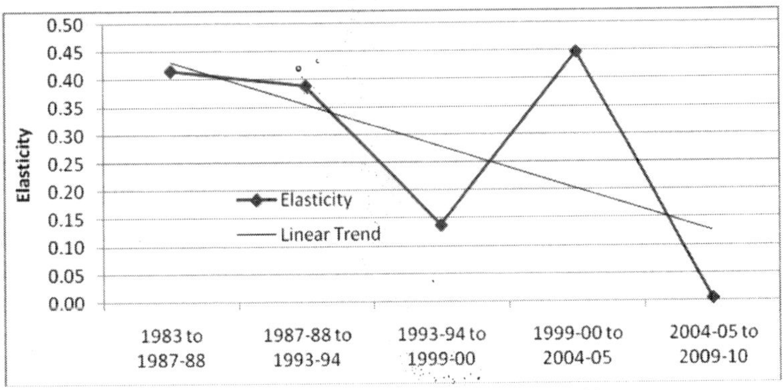

Fig. 7.7: Trends of Employment Elasticity of Output in India

as across sex. But between 2004-05 and 2009-10, there has been hardly any change in the size of the workforce in the country. On one hand there has been an increase in the male employment by 22.4 million between 2004-05 and 2009-10 and on the other there has been a reduction in the female employment by 21.3 million. In total there has been an increase in employment of 1.1 million in the country (Figs. 7.8 and 7.9).

Second, there has been a decline in employment in the rural areas led by a sharp fall in the employment of rural females. In rural India an increase of 13 million male employments along with a fall of 19.5 million

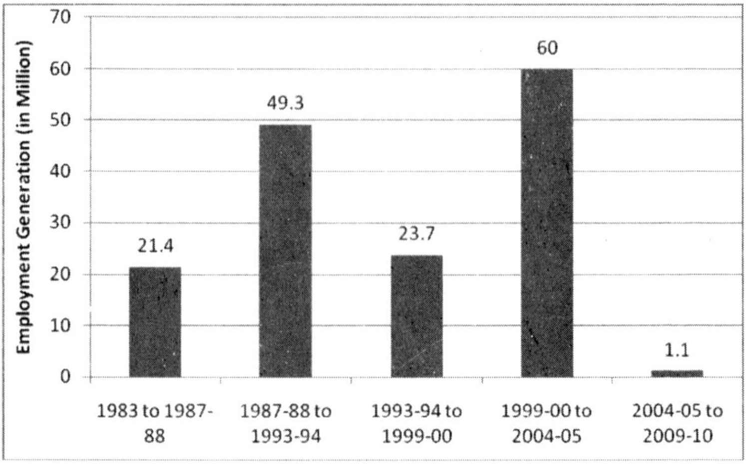

Fig. 7.8: Additional Employments in India

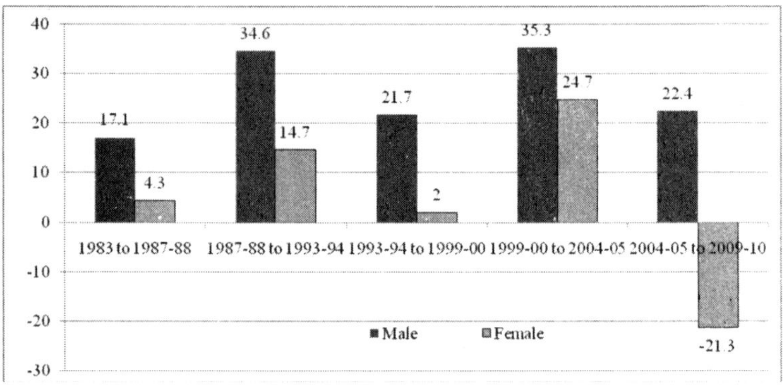

Fig. 7.9: Additional Employments for Male and Female in India

female employments caused for over-all decline of 6.5 million rural employments. It has also been noticed that there has been marginal increase in urban employment mainly due to an increase in male employment, while female employment has come down (Fig. 7.10).

Third, this is the first time the Indian economy has perceived the decline of the number of female workers in contrast with the increase in their male counterpart. The decline of female workers was sharper in rural areas with compound annual growth rate –3.4 per cent in comparison to –1.5 per cent in urban areas (Table 7.4).

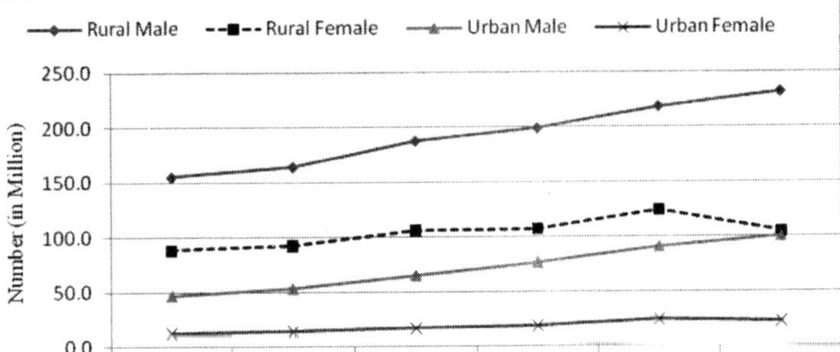

	1983	1987-88	1993-94	1999-00	2004-05	2009-10
Rural Male	155.1	164.0	187.8	199.3	218.9	231.9
Rural Female	88.3	92.4	105.5	107.1	124.0	104.5
Urban Male	46.6	52.9	64.6	76.4	90.4	99.8
Urban Female	12.2	14.1	17.2	18.8	24.6	22.8

Fig. 7.10: Trend of Estimated Employment (in Million) in India by Sex and Region, 1983-84 to 2009-10.

Notes: 1. Workforce figures have been calculated using Census segment-wise population projections and NSS segment-wise Worker Population Ratios.

2. Both principal status and subsidiary status workers taken together.

Source: As in Figure 7.1.

Table 7.4: Compound Annual Growth Rate of Workers in India by Sex and by Region

	Rural		*Urban*		*All*	
	Male	*Female*	*Male*	*Female*	*Male*	*Female*
1983-84 to 1993-94	1.9	1.8	3.3	3.5	2.3	2.0
1993-94 to 2004-05	1.4	1.5	3.1	3.3	1.9	1.8
2004-05 to 2009-10	1.2	–3.4	2.0	–1.5	1.4	–3.0

Source: Calculation is based on number of workers given in Fig. 7.10.

Fourth, at all-India level during the last three decades starting with 1983, the absolute number of male workers gradually increased in both farm and non-farm sectors and during the recent years non-farm employment has out numbered as compared with the farm employment (Table 7.5).

Fifth, in case of females the farm employment has declined in the recent NSSO round 2009-10 and it reaches all time low during the post reform years. Whereas female non-farm employment gradually increased though the rate of expansion is relatively low and, in contrast with male, farm employment has out numbered as compared with non-farm employment.

Sixth, the reduction in the overall female workforce by 21.3 million between 2004-05 and 2009-10 has came from a fall of 21.6 million from the farm with a marginal rise of 0.3 million from non-farm sector. The entire fall of farm employment has been due to the loss of female self-employment because female self-employment has declined 23.1 million during the same period.[6]

Seventh, in both rural and urban India the trend of farm and non-farm employment for male is quite same as it has witnessed at the all- India level. The contrasting feature is that in rural India farm employment has out numbered than non-farm employment.

Eighth, for female rural non-farm sector is the only space where their absorption increased gradually from 11.7 million in 1983-84 to 20.8 million in 2004-05 and further to 21.6 million even in 2009-10. *Last*, during 2004-05 to 2009-10 the female workers declined to the tune of 20.3 million in farm sector of rural India. During the same time the urban female employment declined in both farm (1.3 million) and in non-farm (0.5 million). What was important was that the fall of 21.3 million female employments has been mainly the fall of employment in rural farm sector (Das, 2011).

Growth of Employment in India by Sectors and Location

Highly disparate trends that are discernible for employment growth of male and female during 1983-84 to 1993-94, 1993-94 to 2004-05, and 2004-05 to 2009-10 in various sectors of the rural (and urban) economy (as shown in Tables 7.5 and 7.6) are explained as follows: *Firstly*, the growth rate of rural female and male employment in non-farm sector improved during 1993-94 to 2004-05 than that during the pre-reform period (1983-84 to 1993-94). The growth rate of female RNFE was also higher than that of male during the former period. The global slowdown 2008 has its adverse implications on the Indian economy especially on the employment sphere. During 2004-05 to 2009-10 the growth rates of employment declined in all segments, irrespective of region and sex.

Secondly, for both rural male and rural female workers in construction, manufacturing, transport-storage-communication and trade-commerce were clearly cheering spots, while agriculture, mining, utilities (electricity-gas-water) and other services showed negative growth or slow-down in employment during 1993-94 to 2004-05 over 1983-84 to 1993-94. But during the period of economic slow-down the growth rate of male employment was deteriorated and for female it was negative in all sectors except construction.

Thirdly, growth rate of employment in the construction sector for rural female increased from 1.8 per cent per annum during pre-reform period to 6.3 per cent during the post-reform period, it again substantially increased to 23.9 per cent per annum during 2004-05 and 2009-10. The growth of construction sector has been highest among all other sectors for both male and female. But it has been relatively low for urban female during two post-reform periods. The benefits of improved employment growth rate in the construction sector are duly shared, albeit unevenly, by female and male workers, primarily because of the convenient locale of the construction activities.[7]

Fourthly, the benefit of improved employment growth rate during the first sub-period of post-reform years (i.e., 1993-94 to 2004-05) has also been witnessed in manufacturing sector for both rural male and female. For male (female) that growth steeply declined to –1.8 (–5.5) per cent during 2004-05 to 2009-10 from 2.5 (3.2) per cent during 1993-94 to 2004-05. Trend was similar for urban males and females. Among other two activities of the secondary sector, namely electricity-gas-water and mining and quarrying, for rural female, the first one has negligible (N) employment and the second one has witnessed a decline of employment. For rural male, in contrast, the growth rate has improved in both the sectors. As a whole the rural secondary sector has positive growth rates during two post-reform periods, though the growth has expanded for male and decelerated for female. During the period of economic slow-down the expansion of rural female employment in construction has outnumbered the fall of employment in mining and quarrying and manufacturing. The resultant outcome is the positive growth rate of the secondary sector. But the trend reversed for urban female and growth of secondary sector as a whole was negative during 2004-05 and 2009-10.

Fifthly, while employment for both rural male and female workers in the transport-storage-communication sector increased sizably during 1993-94 to 2004-05, after that it witnessed a steep decline for male and became negative for female. The fast pace of expansion that this sector has witnessed has generally been more conducive to male job seekers, partly because of the physical labour involved and partly because of the shifting locale of the underlying activities. The growth of rural male as well as female employment in trade-commerce and other services increased during 1993-94 to 2004-05 and deteriorated thereafter. On the

Table 7.5: Growth Rate of Employment by Sex in Rural India, 1983-84 to 2009-10

Sector	Male			Female		
	1983-84/ 1993-94	1993-94/ 2004-05	2004-05/ 2009-10	1983-84/ 1993-94	1993-94/ 2004-05	2004-05/ 2009-10
1. Farm (Primary)	1.4	0.4	0.0	1.7	1.2	–4.3
2. Mining and Quarrying	1.9	0.0	7.2	4.8	–1.1	–3.4
3. Manufacturing	1.6	2.5	–1.3	1.9	3.2	–5.5
4. Electricity-Gas-Water Supply	6.1	–2.3	1.2	N	N	N
5. Construction	4.1	8.6	12.0	1.8	6.3	23.9
Secondary (2-5)	2.4	4.4	5.7	2.0	3.3	1.4
6. Trade-Commerce	4.2	5.3	0.9	2.3	3.1	–1.1
7. Transport-Storage Communication	4.0	6.6	2.7	1.8	8.1	–3.4
8. Other Services	2.6	0.4	0.1	2.8	3.0	0.3
Tertiary (6-8)	4.6	3.3	1.0	2.6	3.2	–0.3
Non-Farm (2-8)	3.6	3.8	3.3	2.2	3.3	0.8
Total (1-8)	**1.9**	**1.4**	**1.2**	**1.8**	**1.5**	**–3.4**

Notes and Sources: As in Table 7.5 (Compound annual growth rate is calculated).

Table 7.6: Growth Rate of Employment by Sex in Urban India, 1983-84 to 2009-10

Sector	Male			Female		
	1983-84/ 1993-94	1993-94/ 2004-05	2004-05/ 2009-10	1983-84/ 1993-94	1993-94/ 2004-05	2004-05/ 2009-10
1. Farm (Primary)	1.9	–0.5	1.7	1.0	0.5	–6.6
2. Mining and Quarrying	4.2	–0.3	–3.0	3.5	–6.5	6.8
3. Manufacturing	2.0	3.1	0.5	2.4	4.8	–1.7
4. Electricity-Gas-Water Supply	4.2	–0.6	–0.7	7.8	–0.4	13.1
5. Construction	6.1	5.8	6.5	6.4	2.6	2.8
Secondary (2-5)	2.9	3.5	2.1	3.0	4.3	–1.0
6. Trade-Commerce	4.0	5.4	1.3	4.0	5.2	–1.7
7. Transport-Storage Communication	3.2	3.9	1.4	2.0	4.0	–1.5
8. Other Services	4.0	0.9	3.1	6.2	3.5	0.3
Tertiary (6-8)	3.8	3.3	2.0	5.6	3.9	–0.2
Non-Farm (2-8)	3.5	3.4	2.0	4.5	4.1	–0.5
Total (1-8)	**3.3**	**3.1**	**2.0**	**3.5**	**3.3**	**–1.5**

Notes and Sources: As in Table 7.3.

whole, the growth of employment in tertiary sector for rural female became negative during 2004-05 and 2009-10. The same story unfolds itself for urban female. The growth of tertiary sector has deteriorated for male though it was still positive in rural as well as urban areas.

Conclusion

During recent years there has been large improvement of labour productivity in one hand and on the other a substantial fall of employment elasticity of output. The entire theoretical reasoning regarding growth of labour productivity, output and employment has been shown to be untenable in practice in India. The net implications for employment of this process of growth involving dismal performance in the agricultural sector and a poor employment growth despite high output growth in the manufacturing and services sectors have been adverse.

The pace of growth of output as well as labour productivity has been strongly influenced by the opening up of the Indian economy after economic reforms. However, as the phenomena of labour market are concerned, there was other side of the story where the hopelessness and several zones of darkness loom large. For the entire period the trends of growth of GDP and growth of labour productivity seemed to be upward which was in contrast with the downward trend of growth of employment.

India experiences a slower rate of employment expansion during the recent years, which points to a significant fall in the elasticity of employment with respect to output. Almost jobless growth seems to be prominent features of India's recent economic performance. The sectors like agriculture and manufacturing have experienced the jobloss growth.

The number of workers gradually increased during 1983-84 to 2004-05 for all segments in India, across region as well as across sex. But between 2004-05 and 2009-10, there has been hardly any change in the size of the workforce in the country. There has been a decline in employment in the rural areas led by a sharp fall in the employment of rural females. It has also been noticed that there has been marginal increase in urban employment mainly due to an increase in male employment, while female employment has come down. The decline of female workers was sharper in rural areas in comparison with urban areas. What was important was that the fall of female employment occurred in rural farm sector and the entire fall of female employment has been due to the loss of female self-employment.

The non-farm sector is the only avenue of workers where employment has increased gradually. The growth rate of non-farm employment improved for both male and female during 1993-94 to 2004-05 as compared with pre-reform period. But that growth has decelerated during 2004-05 to 2009-10, for female it is negative in all sectors except construction. Manufacturing sector, an important absorber of workers, has seriously affected during the recent years and as a result the employment has declined.

NOTES

1. In China it was 56 per cent (Chandrasekhar, 2011).
2. All references to rural employment imply such employment for rural workers/households, not necessarily located in the rural areas themselves (Chadha, 2001).
3. The similar methodology has also been used by a number of authors (Vasari, 1995, Sundaram, 2001; Chadha, 2001).
4. The intermediate data set for 1987-88 and 1999-2000 is not used. Weather-wise, the years were not a normal one and was likely to throw up avoidable distortions in rural employment scenario many times more than in urban areas (Chadha, 2001), and, the pre- and post-reform periods need not be shortened (to 1987-88/1993-94 and 1993-94/1999-2000) when data of 1983-84 and 2004-05 are available.
5. In von-Neumann labour itself is perfectly augmentable.
6. The phenomenon has been explained by the withdrawal of unpaid family helpers from the workforce comparison with paid women workers. For detailed see Majumder and Neetha, 2011.
7. The increase of the construction employment during the post-reform periods may be explained in terms of real estate development in urban areas and in terms of implementation of National Rural Employment Guarantee Programme in rural areas.

REFERENCES

Cerruti, Marcela, (2000), "Economic Reform, Structural Adjustment and Female Labour Force Participation in Buenos Aires, Argentina", *World Development*, Vol. 28, No. 5.

Chadha, G.K., (2001), "Impact of Economic Reforms on Rural Employment: No Smooth Sailing Anticipated", *Indian Journal of Agricultural Economics*, Vol. 56, No. 3.

Chandrasekhar, C.P., (2011), "India's New, High-Growth Trajectory: Implications for Demand, Technology and Employment", *IJLE*, 54 (1).

Das, Pinaki, (2012), "Trends of Rural Employment in India: Reflections from Recent NSS Data", *V.U. Journal of Economics*, 13(1); (forthcoming).

Himanshu, (2011), "Employment Trends in India: A Re-examination", *EPW*, Vol. XLVI, No. 37.

Kaldor, N., (1966), *Causes of the Slow Rate of Growth of the United Kingdom* (Cambridge University Press).

Mazumdar, I. and N. Neetha, (2011), "Gender Dimensions: Employment Trends in India, 1993-94 to 2009-10", *Occasional Paper*, No. 56, Centre for Women's Development Studies, New Delhi.

Patnaik, Prabhat, (2011), "Economic Growth and Employment", *EPW*, Vol. XLVI, No. 36.

Sundaram, K., (2001), "Employment-Unemployment situation in Nineties: Some Results from NSS 55th Round Survey", *Economic and Political Weekly*, March 17.

Sundaram, K. and S. Tendulkar, (2006), "Changing Structure of India Workforce, Quality of Employment and Real Earnings, 1983-2000" in *India: Meeting the Employment Challenge*, Conference on Labour and Employment Issues, organized by Institute for Human Development, 27-29 July, New Delhi.

Sundaram, K., (2007), "Employment and Poverty in India: 2000-2005", *Economic and Political Weekly*, 28 July.

Visaria, Pravin, (1995), "Rurul Non-Farm Employment in India: Trends and Issues for Research", *Indian Journal of Agriculture Economics*, Vol. 50, No. 3.

8

Impact of Globalization on Economic Growth

Evidence from India

Sarbapriya Ray, Mihir Kumar Pal and *Ishita Aditya Ray*

Introduction

Today, the term 'globalization' has become a 'buzzword' in any economy all-over the world. The growing integration of economies and societies all-over the universe has been one of the most burning topics in international economics over the past few years. Globalization has many dimensions and has a variety of social, political and economic implications. This term introduced in early 1980, which never precisely defined, is a frequently used word in the political economy. Though there is no appropriate definition of globalization, the term globalization refers to the integration of economies of the world through unrestrained trade and financial flows as well as through mutual exchange of technology and knowledge. Preferably, it also contains free inter-country movement of labour. The process of globalization not only includes opening up of world trade, but also development of advanced means of communication, internationalization of financial markets, growing importance of MNC's, population migrations and more generally increased mobility of persons, goods, capital, data and ideas, but also infections, diseases and pollution. Therefore, it simply means growing integration of the national economies, openness to trade, financial flows, foreign direct investment and the increasing interaction of people in all facets of their lives. Globalization also implies internationalization of production, distribution and marketing of goods and services. International integration implies the adoption of common policies by the individual countries.

India opened up the economy in the early nineties following a major crisis that led by a foreign exchange crunch that dragged the economy close to defaulting on loans. The response was a slew of domestic and external sector policy measures partly prompted by the immediate needs and partly by the demand of the multilateral organizations. The new policy regime radically pushed forward in favour of a more open and market oriented economy. As a participant in the globalization wave, India went through several structural and policy changes only in early 1990s, even if the awareness of need for opening up country's borders was started in late 1980s. The first step towards globalization was taken with the announcement of the devaluation of Indian currency by 18-19 per cent against major currencies in the international foreign exchange market. In fact, this measure was taken in order to resolve the BOP crisis. In order to make the process of globalization smooth, privatization and liberalization policies are moving along as well. By virtue of this programme, intensive charges have been made in industrial policy of Indian Government. Relaxing of licensing rule, reduction of tariff rates, removal of restrictions on import etc. are among those which have been initiated at early stage. Under the privatization scheme, most of the public sector undertakings are being sold to private sector. Licensing policy has been relaxed drastically excepting a few industrial undertaking in India. Some of the recent initiatives taken to further liberalise the FDI regime, *inter alia*, include opening up of sectors such as Insurance, development of integrated townships (up to 100%); defence industry, tea plantation (up to 100% subject to divestment of 26 per cent within five years to FDI); enhancement of FDI limits in private sector banking, allowing FDI up to 100 per cent under the automatic route for most manufacturing activities in SEZs; opening up B2B e-commerce; Internet Service Providers (ISPs) without Gateways; electronic mail and voice mail to 100 per cent foreign investment subject to 26 per cent divestment condition etc. Therefore, wide-ranging financial sector reforms in the banking, capital markets, and insurance sectors, including the deregulation of interest rates, strong regulation and supervisory systems, and the introduction of foreign/private sector competition have already been executed.

The policy reforms undertaken since 1991 had the objectives to make the entire economy more efficient, technologically up-to-date and competitive. This was done with the expectation that efficiency improvement, technological up-gradation and competitiveness would ensure Indian economy to achieve rapid growth. In view of greater openness of Indian economy due to trade liberalization, private sector can build and expand capacity without any regulation. There had been an investment boom in manufacturing sector in the first half of 1990s, (Uchikawa). The advocates of globalization believe that this policy reforms will improve economic growth and performance significantly while critics argue that total withdrawal of restrictions on several matters will have a negative effect on future growth and performance of the economy. There are also negative aspects of globalization. The opponents are of the view that globalization may worsen inequalities both across and within countries, environmental degradation and vulnerability of the poor nations might increase and developed countries establish dominance over these countries culminating in revival of colonialism.

The effects of globalization on growth have also been frequently analyzed with various measures. Until most recently, however, most studies examined them employing cross-sections only. For example, Chanda (2001) uses an index of capital account openness to show that more developing countries have suffered from globalization than not, while Rodrik (1998) as well as Alesina *et al.* (1994) found no effect of capital account openness on economic growth. With respect to foreign direct investment (FDI), there is evidence of a positive growth-effect in countries which are sufficiently rich (Blomström *et al.,* 1992) and a negative one in low income countries (Garrett, 2001). Among others, Dollar (1992) analyzed the relationship between economic performance and openness to trade, Frankel and Romer (1996) those between growth and actual flows. Their results show that both openness to trade and actual trade flows are robustly related to growth. All of these studies present, however, only cross sectional estimates. Moreover, they do not adequately control for endogeneity. Their results might, therefore, reflect unobserved characteristics which do not vary over time instead of being the consequences of globalization or might reflect reverse causality. Streeten (1999) observes that economic liberalization, technological changes, competition in both labour and product markets have contributed to economic failure, weakening of institutions and social support systems, and erosion of established identities and values.

Some recent studies use panel data to examine the relationship between some dimensions of globalization and growth. Among them, Dollar and Kraay (2001) found that an increase in trade flows and foreign direct investment resulted in higher growth rates. Greenaway *et al.* (1999) also report a strong relationship between trade and growth. With respect to FDI, Borensztein *et al.* (1998) provide evidence of a positive growth-effect—given a minimum threshold stock of human capital. Carkovic and Levine (2002), to the contrary, do not find a robust influence of foreign direct investment on growth. A detailed analysis of the impact of several indicators of financial integration and growth is provided by Edison *et al.* (2002a). Their results show that no robust relationship exists. Todaro and Smith (2003) have stated that globalization presents new possibilities for eliminating global poverty and globalization can benefit poor countries directly and indirectly through cultural, social, scientific and technological exchanges as well as trade and finance. Some very important low-income countries like India and China have used globalization to their advantage and have succeeded in achieving enviable economic growth rate and thus reducing some international inequalities. Dollar and Kraay (2004) have studied the effects of globalization on the poor in the developing countries. They note that over half of the developing countries experiencing globalization have gained large increases in trade and considerable reduction in tariffs. These countries are catching-up with the developed countries while the remaining is losing. They have reported that the increase in economic growth leads to a proportionate increases in incomes of the poor.

This chapter attempts to enquire into the fact econometrically whether globalization is a cause of India's economic growth in the long-run. More precisely, the chapter tries to find the causal relationship between globalization and economic growth in India.

Methodology and Database

Data and Variables

The objective of this chapter is to investigate the impact of various factors of globalization on India's economic growth as well as the dynamics of the relationship between globalization and economic growth in India using the annual data for the period, 1990-91 to 2011-12 which includes the 22 annual observations. All necessary data for the sample period are obtained from the *Handbook of Statistics on Indian Economy and Handbook of Statistics on Securities Market of India, 2011-12* published by Reserve Bank of India. All the variables are taken in their natural logarithms to reduce the problems of heteroscedasticity to maximum possible extent.

The real Gross Domestic Product (GDP) is used as the proxy for economic growth in India and we represent the economic growth rate by using the constant value of Gross Domestic Product (GDP) measured in Indian rupee. Economic growth, proxied by real GDP or real per capita GDP, is influenced by a variety of factors. The importance and relevance of these factors may differ from country to country and may also change overtime. Difficulty in obtaining capital stock series for a developing country like India has led us to use gross investment for capital which is again divided into public sector and private sector investments in order to appreciate their relative significance for economic growth. Two measures of openness are used to measure the degree of integration of Indian economy. Openness is the ratio of the sum of imports (M) and exports (X) to GDP and the financial integration is the ratio of sum of capital inflow and capital outflow to the GDP. The latter measure represents financial integration and the international interdependence is represented by the first measure. For capital inflow, we use the sum of official aid, foreign direct investment and portfolio investment in India. Since, consistent and regular time series data is not available for capital outflow, we use debt servicing as a proxy for capital outflow. We use the expenditure on education including medical expenses and health expenditure as a proxy for HRD (Human Resource Development). It is the human resources of a nation that ultimately determine the character and pace of its economic and social development because education makes not only efficient workers but also good citizens.

Econometric Specification

Step I: Ordinary Least Square Method

Primarily, we have studied the effect of globalization on economic growth by a simple regression equation:

$$\text{lnGDP} = \beta_0 + \beta_1 \text{lnPrInv} + \beta_2 \text{lnPubInv} + \beta_3 \text{lnOpenness} + \beta_4 \text{lnFinInt} + \beta_5 \text{lnHRD} + \varepsilon \quad \ldots(1)$$

The expected sign of all the coefficients is positive.

where

ln = natural logarithm.

GDP = nominal gross domestic product.

PubInv = public sector investment.

PrInv = private sector investment.

Openness = trade openness.

FinInt = financial Integration (capital inflow + capital outflow).

HRD = Human resource development.

ε = White noise error term.

Step II: The Stationarity Test (Unit Root Test)

It is suggested that when dealing with time series data, a number of econometric issues can influence the estimation of parametres using OLS. Regressing a time series variable on another time series variable using the Ordinary Least Squares (OLS) estimation can obtain a very high R^2, although there is no meaningful relationship between the variables. This situation reflects the problem of spurious regression between totally unrelated variables generated by a non-stationary process. Therefore, prior to testing Cointegration and Implementing the Granger Causality test, econometric methodology needs to examine the stationarity; for each individual time series, most macro-economic data are non-stationary, i.e. they tend to exhibit a deterministic and/or stochastic trend. Therefore, it is recommended that a stationarity (unit root) test be carried out to test for the order of integration. A series is said to be stationary if the mean and variance are time—invariant. A non stationary time series will have a time dependent mean or make sure that the variables are stationary, because if they are not, the standard assumptions for asymptotic analysis in the Granger test will not be valid. Therefore, a stochastic process that is said to be stationary simply implies that the mean $[(E(Y_t)]$ and the variance $[Var(Y_t)]$ of Y remain constant over time for all t, and the covariance $[covar(Y_t, Ys)]$ and hence, the correlation between any two values of Y taken from different time periods depends on the difference apart in time between the two values for all $t \neq s$. Since, standard regression analysis requires that data series be stationary, it is obviously important that we first test for this requirement to determine whether the series used in the regression process is a difference stationary or a trend stationary.

Several tests of non-stationarity called unit root tests have been developed in the time series econometrics literature. In most of these tests the null hypothesis is that there is a unit root, and it is rejected only when there is strong evidence against it. Most tests of the Dickey-Fuller (DF) type have low power (see Dejong *et al.* 1992). Because of this Maddala and Kim (1998) argue that DF, ADF (augmented Dickey-Fuller) and PP (Phillips and Perron) tests should be discarded. We, therefore, use the KPSS (Kwiatkowski, Phillips, Schmidt and Shin, 1992) test which is considered relatively more powerful (Bahmani-Oskooee, 1999). The KPSS Lagrange Multiplier tests the null of stationarity (H0: $r < 1$) against the alternative of a unit root (H1: $r = 1$).

In *econometrics*, Kwiatkowski–Phillips–Schmidt–Shin (KPSS) tests are used for testing a *null hypothesis* that an observable *time series* is *stationary* around a deterministic trend. The series is expressed as the sum of deterministic trend, random walk, and stationary error, and the test is the *Lagrange multiplier test* of the *hypothesis* that the random walk has zero variance. KPSS type tests are intended to complement *unit root* tests, such as the *Dickey–Fuller tests*. By testing both the unit root hypothesis and the stationarity hypothesis, one can distinguish series that appear to be stationary, series that appear to have a unit root, and series for which the data (or the tests) are not sufficiently informative to be sure whether they are stationary or integrated.

Step III: Testing for Cointegration Test (Johansen Approach)

Co-integration, an econometric property of time series variable, is a precondition for the existence of a long-run or equilibrium economic relationship between two or more variables having unit roots (i.e. Integrated of order one). The Johansen approach can determine the number of co-integrated vectors for any given number of non-stationary variables of the same order. Two or more random variables are said to be co-integrated if each of the series are themselves non-stationary. This test may be regarded as a long-run equilibrium relationship among the variables. The purpose of the Co-integration tests is to determine whether a group of non-stationary series is co-integrated or not.

Engle and Granger (1987) introduced the concept of co-integration, where economic variables might reach a long-run equilibrium that reflects a stable relationship among them. For the variables to be co-integrated, they must be integrated of order one (non-stationary) and the linear combination of them is stationary I(0).

The crucial approach which is used in this study to test co-integration is called the Johansen co-integration approach. The Johansen approach can determine the number of co-integrated vectors for any given number of non-stationary variables of the same order.

If the hypothesis of non-stationarity is established for the underlying variables, it is desirable and important that the time series data are examined for co-integration. Toda and Philips (1993) have shown that ignoring co-integration when it exists, can lead to serious model misspecification. We use the maximum likelihood procedure of Johansen (1991, 1995) because it is based on well-established maximum Likelihood procedure.

Step IV: The Granger Causality Test

Causality is a kind of statistical feedback concept which is widely used in the building of forecasting models. Historically, Granger (1969) and Sim (1972) were the ones who formalized the application of causality in economics. Granger causality test is a technique for determining whether one time series is significant in forecasting another (Granger, 1969). The standard Granger causality test (Granger, 1988) seeks to determine whether past values of a variable helps to predict changes in another variable. The definition states that in the conditional distribution, lagged values of Y_t add no information to explanation of movements of X_t beyond that provided by lagged values of X_t itself (Green, 2003). We should take note of the fact that the Granger causality technique measures the information given by one variable in explaining the latest value of another variable. In addition, it also says that variable Y is Granger caused by variable X if variable X assists in predicting the value of variable Y. If this is the case, it means that the lagged values of variable X are statistically significant in explaining variable Y. The null hypothesis (H_0) that we test in this case is that the X variable does not Granger cause variable Y and variable Y does not Granger cause variable X. In summary, one variable (X_t) is said to Granger cause another variable (Y_t) if the lagged values of X_t can predict Y_t and *vice-versa.*

The spirit of Engle and Granger (1987) lies in the idea that if the two variables are integrated as order one, I(1), and both residuals are I(0), this indicates that the two variables are co-integrated.

Step V: Error Correcting Model (ECM) and Short Term Causality Test

Error correction mechanism was first used by Sargan (1984), later adopted, modified and popularized by Engle and Granger (1937). By definition, error correction mechanism is a means of reconciling the short-run behaviour (or value) of an economic variable with its long-run behaviour (or value). An important theorem in this regard is the Granger Representation Theorem which demonstrates that any set of co-integrated time series has an error correction representation, which reflects the short-run adjustment mechanism.

Co-integration relationships just reflect the long-term balanced relations between relevant variables. In order to cover the shortage, correcting mechanism of short-term deviation from long-term balance could be cited. At the same time, as the limited number of years, the above test result may cause disputes (Christpoulos and Tsionas, 2004). Therefore, under the circumstance of long term causalities, short-term causalities should be further tested as well. Empirical works based on time series data assume that the underlying time series is stationary. However, many studies have shown that majority of time series variables are non-stationary or integrated of order 1 (Engle and Granger, 1987). The time series properties of the data at hand are therefore studied in the outset. Formal tests will be carried out to find the time series properties of the variables. If the variables are I (1), Engle and Granger (1987) assert that causality must exist in, at least, one direction. The Granger causality test is then augmented with an error correction term (ECT).

The acceptance of co-integration between two series implies that there exists a long-run relationship between them and this means that an error-correction model (ECM) exists which combines the long-run relationship with the short-run dynamics of the model. The existence of co-integration implies that unidirectional or bidirectional Granger causality must exist. Therefore, it is necessary that the simple Granger causality test is improved with error-correction mechanism, derived from the residuals of the cointegrating relationship. Based on Engle and Granger (1987 : 255) representation theorem, the error correction model of equation (1) is formulated as follows and the results have been provided in Table 8.5 below:

$$\Delta \text{lnGDPt} = \alpha + \lambda \text{ECM}_{t-1} + \Sigma\beta_i\, \Delta\text{lnGDP}_{t-i} + \Sigma\, \psi i\, \Delta\text{lnPrInv}_{t-i} + \Sigma\varphi i \Delta\text{lnPubInv}_{t-i} + \Sigma\, \eta i\, \Delta\text{lnOpenness}_{t-i} + \Sigma\delta i\, \Delta\text{lnFinInt}_{t-i} + \theta i\, \Delta\text{lnHRD}_{t-i} + \mu_t$$

ECM_{t-1} is the error correction term generated from the Johansen multivariate procedure and the parametre λ is the error correction coefficient that measures the response of the regressor in each period to departures from equilibrium. The presence of ECM_{t-1} reflects the presumption that dependent variable does not adjust instantaneously to its long-run determinants. Therefore, in the short-run an adjustment is made to correct any disequilibrium in the long-run. Therefore, error-correction model shows how system converges to long-run equilibrium. Lagged explanatory variables represent short-run impact and the long-run impact is given by the error correction term.

Empirical Analysis and Interpretation of the Result

The discussion will be divided into two sub-sections. In the first section, we will generally look into the descriptive analysis of the variables. The main target is to understand the behaviour of the variables itself, by looking at the distribution of mean, median, maximum, minimum, standard deviation, skewness and kurtosis of each variable. The next subsection will be focusing on the estimation results of regression, unit root, Johansen co-integration, granger causality analysis etc.

Table 8.1 presents descriptive statistics for the variables used in our estimate. Summary statistics in Table 8.1 include the mean and the standard deviation, minimum and maximum value for Period 1991-92 to 2007-08. The mean, median, maximum, minimum and standard deviation can determine the statistical behaviour of the variables. The relatively smaller figure of standard deviation indicates that the data dispersion in the series is quite small. This finding suggests that almost all independent variables included in the sample were having smaller dispersion level of different independent variables under our study across time series. The descriptive statistics shows negative skewness for private investment, openness and human resource development variables which indicate flatter tails than the normal distribution. Out of five independent variables under our consideration, only financial integration variable (lnFinInt.) shows leptokurtic distribution (kurtosis>3).

Table 8.1: Descriptive Statistics

	lnPrInv.	*lnPubInv.*	*lnOpenness.*	*lnFinInt.*	*lnHRD.*
Mean	9.521809	12.09481	−1.491968	−1.329050	11.20252
Median	9.750453	12.13208	−1.513043	−1.377870	11.43130
Maximum	11.11708	13.74224	−0.568462	−1.072210	12.38344
Minimum	7.548029	10.97454	−2.660567	−1.505240	9.920337
Std. Dev.	0.884445	0.733956	0.609094	0.111184	0.759835
Skewness	−0.439092	0.570509	−0.227997	1.014656	−0.181779
Kurtosis	2.535824	2.921038	2.111347	3.438598	1.859924
Jarque-Bera	0.863332	1.144639	0.872931	3.771664	1.252953
Probability	0.649426	0.564215	0.646317	0.151703	0.534472
Observations	22	22	22	22	22

Source: Own estimate.

In Ordinary Least Squares (OLS) regression, time series residuals are often found to be serially correlated with their own lagged values. Serial correlation means: (a) OLS is no longer an efficient linear estimator; (b) standard errors are incorrect and generally overstated; and (c) OLS estimates are biased and inconsistent. This test is an alternative to the Q-Statistic for testing for serial correlation. It is available for residuals from OLS, and the original regression may include auto-regressive (AR) terms. Unlike the Durbin-Watson Test, the Breusch-Godfrey test may be used to test for serial correlation beyond the first order, and is valid in the presence of lagged dependent variables. The null hypothesis of the Breusch-Godfrey test is that there is no serial correlation up to the specified number of lags. The Breusch-Godfrey test regresses the residuals on the original regressors and lagged residuals up to the specified lag order. The number of observations multiplied by R^2 is the Breusch-Godfrey test statistic.

Table 8.2: Diagnostic Checking: Autocorrelation

Breusch-Godfrey Serial Correlation LM Test:			
F	0.378893	Probability	0.691936
Obs*R-squared	1.156691	Probability	0.560825

The statistic labelled 'Obs*R-squared' is the LM test statistic for the null hypothesis of no serial correlation. The high probability values indicate the absence of serial correlation in the residuals.Therefore, the result from diagnostic checking shows that model does not suffer from auto-correlation.

Table 8.3: Regression Results by Ordinary Least Square Technique

Dependent Variable: lnGDP
Method: Least Squares
Sample: 1990-91 to 2011-12
Included observations: 22

Variable	*Coefficient*	*Std. Error*	*t-Statistic*	*Prob.*
C	7.668327	2.369770	3.235895	0.0055
lnPrInv	0.115559	0.027700	4.171817	0.0008
lnPubInv	0.133156	0.102699	1.296561	0.2144
lnOpenness	0.139912	0.024474	5.716692	0.000
lnFinInt	–0.076663	0.245016	–0.312890	0.7587
lnHRD	0.380466	0.190820	1.993850	0.0647

R-squared 0.977243	Mean dependent var 14.53448
Adjusted R-squared 0.969657	S.D. dependent var 0.490226
S.E. of regression 0.085394	Akaike info criterion-1.848129
Sum squared resid 0.109382	Schwarz criterion-1.549694
Log likelihood 25.40536	F-statistic 128.8254
Durbin-Watson stat 1.409677	Prob (F-statistic) 0.000000

Source: Own estimate.

The OLS results in Table 8.3 show that the primary variables have the expected sign. The regression results show that private investment, openness and human resource development have significant positive impact on economic growth *via* GDP growth. Financial integration variable (capital inflow + capital outflow) has negative impact, although not significant, on economic growth and public investment is also having insignificant positive impact on economic growth.

The KPSS results (Table 8.4) show that all the variables are non-stationary in level form. Table 8.4 presents the results of the unit root test for the variables for their levels and first differences. The results indicate that the null hypothesis of a unit root cannot be rejected for the given variable at levels with both trend and without trend and, hence, one can conclude that the variables are not stationary at their levels. We get mixed results in level form with trend.

To determine the stationarity property of the variable, the same test above was applied to the first differences. Results from Table 8.4 revealed that all the KPSS values both without trend and with trend are smaller than the critical *t*-value at 1 per cent, 5 per cent and 10 per cent level of significance for all variables. Based on these results, the null hypothesis that the series have unit roots in their differences can be rejected. Therefore, all the variables are first difference stationary I (0) thus integrated of order 1.

Table 8.4: Unit Root Test

Variable (log)	*KPSS level*		*KPSS First Difference*	
	Without Trend	*With trend*	*Without Trend*	*With trend*
lnGDP	2.0333	0.3935	0.2874	0.0557706
lnPrInv	0.4114	0.3680	0.12981	0.0525995
lnPubInv	1.8622	0.1567	0.152587	0.0747019
lnOpenness	2.0385	0.2015	0.186322	0.060313
lnFinInt	0.7095	0.2728	0.206787	0.0336542
lnHRD	2.0612	0.3137	0.15061	0.0955587

Ho: series has unit root; H_1: series is trend stationary.

Note: 1 per cent, 5 per cent and 10 per cent critical values for KPSS are 0.739, 0.463 and 0.347 for *without trend.*

1 per cent, 5 per cent and 10 per cent critical values for KPSS *with trend* are 0.216, 0.146 and 0.1199.

Source: Own estimate.

Since, the principal variables are stationary and integrated of order 1, we apply now the Johansen co-integration test to see whether the variables are co-integrated or not suggesting long-run relationship. The test for presence of long-run relationship between the variables using the Johansen and Juselius (1992) LR statistic for co-integration was conducted. It can be seen from the Likelihood Ratio (L.R.) that we have two co-integration equations. In other words, there exist two linear combinations of the variables. Therefore, Economic growth and all right hand side variables are co-integrated thus having long-run relationship.

Table 8.5: Johansen Cointegration Test

Included observations: 21
Test assumption: Linear deterministic trend in the data Series: lnFinInt, lnGDP, lnHRD lnOpenness, lnPrInv, lnPubInv.
Lags interval: No lags

Hypothesized No. of CE(s)	*Eigenvalue*	*Likelihood Ratio*	*5 Per cent Critical Value*	*1 Per cent Critical Value*
None**	0.957328	136.9029	94.15	103.18
At most 1 *	0.877750	73.81849	68.52	76.07
At most 2	0.533268	31.78480	47.21	54.46
At most 3	0.447892	16.54480	29.68	35.65
At most 4	0.199756	4.664555	15.41	20.04
At most 5	0.010335	0.207784	3.76	6.65

Ho: has no co-integration; H1: has co-integration
*(**) denotes rejection of the hypothesis at 5 per cent (1%) significance level.
L.R. test indicates 2 cointegrating equation(s) at 5 per cent significance level.
Source: Own estimate.

The acceptance of co-integration between two series implies that there exists a long-run relationship between them and this means that an error-correction model (ECM) exists which combines the long-run relationship with the short-run dynamics of the model. The existence of co-integration implies that unidirectional or bidirectional Granger causality must exist.

The above results generally show that causality is bidirectional for the majority of the pairs of variables except eight where it is unidirectional. The following pairs of variables are the ones that exhibited unidirectional causality: lnGDP and lnFinInt, lnHRD and lnFinInt, lnFinInt and lnHRD, lnPubInv and lnFinInt, lnFinInt and lnPubInv, lnOpenness and lnGDP, lnOpenness and lnHRD.

If we consider all the other cases considered, we observe that the direction of causality between globalization and economic growth in India is generally bidirectional (causality runs in both directions).

Table 8.6: Pair-wise Granger Causality Tests

Sample: 1990-91 to 2010-11 Lags: 2

Null Hypothesis:	*Obs.*	*F-Statistic*	*Probability*
lnGDP does not Granger Cause lnFinInt	20	4.48040	0.03133*
lnFinInt does not Granger Cause lnGDP		0.18269	0.83498
lnHRD does not Granger Cause lnFinInt	20	2.87988	0.08962**
lnFinInt does not Granger Cause lnHRD		3.86936	0.04595*
lnOpeness does not Granger Cause lnFinInt	20	2.46756	0.12079
lnFinInt does not Granger Cause lnOpenness		0.38558	0.68706
lnPrInv does not Granger Cause lnFinInt	20	0.72978	0.49948
lnFinInt does not Granger Cause lnPrInv		0.91377	0.42365
lnPubInv does not Granger Cause lnFinInt	20	3.00165	0.08226**
lnFinInt does not Granger Cause lnPubInv		9.86485	0.00212*
lnHRD does not Granger Cause lnGDP	20	0.29106	0.75188
lnGDP does not Granger Cause lnHRD		1.59103	0.23843
lnOpeness does not Granger Cause lnGDP	20	3.71120	0.05091**
lnGDP does not Granger Cause lnOpeness		1.50974	0.25484
lnPrInv does not Granger Cause lnGDP	20	1.50397	0.25605
lnGDP does not Granger Cause lnPrInv		1.43881	0.27022
lnPubInv does not Granger Cause lnGDP	20	0.91891	0.42172
lnGDP does not Granger Cause lnPubInv		6.06310	0.01269*
lnOpenness does not Granger Cause lnHRD	20	2.89771	0.08850**
lnHRD does not Granger Cause lnOpenness		1.37712	0.28446
lnPrInv does not Granger Cause lnHRD	20	0.37594	0.69337
lnHRD does not Granger Cause lnPrInv		0.25024	0.78202
lnPubInv does not Granger Cause lnHRD	20	0.75855	0.48666
lnHRD does not Granger Cause lnPubInv		1.19786	0.33097
lnPrInv does not Granger Cause lnOpenness	20	2.11038	0.15810
lnOpenness does not Granger Cause lnPrInv		0.47133	0.63372
lnPubInv does not Granger Cause lnOpenness	20	0.21961	0.80555
lnOpenness does not Granger Cause lnPubInv		8.28019	0.00423
lnPubInv does not Granger Cause lnPrInv	20	0.37392	0.69470
lnPrInv does not Granger Cause lnPubInv		1.91013	0.18471

Notes:

(a) The Schwartz criterion was used to determine the order of the lags on the bivariate (bVAR) relationships. The number of observations is the one that restricted us to two lags.

(b) The estimates were achieved by using the integrated variables first differences. *(**) denotes significance at 5 (10) per cent level.

Source: Own estimate.

Lagged explanatory variables represent short- run impact and the long-run impact is given by the error correction term. Error correction results show that the error correction term ECT t-1 has the correct negative sign and is significant for GDP, public sector investment, private sector investment and financial integration indicate the long-run equilibrium between the foresaid variables. An estimate of –0.037 for GDP indicates that 3.7 per cent of the preceding year disequilibrium is eliminated in the current year.

Table 8.7: Error-correction Results

	d_lnGDP	*d_lnprinv*	*d_lnpubinv*	*d_lnopennes*	*d_lnFI*	*d_lnHRD*
ECT	–0.037	–0.59	0.12	–0.041	–0.084	–0.0148
	(–2.31) *	(–1.75) *	(2.64)*	(–1.14)	(–2.98)*	(–0.456)
d_lnGDP_1	0.659	–2.501	2.13	–0.865	0.0623	0.0411
	(1.542)	(–0.49)	(3.00)*	(–1.57)	(0.146)	(0.084)
d_lnprinv_1	0.017	0.225	–0.157	0.071	–0.0155	0.0021
	(0.605)	(0.67)	(–3.35)*	(1.986)*	(–0.548)	(0.068)
d_lnpubinv_1	–0.236	3.90	–0.53	0.391	0.465	0.0667
	(–1.039)	(1.44)	(–1.41)	(1.337)	(2.047)*	(0.256)
d_lnopennes_1	–0.315	12.59	–0.274	0.517	1.276	0.431
	(–0.517)	(1.73)	(–0.27)	(0.659)	(2.09)*	(0.616)
d_lnFI_1	–0.462	7.66	0.255	0.308	1.62	0.617
	(–0.910)	(1.27)	(0.303)	(0.472)	(3.19)*	(1.062)
d_lnHRD_1	0.0119	–2.41	0.724	–0.498	–0.0097	0.418
	(–0.046)	(–0.78)	(1.67)	(–1.48)	(–0.037)	(1.399)

Source: Own estimate.

Conclusion

This chapter explores the impact of globalization on economic growth of India for the period 1990-91 to 2011-12. In order to assess the impact of globalization empirically, we consider trade openness and financial integration, public and private investment, human resource development etc. as macro-economic independent variables expected to influence the economic growth in the regression framework. The regression results show that private investment, openness and human resource development have significant positive impact on economic growth *via* GDP growth. Financial integration variable (capital inflow+capital outflow) has negative impact, although not significant, on economic growth and public investment is also having insignificant positive impact on economic growth. Johansen's co-integration procedure showed that all the above-mentioned variables are cointegrated implying these macro-economic variables have long-run equilibrium relationship with economic growth *via* GDP growth. Error-correction model results also supported the co-integration results. We observe that the direction of causality between globalization and economic growth in India is generally bidirectional (causality runs in both directions) excepting a few where it is unidirectional. Main finding of this chapter is that India's economic growth has received a strong impetus in post, 1991 era. This increased economic growth is mainly and directly is a result of free trade movement that started in 1991. The government is committed to accelerate economic reforms and developing basic infrastructure further to improve lives of the rural poor and boost economic performance.

REFERENCES

Alesina, Alberto, Vittorio Grilli and Gian M. Milesi-Ferretti, (1994), "The Political Economy of Capital Controls", in: Leonardo Leiderman and Assaf Razin (eds.), *Capital Mobility: The Impact on Consumption, Investment and Growth*, Cambridge University Press, Cambridge: 289-321.

Bahmani-Oskooee, Mohsin, (1999), Cointegration Approach to Estimating Bilateral Trade Elasticities Between US and Her Trading Partners, *International Economic Journal,* Vol. 13(4), pp. 119-128.

Borensztein, E., J. de Gregorio, J.W. Lee, (1998), "How Does Foreign Direct Investment Affect Economic Growth?", *Journal of International Economics*, Vol. 45, pp. 115-135.

Blomström, Magnus, Robert E. Lipsey, Mario Zejan, (1992), What Explains Developing Country Growth?, NBER Working Paper 4132.

Dimitris K. Christopoulos and Efthymios G. Tsionas, (2004), "Convergence and regional productivity differences: Evidence from Greek prefectures," *The Annals of Regional Science*, Springer, Vol. 38 (3), pp. 387-396.

Carkovic, Maria, Ross Levine, (2002), Does Foreign Direct Investment Accelerate Growth?, *mimeo*, University of Minnesota.

Chanda, Areendam, (2001), The Influence of Capital Controls on Long Run Growth: Where and How Much?, North Carolina State University, *mimeo.*

Dollar, David, (1992), "Outward-Oriented Developing Economies Really Do Grow More Rapidly: Evidence from 95 LDCs, 1976-85", *Economic Development and Cultural Change*: 523-544.

Dollar, David, Aart Kraay, (2001), Trade, Growth, and Poverty, World Bank Discussion Paper, Washington, D.C.

Edison, Hali J., Ross Levine, Luca Ricci, Torsten Sløk, (2002), International Financial Integration and Economic Growth, IMF Working Paper 02/145, Washington, D.C.

Engle, R.F. and C.W.J. Granger, (1987), Cointegration and Error—Correction: Representation, Estimation, and Testing, *Econometrica*, Vol. 55(2), pp. 251-276.

Frankel, Jeffrey A., David Romer, (1996), Trade and Growth: An Empirical Investigation, NBER Working Paper 5476.

Granger, C.W.J, (1986), Developments in the Study of Cointegrated Economic Variables, *Oxford Bulletin of Economics and Statistics*, nr. 48.

Granger, C.W.J. and P. Newbold, (1974), "Spurious regressions in econometrics". *Journal of Econometrics*, Vol. 2 (2), pp. 111-120.

Greenaway, David, Wyn Morgan, Peter Wright, (1999), Exports, Export Composition and Growth, *Journal of International Trade and Economic Development*, Vol. 8, no.1, pp. 41-51.

Garrett, Geoffrey, (2001), The Distributive Consequences of Globalization, UCLA, MS.

Johansen, S., (1996), Likelihood-Based Inference in Cointegrated Vector Autoregressive Models, 2nd edition, Oxford University Press.

Johansen, S., (1988), "Statistical Analysis of Cointegrating Vectors." *Journal of Economic Dynamics and Control*, Vol. 12, pp. 231-54.

Johansen, S., K. Juselius, (1992), Structural hypotheses in a multivariate co-integration analysis of the PPP and UIP for UK. J. *Economics*, Vol. 53, pp. 211-44.

Maddala, G.S. and I.M. Kim, (1998), *Unit Roots, Cointegration, and Structural Change*, Cambridge: Cambridge University Press.

Phillips, Peter and Pierre Perron, (1998), "Testing for a Unit Root in Time Series Regression", *Biometrica*, Vol. 75, (June), pp. 335-346.

Rodrik, Dan, (1998), "Who Needs Capital Account Convertibility?", in: Stanley Fischer *et al.* (eds.), Should the IMF Pursue Capital Account Convertibility?, *Essays in International Finance 207*, Department of Economics, Princeton University, Princeton, NJ: 55-65.

Sims, C.A., (1972), Money, income and causality, *American Economic Review*, Vol. 62, pp. 540-552.

Streeten, Paul F., (1999), *Globalization: Threat or Opportunity*, 14th Annual General Meeting and Conference, 28th-31st January, 1999, Islamabad, Pakistan Institute of Development Economics.

Toda, H.Y. and P.C.B. Phillips, (1993), Vector auto regressions and causality, *Econometrica*, Vol. 61 (6), pp. 1367-1393.

Uchikawa, S., (2001), "Investment boom and underutilization of capacity in the 1990s," *Economic and Political Weekly*, August 25, pp. 3247-3253.

9

Impact of Foreign Capital Inflow in the Presence of Employment Subsidy

A Theoretical Analysis

Anindita Basu (Chowdhury)

Introduction

The formation of World Trade Organization (WTO) has brought some revolutionary changes in liberalizing international trade across countries, whether developed or developing. Liberalization includes both inflow of foreign capital as well as reduction of protection to domestic industries. Empirically, it has been observed that many developing economies, notably the non-OECD countries, have not implemented tariff reforms to any significant extent, even after formally choosing free trade as their developmental strategy. So, the countries which welcome huge inflow of foreign capital may be reluctant to implement tariff reform seriously. There is a vast empirical as well as theoretical literature related to the role of foreign capital inflow in economic development of a developing economy. Some of the theoretical models have been developed to meet the empirical challenges: again, some of the empirical works have been conducted to examine the validity of certain established theoretical propositions. A large number of theoretical works have been developed to provide theoretical structures to examine the role of foreign capital inflow in developing economies from different angles. On the basis of the works of Bhagwati (1958) and Johnson (1967), Bhagwati (1973) related to immiserising growth in a tariff ridden economy Brecher and Alejandro (1977) have analyzed the welfare effects of foreign capital inflow in a two commodity, two factor full employment framework. According to them foreign capital inflow with full repatriation of its earning is necessarily immiserizing if the import-competing sector is capital-intensive and is protected by a tariff. However, in the absence of any tariff, the inflow of foreign capital with full repatriation of its earning does not affect the social welfare. This is the well-known Brecher-Alejandro proposition of trade theory. Khan (1982) has reexamined the Brecher Alejandro proposition in a two-sector Harris-Todaro (1970) framework and reached to the same conclusion. In latter period this two-sector framework has been extended to three sector frameworks, where third sector may be an export processing zone or duty free zone or foreign enclave as in the works of Beladi and Marjit (1992), Marjit (1994) etc. or it may be an urban informal sector as in the works of Grinols (1991), Chandra and Khan (1993), Gupta (1997) Chaudhuri (2001) etc.[1]

In spite of liberalization in some developing economy like India there exists a case of employment subsidy or wage subsidy. Thus, different economists and policy-makers have tried to test its impact on economy. Yabuuchi and Beladi (2000) have shown that wage subsidies to the agricultural and informal sectors increase welfare and decrease urban unemployment. The effects of a wage subsidy to manufacturing sector on welfare and unemployment are conditional. Gupta and Basu (2008) have shown that increase in employment subsidy to the formal manufacturing sector decreases the urban unemployment rate of the economy and it also increases the level of welfare of the economy.

The main motivation behind this study generates from the fact that in spite of few empirical works only a few theoretical works have been made to examine the impact of foreign capital inflow on the level of welfare in the presence of employment subsidy. Unlike the existing literature here we have considered the combination of specific-factor and Heckscher-Ohlin-Samuelson type full employment and mobile factor model framework instead of Harris-Todaro framework of urban unemployment. This type of structure justifies the characteristics of the production and trade patterns of LDCs. Here, we have examined the impact of foreign capital inflow on the level of output of different sectors and on the level of welfare.

The major results of the chapter are as follows: In the presence of employment subsidy to the manufacturing sector the production of the foreign enclave and agricultural goods sector increases and the production of manufacturing goods sectors decreases due to inflow of foreign capital. Under some sufficient condition this foreign capital inflow is welfare improving.

The plan of this chapter is as follows. Section 2 specifies and explains the working of the basic three-sector model. The comparative static analysis regarding the effects of foreign capital inflow on the level of output of different sectors and social welfare are considered in this section. Finally, the concluding remarks are made in Section 3.

The Model

We consider a small openless developed economy consisting of three sectors in a Heckscher-Ohlin-Samuelson framework. There are two types of labour available in the economy: Unskilled labour (L) and skilled labour (S). Unskilled labour (L) has been considered as mobile only between domestic agricultural sectors, sector-A and manufacturing sector, sector-M. Skilled labour (S) has been considered as mobile only between domestic manufacturing sector, M, and foreign enclave, F. Domestic capital (K_D) has been considered as mobile between domestic manufacturing sector, M, and the agricultural sector, A. Foreign capital (K_F) on the other hand has been considered as specific to the foreign enclave. Here the manufacturing sector, M produces its commodity (X_M) with the help of skilled labour, unskilled labour and domestic capital. The agricultural sector, A, produces its commodity (X_A) with the help of unskilled labour and domestic capital. The foreign enclave produces its commodity (X_F) with the help of skilled labour and foreign capital. Owing to our small open economy assumption, we consider prices of all goods to be given internationally. The agricultural product is considered as numeraire and its price is set equal to unity. We assume that the manufacturing sector is the import competing sector and the agricultural sectors is the sector that produces exportable commodity. Here, we have assumed that employment subsidy is given to the manufacturing sector. This subsidy is financed by lump sum taxes. Production functions exhibit constant returns to scale with diminishing marginal productivity to each factor. All inputs are fully employed. The entire foreign capital income is assumed to be fully repatriated.

For specifying our model on the basis of the above assumption we use the following notations:

X_i = Product produced by the ith sector, i = M, A, F
P_i = World price of the ith commodity, i = M, A and F
L = Fixed endowment of unskilled labour
S = Fixed endowment of skilled labour

K_D = Fixed endowment of domestic capital
K_F = Fixed amount of foreign capital
w = Common wage rate of unskilled labour
w_S = Common wage rate of the skilled labour
r = Rate of return on domestic capital
r_F = Rate of return on foreign capital[1]
a_{ji} = Quantity of *j*th factor for producing one unit of output in the *i*th sector.
$j = L, S, K_D, K_F$, and
i = M, A and F
α_M = employment subsidy in sector M.
λ_{ji} = Proportion of *j*th factor used in the production of the *i*th sector
$\wedge$ = Proportional change
θ_{ij} = Distributive share of the *j*th input in the *i*th industry
Ω = A measure of welfare

The competitive equilibrium condition in the product market for the four sectors implies the following equations:

$$w_S a_{SM} + (w - \alpha_M) a_{LM} + r a_{KM} = P_M \tag{1}$$
$$w a_{LA} + r a_{KA} = 1 \tag{2}$$
$$w_S a_{SF} + r_F a_{KF} = P_F \tag{3}$$

The sector specificity of foreign capital is given by the following equation:

$$a_{KF} X_F = K_F \tag{4}$$

Mobility of domestic capital can be expressed as

$$a_{KA} X_A + a_{KM} X_M = K_D \tag{5}$$

Full employment of unskilled labour implies the following equation:

$$a_{LA} X_A + a_{LM} X_M = L \tag{6}$$

Full employment of skilled labour implies the following equation:

$$a_{SM} X_M + a_{SF} X_F = S \tag{7}$$

In this model we have 7 equations with seven variables w, w_S, r, r_F, X_M, X_A, X_F. So, the system is consistent. Due to variable coefficient technology input-output coefficients are the functions of factor prices (of the factors used by the particular sector).[2] The parametres of the system are P_M, P_F, K_F, K_D, L and S that are assumed to be given exogenously.

The working of the model can be explained in the following manner. From equation (3) we find that, given P_F, r_F is a decreasing function of w_S, i.e. $(\partial r_F/\partial w_S) < 0$. Again, from equation (2) we find that, given w is a decreasing function of *r*, i.e. $(\partial w/\partial r) < 0$. From equation (1) we find that, given P_M, w_S is a decreasing function of *r*, i.e. $(\partial w_S/\partial r) < 0$. From these relations we can say that r_F is a positive function of *r*, i.e. $(\partial r/\partial r_F) > 0$. Thus, it can be concluded that both r_F and w_S are functions of *r*. Here, the endogenous variables are to be solved simultaneously and decomposability property is not applicable here.[3]

Using equation (4), equation (7) can be written as

$$a_{SM} X_M + a_{SF} (K_F/a_{KF}) = S$$

$$\Rightarrow a_{SM} X_M + \Psi(r)K_F = S \tag{7.1}$$

where $\Psi = (a_{SF}/a_{KF})$.

As $r_F = r_F(r)$ and $w_S = w_S(r)$ we can write

$$a_{SF} = a_{SF} (w_S/r_F) = a_{SF} (r) \text{ and } a_{KF} = a_{KF} (w_S/r_F) = a_{KF} (r)$$

Since $a'_{SF} > 0$ and $a'_{KF} < 0$; thus, we can write $\Psi' > 0$ where $\Psi = \Psi(r)$.

The combination of *r* and X_M which maintains equilibrium in the market for skilled labour is given by the SS locus, in Figure 9.1.

The slope of this locus, as obtained from equation (7.1) is given by

$$(dr/dX_M)|_{SS} = -a_{SM}/(K_F\Psi' + X_M a'_{SM})$$

Since, the input-output ratio is positive and the function Ψ along with the input–output ratio a_{SM} varies directly with *r*[4], therefore the curve SS is negatively sloped. This is shown in Figure 9.1.

Using equation (6), equation (5) can be written as

$$a_{KM}X_M + a_{KA}\{(L/a_{LA}) - (a_{LM}/a_{LA}) X_M\} = K_D$$

$$\Rightarrow \quad a_{KM}X_M + \xi(r)L - \mu X_M = K_D \tag{5.1}$$

where $\xi = a_{KA}/a_{LA}$ and $\mu = a_{KA}a_{LM}/a_{LA}$

As $w = w(r)$, $r_F = r_F(r)$ and $w_S = w_S(r)$ we can write

$$a_{KA} = a_{KA}(w/r) = a_{KA}(r) \text{ and } a_{LA} = a_{LA}(w/r) = a_{LA}(r)$$

Since $a'_{LA} > 0$ and $a'_{KA} < 0$; thus, we can write $\xi' < 0$ and where $\xi = \xi(r)$.

The locus of r and X_M, which maintains the equilibrium of the domestic capital market, is given by the KK curve in Figure 9.1. The slope of this curve as obtained from equation (5.1) is given by

$$(dr/dX_M)|_{KK} = -(a_{KM} - \mu)/(X_M a'_{KM} + L\,\xi' - \mu' X_M)$$

Now $(a_{KM} - \mu) > 0$ if M sector is more capital intensive compared to A sector.

Again $L\xi' - \mu' X_M = \xi'(L - a_{LM} X_M) - X_M \xi a'_{LM}$ which is negative as $\xi' < 0$.

Since $a_{KM} = a_{KM}(w_S/r) = a_{KM}(r)$, $a_{LM} = a_{LM}(w_S/r) = a_{LM}(r)$ where $a'_{KM} < 0$, $a'_{LM} > 0$ and the input-output ratio is positive, therefore, the curve KK is positively sloped. This is shown in Figure 9.1.

The intersection of SS and KK locus in Figure 9.1 gives us the equilibrium values of r and X_M. In other words, r and X_M can be determined from equations (5.1) and (7.1), when solved simultaneously. Once r is known, all other factor prices and the input-output coefficients are known.

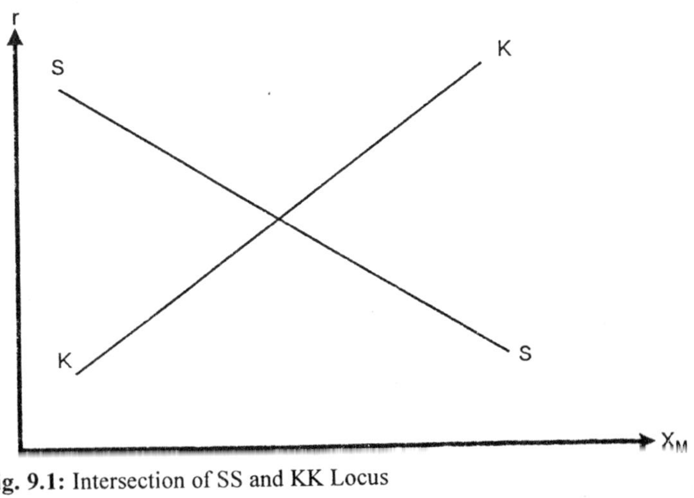

Fig. 9.1: Intersection of SS and KK Locus

Again when X_M is determined, one can easily determine the values of X_A and X_F from the model. This completes the working of our model.

The Comparative Statics

In this section of the chapter, our main focus is to analyze the impact of foreign capital inflow on the level of national welfare of a developing economy. In this context at first we have to find out the impact of foreign capital inflow on the level of factor prices as well as sectoral composition of output. With larger inflow of foreign capital into the economy, the level of output of the sector using it increases. For given r and hence for given input-output ratios a_{KF} and a_{SF}, larger inflow of foreign capital into the economy, leads to an increase in output of the sector which uses this foreign capital, i.e. an increase in K_F implies an increase in the level of output of sector X_F, which leads to *Rybczynski type effect* through change in the availability of effective supply of skilled labour in the other domestic sector. An increase in foreign capital stock (K_F) leads to an increase in the output of foreign enclave (X_F), which draws skilled labour away from domestic manufacturing sector, M. As the endowment of skilled labour force, S, is given it implies a contraction of X_M. In other words, from equation (7.1) we find that for given *r*, an increase in K_F implies a reduction in X_M, i.e. a leftward shift of SS locus. However, there will be no effect on the KK curve. Hence, a new equilibrium has been obtained, where both r and X_M fall. As a result of decrease in r, both w and w_S rise (as product prices are given). Hence, from competitive equilibrium conditions we find that r_F falls.

Now, we want to show this result mathematically. Using equation (2) we get

$$(\hat{w}/\hat{K}_F) = D(\hat{r}/\hat{K}_F) \text{ [see appendix for details]} \quad (8)$$

where $D = -(\theta_{KA}/\theta_{LA})$ which is negative.

Totally differentiating equation (1) and using equation (8) we get

$$(\hat{w}_s/\hat{K}_F) = E(\hat{r}/\hat{K}_F) \text{ [see appendix for details]} \quad (9)$$

where $E = \{(\theta_{LM}\theta_{KA} - \theta_{KM}\theta_{LA})/\theta_{SM}\theta_{LA}\}$

Since, the M sector is more capital intensive (with respect to unskilled labour) comparing to the A sector so that $\theta_{LA}\theta_{KM} - \theta_{LM}\theta_{KA} > 0$, i.e. $E < 0$.

Using the envelope condition (or the concept of unit isoquant) we find $wda_{LF} + r_F da_{KF} = 0$ so that equation (3) implies $a_{LF}dw + a_{KF}dr_F = 0$

$$\therefore \qquad (\hat{r}_F / \hat{K}_F) = F(\hat{r} / \hat{K}_F) \text{ [see appendix for details]} \quad (10)$$

where $F = -(\theta_{SF}/\theta_{KF})\{(\theta_{LM}\theta_{KA} - \theta_{KM}\theta_{LA})/\theta_{SM}\theta_{LA}\}$ which is positive.

The above expressions show that the impacts of foreign capital on the factor prices are dependent on the impact of foreign capital inflow on the price of domestic capital.

Now, differentiating equation (4) we can get [see appendix for details]

$$\hat{X}_F / \hat{K}_F = 1 - N(\hat{r} / \hat{K}_F) \quad (11)$$

As N is negative, we can say that $\hat{X}_F$ is positive.

From equation (5) we can get [see appendix for details]

$$\lambda_{KDA}(\hat{X}_M / \hat{K}_F) + \lambda_{KDI}(\hat{X}_A / \hat{K}_F) = G(\hat{r} / \hat{K}_F) \quad (12)$$

where $G = -E\lambda_{KDM}S^M_{KDS} - D\lambda_{KDM}S^M_{KDL} - \lambda_{KDM}S^M_{KDKD} - D\lambda_{KDA}S^A_{KDL} - \lambda_{KDA}S^A_{KDKD}$ which is positive.

From equation (6) we can get [see appendix for details]

$$\lambda_{LM}(\hat{X}_M / \hat{K}_F) + \lambda_{LA}(\hat{X}_A / \hat{K}_F) = H(\hat{r} / \hat{K}_F) \quad (13)$$

where $H = -E\lambda_{LM}S^M_{LS} - D\lambda_{LM}S^M_{LL} - \lambda_{LM}S^M_{LKD} - D\lambda_{LA}S^A_{LL} - \lambda_{LA}S^A_{LKD}$.

As the substitutability between skilled labour and unskilled labour is negligible so we can say that the value of H is negative.

From equation (7) we can get [see appendix for details]

$$\lambda_{SM}(\hat{X}_M / \hat{K}_F) + \lambda_{SF}(\hat{X}_F / \hat{K}_F) = I(\hat{r} / \hat{K}_F) \quad (14)$$

where $I = -E\lambda_{SM}S^M_{SS} - D\lambda_{SM}S^M_{SL} - \lambda_{SM}S^M_{SKD} - D\lambda_{SF}S^A_{SL} - F\lambda_{SF}S^A_{SKD}$ which is negative.

Using equation (11) equation (14) can be written as

$$\lambda_{SM}(\hat{X}_M / \hat{K}_F) = \lambda_{SF} + J(\hat{r} / \hat{K}_F) \quad (15)$$

where $J = (I + N)$ which is negative.

Solving equation (12), (13) and (15) by Cramer's rule we can get the following expressions [see appendix for details]

$$\hat{X}_M/\hat{K}_F = (H\lambda_{KA}\lambda_{SF} - G\lambda_{LA}\lambda_{SF})/|\lambda|$$
$$\hat{X}_A/\hat{K}_F = (-H\lambda_{KM}\lambda_{SF} + G\lambda_{LM}\lambda_{SF})/|\lambda|$$
$$\hat{r}/\hat{K}_F = (-\lambda_{KM}\lambda_{LA}\lambda_{SF} + \lambda_{KA}\lambda_{LM}\lambda_{SF})/|\lambda|$$

where $|\lambda| = -J\lambda_{LA}\lambda_{KM} - \lambda_{KA}(-J\lambda_{LM} + H\lambda_{SM}) - G(-\lambda_{LA}\lambda_{SM})$

Now $|\lambda|$ is positive under the sufficient condition $\lambda_{KM}\lambda_{LA} > \lambda_{KA}\lambda_{LM}$.

Under the above sufficient condition we can say that $(\hat{X}_M/\hat{K}_F) < 0$, $(\hat{X}_A/\hat{K}_F) > 0$ and $(\hat{r}/\hat{K}_F) < 0$.

As $(\hat{r}/\hat{K}_F) < 0$ so we can get that $(\hat{w}/\hat{K}_F) > 0$, $(\hat{w}_s/\hat{K}_F) > 0$ and $(\hat{r}/\hat{K}_F) < 0$. Thus, foreign capital inflow produces a favourable impact on the return of labour and negative impact on the return of domestic as well as foreign capital.

We next consider the impact of foreign capital inflow on the national welfare.[5] Now, we consider quasi-concave social utility function, denoted by U that depends on consumption demand for four final goods denoted by D_A, D_B, D_M and D_F. Thus, it is shown as

$$U = U(D_M, D_A, D_B, D_F) \tag{16}$$

Taking total differential of equation (16) and the using the fact $(U_M/U_A) = P_M$ and $(U_F/U_A) = P_F$ (where $U_A = \partial U/\partial D_A$, $U_M = \partial U/\partial D_M$ and $U_F = \partial U/\partial D_F$) it is possible to write

$$d\Omega = dD_A + P_B dD_B + P_M dD_M + P_F dD_F \tag{16.1}$$

Here $d\Omega = dU/U_A$.

Following Caves, Frankel and Jones (1996) we find that $d\Omega$ implies a measure of change in welfare measured in units of the product of sector A. Here in the absence of tariff world price is equal to domestic price.

The trade balance equation requires that

$$D_A + P_M D_M + P_F D_F = X_A + P_M X_M + P_F X_F - r_F K_F \tag{17}$$

We know that $X_A + P_B X_B + P_M X_M + P_F X_F$ is the value of output measured at domestic price which is nothing but $w.L + w_S S + r.K_D + r_F K_F$

$$X_A + P_B X_B + P_M X_M + P_F X_F = w.L + w_S S + r.K_D + r_F K_F - \alpha_M a_{LM} X_M \quad (17.1)$$

Taking total differential of equation (17) we can get
$dD_A + P_M dD_M + P_F dD_F = dX_A + P_M dX_M + P_F dX_F - r_F dK_F - K_F dr_F$

Using equation (16.1) and also using equation (17.1) we get

$$d\Omega = wdL + Ldw + w_S dS + Sdw_S + r.dK_D + K_D.dr - \alpha_M a_{LM} dX_M - \alpha_M X_M da_{LM}$$

When $dK_F > 0$, $dL = dS = dK_D = 0$.

$$\therefore \Omega(\hat{\Omega}/\hat{K}_F) = wL(\hat{w}/\hat{K}_F) + w_S S(\hat{w}_S/\hat{K}_F) + r.K_D(\hat{r}/\hat{K}_F) - \alpha_M a_{LM} X_M(\hat{X}_M/\hat{K}_F) - \alpha_M \lambda_{LM} S^M_{LS}(\hat{w}_S/\hat{K}_F) - \alpha_M \lambda_{LM} S^M_{LL}(\hat{w}/\hat{K}_F) - \alpha_M \lambda_{LM} S^M_{LKD}(\hat{r}/\hat{K}_F)$$

As a result of foreign capital inflow we find that output of manufacturing sector decreases under the sufficient condition that $\lambda_{KM}\lambda_{LA} > \lambda_{KA}\lambda_{LM}$. It produces a positive impact on welfare by reducing the social cost of protection. Again foreign capital inflow produces a positive impact on welfare by increasing the wage rate of both skilled and unskilled labour under above sufficient condition. This foreign capital inflow also produces some negative impact on welfare by reducing the rate of return on capital and by increasing social cost of protection. Now, the total welfare effect is dependent on the relative strength of these two opposite effects. We thus find $(\hat{\Omega}/\hat{K}_F)$ is positive if the positive effects of foreign capital inflow is greater than the negative effects of foreign capital inflow, i.e. if the reduction of the rate return on capital and increase in the social cost of protection is lower than the increase in the wage rate of both skilled and unskilled labour. Thus, we can say that under some condition foreign capital inflow is welfare improving.

Concluding Remarks

The impact of foreign capital inflow on the level of welfare of a small open economy is considered as one of the most important issues in the context of the developmental problems of a developing economy. The present chapter shows that under some reasonable condition foreign capital inflow may improve national welfare in the presence of employment subsidy to the manufacturing sector.

Our result may encourage the policy-makers who are in favour of foreign capital inflow in developing countries. Our results are thus consistent with WTO prescriptions in developing economies. This interesting issue can be resolved once we consider the empirical aspects of the above study for developing economies, especially India. Such an analysis is beyond the empirical scope of the present chapter though it can be considered as an important area of research for the researchers who are interested in gains and losses of foreign capital inflow in developing economies. The present research can be considered as a theoretical guideline for this future research agenda.

Appendix

Derivation of the expressions for $(\hat{w}/\hat{K}_F)$, $(\hat{w}_S/\hat{K}_F)$ $(\hat{r}/\hat{K}_F)$ and $(\hat{r}_F/\hat{K}_F)$.

Totally differentiating equation (2) we can get

$$\theta_{LA}\,\hat{w} + \theta_{KA}\,\hat{r} = 0$$

$$\therefore \quad \hat{w}/\hat{K}_F = D(\hat{r}/\hat{K}_F) \tag{8}$$

where $D = -(\theta_{KA}/\theta_{LA})$ which is negative.

Totally differentiating equation (1) and using equation (8) we get

$$\theta_{SM}\,\hat{w}_S + \{(-\theta_{LM}\theta_{KA} + \theta_{KM}\theta_{LA})/\theta_{LA}\}\,\hat{r} = 0$$

$$\therefore \quad \hat{w}_S/\hat{K}_F = E(\hat{r}/\hat{K}_F) \tag{9}$$

where $E = \{(\theta_{LM}\theta_{KA} - \theta_{KM}\theta_{LA})/\theta_{SM}\theta_{LA}\}$

Since, the M sector is more capital intensive (with respect to unskilled labour) comparing to the A sector so $\theta_{KM}/\theta_{LM} > \theta_{KA}/\theta_{LA}$, i.e. $\theta_{LA}\theta_{KM} - \theta_{LM}\,\theta_{KA} > 0$ and $E < 0$.

Using the envelope condition (or the concept of unit isoquant) we find $w da_{LF} + r_F da_{KF} = 0$ so that equation (3) implies $a_{LF}dw + a_{KF}dr_F = 0$

$$\text{or,} \quad \theta_{SF}\,\hat{w}_S + \theta_{KF}\,\hat{r}_F = 0$$

$$\text{or,} \quad \hat{r}_F = -(\theta_{SF}/\theta_{KF})\,\hat{w}_S$$

$$\therefore \quad \hat{r}_F/\hat{K}_F = F(\hat{r}/\hat{K}_F) \tag{10}$$

where $F = -(\theta_{SF}/\theta_{KF})\{(\theta_{LM}\theta_{KA} - \theta_{KM}\theta_{LA})/\theta_{SM}\theta_{LA}\}$ which is positive.

Derivation of the expressions for $(\hat{X}_A/\hat{K}_F)$, $(\hat{X}_M/\hat{K}_F)$ and $(\hat{X}_F/\hat{K}_F)$.

Differentiating equation (4) we can get

$$a_{KFF}dX_F = dK_F - X_F da_{KFF}(w_S, r_F)$$

$$\text{or,} \quad \lambda_{KFF}\,\hat{X}_F = \hat{K}_F - \lambda_{KFF}\,S^F_{KFKF}\,\hat{r}_F - \lambda_{KFF}\,S^F_{KFS}\,\hat{w}_S$$

$$\text{or,} \quad \hat{X}_F = \hat{K}_F - F\,S^F_{KFKF}\,r - E\,S^F_{KFL}\,r \;[\text{as } \lambda_{KFF} = 1]$$

$$\therefore \quad \hat{X}_F/\hat{K}_F = 1 - N(\hat{r}/\hat{K}_F) \tag{11}$$

As N is negative, we can say that $\hat{X}_F$ is positive.
From equation (5) we can get

$$a_{KDM}dX_M + a_{KDA}dX_A = -X_M da_{KDM}(w_S, w, r) - X_A da_{KDA}(w, r)$$

$$\text{or, } \lambda_{KDM}\hat{X}_M + \lambda_{KDA}\hat{X}_A = -\lambda_{KDM}S^M_{KDS}\hat{w}_S - \lambda_{KDM}S^M_{KDL}\hat{w} - \lambda_{KDM}S^M_{KDKD}\hat{r} - \lambda_{KDA}S^A_{KDL}\hat{w} - \lambda_{KDA}S^A_{KDKD}\hat{r}$$

$$\text{or, } \lambda_{KDM}\hat{X}_M + \lambda_{KDA}\hat{X}_A = -E\lambda_{KDM}S^M_{KDS}\hat{r} - D\lambda_{KDM}S^M_{KDL}\hat{r} - \lambda_{KDM}S^M_{KDKD}\hat{r} - D\lambda_{KDA}S^A_{KDL}\hat{r} - \lambda_{KDA}S^A_{KDKD}\hat{r}$$

$$\therefore \lambda_{KDM}(\hat{X}_M / \hat{K}_F) + \lambda_{KDA}(\hat{X}_A / \hat{K}_F) = G(\hat{r} / \hat{K}_F) \tag{12}$$

where $G = -E\lambda_{KDM}S^M_{KDS} - D\lambda_{KDM}S^M_{KDL} - \lambda_{KDM}S^M_{KDKD} - D\lambda_{KDA}S^A_{KDL} - \lambda_{KDA}S^A_{KDKD}$ which is positive.

From equation (6) we can get

$$a_{LM}dX_M + a_{LA}dX_A = -X_M da_{LM}(w_S, w, r) - X_A da_{LA}(w, r)$$

$$\text{or, } \lambda_{LM}\hat{X}_M + \lambda_{LA}\hat{X}_A = -\lambda_{LM}S^M_{LS}\hat{w}_S - \lambda_{LM}S^M_{LL}\hat{w} - \lambda_{LM}S^M_{LL}\hat{w} - \lambda_{LM}S^M_{LKD}\hat{r} - \lambda_{LA}S^A_{LL}\hat{w} - \lambda_{LA}S^A_{LKD}\hat{r}$$

$$= -E\lambda_{LM}S^M_{LS}\hat{r} - D\lambda_{LM}S^M_{LL}\hat{r} - \lambda_{LM}S^M_{LKD}\hat{r} - D\lambda_{LA}S^A_{LL}\hat{r} - \lambda_{LA}S^A_{LKD}\hat{r}$$

$$\therefore \lambda_{LM}(\hat{X}_M / \hat{K}_F) + \lambda_{LA}(\hat{X}_A / \hat{K}_F) = H(\hat{r} / \hat{K}_F) \tag{13}$$

where $H = -E\lambda_{LM}S^M_{LS} - D\lambda_{LM}S^M_{LL} - \lambda_{LM}S^M_{LKD} - D\lambda_{LA}S^A_{LL} - \lambda_{LA}S^A_{LKD}$.

As the substitutability between skilled labour and unskilled labour is negligible so we can say that the value of H is negative.
From equation (7) we can get

$$a_{SM}dX_M + a_{SF}dX_F = -X_M da_{SM}(w_S, w, r) - X_A da_{SF}(w_S, r_F)$$

$$\text{or, } \lambda_{SM}\hat{X}_M + \lambda_{SF}\hat{X}_F = -\lambda_{SM}S^M_{SS}\hat{w}_S - \lambda_{SM}S^M_{SL}\hat{w} - \lambda_{SM}S^M_{SKD}\hat{r} - \lambda_{SF}S^A_{SL}\hat{w}_S - \lambda_{SF}S^A_{SKD}\hat{r}_F$$

$$= -E\lambda_{SM}S^M_{SS}\hat{r} - D\lambda_{SM}S^M_{SL}\hat{r} - \lambda_{SM}S^M_{SKD}\hat{r} - D\lambda_{SF}S^A_{SL}\hat{r} - F\lambda_{SF}S^A_{SKD}\hat{r}$$

$$\therefore \qquad \lambda_{SM}(\hat{X}_M/\hat{K}_F) + \lambda_{SF}(\hat{X}_F/\hat{K}_F) = I(\hat{r}/\hat{K}_F) \qquad (14)$$

where $I = -E\lambda_{SM}S^M_{SS} - D\lambda_{SM}S^M_{SL} - \lambda_{SM}S^M_{SKD} - D\lambda_{SF}S^A_{SL} - F\lambda_{SF}S^A_{SKD}$ which is negative.

Using equation (11) equation (14) can be written as

$$\lambda_{SM}\hat{X}_M = -\lambda_{SF}\hat{K}_F + I\hat{r} + \lambda_{SF}N\hat{r}$$

$$\therefore \lambda_{SM}(\hat{X}_M/\hat{K}_F) = -\lambda_{SF} + J(\hat{r}/\hat{K}_F) \qquad (15)$$

where $J = (I + \lambda_{SF}N)$ which is negative.

From equation (12), (13) and (15) we can write

$$\begin{bmatrix} \lambda_{KM} & \lambda_{KA} & -G \\ \lambda_{LM} & \lambda_{LA} & -H \\ \lambda_{SM} & 0 & -J \end{bmatrix} \begin{bmatrix} \hat{X}_M/\hat{K}_F \\ \hat{X}_A/\hat{K}_F \\ \hat{r}/\hat{K}_F \end{bmatrix} = \begin{bmatrix} 0 \\ 0 \\ -\lambda_{SF} \end{bmatrix}$$

Solving above equation by Cramer's rule and simplifying one gets

$$\hat{X}_M/\hat{K}_F = (H\lambda_{KA}\lambda_{SF} - G\lambda_{LA}\lambda_{SF})/|\lambda|$$

$$\hat{X}_A/\hat{K}_F = (-H\lambda_{KM}\lambda_{SF} + G\lambda_{LM}\lambda_{SF})/|\lambda|$$

$$\hat{r}/\hat{K}_F = (-\lambda_{KM}\lambda_{LA}\lambda_{SF} + \lambda_{KA}\lambda_{LM}\lambda_{SF})/|\lambda|$$

where $\qquad |\lambda| = -J\lambda_{LA}\lambda_{KM} - \lambda_{KA}(-J\lambda_{LM} + H\lambda_{SM}) - G(-\lambda_{LA}\lambda_{SM})$

Now, $|\lambda|$ is positive under the sufficient condition $\lambda_{KM}\lambda_{LA} > \lambda_{KA}\lambda_{LM}$.

NOTES

1. Our implicit assumption is that $r_F \geq r_F^w$, where r_F^w is the exogenously given world rate of return on foreign capital. For this reason foreign capital will be invested in the small open economy but due to government control the amount of foreign capital, which enters in this country, is also fixed at a particular point of time. It may be noted in this connection that in many developing countries we find that the shift towards more liberalized regime is a gradual one instead of drastic shift. Drastic policy changes may lead socio-political tension in the economy in the short-run. The assumption of

exogenously given foreign capial stock can thus be justified as the government directly regulates the entry of foreign capital. *See* Marjit (1994) for details. *See* also Gupta and Gupta (1998).

2. Thus, for example $a_{LA} = a_{LA}(W,r)$. It is to be noted that a_{Ly} can be interpreted as demand for labour to produce one unit of the product of sector 'A'. As (input) demand functions are homogeneous of degree zero we can write $a_{LA} = a_{LA}(W/r)$.
3. When the factor prices are determined independently of factor endowments we refer to the structure as a decomposable one.
4. One can consider the unit demand function as $a_{SM} = a_{SM}[w_S(r)/r]$. Now, as r decreases, w_S increases, therefore (w_S/r) increases due to which the producers will substitute skilled labour by capital, which in turn will increase the demand for capital and decrease the demand for skilled labour. Thus, $a'_{SM} > 0$.
5. Here, we have assumed that due to balanced budget lump sum tax revenue is equal to total amount of subsidy.

REFERENCES

Bhagwati, J.N., (1958), "Immiserizing Growth: A General Note", *Review of Economic Studies,* 25: 201-205.

Bhagwati, J.N., (1973), "The Theory of Immiserising Growth: Further Application", *International Trade and Money;* University of Toronto Press: 45-54.

Brecher, R.A. and Alejandro, C.F.D., (1977), "Tariff, Foreign Capital and Immiserising Growth", *Journal of International Economics,* 7: 317-322.

Caves, R.E., J.A. Frankel and R.W. Jones, (1990), *"World Trade and Payments"* (5th edition), Scott, Foresman and Little, London: Brown Higher Education.

Chandra, V. and M.A. Khan, (1993), "Foreign Investment in the Presence of an Informal Sector", *Economica,* 60: 79-103.

Corden, W.M. and R. Findlay, (1975), "Urban Unemployment, Intersectoral Capital Mobility and Development Policy", *Economica,* 29:59-78.

Chaudhuri, S., (2001), "Foreign Capital Inflow; Technology Transfer and National Income", *The Pakistan Development Review*: 40(1) spring, 49-56.

Grinols, E.L., (1991), "Unemployment and Foreign Capital: *The Relative Opportunity Cost of Domestic Labour and Welfare Economics,* 57: 107-122.

Gupta, K. and T. Basu, (2007), "Urban Employment Subsidy, Capital Market Distortion and Urban Unemployment in the Presence of Informal Sector: A Theoretical Analysis", *Asian Economic Review,* 49: 299-314.

Gupta, M.R., (1997), "Informal Sector and Informal Capital Market in a Small Open Less Developed Economy", *Journal of Development Economics,* 52: 409-428.

Harris, J.R. and M.P. Todaro, (1970), "Migration, Unemployment and Development: A Two Sector Analysis", *American Economic Review*, 60: 126-142.

Johnson, H.G., (1967), "The Possibility of Income Losses from Increased Efficiency of Factor Accumulation in the Presence of Tariff", *Economic Journal*, 77: 151-154.

Khan, M.A., (1982), "Tariff, Foreign Capital and Immiserizing Growth with Urban Unemployment and Specific Factors of Production", *Journal of Development Economics,* 10: 245-256.

Marjit, S., (1994), "On the Participation of Local Capital in a Foreign Enclave: A General Equilibrium Analysis", *Journal of Economic Integration,* 9(4): 489-501.

Yabuuchi, S. and H. Beladi, (2000), "Urban Unemployment, Informal Sector and Development Policies", *Journal of Economics*, Vol. 74, No. 3.

10

Effect of Per Capita Expenditure and Income on Student Enrolment in Higher Education

Jagabandhu Mandal, Ashit Baran Aich and *Sanjib Basu*

Introduction

So long the main emphasis was on growth literature following the Western tradition and based on the principle of efficiency, but now for less developed country like India we need a literature on development on economics where along with efficiency the question of equity is also important. Again Nurksian logic of vicious circle of poverty mainly rests on material capital and for capital accumulation of UD country mainly two methods are suggested: (1) Primitive capital accumulation, and (2) Mercantile capital accumulation. But our emphasis should shift to human capital which is population driven, a combination of mental and physical strength acts as a stock for repeated use. This includes education and health and growth theory is subsequently endogenous using technology and knowledge as a shock from within. Then we come to social capital which mainly includes power, road, and transport and finally natural capital, which falls under the area of environmental economics closely related to development literature. Here, we try to distinguish between renewable resources like air, water, fish etc. and non-renewable resources like mineral oil, certain species of plants and animals. Finally, we come across a latest emphasis on sustainable development which meets the needs of the present without compromising the ability of future generation to meet their own needs.

Our present chapter is an attempt to locate the factors affecting demand for higher education in India comprising conventional system as well as open and distance learning (ODL) system. The main objective is to identify a set of explanatory variables explaining enrolment in Higher Education in Indian States.

Data Source

Our data source is secondary mainly based on NSSO 64th round "Education in India (2007-08) Participation and Expenditure", *RBI Bulletin*, and Ministry of Human Resource Development (MHRD) data, we take 2007-08 as our reference period and data covers 29 States in India and nature of the data is cross-section.

The Background of the Study

The Eleventh Five Year Plan has set the objective of 15 per cent GER by the end of the plan period against the world average of 23 per cent. A few comments about the notion of gross enrolment ratio (GER) may be made here. GER is widely used to express the general level of participation by an age-specific group of learners in a given level of education. It indicates the capacity of the system to enroll students of a particular age-group. The gross enrolment ratio for higher education, expressed as percentage, is given by

$$GER = [(X + Y)/Z] \times 100\%, \qquad (1)$$

where

X = Total enrolment at the post-higher secondary level with ages of the learners falling in the group 18-23 years;

Y = Total enrolment at the post-higher secondary level with ages of the learners greater than 23 years (the case of over-age learners); and

Z = Total population in the 18-23 age group.

In the definition (1), it is assumed that the age-group for higher education is typically 18-23 years while the quantity Y captures the scenario encountered in the ODL system where age is no hindrance to go for higher education. One defect of GER as given in (1) is that it can exceed 100 per cent because the sum X + Y may theoretically exceed the quantity Z. Moreover, there is a problem of compatibility as the coverage of X and Z is different.

In contrast to the formula (1) above, the net enrolment ratio (NER), expressed as percentage, may likewise be defined as

$$\text{NER} = (X/Z) \times 100\%, \tag{2}$$

Which, however, does not exceed 100 per cent. To ensure statistical regularity, we take enrolment per 1000 in higher education as dependent variable (Y) and enrolment per 1000 in higher secondary level as explanatory variable (X_1). In our chapter we have also shown gross attendance ratio (GAR) and net attendance ratio (NAR).

Demand for higher education is affected by the several factors like student enrolment in higher secondary level and per capita income of the country, number of higher educational institution and also student expenditure, population growth, literacy rate, employment generation or job opportunity, good governance etc. We approximately suggest enrolment in post-higher secondary level as an index of demand for higher education.

Estimation of demand for higher education and forecasting of the future demand is necessary mainly for two purposes: (1) To get prepared with requisite infrastructure to meet the demand; and (2) To formulate policy for the future and also to prepare the budget.

Regression Model

We have used linear as well as double log form so far as regression equation are concerned. Log linear relation gives us lower value of R^2 indicating that linear relation is better fit. But the advantage of log linear form is that every regression coefficient represents the elasticity of dependent variable with respect to explanatory variable.

Here, we use a demand function expressed by regression equation form—

$$Y_i = b_0 + b_1X + b_2\,Z_i + b_3I_i + b_4\,C_i + U_i$$

$$(i = 1, 2, 3, \ldots 29)$$

Here, certain observations on enrolment in higher education (Y_i) which is taken as dependent variable and higher secondary enrolment (X_i), per-capital state domestic product (I_i), per student expenditure (Z_i) number of colleges (C_i) are taken as explanatory variables variable. Here, I and Z are monetary factors and previous enrolment (X) is quantitative factors behind demand for higher education. We will fit a linear regression to these observations and test the overall goodness of fit (with R^2) as well as the statistical reliability of the estimates $\hat{b}_0$, $\hat{b}_1$, $\hat{b}_2$, $\hat{b}_3$, $\hat{b}_4$. Good Governance is a qualitative variable which can be tackled by a Dummy using (0,1) combination.

The fitted regression equation is found to be

$$Y_i = -12.103 + 0.24X_i + 0.001Z_i + 0.001I_i + 0.010\,C_i$$

SE(^bj) (9.495) (0.071) (0.002) (0.000) (0.001)

t-value (–1.275) (3.276) (0.653) (5.192) (4.403) with

$$R^2 = 0.811$$

and $\text{Log}(Y_i) = -2.703 + 0.338\text{Log}X_i + 0.274\text{Log}Z_i + 0.548\text{Log}I + 0.111\text{Log}C$ with $R^2 = 0.685$

Percentage of variation in dependent variable is 81 per cent explained by the independent variable chosen by us. The t-value of Z coefficient in regression equation is un-usually low which suggest omission of Z. When we consider log linear relation which gives us lower value of R^2 indicating that linear relation is better fit.

If we consider gross attendance ratio (GAR) we consider linear estimation given by

$$Y_i = 0.432 + 0.131X + 0.00002Z + 0.000I + 0.002C$$

SE(^bj) (2.944) (0.041) (0.000) (0.001) (0.001)

t-value (0.147) (3.242) (0.075) (2.377) (2.551) with

$$R^2 = 0.566$$

and $\text{Log}(Y_i) = -1.666 + 0.397\text{Log}X + 0.076\text{Log}Z + 0.356\text{Log}I + 0.084\text{Log}C$ with $R^2 = 0.572$

And if we consider net attendance ratio (NAR) we have linear demand function given by

$$Y_i = 2.757 + 0.232X + 0.000Z + 0.00003I + 0.00C$$

SE(^bj) (2.219) (0.057) (0.000) (0.000) (0.001)

t-value (1.242) (4.089) (0.578) (0.605) (0.274) with

$$R^2 = 0.602$$

and $\text{Log}(Y_i) = -1.012 + 0.310X_i + 0.142\text{Log}Z + .220\text{Log}I + 0.037\text{Log}C$ with $R^2 = 0.488$

Here t-value of Z, I and C coefficient in regression equation is un-usually low which are also not significant. In case of attendance, behavioural factors are more relevant as compared to traditional factors.

Measure of Elasticity

In the literature on Income elasticity of demand, non-availability of data suggests expenditure as proxy of income. The logic behind such formulation is that income determines expenditure which finally determines enrolment. Intuitively, dlogY/dlogE<1 and expenditure elasticity is an overestimate.

$$\frac{d\log Y}{d\log I} = \frac{d\log Y}{d\log Z} \cdot \frac{d\log Z}{d\log I}$$

Value of first term on the left hand side is 0.739 and first term of the right hand side is 0.661 last term of the right hand side is 0.200 that means income elasticity is over estimated then expenditure elasticity. But our empirical findings contradicts our intuitive guess.

When we consider enrolment in higher education in value terms then V = ZY, logV = logZ + logY

or, $$\frac{d\log V}{d\log I} = \frac{d\log Z}{d\log I} + \frac{d\log Y}{d\log I}$$

Therefore, value elasticity can be decomposed into two parts—quantity elasticity and quality elasticity and the result is empirically verified as follows—

$$\log V = 1.432 + 0.939 \log I (e = 0.939)$$
$$\log Z = 2.984 + 0.200 \log I (e_1 = 0.200) \text{ and}$$
$$\log Y = -1.552 + 0.739 \log I (e_2 = 0.739).$$

Therefore, $e = e_1 + e_2$, which correlates our theoretical result.

Problems of Multicollinearity

The term multicollinearity is used to denote the presence of linear relationships (or near linear relationships) among explanatory variables. It may arise when some or all of explanatory variables in a regression are highly correlated with one another. If the explanatory variables are perfectly linearly correlated the model in matrix form can be written as

$$Y = X\beta + \in$$

where

OLS estimate $\beta\,\hat{} = (X'X)^{-1} X'Y$ and

$(X'X)^{-1} = adj(X'X)/|X/X|$.

But, $|X'X| = 0$ and OLS estimate is indeterminates.

Measure of Multicollinearity

Theil's measure of multicollinearity: Theil (1971, p.179) considers a multicollinearity measure which is

$$m = R^2 - \Sigma\,(R^2 - R^2_{-j}) \tag{3}$$

where R^2 is the square of the multiple correlation coefficient and R^2_{-j} is the same excluding the jth explanatory variable. The quantity $(R^2 - R^2_{-j}) \geq 0$ is termed the "incremental contribution" of the jth regressor by Theil. If all the explanatory variables are mutually uncorrelated, then m will be zero because the incremental contributions all add up to R^2. In other cases, m can be negative as well as highly positive.

As reported by Mehta, Swamy and Iyengar (1993), the Theil's measure is preferable to other measures used in the statistics literature to diagnose multicollinearity. They have also obtained the exact distribution of m which can be used to test the significance of any observed value of m from data.

Value of $m = 0.364$ that indicates presence of near exact multicollinearity and impact is not severe.

Variance Inflation Function (VIF) = $1/(1 - R_i^2)$ where R_i^2 is squared multiple correlation coefficient between X_i and the other explanatory variable. It can also be interpretated as the ratio of actual variance of $\beta_i\hat{}$ to what the variance of $\beta_i\hat{}$ would have been if X_i were to be un-correlated with the remaining X's. In case of four explanatory variable, Variance Inflation Function are VIF(X) = 1.297, VIF(Z) = 1.074, VIF(C) = 1.02, VIF(I) = 1.4577. Income is mainly responsible for the increasing the variance of regression coefficient or in other words income is mainly responsible for failure of ordinary least square estimate. As it loses its efficiency property.

Test of Multicollinearity

Farrar-Glauber Test for Multicollinearity: It is really a set of three tests, that is the authors use three statistics for testing for multicollinearity. The first test is a chi-square test for the detection of the existence and the severity of multicollinearity in a function including several explanatory variables. The second test is an F test for locating which variables are multicollinear. The third test is a t test for finding out the pattern of multicollinearity, that is for determining which variable are responsible for the appearance of multicollinear variables. We use second and third part for our analysis.

F-Test for the Location of Multicollinearity

$$F^* = \{R^2/(k-1)\}/\{(1-R^2)/(n-k)\}$$

where R^2 is square of multiple correlation coefficients (square of correlation between actual dependent variable and estimated value from the entire explanatory variable), n = size of the sample, k = number of explanatory variables.

Here total number of observations $n = 29$ and explanatory variable $k = 4$. Therefore, $F^* = 35.30$. Since, theoretically $F_{0.05}$ value with $V_1 = 4$ and $V_2 = 25$ degrees of freedom is 2.78 (i.e., $F^*_{0.05} > F_{0.05}$) we reject the null hypothesis, accepting the alternative that there is a significant between enrolment in higher education and the explanatory variables. Here null hypothesis is H_0 = There is no multicollinearity and alternative hypothesis is H_1 = There is multicollinearity.

T-test for Pattern of Multicollinearity

$$t^* = [(rx_ix_j{\cdot}x_1{\cdot}x_2\ldots x_k)\surd(n-k)]/\surd(1 - r^2x_ix_j{\cdot}x_1{\cdot}x_2\ldots x_k)$$

If $t^*>t$ we accept that the partial correlation coefficient between the variables X_i and X_j are responsible for the multicollinearity in function.

From the following table we conclude that only X and I contribute multicollinearity.

Table 10.1: Partial correlation value and significant level

Partial Correlation	*Value*	*t*-value*	*Compared with t* and table value*
r XI.ZC	0.515	3.504	t*>t
r XZ.IC	0.044	0.220	t*<t
rXC.IZ	0.098	0.495	t*<t
rIZ.XC	0.194	1.008	t*<t
rIC.XZ	–0.108	–0.546	t*<t
rZC.XI	0.069	0.347	t*<t

Obtained from above table only X I are contribute multicollinearity. Which is also statistically significant.

Selection of Regressors'

Generally, in empirical work the statistical model underline the data is assumed to known at the outset and the problem is merely obtained good estimates of the parametres in the model. In reality, however, the choice of a model is almost always made after some preliminary data analysis. Hence, for an econometrician model selection is a primary problem then comes chronologically the problem of selection of regressors. Suppose we have a multiple repressors' framework with *k* explanatory variable. $x_1, x_2, x_3, \ldots, x_k$. But we face the problem of elimination of some repressors'. Hence, step-wise regression is suggested which may be either backward and forward. In the first case we start with all the explanatory variables and gradually eliminate variables with *t*-ratios less than one. Because, in only one case t-ratio is less than one. We ranked *t*-values greater than one and eliminate accordingly.

In the second case we started with a single variable which had highest correlation with Y then pick at each state the variable with highest partial correlation coefficient. However, the backward selection procedure can help us in formulating droping variable method which is a solution for multicollinearity.

Table 10.2: Values of R^2 for different choices of the explanatory variables using Forward Inclusion and Backward Elimination

Forward Inclusion		*Backward Elimination*	
Function	R^2	*Function*	R^2
Y = f(I)	0.538	Y = f (X, Z, I, C)	0.811
Y = f(I, C)	0.721	Y = f (X, I, C)	0.808
Y = f(I, C, X)	0.808	Y = f (I, C)	0.721
Y = f(I, C, X, Z)	0.811	Y = f (I)	0.538

Conclusion

The best fit demand function is Y = *f* (X, I, C), this is also perfect in case of ODL system because income (I) which is also major contribute enrolment in higher education. In the Open system large number of student are engaged in different types of job and also earn income and they want to continuing education. So as per capita state income increases it is likely that job opportunity of the state also increases and private income of the people, especially that young generation increases. On economic ground income is the main motivating factor, but statistically it introduces some problems, we can also enquire whether other infrastructural development (media use, video conference, online admission etc.) are more effective in shaping up open and distance learning system.

Further scope of the study:

(1) If we can develop as simultaneous equation framework, then the main equation described above can be identified as demand function or supply function using the rank and order condition.
(2) The equation can be converted in ratio form to avoid the menace of multicollinearity.
(3) Other single equation problem like auto-correlation and heteroscadisticity should be properly considered.
(4) Using auto-regressive model it can be shown that previous enrolment in higher education significantly affects present enrolment in higher education. One can use Grangeur causality test in this context.

REFERENCES

Aich, A.B., (2010), Open and Distance Learning—The way to Access and Equity in Higher Education. *The Communications,* Vol.19, No.1, 45-52.

Draper, N.R. and H. Smith, (1981), *Applied Regression Analysis*, 2nd ed., Wiley, New York.

Koutsoyiannis, A., (1977), *Theory of Econometrics*, 2nd edition., MacMillan Press Ltd.

Maddala, G.S., (2005), *Introduction to Econometrics*, Wiley, New Delhi.

Mehta, J.S., P.A.V.B. Swamy and N.S. Iyengar, (1993), Finite Sample Properties of a Measure of Multicollinearity. *Sankhya* Ser, B., 56: 353-371.

Mishra, S., (2003), Human Resource Planning and Development for Distance Education in India, *University News,* Vol. 41, No. 46, November 17-23, pp. 8-13.

Rao, C.R., (1973), *Linear Statistical Inference and Its Applications*, 2nd edition. Wiley, New York.

Swamy, P.A.V.B., J.S. Mehta, S.S. Thurman and N.S. Iyengar, (1985), A generalized multicollinearity index for regression analysis. *Sankhya* Ser. B, 47: 401-431.

11

High Value Crop Production in Neighbouring Country of India

The Case Study of Nepalese Rural Village

Dil Nath Fuel

Introduction

Nepal is characterized by heavy reliance on subsistence agriculture sector like the other developing countries in the world (Adhikari, 2006). Agriculture is considered to be backbone of the economy and is the major source of livelihood of Nepalese people. A total of 74 per cent of the total population still depends on agriculture for their subsistence (NPC, 2010). The agricultural products contribute the country's 80 per cent of the total foreign exchange and contribute 39 per cent in GDP approximately (CBS, 2003). Among the agricultural products high value crops or cash crops like ginger, oilseed, sugarcane, tobacco, potato, cardamom and tea are no less important in our economy. These crops are used for local consumption and for earning foreign exchange (Takahatake and Maharjan, 2003).

The ginger (*Zingiber officinale* Roscoe) is a perennial root crop, lies on Zingiberaceae family. Its cultivation began in South Asia and has since spread to East Africa and the Caribbean. It is cultivated in almost all the tropical and subtropical regions of the world such as in West Indies, South America, West Africa, India South and South-East Asia (Panhwar, 2005). It is a product that grows underground the soil. The edible part is called rhizome, which is either fibrous or fleshy. Ginger is included different crop rotations and is also grown as a mixed crop or intercrop with maize and vegetables. A piece of 25-60 gm. young rhizome is used as a seed and is planted in *Phalgun-Baishakh* (February-April) and harvested in *Margsirsha* (November-December) of same year. It is generally cultivated on upland (*badi*). It is nutritious and export oriented agro-product. It has been exported in raw or dried form. It has been cultivated in Nepal since the long time. Ilam district is famous for ginger production in Nepal (CADP, 2008; Chapagain, 2006).

Ilam district is located in the easternmost part of Nepal is bordered by Panchthar in the North and West, Morang in the South-West, Jhapa in the South and Darjeeling district of West Bengal (WB), India in the East. This district is popular for commercial farming in cash crops, namely large cardamom (*alainchi),* ginger (*aduwaa*), broomgrass (*amriso*), potato (*aaloo*), round chilly (*akabare*), milk (*olan*) and tea of orthodox variety (Parajuli, 2011). These crops have been used by farmers to earn money in order to buy food and other necessities of life and thus increase their ability to achieve food security. It is important to note, however, that cash crops were introduced prior to the changes in government policies on high value crops. Thus, the pioneering nature of Ilam District makes it an interesting and important one to study (Takahatake, 2001).

This chapter brings the production approach of ginger farming in Ilam-adjoining district of Darjeeling, India. The contents of the chapter have been arranged into four sections. The present section provides the introduction, subject and context, rationale, objectives and hypothesis of the study. The second section presents the research methodology. The empirical findings with their interpretation are given in third section. Finally, findings and conclusions will be revealed in section four.

The Subject and the Context

In Nepal, 85.8 per cent of the total population resides in the rural areas and suffers from acute poverty and lack of basic needs (CBS, 2006). The poverty in Nepal is predominantly a rural phenomenon (LDTA, 2002) and it could be alleviated only by reforming in agriculture sector (NPC, 2010). The economic status of rural people could be increased by production and productivity of agriculture and livestock commodities in line with the requirements of farmers and other stakeholders.

The livelihood strategies for rural households include high value crop production and foodgrain production for own consumption can be the source of considerable cash income and provide a high degree of food security. It is the causative factor to the development of rural small towns and physical infrastructures. In all castes and religious groups alternative income strategies as commercial crop farming was adopted when the then prevailing strategies were scarce (Raithelhuber, 2001).

There are many options and opportunities are adapted to minimize the consequences of climatic change. The strategies would be more successful if they are identified and developed by the local residents. For this, the cash crop farming is found a successful attempt to minimize the effects and hazards due to climatic change (Khadka, 2011).

Ginger is one of the main cash crops for small-holders farmers in the village and most important crop in India (Indo-Swiss Project Sikkim, 2005). India, with over 30 per cent of the global share, now leads in global production of ginger, replacing China, which has slipped to the second position (~20.5%), followed by Indonesia (~12.7%), Nepal (~11.5%) and Nigeria (~10%) (http://en.wikipedia.org/wiki/ginger, 25th November, 2011).

It is quick growing, aromatic rhizome and is suitable for cropping in wide range of climate (Panhwar, 2005). Ginger has been farming since the long time for commercial and own consumption purpose. It is one of the major spices exported to international market from Nepal (CADP, 2007). India still remains only one foreign market for Nepalese ginger. The trend of raw and dried ginger export to India is given in figure 11.1, below:

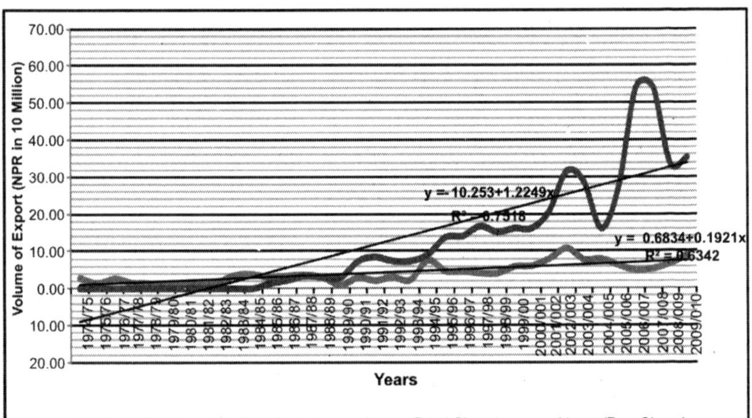

Note: NPR stands for Nepali currency, 1.6 NPR = 1 INR.

Data Source: MoF (2011).

Fig. 11.1: Dried and Raw Ginger Export to India (1974/85-2009/10)

More than 60 per cent of the total production of the country is exported to India as raw (fresh) or dried form and the remaining 40 per cent is for local consumption and seeds (CADP, 2008). The export of dry ginger (*sutho*) is less than the raw ginger. Around 75 per cent of the total ginger export (in monetary values) is comprised raw ginger and remaining 25 per cent is *sutho* one. Ilam is adjoining part of WB, India and main market for ginger (Takahatake, 2001). The ginger is a compulsory spice in Bengali food items, namely: tea, pulse (*daal*), curry, meat, fast foods, and fish. The crowded population of WB is the reliable consumer for Ilam produced ginger (Internee, 2002). The Ilam produced raw ginger is ultimately sold in Siliguri of WB, India. It is the main source of income for the district.

Ginger is better option for earning money in place of other cereal crops. The price of ginger is more attractive and the cost of production is lower than the same (ABTRACO, 2005). The government policy is supportive in ginger farming. It is the focal area for INGOs, local NGOs, community based organizations (CBOs) and cooperatives to boost up the rural livelihood. (Raithelhuber, 2001; Takahatake and Maharjan, 2003). There are scores of government and non-government agencies working to promote it.

For over 5000 years ginger has been recognized as the 'universal medicine' by the ancient Orientals of China and India. It is a component of more than 50 per cent of the traditional herbal remedies and has been used to treat nausea, indigestion, fever and infection and to promote vitality and longevity. It is effective in the treatment of illnesses and discomforts, namely: disorders, flatulence, nausea, intestinal infection, food poisoning, high blood pressure, chilblains, fever, clotting, motion sickness, morning sickness, cold and flu, arthritis pain, skin cancer, weight loss, thirst, depression, gastrointestinal disorders, bone fragility (Internee, 2002). In Nepal as an indigenous medicine it is used in common cold, menstrual pain, post-natal confinement, cough and other religious-*cum*-cultural occasions (Fuel, 2004). The rhizome of ginger is nutritious. Dry ginger contains 1-3 per cent essential oil, 5-10 per cent oleoresin, 50-55 per cent starch and 7-12 per cent moisture, with protein, fibre, fat and ash as its other constituents. So, it could be consumed for better health (http://en.wikipedia.org/wiki/ginger, 25th November, 2011).

To get returns from cash crops like broom-grass, large cardamom and tea takes 4-5 years after its cultivation, where as the returns from ginger is start after two months of its plantation (Pokhrel, 2011; Shrestha, n. d.). It is propagated through rhizomes, after 2-3 months of its plantation; the mother rhizome is retrieved and sold. After 9-10 months of its plantation, the rhizomes would be matured then it should be harvested

(Panhwar, 2005). In this way from the same bush, the product is obtained two times; is also the means of earning twice within a year.

It is found that the way of ginger farming is easier. Unskilled labour could be used in soil preparation, planting, mulching, weeding, harvesting and transportation up to collection centre in the selling process. It is as a part time employment opportunity for family member of the farmer. In some extent, it has blocked the labour migration from the village. Hence, involvement in ginger farming is now seen particularly for small holding farmers.

Ginger is not grown as sole crop. It is always grown in intercrop with maize and sometimes with legumes, and vegetables. It is also rotated with paddy, maize, potato and vegetables, which improve the physical condition of the soil. It is shade lover plant. It is most adapted cash crop having spread fibrous roots (Yadav *et al.*, 2004). It is observed that it the mulching is well understood by the farmers and is generally adopted practice in the study area. It is done immediately after planting using various mulching materials like dry leaves, straw, fodders. It protects the planted seeds from direct heat from the sun, maintained moisture in soil and protects to grow the unnecessary weeds. This way of farming is farmers' friendly, which preserves the fertility of soil and protects it from erosion.

Ginger is pungent by the cause of rich content of aromatic compound, called oleoresin and oils. Dry ginger contains 1-3 per cent essential oil, 5-10 per cent oleoresin, 50-55 per cent starch. Its rhizome is used as the raw material for culinary, beverage, confectionary, pharmaceutical and perfumery industries (http://en.wikipedia.org/wiki/ginger, 25th November, 2011).

In rural village of Nepal, the collection centres were established to sell the locally produced ginger. These centres were developed as a rural market, the point of economic transaction (Chapagain, 2006). For the transportation of this product human labour and animals were used. Gradually, the rural road and other infrastructures were built.

In conclusion, the cultivating subsistence and cash crops are interrelated and interlinked with ecological, social, economic perspectives and the better livelihood options for the villagers even at the adverse situation.

Rationale

Nepal is bordering by Republic of India in the South, East and West. It is a landlocked country with varying topography—mountain ranges in the north, hills in the middle and plains in the south. The country is often described as a country with a large rural population working in agriculture. It is the backbone of national economy, means of livelihood for majority of population, main source of GDP, income and employment opportunities. The high value crops are the important component of agriculture. It has potential benefits to improve the life of farmers. The ginger is main cash crop and has been ranging from mountains hills to plains (*terai*). It is cultivated for commercial purpose in more than 50 districts of the kingdom. Comparing to other cash crops, the ginger is easier to produce, because this crop is suitable for wide range of climate and be produced by labour intensive technique. Realizing this fact, the present study aims to fill a void in the ginger farming as a means of foreign exchange in Nepal.

There have been a number of theoretical and empirical works carried out at different times on high value crops. Very few studies have been conducted on ginger farming in Nepal. Almost all the theoretical and empirical works have been conducted for other high value crops of other districts/regions. It has not been taken as a principal high value crop in the government published literature. To the best of my knowledge, the production function of ginger rarely had been the subject of study in Nepal. In this context, the present study is the picture of productivity, production function, responsiveness of inputs to the output, marginal physical productivity, economies of scale and isoquant of ginger for the study area.

Objectives

The main aim of this chapter is to assess the importance of ginger as a high value export oriented cash crop of rural Nepal. The specific objectives of this study are:

(i) To estimate ginger production function in relation to four inputs: labour (L), farmyard manure (FYM), bullock labour (BL) and seed (S);
(ii) To calculate the responsiveness inputs to the output;
(iii) To find out the marginal physical productivity (MPP) of the different inputs: L, FYM, BL and S;
(iv) To investigate the economies of scale in production; and
(v) To predict ginger isoquant, isocline indicating marginal rate of technical substitution (MRTS) between two inputs: L and BL.

Hypothesis

The hypothesis of this study is that there is significant statistical relationship between inputs and output of ginger.

Research Methodology

In this section, the analytical foundations behind measuring production function and introduction of study area is elucidated.

Study Area

There are 3 Electoral Constituencies in Ilam district, comprising 11 Sub-districts (*Ilakas*), 48 Village Development Committees (VDCs) and 1 municipality (IDDC, 2011). Chisapani VDC, a rural hilly village of Ilam, Nepal has been purposively selected as study area. It is situated at a distance of 15 km south from Ilam district headquarters and ranges ~500 metre to ~950 metre from the mean sea level. The temperature is ranging from 8.6 degree Celsius to 35 degree Celsius and average annual rainfall is 330.5 millimetre.

The villagers of this VDC are involved in ginger farming commercially by which they got negotiable economic earning. More than 50 per cent of the total households had been cultivating ginger. Mainly, local medium size ginger is used to cultivate here. Rice, maize, and millet are the main crops. Socially diversified castes like *Brahmin, Kshatriya, Tamang, Rai, Limbu, Gurung, Magar* and other occupational (scheduled) castes reside in this area. This VDC has been selected because it is representative of the VDCs of this district in respect of soil, productivity, climate, other socio-economic factors and topographic features. Furthermore, this VDC being semi-rural one is characterized by traditional as well as modern farming methods.

Nature and Source of Data

This study is mainly based on primary data; field survey was conducted to collect primary data. All necessary data of inputs and output have been collected in physical units of local measurements like *doko/bhari*, at first hand with the help of pre-tested questionnaire then these were converted into standard units of measurement.

The prices of inputs and output have been computed approximately which was prevailing in the study area. The output was valued at the post-harvest period while other inputs were valued at the time of their use.

Data Collection Procedure and Sampling Size

Simple random sampling has been used to collect primary data. The total household of this VDC is 838. Out of these about 490 farm families are engaged in ginger production. All of these ginger producers constitute the population of this study. As a sample 99 farm families were drawn randomly by using random table as a representative of the total population. Thus, the sampling fraction is only 20.20 per cent.

To develop the idea, informal discussion and interview with key informant was done. The model farmers, teachers, village's elders, VDC's Office, VDC Secretary, technical staff of District Agricultural Development Office (DADO), Officers of Soktim Tea Estate (STE) and other knowledgeable persons were taken as the key informants. Formal and Informal discussion was carried out with different farmer group in different wards of VDC. Direct observation was carried out around the research sites for additional information and the field verification.

Secondary data were obtained from annual reports, newsletters, bulletins and relevant articles from DADO, STE, Nepal Agriculture Research Council (NARC), Tribhuvan University, Central Library, Nepal and internet.

Data Processing Procedure

For the processing of data and mathematical computation, scientific calculator and Statistical Package for Social Sciences (SPSS) package in computer were used. The equations of C-D production function have been estimated by using ordinary least square (OLS) method. The output of ginger (Q) was taken as endogenous variable; human labour (L), farmyard manure (FYM), bullock labour (BL) and seeds of ginger (S) were the exogenous or explanatory variables in the production function.

Choice of the Production Function

To calculate the elasticities of different inputs the renowned C-D production function and its log linear form have been applied (Koutsoyiannis, 1994). Because, it is easier to manipulate and is extensively used in agricultural sector for input-output analysis (Bhujel and Ghimire, 2006).

On the basis of above mentioned inputs, the C-D production function in non-linear form can be written as:

$$Q = b_0 L^{b_1} FYM^{b_2} BL^{b_3} S^{b_4} e^u \quad \dots (1)$$

where, Q = Total output of ginger (in NPR/*Ropani*)
L = Human labour (in NPR/*Ropani*)
FYM = Farm yard manure (in NPR/*Ropani*)
BL = Bullock Labour (in NPR/*Ropani*)
S = Seed of ginger (in NPR/*Ropani*)
b_i = Elasticities of inputs to be estimated, i = 0, 1, 2, 3, 4.

The linear logarithmic form of (1) can be written as,

$$\log Q = \log b_0 + b_1 \log L + b_2 \log FYM + b_3 \log BL + b_4 \log S + u \quad \dots (2)$$

And it can be expressed algebraically as,

$$Y = b^{+}_0 + b_1 x_1 + b_2 x_2 + b_3 x_3 + b_4 x_4 + u \quad \dots (3)$$

where, u = Disturbance term (as the value zero).

$$Y = \log Q, b^{+}_0 = \log b_0, x_1 = \log L, x_2 = \log FYM, x_3 = \log BL \text{ and } x_4 = \log S$$

[*Note: Ropani* refers to the area of 72 feet × 72 feet land, NPR Stands for Nepalí currency and 160 NPR = 100 Indian rupees]

Empirical Findings with their Interpretations

In this section, the empirical results of the study along with its economic analysis are presented.

Presentation of Models

There are seven models presented below:

Model-1

In this model, all the four independent variables were taken into consideration. The estimated production function in linear and non-linear forms are given as

Linear form

$$\log Q = 1.73487 + 0.27241 \log L + 0.39292 \log FYM - 0.0749 \log BL + 0.13142 \log S$$

Non-linear form

$$Q = 54.30877\ L^{0.27241}\ FYM^{0.39292}\ BL^{-0.07490}\ S^{0.13142}$$

The estimated results have been presented in the following Table 11.1:

Table 11.1: Estimated values of Regression Constant, Coefficients, *t*-Ratio, F-Ratio, D-W stat, R^2 and $\bar{R}^2$

Constant and Coefficients	*Values*	*Correlation*	*t-Ratio*
b_0^+(Constant)	1.73487 (0.84174)	—	2.061**
b_1	0.27241 (0.15156)	0.21447	1.797***
b_2	0.39292 (0.12230)	0.35700	3.213*
b_3	–0.07490 (0.21033)	0.3609	–0.356
b_4	0.13142 (0.20402)	0.23566	0.644

Multiple R = 0.41413 N = 99 d.f. = 95

R^2 = 0.17150 S.E. of regression = 0.28174

$\bar{R}^2$ = 0.13625 Mean of dependent variable = 3.85452

F^3_{95} = 4.86464* S.D. of dependent variable = 0.05985

D-W stat = 1.99866 (Standard errors are bracketed)

* Significant at 0.01 level

** Significant at 0.05 level

*** Significant at 0.10 level

In this model, the regression constant b^+_0 is positive and significant at 0.05 level. So, alternative hypothesis is accepted that $b^+_0>0$. That is, inputs have positive effect on output. The elasticity of input BL is negative and insignificant which may be due to the excess use of BL as required in ginger farms. Most of the farmers used own bullock often it is not considered to account in the survey. The regression coefficients of L and FYM are statistically significant at 0.10 and 0.01 level respectively. So, for b_1 and b_2 alternative hypothesis is accepted that $b_1 \neq 0$, $b_2 \neq 0$, but the null hypothesis is accepted for BL and S that $b_3 = 0$,

$b_4 = 0$. The elasticity of S is positive and insignificant, which may be due to the rotten, improper size, quantity, quality and not taken that account of self produced seeds.

The value of R^2 is 0.17150 which show only 17.15 per cent of the total variation of dependent variable is explained by independent variables. It indicates that excluded variables (explanatory) like mulching, pesticides, chemical fertilizers have been playing important role in ginger farming. The value of adjusted R^2 is 0.13625 and it means 13.62 per cent of the total variance in the dependent variable is explained by this model.

The value of F-stat is 4.86462 and is significant at 0.01 level. It leads to the acceptance of alternative hypothesis indicating significant relationship between output and inputs. The value of D-W stat is 1.99866 and is approximately equal to 2. It means there is no auto-correlation in the model.

Model-2

In this model the first independent variables L from Model-1 has been dropped out so that the production function with three inputs FYM, BL and S has been estimated. Then the production functions are:

Linear form

$$\log Q = 2.06364 + 0.37546 \log FYM - 0.02705 \log BL + 0.24679 \log S$$

Non linear form

$$Q = 116.04595\ FYM^{0.37546}\ BL^{-0.02705}\ S^{0.24679}$$

Table 11.2: Estimated values of Regression Constant, Coefficients, t-Ratio, F-Ratio, D-W stat, R^2 and $\bar{R}^2$

Constant and Coefficients	Values	Correlation	t-Ratio
b^{+}_{0} (Constant)	2.06463 (0.83110)	—	2.484**
b_2	0.37546 (0.12334)	0.35700	3.044*
b_3	–0.2705 (0.21107)	0.03609	–0.128
b_4	0.24679 (0.19593)	0.23566	1.260

Multiple R = 0.37819 | N = 99 d.f. = 96

R^2 = 0.14303 | S.E. of regression = 0.28503

$\bar{R}^2$ = 0.11597 | Mean of dependent variable = 3.84669

F^{3}_{96} = 5.28513** | S.D. of dependent variable = 0.06963

D-W stat = 2.07562 | (Standard errors are bracketed)

* Significant at 0.01 level

** Significant at 0.05 level

The estimated results have been given in the Table 11.2

In this model the regression constant b^{+}_{0} is positively significant at 0.05 level. Thus, we accept the alternative hypothesis that $b^{+}_{0}>0$. Only the coefficient of FYM is significant statistically at 0.01 level but the value is smaller than model-1. So, for b^{+}_{0} and b_2 the alternative hypothesis is accepted that $b_2 \neq 0$. But the null hypothesis is accepted for S and BL that $b_3 = 0$, $b_4 = 0$. This result shows that there is significant relationship between FYM and output. But the elasticities of most important input BL is negative and is insignificant which may be due to the less use of BL in ginger farming. The coefficient of S is positive but insignificant which may be due to the neglect of cost of self produced seeds of ginger. This may also the cause of rejection other essential variables like mulching, irrigation, chemical fertilizer, pesticides in the model.

The R^2 in this model is 0.14303 depicts only 14.30 per cent of the total variation of dependent variable is explained by explanatory variables. Similarly, the value of adjusted R^2 is 0.11597 and it means only 11.59 per cent of the total variance in the dependent variable is explained by this model.

The value of F-stat is 5.28513 and is significant at 0.05 level. It leads to the acceptance of the alternative hypothesis indicating significant relationship between output and inputs. The D-W stat is 2.07562 and it lies between du and (4-du). It indicates there is no auto-correlation with a first order scheme.

Model-3

In this model, the input FYM has been removed from model-1 and an attempt has been made to find out the relationship between output of ginger and the rest of inputs L, BL and S. The estimated production functions are:

Linear form

$$\log Q = 1.64008 + 0.23374 \log L + 0.09959 \log BL + 0.37304 \log S$$

Non-linear form

$$Q = 43.65962\, L^{0.23374}\, BL^{0.9959}\, S^{0.37304}$$

The estimated results have been given in table 11.3 below:

Table 11.3: Estimated values of Regression Constant, Coefficients, t-Ratio, F-Ratio, D-W stat, R^2 and $\overline{R}^2$

Constant and Coefficients	Values	Correlation	t-Ratio
b_0^+(Constant)	1.64008 (0.88153)	—	1.860***
b_1	0.23374 (0.18832)	0.21447	1.476
b_3	0.09959 (0.21293)	0.03609	0.468
b_4	0.37304 (0.19875)	0.23566	1.877***

Multiple R = 0.28377 N = 99 d.f. = 95

R^2 = 0.8053 S.E. of regression = 0.29524

$\overline{R}^2$ = 0.5249 Mean of dependent variable = 3.85362

F^3_{95} = 2.77336 S.D. of dependent variable = 0.06097

D-W stat = 1.95861 (Standard errors are bracketed)

*** Significant at 0.10 level.

In this model, regression constant b^+_0 is positively significant at 0.10 level. So, the alternative hypothesis is accepted that $b_0^+>0$. All the coefficients of inputs are positive but the coefficient of S is only statistically significant at 0.10 level. So, for b_4 the alternative hypothesis is accepted that $b_4 \neq 0$ but the null hypothesis is accepted for L and BL that $b_1 = 0$, $b_3 = 0$. This shows that there is statistically significant relationship between S and output, but for L, BL and output the relation is statistically insignificant. It means by increasing L and BL the output may increase but not significantly and *vice versa.* Which may be the cause of neglecting the other essential variables?

The value of R^2 is 0.08053, this indicates only 8.05 per cent of the total variation in the dependent variable is explained by explanatory variables. Similarly, the value of adjusted R^2 is 0.05149 and it means 5.14 per cent of the total variance in the dependent variable is explained by explanatory variables in this model.

The value of F-stat is 2.77336 and is insignificant, it lead us to acceptance of null hypothesis indicating statistically insignificant between inputs and output of ginger. The value of D-W stat is 1.95861, which is it is approximately equal to 2. It concludes there is no auto-correlation between variables.

Model-4

In this model, third independent variable BL from model-1 has been dropped out and the production function with three inputs L, FYM and S has been estimated. The estimated production functions are:

Linear form

$$\log Q = 1.55108 + 0.26558 \log L + 0.38167 \log FYM + 0.14734 \log S$$

Non-linear form

$$Q = 35.56968\ L^{0.26558}\ FYM^{0.38167}\ S^{0.14734}$$

The following table presents the estimated values:

Table 11.4: Estimated values of Regression Constant, Coefficients, t-Ratio, F-Ratio, D-W stat, R^2 and $\bar{R}^2$

Constant and Coefficients	*Values*	*Correlation*	*t-Ratio*
b_0^+ (Constant)	1.55108 (0.66190)	—	2.343**
b_1	0.26558 (0.14964)	0.21447	1.775**
b_2	0.38167 (0.11761)	0.35700	3.245*
b_4	0.14734 (0.19815)	0.23566	0.45

Multiple R = 0.41278 N = 99 d.f. = 96

R^2 = 0.17039 S.E. of regression = 0.28044

$\bar{R}^2$ =0.14419 Mean of dependent variable = 3.85581

F^2_{96} = 6.50369* S.D. of dependent variable = 0.05823.

D-W stat = 200781 (Standard errors are bracketed)

* Significant at 0.01 level

** Significant at 0.05 level

*** Significant at 0.10 level

This model is found some how different as previous models, because here only one coefficient is statistically insignificant. The regression constant b^+_0 is positively significant at 0.05 level, it means the alternative hypothesis is accepted that $b^+_0>0$. Similarly, the regression coefficient for L is significant at 0.10 level. So, for b_1 alternative hypothesis has been accepted. But the regression coefficient of S is positive but statistically insignificant so null hypothesis is accepted for it that $b_4 = 0$, this may be due to rotten of seeds, improper size, quality and self-produced seeds as the reasons of previous models-1 and 2.

The value of R^2 is 0.17039 reveals only 17.04 per cent of the total variation of the dependent variable is explained by explanatory variables. Again the value of adjusted R^2 is 0.14419 and it means that only 14.42 per cent of the total variance is explained by this model. F-stat is 6.50369 and is significant at 0.01 level. It leads to the acceptance of alternative hypothesis indicating significant relationship between output and inputs. The value of D-W stat is closer, to 2 showing absence of auto-correlation.

Model-5

In this model the fourth independent variable S has been deleted from model-1 and the production function with other three variables L, FYM and BL has been estimated. The estimated production functions are:

Linear form

$$\log Q = 2.08614 + 0.30313 \log L + 0.42196 \log FYM - 10458 \log BL$$

Non-linear form

$$Q = 121.93826 L^{0.30313} FYM^{0.42196} BL^{-0.10458}$$

The estimated values have been given in the following Table 11.5:

Table 11.5: Estimated values of Regression Constant, Coefficients, t-Ratio, F-Ratio, D-W stat, R^2 and $\bar{R}^2$

Constant and Coefficients	Values	Correlation	t-Ratio
b^{+}_{0} (Constant)	2.08614 (0.63923)	—	3.264*
b_1	0.30313 (0.14342)	0.21447	3.264**
b_2	0.42196 (0.11334)	0.35700	2.114*
b_3	−0.10458 (0.20459)	0.03609	−0.511

Multiple R = −0.40969 N = 99 d.f. = 96

R^2 = 0.16785 S.E. of regression = 0.28087

$\bar{R}^2$ = 0.14157 Mean of dependent variable = 3.85283

F^2_{96} = 6.38722* S.D. of dependent variable = 0.06193

D-W stat = 2.02169 (standard errors are bracketed)

* Significant at 0.01 level

** Significant at 0.05 level

In this model, the regression constant, regression coefficient of L and FYM are positive and significant, but the BL is negative and insignificant. The regression constant b_0^{+} is positively significant at 0.01 level. So, the alternative hypothesis is accepted that $b_0^{+}>0$. The regression coefficient of FYM and BL are positive and significant at 0.05 and 0.01 level respectively. So, for b_1 and b_2 alternative hypothesis is accepted that $b_1 \neq 0$, $b_2 \neq 0$ but the null hypothesis is accepted for BL that $b_3 = 0$. It means if the input BL increases then the output will decrease and *vice versa*. It is negative and insignificant which may be due to the excess use of bullock labour in ginger forms. This result shows that there is statistically significant relationship between L, FYM and output.

The value of R^2 in this model is 0.16785, which means only 16.78 per cent of the total variation of dependent variable is explained by explanatory variables. Similarly, adjusted R^2 is 0.14157 and it depicts only 14.15 per cent of the total variance in the dependent variable is explained by the explanatory variable in this model. The value of F-stat is 6.38722 and is significant at 0.01 levels. It indicates that there is strong relationship between inputs and output. The value of D-W stat is 2.02169, so the condition du< d (4-du) is fulfilled. It means there is no auto-correlation between the variables.

Model-6

In this model, only two independent variables L and BL have been taken into consideration with all 99 observations in order to estimate production function, to predict ginger isoquant, isocline, MRTS between them. The following are the production functions:

Linear form

$$\log Q = 2.77094 + 0.32524 \log L + 0.04445 \log BL$$

Non-Linear form

$$Q = 590.10595\ L^{0.32524}\ BL^{0.04445}$$

The following are the estimated values:

Table 11.6: Estimated values of Regression Constant, Coefficients, t-Ratio, F-Ratio, D-W stat, R^2 and $\overline{R}^2$

Constant and Coefficients	*Values*	*Correlation*	*t-Ratio*
b^{*}_{0} (Constant)	2.77093 (0.65191)	—	4.250*
b_1	0.32524 (0.15259)	0.21447	2.131**
b_3	0.4445 (0.21365)	0.03609	0.208

Multiple R = –0.21548 N = 99 d.f. = 97
R^2 = 0.04643 S.E. of regression = 0.29910
$\overline{R}^2$ = 0.02656 Mean of dependent variable = 3.83435
F^{1}_{97} = 2.33713 S.D. of dependent variable = 0.8506
D-W stat = 1.98023 (Standard errors are bracketed)

* Significant at 0.01 level

** Significant at 0.05 level

In this model, all the coefficients are positive. The regression constant is positively significant at 0.01 level. So, alternative hypothesis is accepted that $b^{*}_{0}>0$. The regression coefficient of L is statistically significant at

0.05 level, so for bi-alternative hypothesis is accepted that $b_1 \neq 0$, but the null hypothesis is accepted for BL that $b_3 = 0$. This result depicts that there is significant relationship between L and output whereas BL is statistically insignificant. This may be due to the less use of BL in comparison to L for ginger farming. The next cause may be due to not maintained the appropriate account of the farmers own BL in the ginger farming.

The value of R^2 in this model is 0.04643, it means only 4.64 per cent of the total variation of dependent variable is explained by explanatory variables. On the other hand, the value of adjusted R^2 is 0.02656 depicts 2.65 per cent of the total variance in the dependent variable is explained by this model. The value of F-stat is 2.33713 and is not significant. It means null hypothesis is accepted. It leads there is insignificant relationship between inputs and output. The value of D-W stat is 1.98023 and is closer to 2 indicates there is no auto-correlation with a first order scheme.

Model-7

This model is as model-1, but here linear production function has been used. In this model all inputs have been considered as explanatory variables. The estimated model is as follows.

The estimated linear production function can be written as,

$$Q = 4003.49995 + 1.07776L + 4.88802FYM$$

Table 11.7: Estimated values of Regression Constant, Coefficients, t-Ratio, F-Ratio, D-W stat, R^2 and $\bar{R}^2$

Constant and Coefficients	*Values*	*Correlation*	*t-Ratio*
b^*_0 (Constant)	4003.49995 (1759.31504)	—	2.276**
b_1	1.07776 (1.19829)	0.20145	0.889
b_2	4.88802 (2.19676)	0.31840	2.225**
b_3	–4.74886 (4.84658)	–0.04704	0.980
b_4	0.75300 (0.46344)	0.32446	1.625***

Multiple R = 0.39882 N = 99 d.f. = 95

R^2 = 0.15906 S.E. of regression = 4027.81475

$\bar{R}^2$ = 0.12328 Mean of dependent variable = 6213.82616

F^1_{95} = 4.44494* S.D. of Dependent variable = 2216.76730

D-W stat = 1.93723 (Standard errors are bracketed)

** Significant at 0.05 level

** * Significant at 0.10 level

$$-4.74886BL + 0.0753S$$

The estimated values are given in Table 11.7.

In this model, the value of regression constant is 4003.49995 and is significant at 0.05 level. So, alternative hypothesis is accepted that $b^{+}_{0}>0$. All the coefficients except bullock labour are positive. The regression coefficient of FYM and S are significant at 0.05 and 0.10 level respectively. But the regression coefficient of L and BL are positive and negative respectively and both are insignificant. So, for b_2 and b_4, alternative hypothesis is accepted that $b_2 \neq 0$, $b_4 \neq 0$; but null hypothesis is accepted for L and BL that $b_1 = 0$, $b_3 = 0$. This result shows that there is statistically significant relationship between FYM, S and output. But the most important input L is insignificant, it may the reason same as before only because of the tendency of using labour force in the ginger farming. This shows the situation of disguised unemployment. Similarly, the input BL is negative and insignificant means when BL increase the output will be ultimately decreases in the ginger production and *vice versa*. The cause of this both type of labours are insignificant may due to low technology and neglecting of other important variables.

The value of R^2 in this model is 0.15906 means only 15.90 per cent of the total variation of dependent variable is explained by explanatory variables. Similarly, the value of adjusted R^2 is 0.12328, thus, it depicts 12.33 per cent of the total variance in the dependent variable is explained by this model. The value of F-stat is 4.44494 and is significant at 0.01 level. It means the alternative hypothesis is accepted indicating that significant relationship between output and inputs. The value of D-W stat is lies in between du and (4-du), indicates there is no auto-correlation between the variables.

Estimation of Isoquant, MRTS and Isocline Equations

Isoquant Equation

To estimate isoquant equation we assumed output Q is fixed, then from Model-6 we get,

$$Q_0 = 590.10595L^{0.32524}\,BL^{0.04445}$$

Therefore, $L = \left[\frac{Q_0}{590.10595\ BL^{0.04445}}\right]^{3.074645}$

and similarly, $BL = \left[\frac{Q_0}{590.10595\ \ L^{0.32524}}\right]^{22.49719}$

Marginal Rate of Technical Substitution (MRTS) Equation

From model-6, the MRTS with respect to L and BL respectively are calculated as

$$\frac{\partial Q}{\partial L} = 191.92606\ L^{-0.67476}\ BL^{0.04445} \quad \ldots(1)$$

and

$$\frac{\partial Q}{\partial BL} = 26.23021 L^{0.32524}\ BL^{-0.95555} \quad \ldots(2)$$

From relation (1) and (2), we get the MRTs equations as,

$-\frac{\partial BL}{\partial L} = 7.31699\frac{BL}{L}, -\frac{\partial L}{\partial BL} = 0.13667\frac{L}{BL}$ respectively. The negative (–) sign indicates that the substitution in between BL and L to keep the Q at the same level.

Isocline Equation

By setting the MRTS equation equal to a constant k, we get the isocline equation for L and BL as; $L = \frac{k}{0.13667}BL$ and $BL = \frac{k}{7.31669}L$ respectively.

Returns to Scale

The sum of regression coefficients of Model-1 to 6 show the degree of returns to scale in production. The following Table 11.8 shows the nature of returns to scale of ginger production in the study area.

Table 11.8: Sum of Input Elasticities and the Nature of Returns to Scale

Models	b_1	b_2	b_3	b_4	*Sum of the elasticities*	*Returns to scale*
1.	0.27241	0.39292	–0.07490	0.13142	0.72185	DRS
2.	—	0.37546	–0.02705	0.24679	0.59520	DRS
3.	0.23374	—	0.09959	0.37304	0.70673	DRS
4.	0.26558	0.38167	—	0.14734	0.79459	DRS
5.	0.30313	0.42196	–0.10458	—	0.62051	DRS
6.	0.32524	—	0.04445	—	0.36969	DRS

Note: DRS stand for decreasing returns to scale in ginger production.

The highest and lowest sum of regression coefficients are 0.79459 and 0.36969 respectively. All these values are less than 1, it can be concluded that there is decreasing returns to scale operating in ginger production in the study area.

The Average Output and Inputs

The average output and inputs have been calculated by putting the average values of Q, L, FYM, BL and S in respective models are presented in following Table 11.9.

Table 11.9: Average Output and Inputs of Ginger (NPR per *Ropani*)

Models	*Q*	*L*	*FYM*	*BL*	*S*
1.	7153.52	834.06	457.47	303.37	2398.85
2.	7025.71	—	471.25	259.44	2696.82
3.	7138.71	967.82	—	332.92	2801.24
4.	7174.80	870.17	471.25	—	2621.94
5.	7125.74	870.95	471.50	259.99	—
6.	6828.89	870.93	—	260.73	—
Average	**7074.56**	**882.79**	**467.88**	**283.29**	**2629.71**

From the above Table 11.9, the average output of ginger is NPR 7074.56 (i.e. 813.87 kgs) per *Ropani* and the average use of L, FYM, BL and S are NPR 882.79 (i.e. 2874 man days), NPR 467.88 (i.e. 2026.88 kgs), NPR 283.29 (i.e. 3.8 bullock days) and Rs. 2629.71 (i.e. 267.55 kgs) respectively. These values differ in different, but not outstandingly. Thus, the average productivity (AP) of ginger in Study area is 0.813 MT per *Ropani* or 16.27 MT per Hectare is calculated, is little greater than the AP of ginger in Ilam of about 14 MT per Hectare.

The Marginal Physical Productivities (MPPs)

The MPPs have been calculated and presented in the following Table 11.10.

Table 11.10: Marginal Physical Productivities (MPPs) of Various Inputs

Model	MPP_L	MPP_{FYM}	MPP_{BL}	MPP_S
1.	2.49966	6.65906	–2.30626	0.40045
2.	—	6.36315	–0.83290	0.75200
3.	2.14482	—	3.06650	1.13669
4.	2.43699	6.46840	—	0.44896
5.	2.78155	7.15121	–3.22014	—
6.	2.98443	—	1.36867	—

The above table 11.10 depicts that in all models, MPP of FYM is positive and very high in comparison to other inputs. Therefore, it is better to increase the use of FYM to increase output of ginger. But the MPP of BL and S are insignificant in most of the models. The MPP_{BL} is negative in some cases. So, the quantity of BL and S should be decreased whereas the quantity of L and FYM must be increased for better output of ginger.

Findings and Conclusions

The findings and conclusions are presented here on the basis of previous sections for the policy prescriptions:

(i) Agriculture is the means of livelihood for Nepalese people. The agricultural products are the main source of foreign exchange and national GDP. Among the agricultural products, the cash crop or high value crop like ginger is cultivated for local consumption and for earning foreign exchange since the long time in the villages.

(ii) India is the main foreign market of Nepalese agricultural products. More than 60 per cent of the total produced ginger is exported to India as a raw or in dried form.

(iii) Ginger is nutritious, high impact, high value crop and could be used as spices, medicines, beverages, confectionaries, cosmetics and vegetables.

(iv) It is easier to produce and is suitable for wide range of climate and be produced by labour intensive technique. It is a reliable means for sustainable better rural livelihood in Nepal.

(v) The analysis of the previous chapter shows that L and FYM are most significant variables, so it is recommended to use more of these two inputs for produce more ginger relative to other inputs.

(vi) In most of the models and coefficient of BL is negative and the coefficient of S is small and insignificant. So, the BL should be shifted to L.

(vii) The value of R^2 is below 0.20 in all models. This is small value shows, the explanatory variables contribute below than 20 per cent to the output in the production process.

(viii) The value of D-W stat is around 2 indicates the explanatory variables are not auto correlated with the first order scheme.

(ix) In all models, the sum of the input elasticities being less than one show the diminishing returns to scale operates in ginger farming.

(x) The average values of four inputs (L, FYM, BL and S) and output (Q) differ in different models but not notably.

(xi) The average output of ginger in each model is higher than the district level average output.

(xii) The MPP of L and FYM are greater than one. Thus, it revealed no diminishing marginal physical productivities due to these variables. But for BL and S are less than one or negative indicates diminishing marginal physical productivities.

(xiii) Many important variables like mulching, to escape and sale of the mother seeds during the time of weeding, pesticides, chemical fertilizers, credit facilities, consumption pattern, time factor and other inter cropping crops like maize, vegetables, legumes have not been included due to limited availability of data and difficulties in computation. So, it is hope that in the future study these variables will be taken into consideration to know the actual status of inputs and output combination in ginger farming.

REFERENCES

ABTRACO, (2005), *Trade Competitiveness of Off-season Vegetables and Ginger in Selected Districts in Western Development Region of Nepal,* Report Submitted by Agri-Business and Trade Promotion Multipurpose Cooperative Limited (ABTRACO) to Agro-Enterprise Centre, Federation of Nepalese Chamber of Commerce and Industry, Teku, Kathmandu.

Adhikari, Damodar, (2006), *Towards Local Democracy in Nepal: Power and Participation in District Development Planning,* Spring Centre, Kathmandu.

Bhujel, Ram B. and Surya P. Ghimire, (2006), Estimation of Production Function of Hiunde (Boro) Rice, in *Nepal Agriculture Research Journal,* Vol. 7, pp. 88-97.

CADP, (2008), *Product Chain Study: Ginger,* Final Report, Commercial Agriculture Development Project (CADP), Biratnagar, Nepal.

CBS, (2001), *Population Census 2001*, Central Bureau of Statistics (CBS), National Planning Commission, Kathmandu, Nepal.

_______, (2003), *Population Monograph of Nepal,* (Vol. 1), CBS, National Planning Commission, Nepal.

_______, (2006), *Resilience amidst Conflict: An Assessment of Poverty in Nepal, 1995-96 and 2003-04,* CBS, National Planning Commission, Nepal.

Chapagain, Prem Sagar, (2006), Involution or Evolution? Conceptualizing the Changes in Farming System of Eastern Nepal, in *The Himalayan Review,* Vol. 37, pp.1-17.

Ellis, Frank, (1999), Rural Livelihood Diversity in Developing Countries: Evidence. Implications, in *ODI Natural Resource Perspectives,* No. 40.

Fuel, Dil Nath, (2004), Ginger Cultivation in Ilam: Patterns, Productivity and Problems (Nepali Version), in *Anveshan* (Journal of Tribhuvan University Teachers' Association, Mahendra Ratna Multiple Campus Unit), Ilam, Nepal, Vol.14 (3).

IDDC, (2011), *District Climate and Energy Plan: Ilam District,* Ilam District Development Committee (IDDC), Ilam, Nepal.

Indo-Swiss Project Sikkim, (2005), *Addressing Sustainable Livelihoods in Rural Sikkim: Experiences with Participatory Technology Development in Ginger Cultivation,* Intercooperation India, Programme Series 2, Intercooperation Delegation, Hyderabad, India.

Internee, Heidi Arnaudon, (2002), *An International Market Study of Ginger,* A Report to Micro-Enterprise Development Programme (MEDP) and District Ginger Entrepreneurs, MEDP, Nepal.

Khadka, Chhatra Bahadur, (2011), *Impacts of Climate Change on Production of Cash Crops in Annapurna Conservation Area: A Case Study from Lwang Ghalel Village Development Committee, Kaski,* Unpublished B. Sc. Forestry Research Thesis Submitted to Tribhuvan University, Institute of Forestry, Pokhara, Nepal.

Koutsoyiannis, A., (1978), *Theory of Econometrics,* The MacMillan Press Limited.

_______, (1994), *Modern Microeconomics,* (2nd ed.), The MacMillan Press Limited.

LDTA, (2002), *Poverty Reduction and Decentralization: A Linkage Assessment Report (2002),* Local Development Training Academy (LDTA), Lalitpur, Nepal.

MoF, (2011), *Economic Survey: Fiscal Year 2010/11,* (Vols. I & II), Ministry of Finance (MoF), Nepal.

NEFIN, (2004), *Protecting What's Ours: Indigenous Peoples' Initiatives to Biodiversity Conservation in Nepal (A Case Study of Lapcha Community from Ilam District of East Nepal),* National Federation of Indigenous Nationalities (NEFIN), Kathmandu, Nepal.

NPC, (2010), *Three Year Plan Approach Paper (2010/11–2012/13),* National Planning Commission (NPC), Government of Nepal.

Panhwar, Farzana, (2005), *Ginger (Zingiber officinale* Rosc.*) Cultivation in Sindh, Pakistan,* Digitalverlag GmbH, Germany

Pant, Shastra Dutta, (2000), *Aspect of Decentralization in Nepal,* (2nd ed.), Sajha Prakashan, Kathmandu.

Parajuli, Santosh, (2011), Socio-Economic Condition and Environmental Impact of Ilam Tea Estate—A Sociological Study, in *Mahendra Ratna Multiple Campus Research Journal,* Mahendra Ratna Multiple Campus, Ilam, Nepal, Vol. 1(1), pp. 128-135.

Pindyck, Robert S. and Daniel L. Rubinfeld, (1998), *Econometric Models and Econometric Forecasts,* (4th ed.), Irwin McGraw-Hill, USA.

Pokhrel, Bimala, (2011), Problems of Women Workers in Tea, in *Mahendra Ratna Multiple Campus Research Journal,* Mahendra Ratna Multiple Campus, Ilam, Nepal, Vol. 1(1), pp. 103-112.

Purseglov, J.W., (1968), *Tropical Crops: Dicotyledons,* Longman Group Limited, London.

_______, (1972), *Tropical Crops: Monocotyledons,* Longman Group Limited, London.

Raithelhuber, Martin, (2001), The Significance of Towns for Rural Livelihood in Nepal: Two Case Studies from Western Nepal, in *Contributions to Nepalese Studies,* Centre for Nepal and Asian Studies, Tribhuvan University, Nepal, Vol. 28 (1), pp. 35-52.

Shrestha, Yogendra Man, (n.d.), *Ginger Farming Technology,* Unpublished Paper, Namsaling Community Development Centre (NCDC), Ilam, Nepal.

Takahatake, Takashi, (2001), The Benefits and Problems of Cash Crops farming in Eastern Nepal: A Case Studies of Ilam District, in *Journal of International Development and Cooperation,* Vol. 8(1), pp. 127-126.

Takahatake, Takashi and Keshav Lall Mahajan, (2003), The Effect of Altitude on Crop Farming and Cash Crop Use in Ilam District: Some Implications for Agricultural Policy, in *Contributions to Nepalese Studies,* Centre for Nepal and Asian Studies, Tribhuvan University, Nepal, Vol. 30 (2), pp. 253-293.

UN-EUE, (2002), *Livelihood disruption in cash crop and surplus producing areas—Consequences of persistent low cereal market prices in Ethiopia,* United Nations-Emergencies Unit for Ethiopia (UN-EUE), Ethiopia.

Yadav, R.K., *et al.*, (2004), Commercial Prospects of Ginger Cultivation in North-Eastern Region, in *ENVIS Bulletin: Himalayan Ecology,* G.B. Pant

Institute of Himalayan Environment and Development, Almora, Uttarakhand, India, Vol.12 (2), pp. 4-8.

Zakka, U., N.E.S. Lale and V.C. Okereke, (2010), A Survey of Pests of Stored Ginger [*Zingiber officinale* (Rosc.)] in Some Selected Markets in Rivers State, Nigeria, in *African Journal of Agricultural Research,* Vol. 5 (18), pp. 2529-2534.

12

Prospects of Marigold Flower Cultivation in East Midnapur District of West Bengal

Joydeb Bera and *Sankar Majumder*

Introduction

A number of floricultural crops like Rose, Chrysanthimum, Gladiolous, Tuberose, Lotus, Marigold, Jasmine, Tagar, Jawba, Atasi, Belly etc. are grown in West Bengal. Among these flowers Rose, Chrysanthimum, Gladiolous, Tuberose, Lotus, Jasmine etc. are high-priced and are used mainly for festivals, social ceremonies and other aesthetic and decorative purposes. Whereas Marigold, Tagar, Jawba, Atasi etc. are low-priced and are used mainly for worshipping and religious purposes. Traditionally, these were grown in the homestead land. But now these flowers have become important commercial crops. Marigold is also common man's flower for decorative purposes. Among the commercial flowers, both in terms of area under cultivation and quantity of production, marigold occupies the first position in West Bengal. This chapter is an attempt to understand the prospects of marigold flower cultivation by analyzing (i) the economic feasibility of investment in marigold cultivation and its advantages over other major competing crops; and (ii) its employment generating prospects.

The duration of Marigold crop is six months. Marigold crop starts flowering after around two months from the planting period. There are three seasons for marigold cultivation: Summer season (January to June), Rainy season (June to November) and Winter season (September to February). But a farmer does not cultivate Marigold in a particular land during all the three seasons. The present study relates to Marigold cultivation during Winter season in the agricultural year 2007-08.

Methodology

The study is based on primary data. The important regions for flower cultivation in West Bengal are Kolaghat-Panskura region and Ranaghat region in the South-Bengal and Kalimpong-Darjeeling region in the North-Bengal. Kolaghat-Panskura region in the district of erstwhile undivided Midnapore was fore-runner in flower cultivation and was selected for the present study. This region now falls under the jurisdiction of newly formed East Midnapur district. Panskura I and Panskura II are known as the flower producing blocks and were selected purposively for the present study. Two Gram panchayats from each of these two blocks have been selected following the information from the Agricultural Development Officer (ADO) of these blocks regarding the concentration of flower growers in the constituent GPs under each block. Four separate lists of flower growers for each of these four GPs were prepared with the help of the panchayat members and the Krishi Prajukti Sahayak (KPS) of the concerned GPs. From each list 25 flower growers were selected. Thus, there were 100 sample flower growers. Out of these 100 sample flower growers 48 were engaged in marigold cultivation. These 48 sample marigold cultivators have been classified into four groups based on the total land holding of the sample farmers: Group I (up to 0.50 ha)—11 farmers, Group II (between 0.51 ha to 1.00 ha)—24 farmers, Group III (between 1.01 ha to 2.00 ha)—11 famers and Group IV (2.01 ha and above)—02 farmers. Simple statistical techniques like tables, averages, percentages, regression etc. have been used and the standard measures of costs and revenues have been followed.

Results and Discussion

The economic feasibility of investment in marigold cultivation has been analysed by considering its profitability and return from resource use. For profitability calculation, costs of and returns from marigold cultivation have been analysed. Its employment generating prospects have been analysed by considering the pattern and characteristics of labour used.

Costs

Table 12.1 exhibits the estimation of different cost concepts of and returns from the cultivation of marigold flower. From Table 12.1, it is observed that, on an average, per hectare cost of cultivation, using the concept of

Cost A_1 is worked out to be Rs.1,09,360. This cost varies from Rs. 97,101 (for Group I) to Rs. 1,21,033 (for Group IV). Using the concept of Cost A_2, where rent is paid for leased in land, it is Rs.1,10,065. Cost A_2 varies from Rs. 1,01,165 (for Group I) to Rs. 1,21,033 (for Group IV).

If imputed rent for the owned land and imputed interest for the owned fixed capital are taken into account, then the cost of cultivation of marigold for one hectare of land as per cost B concept becomes Rs. 1,24,081. This cost is minimum in case of farmers belonging to Group I and it is maximum in case of farmers belonging to Group IV.

Cost C is a business-like concept in which even the imputed cost of the family labour is considered. Value of cost C is Rs. 1,87,960 per hectare of marigold cultivation. Value of this cost varies from Rs. 1,80,296 for Group II to Rs. 2,01,918 for the farmers belonging to Group IV.

Farmers' marketing cost including labour cost for marketing is Rs. 24,404 per hectare. Marketing cost varies from Rs. 21,850 for Group III to Rs. 31,367 for Group I farmers.

Total cost borne by the farmers up to the point of selling the flowers in the market, is Rs. 2,12,364 for one hectare of marigold cultivation and it varied from Rs. 2,04,082 for Group II to Rs. 2,28,488 for Group IV farmers.

Return

Average gross return is Rs. 2,34,797 per hectare of marigold cultivation. Gross return varies from Rs. 2,27,781 for Group II to Rs. 2,71,739 for Group IV farmers. Gross return of Group IV is higher because some farmers in this group sell the flower directly in the main local market and city market at Kolkata where price is relatively high.

Profitability

Profitability of the crop under consideration is measured in terms of (i) surplus over cost, and (ii) gross return cost-ratio. These two measures have also been worked out on the basis of Cost A_1, Cost A_2, Cost B, Cost C as well as total cost including marketing cost.

Table 12.1 shows that, on an average, surplus over Cost A_1 concept is Rs. 1,25,437 per hectare of marigold cultivation. Surplus over Cost A_1 is lower for Group II farmers and higher for Group IV farmers. Surplus over Cost A_2 concept is Rs. 1,24,733 per hectare of marigold cultivation. This surplus varies from Rs. 1,17,682 for Group II farmers to Rs. 1,50,707 for

Group IV farmers. Surplus over Cost B concept is Rs. 1,10,716 per hectare. This surplus varies from Rs. 1,02,719 for Group II farmers to Rs.1,36,010 for Group IV farmers. Surplus over Cost C concept is Rs. 46,838 per hectare of marigold cultivation and it is highest for Group IV (Rs. 69,821) farmers.

Surplus over total cost including marketing cost which shows the return to management for his managerial functions which indicate costs of taking risks and uncertainties is Rs. 22,433 for one hectare of marigold cultivation. This is net return and it is lowest for Group I (Rs. 13,199) farmers and highest for Group IV (Rs. 43,251) farmers.

Table 12.1: Group-wise Cost (Including marketing cost) and Returns Analysis of Marigold Flower Cultivation by the Sample Farmers (2007-08)

(Rs. per Hectare)

Items	*Group-I (.01–.5ha)*	*Group-II (.51–1ha)*	*Group-III (1.01–2ha)*	*Group-IV (2.01ha–)*	*Overall*
1. Cost A_1	97101	110099	110902	121033	109360
2. Cost A_2	101165	110099	111219	121033	110065
3. Cost B	111464	125062	125494	135729	124081
4. Cost C	186753	180296	194209	201918	187960
5. Farmer's Marketing Cost	31367	23786	21850	26570	24404
Total Cost	218120	204082	216059	228488	212364
Gross Return	231319	227781	236233	271739	234797
Surplus Over					
(a) Cost A_1	134218	117682	125331	150706	125437
(b) Cost A_2	130154	117682	125015	150706	124733
(c) Cost B	119855	102719	110740	136010	110716
(d) Cost C	44566	47485	42024	69821	46838
(e) Total Cost	13199	23699	20174	43251	22433
Return Cost Ratio at					
(a) Cost A_1	2.38	2.07	2.13	2.25	2.15
(b) Cost A_2	2.29	2.07	2.12	2.25	2.13
(c) Cost B	2.08	1.82	1.88	2.00	1.89
(d) Cost C	1.24	1.26	1.22	1.35	1.25
(e) Total Cost	1.06	1.12	1.09	1.19	1.11
Net Return per one rupee of invstment	0.06	0.12	0.09	0.19	0.11

Return-Cost Ratio

Table 12.1 also showed that the ratios of gross return to cost at either of cost concepts is more than unity. The ratios are 2.15, 2.31, 1.89, 1.25 and 1.11 at Cost A_1, Cost A_2, Cost B, Cost C and Total Cost respectively. It indicates the remunerativeness concept of the marigold flower. Net return to management for his managerial function is Rs. 0.11 for one rupee of investment and it varied from Rs. 0.06 for Group I farmers to Rs. 0.19 Group IV farmers. Ratios of gross return to cost concepts (Cost A_1, Cost A_2 and Cost B) are higher for the farmers belonging to Group I. But ratios of gross return to Cost C and to total cost are higher for Group IV farmers.

Returns to Inputs in Marigold Cultivation

Cobb-Douglas production function in its log linear form has been estimated for the marigold flower for the following size groups of the farmers: (1) Group-I farmers (up to 0.50 ha), (2) Group-II farmers (0.51 ha to 1.00 ha), (3) Group-III and Group-IV farmers (0.01 ha and above); and (4) Overall Farmers (all the farmers taken together).

Form of the production function used is

$$\log Y = \log a + b_1 \log (L) + b_2 \log (M) + u$$

where, Y = value of production per hectare (Rs.)

L = labour input in value term (Rs.)

M = Material input in value term (Rs.)

a, b_1 and b_2 are the parametres; 'u' is the disturbance term.

Table 12.2: Estimated Production functions of Marigold Flower in different Groups of farm Families (2007-08)

Categories of Farmers	*Constant term (a)*	*Regression co-efficient*		*R2*
		Labour input (b_1)	*Material input (b_2)*	
1. Group-I (.01–.5 ha)	1.805** (2.538)	0.127 (1.271)	.599*** (4.605)	0.77
2. Group-II (0.51–1.0 ha)	3.049*** (4.25)	0.22 (1.407)	0.248** (2.095)	0.35
3. Group-III (1.01 ha above)	3.41** (2.459)	0.052 (0.384)	0.35 (1.272)	0.17
4. Overall farmers	2.867*** (6.315)	0.134* (1.737)	0.374*** (4.663)	0.42

Note: "t" values are given in parentheses.

"*","**" and "***" indicate levels of significance at 10%, 5% and 1% level respectively.

Value Marginal Productivity of Labour (VMPL) has been calculated by multiplying Labour input parametre (b_1) by the ratio of the geometric means of the output and labour input.

Similarly, Value Marginal Productivity of Material inputs (VMPM) has been calculated by multiplying the Material input parametre (b_2) by the ratio of the geometric means of the output and material input.

The results of the estimated production function (Table 12.2) show that there are decreasing returns to scale for all types of cultivators of marigold flower. This result indicates that for all categories of farmers overall efficiency of management in production and marketing tasks undertaken by them decreases. The prospects of marigold cultivation depend to a large extent on how the different aspects of managerial decisions are tackled by these flower cultivators. Farmers are becoming entrepreneurs. An increase in scale may come to a point where the abilities and skills of these farmer-entrepreneurs may be fully or over utilized. An increase in the scale beyond this point may decrease the efficiency of these entrepreneurs. This gives rise to diseconomies of scale. Another factor responsible for the diminishing returns may be the limitation of natural sources, *viz.*, soil quality.

The results of estimation of marginal productivities of different inputs for different groups of farmers are shown in Table 12.3. Values of the marginal productivity of labour input (VMPL) for all groups are positive, but well below unity implying diminishing return to labour input. This implies that the labour was paid much below its contribution. The values of marginal productivity of material inputs (VMPM) in marigold cultivation for different groups of farmers are greater than unity except for the Group-II farmers. Material inputs, therefore, appear to be under-used in marigold cultivation except for the farmers belonging to Group-II.

Table 12.3: Values of Marginal Productivities (VMP) of different Inputs in the Cultivation of Marigold flower in the different Groups of Farm Families (2007-08)

Categories of Households	*VMP of Labour (Rs.)*	*VMP of Material Inputs (Rs.)*
1. Group-I (.01–.5 HA)	0.43	1.63
2. Group-II (0.51–1.0 HA)	0.63	0.68
3. Group-III (1.01–above)	0.16	1.08
All Farmers	**0.41**	**1.05**

Human Labour Utilization in Marigold Flower Cultivation

Group-wise human labour utilization in marigold flower cultivation is shown in Table 12.4. It is noted that, on an average, 1,233 person days were used per hectare of marigold flower cultivation and it varies from 1,134 person days for Group II to 1,423 person days for Group IV.

Out of total labour use in one hectare of marigold cultivation, on an average, 912 person days (73.97%) are family labour and 321 person days (26.03%) are hired labour. So, marigold is mainly a family labour based cultivation. Out of total labour used by a group of farmers, percentage of use of family labour ranges from 66.41 per cent for Group IV to 93.24 per cent for Group I. Percentage use of hired labour ranges from 6.76 per cent for Group I to 33.59 per cent for Group IV.

Consideration of total labour (family plus hired) use revealed that 51.26 per cent is male labour, 47.77 per cent is female labour and 0.97 per cent is child labour. It is found that percentage use of male labour decreases with the increase in landholding size. It decreases from 61.27 per cent for Group I to 26.21 per cent for Group IV. Percentage of female labour use in marigold cultivation increases with the increase in landholding size. The percentage varies from 38.04 per cent for Group I to 70.20 per cent for Group IV. Child labour utilization varies from 0.44 per cent (Group II) to 3.58 per cent (Group IV) among the four groups of farmers. This shows that there is significant use of child labour.

Marigold farmers also undertake a part of marketing of their produce. Consideration of marigold cultivation and its marketing shows that on an average, 1,434 person days are utilized per hectare. Out of this 201 person days (14.02%) are for marigold marketing. Only family male labour is used for marketing purposes. 1,233 person days (85.98%) are utilized per hectare of marigold cultivation. Percentage of labour utilization in marigold marketing decreases as landholding size increases. Farmers having less amount of land under flower cultivation face a higher labour cost for sending his produce to the flower-market. This is because of the fact that at least one person is required to be engaged for sending the flower to the market, but the amount of flower that is handled by the person is usually much less than the amount which he can handle. Whereas the flower cultivator having larger area under flower sends much more flower to the market by engaging the same amount of labour. This implies that labour cost for sending the flower to the market remains lower for flower growers having large amount of land under flower cultivation

Table 12.4: Group-wise Human Labour Utilization in Marigold Flower Cultivation and its Marketing (2007-08)

(Person Days per Hectare)

(Person Days per Hectare)									
Categories of Households	*Total Labour*			*Total Labour*			*Labour for Marketing*	*Labour for Cultivation*	*Total Labour use*
	Family	*Hired*	*Total*	*Male*	*Female*	*Child*			
1. Group-I (.01–.5 HA)	1076 (93.24)	78 (6.76)	1154 (100)	707 (61.27)	439 (38.04)	8 (0.69)	307 (21.01)	1154 (78.99)	1461 (100)
2. Group-II (0.51–1.0 HA)	788 (69.49)	346 (30.51)	1134 (100)	615 (54.23)	514 (45.33)	5 (0.44)	211 (15.69)	1134 (84.31)	1345 (100)
3. Group-III (1.01–2HA)	982 (73.28)	358 (26.72)	1340 (100)	680 (50.75)	647 (48.28)	13 (0.97)	156 (10.43)	1340 (89.57)	1496 (100)
4. Group-IV (2.01–Above)	945 (66.41)	478 (33.59)	1423 (100)	373 (26.21)	999 (70.20)	51 (3.58)	156 (9.88)	1423 (90.12)	1579 (100)
Overall	**912 (73.97)**	**321 (26.03)**	**1233 (100)**	**632 (51.26)**	**589 (47.77)**	**12 (0.97)**	**201 (14.02)**	**1233 (85.98)**	**1434 (100)**

Note: Figures in the parentheses indicate percentage to total.

compared to that of the flower growers having small amount of land under flower cultivation.

Comparison of Marigold Flower Cultivation with Other Major Competing Crops

Cucumber, potato, mustard, cabbage, boro paddy, groundnut, brinjal and cauliflower are the crops which compete for resources used in the cultivation of marigold flower in the winter season.

The revenue pattern of marigold and other competing crops of marigold in four groups of farm families are shown in Table 12.5. In all the four groups, marigold earned higher gross return than the other competing crops. This indicates that marigold is a more income generating crop in comparison to the other crops here. It is also observed that marigold flower is more expensive in comparison to other competing crops (Table 12.5). In terms of return net of total costs concept, it is observed that marigold is highly lucrative (except for cucumber farmers of Group I farmers and cabbage cultivation by Group II farmers).

Farmers in Group I earned a net return of Rs. 13,199 per hectare from marigold cultivation, which is 0.24 and 1.81 times higher than that of the net returns from cucumber and from potato cultivation respectively. But farmers in this Group earned negative profit (Rs. –5,250 per hectare) from mustard cultivation though imputed value of family labour is Rs. 11,411. In this group, net return per one rupee of investment is high (Rs. 0.86) for cucumber cultivation, followed by potato (Rs. 0.11) and marigold (Rs. 0.06). But imputed value of family labour (i.e. family labour income) for marigold is Rs. 96,800 per hectare, which is 4.59, 25.15 and 8.48 times more than that of cucumber, potato and mustard respectively.

Farmers belonging to Group II earned a net return of Rs. 23,699 per hectare from marigold cultivation, which is 0.64, 5.81 and 74.29 times higher than that of the net returns from cabbage, potato and boro paddy cultivation respectively. Net return per one rupee of investment by this Group is highest (Rs. 0.33) from cabbage cultivation, followed by marigold (Rs. 0.12), potato (Rs. 0.05) and boro paddy (Rs. 0.01) respectively. Imputed value of family labour in marigold in this Group of farmers is Rs. 69,999 per hectare, which is 2.11, 6.25 and 8.29 times more than that of cabbage, potato and boro paddy respectively.

Net return from marigold cultivation by the farmers belonging to Group III is Rs. 20,174 per hectare, which is 39.49 and 34.30 times higher than that of the net return from groundnut and potato cultivation

Table 12.5: Comparison of costs of and returns from Marigold Flower Cultivation over other Major Competing Crops (2007-08)

Categories of Farmers	*Crops and Crop Rotation*	*Total cost Rs. per ha*	*Gross Return per ha*	*Net Return per ha*	*Return-cost ratio*	*Imputed value of family lab Rs./ha (cult +market)*	*Labour Utilisation (cult+mkt) Mandays per ha*	*Net Return per rupee of investment*
1. Group-I	Marigold	218120	231319	13199	1.06	96800	1461	0.06
(.01–.5 ha)	Cucumber	64365	119890	55525	1.86	21071	598	0.86
	Potato	63535	70827	7292	1.11	3850	249	0.11
	Mustard	32601	27351	–5250	0.84	11411	181	–0.16
2. Group-II	Marigold	204082	227781	23699	1.12	69999	1343	0.12
(.51–1 ha)	Cabbage	111586	148833	37247	1.33	33180	760	0.33
	Potato	74234	78311	4077	1.05	11200	235	0.05
	Boro	40981	41300	319	1.01	8440	177	0.01
3. Group-III	Marigold	216060	236233	20174	1.09	79622	1496	0.09
(1.01–2 ha)	Groundnut	33990	34501	511	1.02	9170	210	0.02
	Potato	75963	76552	588	1.01	10430	264	0.01
	Brinjal	185417	149915	-35502	0.81	56350	1305	–0.19
4. Group-IV	Marigold	228488	271739	43251	1.19	77098	1579	0.19
(2.01 ha)	Cauliflower	127565	150406	22841	1.18	42199	927	0.18
	Mustard	35776	25986	–9790	0.73	11877	210	–0.27
	Groundnut	34809	36106	1296	1.04	4480	213	0.04

Source: Primary Survey.

respectively. In this group, net return from brinjal cultivation is negative (Rs. –35,502 per hectare), but imputed value of family labour in brinjal cultivation is Rs. 56,350. Imputed value of family labour for marigold cultivation is Rs. 79,623 per hectare for this group, which is 8.68, 7.63 and 1.41 times than that of groundnut, potato and brinjal cultivation respectively. Net return per one rupee of investment is highest (Rs. 0.09) from marigold cultivation, followed by groundnut, potato with Rs. 0.02, Rs. 0.008 respectively.

Farmers belonging to Group IV earned net return of Rs. 43,251 per hectare from marigold cultivation which is 1.89, 33.36 times higher than the net return from cauliflower and groundnut cultivation respectively. In this group net return from mustard cultivation is negative (Rs. –9,790 per hectare), but imputed value of family labour is Rs. 11,877. Imputed value of family labour for marigold cultivation is Rs. 77,098 per hectare for this group of farmers, which is 1.83, 6.49 and 17.21 times higher than that of for cauliflower, mustard and groundnut cultivation respectively. Net return per one rupee of investment is Rs. 0.19 from marigold cultivation followed by cauliflower, groundnut cultivation with Rs. 0.18, Rs. 0.04 respectively.

Conclusion

The cultivation of marigold flower is very expensive. There is intensive use of human labour and especially family labour in marigold flower cultivation. Surpluses over different cost concepts are quite lucrative. Net return to management for his managerial function for one rupee of investment is significant. There are decreasing returns to scale for all types of cultivators of marigold flower. The prospects of marigold cultivation depend to a large extent on how the different aspects of managerial decisions are tackled by these flower farmers-*cum* entreprenuers. Percentage of use of female labour in marigold cultivation increases with the increase in land holding size. Marigold is a high income generating crop over other competing crops. Labour utilization in marigold cultivation and imputed value of family labour is highest in comparison to all other competing crops. Marigold being a common man's flower has high market demand and in a labour abundant and employment-scarce rural families in our rural areas this marigold cultivation is a good proposition.

REFERENCES

Sinha, M., Md. H. Ali, B.N. Banarjee and M.S. A. Choudhury (2008) "Economic Analysis on Production of Marigold Flower in Ranaghat Region of West Bengal," *Economic Affairs*, Vol. 53, Qr. 1, January-March.

Sharma, P. (2001), "Economics of production and marketing of marigold in Joipur District of Rajasthan," *Journal of the Agricultural Economics Research Review*, India, July-December, Vol. 14, No.2, 163-169.

13

Tank Irrigation in the Dry Zones of West Bengal

A Regional Analysis

Sebak K. Jana and *Amit Das*

Introduction

According to Tank Improvement Act (GoWB, 1967) "tank means a reservoir, or place which has been used as a reservoir, for the storage of water whether formed by excavation or by the construction of one or more embankments or place where water naturally accumulates, and includes any part of a tank and the banks thereof except such portions of the banks as are homestead garden or orchard lands." Tank irrigation, in certain parts of India particularly in the dry zones, provides a good alternative for irrigation development. Tanks can have a wider geological distribution than large-scale projects. Income distribution and employment generation effects are not limited to one area in case of tanks. Tank investments tend to be less capital intensive, have fewer negative environmental impacts and can better involve local communities in improvement and construction works. In spite of the advantages of irrigation development, development of tank irrigation deteriorated in almost every State in India. There are various causes behind this phenomenon.

Causes of Degradation of Traditional Methods

The main causes of degradation of traditional methods like tanks as has been observed in the literature are as follows (Dhawan, 1986; Agarwal, 2009; Shah, 2009; Palanisami *et al.*, 2007).

1. The massive increase in demographic pressure on land has contributed significantly to extension of cultivation to marginal lands, encroachment of common lands, government and forestlands, and deforestation. Deforestation of upper catchments aggravates soil erosion and siltation of natural drainage channels and reservoirs. Encroachment of tank foreshore areas and feeder channels and conversion of tank beds to residential and industrial sites are again due to growing demographic pressure.
2. The introduction of drilling methods and energized pumping permit tapping deeper strata of ground water enable larger volumes of water to be lifted per unit of time.
3. The construction of dams/reservoirs in the upper catchments results in a less quantity of water reaching the downstream tanks.
4. The faulty design features of the newly constructed tanks resulted in the low performance of the tanks (Narayanmoorthy and Deshpande, 2005).
5. The deterioration of traditional local systems is also due to the weakening of local institutions for maintaining the existing facilities and managing them.
6. Due to government emphasis on more convenient systems of centralized storage arrangements in the form of water reservoirs and canals, extension of traditional to individual beneficiary schemes by the government simultaneously lead to neglect of active community participation in maintenance of traditional systems.
7. Commercialization of agriculture and large-scale cultivation of cash crops give short-term profit, but create grave problems in the long-run.
8. As investment system of colonization period did not change; small systems of irrigation have neglected.
9. Expectation of instant benefit at the personal level generally discourages community cooperation in tank irrigation.
10. Inability of government agencies to consider water as a gift of nature for environmental management.
11. The control and administration has moved to a distant place making tank as a mere physical structure.
12. Emergence of livelihood patterns that are increasingly independent of tank based occupation.
13. Inadequate government expenditure for the construction/ renovation of tanks.

Trends in Tank Irrigation Development in India

The gross irrigated area in India was 5.276 crores hectares in 2003-04 which has been increased from 3.1103 crores hectare in 1970-71. On the contrary, the tank-irrigated area had decreased from 41.12 lakhs hectares to 19.43 lakhs hectares during the same period. The share of tank irrigated area has consistently decreased from 13.2 per cent in 1970-71 to 3.5 per cent in 2003-04. The share of canals has decreased from 41.3 per cent in 1970-71 to 27.5 per cent in 2003-04. On the other hand, the share of wells has increased from 38.2 per cent in 1970-71 to 64 per cent in 2003-04. The growth of tank-irrigated area in India was positive for the period 1950-51 to 1960-61, after that the growth of tank-irrigated area declined consistently for three consecutive decades and growth rate was positive in the decade of 1990s.

In Figure 13.1, we have presented that percentage share of irrigation by tanks in India.

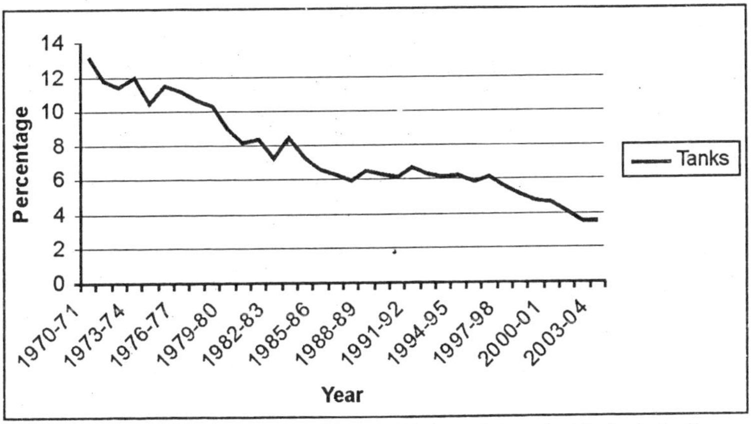

Fig. 13.1: Year-wise Percentages Share of Irrigated Area by Tanks in India.

Tank Irrigation in West Bengal

Out of 30.48 lakh hectares of irrigated land in West Bengal, source-wise irrigated land are as follows: Government canal—10.65 lakh hectares, Tubewell—11.53 lakh hectares, tanks—2.45 lakh hectares. District-wise share of different sources of irrigation in 2005-06 is presented in Table 13.1.

Table 13.1: District-wise Share of Different Sources of irrigation in West Bengal (2007)

	Govt. Canal	Tank	DTW	STW	RLI	Others	Total
Bankura	64	12.1	1.0	17.3	2.0	3.2	100
Birbhum	54.8	8.7	1.3	15.7	0.7	18.9	100
Burdwan	89.2		7.0	0.0	3.7	0.0	100
Coochbhar	1.6	5.5	20.9	47.2	13.4	11.4	100
Dakshin Dinajpur	–	36.9	22.3	20.2	20.6	0.0	100
Darjeeling	27.0	–	0.0	22.5	47.2	3.4	100
Hooghly	29.8		4.6	41.6	12.8	0.0	100
Howrah	68.8	17.4	5.4	3.9	4.5	0.0	100
Jalpaiguri	62.4	2.2	2.5	4.7	9.5	18.7	100
Malda	–	1.0	6.0	65.9	7.3	19.9	100
Murshidabad	16.1	3.8	5.4	0.2	5.4	69.1	100
Nadia	–	–	9.7	80.5	5.2	4.6	100
North 24-Parganas	4.8	9.7	4.9	70.6	7.6	2.4	100
Paschim Medinipur	21.7	8.1	10.6	37.2	5.2	17.2	100
Purba Medinipur	30.4	12.6	12.9	23.3	1.8	19.0	100
Purulia	42.0	39.3	0.0	0.0	1.8	16.9	100
South 24-Parganas	41.0	11.2	0.3	12.4	3.7	31.3	100
Uttar Dinajpur	1.8	4.1	6.7	82.8	4.7	0.0	100
West Bengal	**34.9**	**8.0**	**6.4**	**31.5**	**5.7**	**13.5**	**100**
% in WB	**34.9**	**8.0**	**6.4**	**31.5**	**5.7**	**13.5**	**100**

Source: *Government of W.B., District Statistical Handbook.*

The Table 13.2 shows the district-wise area irrigated by Tank of West Bengal during the period 2001-02 to 2005-06 (in thousand hectares). We pointed out from table 13.2 that area irrigated by Tank in Bankura, Purulia and Paschim Medinipur are 20.8, 22.4 and 26.4 thousand hectares respectively in the year 2001-02. During the above-mentioned period, the tank-irrigated area decreased in Paschim Medinipur but increased in Bankura and Purulia.

Though there is wide literature on irrigation in India, the study on tank irrigation in India particularly for the State of West Bengal is very limited. Sengupta (1985) emphasized that the knowledge of tradition is necessary to alter the distorted course of development in science and society under colonial rule. The book by Chiraneevulu (1992) discusses the problems of improvements of efficiency under conditions of tank irrigation in Andhra Pradesh and recommends for public policy for improvement of storage capacity. According to Sakthivadivel (2004) despite several state-sponsored tank rehabilitation programmes in many states, the number of tanks rehabilitated effectively is negligible as compared to the total number of tanks. The focus of the enquiry of Dhawan

Table 13.2: District-wise Area Irrigated Area by Tank of West Bengal in the Year 2001-02 to 2005-06 ('000 hectares)

Districts	*2001-02*	*2002-03*	*2003-04*	*2004-05*	*2005-06*
Bankura	20.8	24.9	26.7	32.4	33.1
Birbhum	40.8	40.5	25.4	25.4	25.3
Burdwan	—	—	—	—	—
Coochbehar	5.9	5.9	5.9	5.9	5.9
Dakshin Dinajpur	10.4	10.4	10.4	10.4	10.4
Darjeeling	—	—	—	—	—
Hooghly	35.2	33.3	33.4	37.5	37.5
Howrah	8.4	8.4	8.4	8.4	9.0
Jalpaiguri	2.3	2.3	2.3	2.1	2.1
Malda	1.3	1.3	1.3	1.3	1.3
Murshidabad	10.2	7.9	8.6	8.3	7.8
Nadia	—	—	—	—	—
North 24-Parganas	16.7	16.7	17.0	15.1	15.1
Paschim Medinipur	26.4	22.1	24.7	24.7	24.7
Purba Medinipur	40.0	26.3	26.3	26.3	26.3
Purulia	22.4	22.8	27.1	27.8	28.3
South 24-Parganas	34.3	35.7	40.0	34.7	12.3
Uttar Dinajpur	14.8	14.8	8.9	6.0	6.0

Source: Government of W.B., District Statistical Handbook.

(1986) is to highlight regional differential in tubewell expansion, within the plains of the Ganges and the Indus rivers. Anbumozhi, *et al.* (2007) observe that deferred maintenance of surface irrigation infrastructure over years has led to further deterioration of its physical service. According to Sreedhar (2007) while designing and implementing tank rehabilitation projects, it is important that these projects should be made an integral part of the poverty reduction programmes of the government because the decline in collective management of tanks would adversely affect the poorer sections and stricter rules of well irrigation should be implemented. The chapter of Chakravorty, *et al.* (1991) shows that in the presence of conveyance losses, efficient spatial allocation of irrigation water implies that the quantity of water applied should fall with distance from the water source. According to Palanasami, *et al.* (1984), government should establish demonstration tanks in different agro-climatic zones with successful experiments on tank investments as well as new management strategies. Shah (2009) argues that Integrated Water Resources Management (IWRM) paradigm of direct demand management is not feasible in informal water economies. The rise of a class of intermediaries, i.e. water service providers between users and natural resources of water is a precondition to meaningful demand management. The central research question of Shah (2003) is to understand how democratic the water utilization practices in tank irrigated areas are. Bardhan (2000) explores how inequality among members of an integrating community affects the success of community undertaking of collective tasks like managing tank irrigation.

Objectives, Methodology and Data Source

The main objective of the chapter is to investigate the different characteristics of tank irrigation in the dry zones of West Bengal. We have selected 181 tanks for our study. In order to examine the nature of the tanks, we select the study area to suit our purpose. The precondition for dry zones in the three districts of Purulia, Bankura and Paschim Medinipur did not allow us to adopt random sampling. We used purposive sampling procedure for the selection of blocks and villages. The blocks have been selected with the discussion of the officials of the departments of irrigation, Principal Agricultural Officer and other officials in the district. The villages have been selected in consultation with GP offices. But for the selection of tanks we have used random sampling procedure. Table 13.3 presents the number of districts, blocks, villages and households selected in West Bengal for our survey.

Table 13.3: Number of Districts, Blocks, Villages and Tanks Selected in West Bengal

Districts	*No. of blocks selected*	*No. of GPs/Municipality selected*	*No. of villages selected*	*No. of tanks selected*
Bankura	2	5	26	52
Purulia	3	8	27	60
Paschim Medinipur	6	14	49	69
Total Sample	**11**	**27**	**102**	**181**

Source: Based on Primary (Field) Survey.

The data used for this project has used both primary and secondary data though the work is based more on primary data. The primary data used in this study have been collected using the structured questionnaire during the period of 2008-09.

Tank Characteristics

Out of the 181 tanks surveyed the ownership-wise distribution of tanks are as follows in Table 13.4: Government-19, Personal-69, Community-77, Gram Samsad-13 and others-3. Therefore, the community ownership is highest in our sample followed by personal and Government. The percentage distributions of the whole sample are as follows: Government-10.5, Personal-38.1, Community-42.5, Gram Sansad-7.2 and Others-1.7.

Table 13.4: Districts-wise Number and percentage of Tanks by Ownership

Districts	*Government*	*Personal*	*Community*	*Gram Samsad*	*Others*	*Total*
Bankura	1	31	20	0	0	52
Paschim Medinipur	14	32	9	12	2	69
Purulia	4	6	48	1	1	60
Grand Total	19	69	77	13	3	181
		Percentage				
Bankura	1.9	59.6	38.5	0.0	0.0	100.0
Paschim Medinipur	20.3	46.4	13.0	17.4	2.9	100.0
Purulia	6.7	10.0	80.0	1.7	1.7	100.0
Grand Total	**9.7**	**38.7**	**43.8**	**6.4**	**1.5**	**100.0**

Source: Based on Primary (Field) Survey.

The percentages of tanks by types of irrigation have presented in the Table 13.5. As Table 13.5 shows, 62 per cent of the tanks are of dual in nature, i.e. both lift and flow irrigation types while 10 per cent of the tanks are of the only lift irrigation and 28 per cent of the tanks are of the only flow irrigation type.

Table 13.5: Districts-wise Percentages of Tanks by Types of Irrigation

Districts	*Lift Irrigation*	*Flow Irrigation*	*Lift and Flow Irrigation*	*Total*
Bankura	4	33	63	100
Paschim Medinipur	9	20	71	100
Purulia	18	32	50	100
Grand Total	**10**	**28**	**62**	**100**

Source: Based on Primary (Field) Survey.

We have divided the tanks by their nature into 6 groups. These groups are—Old Bund, Old Tank, New (NREGS), New (RSVY), New (BCW)

and New (Others). Table 13.6 shows that the distributions of tanks according to their categories are as follows: Old Bund—117, Old Tank—4, New (NREGS)—4, New (RSVY)—8, New (BCW)—1 and New (Others) —2. The percentage distribution of the different categories for the whole sample is Old Bund—65, Old Tank—27, New (NREGS)—2, New (RSVY)—4, New (BCW)—1 and New (Others)—1. All the new tanks under our survey have been constructed under some government schemes.

Table 13.6: Districts-wise Numbers of Tanks by Nature

Districts	Old Bund	Old Tank	New (NREGS)	New (RSVY)	New (BCW)	New (Others)	Total
Bankura	29	20	1	0	0	2	52
Paschim Medinipur	30	29	1	8	1	0	69
Purulia	58	0	2	0	0	0	60
Grand Total	**117**	**49**	**4**	**8**	**1**	**2**	**181**

Source: Based on Primary (Field) Survey.

We have collected the data about the actual area cultivated in the command area for all the tanks in our sample. Here, we see that in Table 13.7 the average actual gross cultivated area of the tank for the sample is 57 acres of which acreage for different crops are: Aman paddy –49.6 acre, Boro –0.9 acre, Others –5.3 acres. District-wise actual cultivated area per tank is presented in Table 13.7.

Table 13.7: Districts-wise Average Actual Cultivated Area (in acre) per Tank

Districts	Aman	Boro	Other	Total
Bankura	37.6	0.2	5.9	43.7
Paschim Medinipur	62.3	1.8	6.3	70.4
Purulia	48.8	0.5	3.6	53.0
Grand Total	**49.6**	**0.9**	**5.3**	**55.7**

Source: Based on Primary (Field) Survey.

In Table 13.8, we have presented that the average expenditure of reconstruction/re-excavation of old tanks/old Bunds upon the available data from our field survey. Here we see that the average expenditures are Rs. 3.41 lakhs, Rs. 1.54 lakhs and Rs. 2.8 lakhs in the districts of Bankura, Paschim Medinipur and Purulia respectively.

Table 13.8: Districts-wise Average Expenditure (in Rs.) of Reconstruction/ Re-excavation of old Bunds/old tanks

Districts	*No. of Old Tanks and Old Bunds*	*No. of Tanks Newly Constructed*	*Average Expenditure of Reconstruction/ Re-excavation of old Bunds/old tanks*
Bankura	49	3	341526.8
Paschim Medinipur	59	10	154045.4
Purulia	58	2	289894.1
Grand Total	**166**	**15**	**261822.1**

Source: Based on Primary (Field) Survey.

It is important to examine the land ownership patterns in the tank command areas in terms of caste and land holding size which are regarded as crucial determinants of collective action. The percentages for different castes for the whole sample are as follows General—30 per cent, OBC—30 per cent, SC—22 per cent ST—18 per cent. Therefore, the backward caste for the whole sample consists of 60 per cent. The district-wise caste composition in the tank command area is given in Table 13.9.

Table 13.9: Districts-wise Nos. and Percentages of Caste of Beneficiaries under Tank Command Area

Districts	*Number*				*Total*	*Percentage*				*Total*
	Gen.	*OBC*	*SC*	*ST*		*Gen.*	*OBC*	*SC*	*ST*	
Bankura	837	556	1000	401	2794	30	20	36	14	100
Paschim Medinipur	1478	1908	881	1285	5552	27	34	16	23	100
Purulia	1385	1185	798	458	3826	36	31	21	12	100
Grand Total	**3700**	**3649**	**2679**	**2144**	**12172**	**31**	**28**	**24**	**16**	**100**

Source: Based on Primary (Field) Survey.

We have divided the land classes into 7 categories. The percentage of beneficiaries belonging to these 7 categories for all the beneficiaries are as follows (given in Table 13.7): upto 0.5 ha –48 per cent, (0.5 –1) ha –33 per cent, (11.15) ha –12 per cent, (1.5 –2) ha –4 per cent, (2–2.5) -2 per cent, (2.5 –3) –1 per cent. So, 81 per cent of the beneficiaries are marginal. District-wise distribution have presented in the Table 13.10.

Table 13.10: Districts-wise Percentage of Beneficiaries by Land Distribution (in Hectare) under Tank Command Area

Districts	*Up to 0.50*	*0.5-1*	*1-1.5*	*1.5-2.00*	*2.00-2.5*	*2.5-3.00*	*Above 3.00*	*Total*
Bankura	58	31	9	2	0	0	0	100
Paschim Medinipur	50	35	10	3	1	1	0	100
Purulia	37	31	17	7	4	3	1	100
Grand Total	**48**	**33**	**12**	**4**	**2**	**1**	**0**	**100**

Source: Based on Primary (Field) Survey.

The average numbers of beneficiaries from tank irrigation for different land distributions have been given in Table 13.11. The land class-wise average number of beneficiaries for the whole sample are as follows: up to 0.5 ha –32, (0.5 –1) ha –22, (1–1.15) ha –8, (1.5 –2) ha –2.7, (2–2.5) –1.2, (2.5 – 3) – 0.9. Obviously, beneficiaries are mostly within the land class of (0-1) ha.

Table 13.11: Districts-wise Average Nos. of Beneficiaries Per Tank by Land Distribution (Hectare) under Tank Command Area

Districts	*Up to 0.50*	*0.5–1*	*1–1.5*	*1.5–2.00*	*2.00-2.5*	*2.5–3.00*	*Above 3.00*	*Total*
Bankura	31.3	16.5	4.9	0.9	0.0	0.1	0.1	53.7
Paschim Medinipur	40.1	28.1	8.0	2.5	0.9	0.5	0.4	80.5
Purulia	23.4	19.7	10.8	4.5	2.6	1.9	0.8	63.8
Grand Total	**32.0**	**22.0**	**8.0**	**2.6**	**1.2**	**0.8**	**0.4**	**66.0**

Source: Based on Primary (Field) Survey.

Tank Condition and Tank Performance

We have assessed tank condition on 5-point scale (Very good, good, medium, bad and very bad) for 5 parametres, namely the condition of

Table 13.12: Districts-wise Condition of the Tanks Based on the Scale Values

Districts	*Bund Condition*	*Enter water*	*Exit Water*	*Channel Maintenance*	*Desiltation*
Bankura	Medium	Good	Good	Very Bad	Very Bad
Paschim Medinipur	Medium	Good	Good	Very Bad	Very Bad
Purulia	Medium	Good	Medium	Very Bad	Very Bad
Grand Total	**Medium**	**Good**	**Good**	**Very Bad**	**Very Bad**

Source: Based on Primary (Field) Survey.

bund, system of entering water, exit system of water, channel maintenance and desiltation. In Table 13.12, we have presented district-wise condition of the tanks based on the average scale values for the above mentioned 5 parametres.

In Table 13.13, we have given the average of the area and depth of the sample tanks district-wise. Here, we see that the average area and depth are 6.7 acre and 8.4 ft in Bankura respectively, the average area and depth are 8.5 acre and 10.7 ft in Paschim Medinipur respectively and the average area and depth are 6.2 acre and 11.2 ft in Purulia respectively. The grand average of the three districts for tank area is 7.2 acre and for depth is 10.1 acre.

Table 13.13: Districts-wise Average Area (acre) and Depth (ft) of the Tanks

Districts	*Area (in Acre)*	*Depth (ft)*
Bankura	6.7	8.4
Paschim Medinipur	8.5	10.7
Purulia	6.2	11.2
Grand Total	**7.2**	**10.1**

Source: Based on Primary (Field) Survey.

Water in most of the tanks get dried out in the summer season. We have first calculated average availability of water measured in terms of months. As the water is used for some other purposes also like fishery and bathing, the availability of water for irrigation is less than average availability. We have calculated water availability and water uses for irrigation for the sample tanks by the number of months in Table 13.14. Here, we have seen that the average availability for the whole sample is 10.3 months and the water used for irrigation purposes for 6.2 months on average.

Table 13.14: Districts-wise Average of Water Availability (months), Water Uses (months) for Cultivation and Bathing

Districts	*Water Availability for Cultivation and bathing (months)*	*Water Uses for Cultivation (months)*
Bankura	9.6	5.8
Paschim Medinipur	10.2	5.9
Purulia	11.2	6.9
Grand Total	**10.3**	**6.2**

Source: Based on Primary (Field) Survey.

Table 13.15: Districts-wise Numbers of Tanks by Cultivating Crops in Tank Command Area

Districts	*Aman*	*Boro*	*Wheat*	*Potato*	*Seasmum*	*Mustard*	*Sunflower*	*Veg.*	*Onion*	*Cauli-flower*	*Gourd*	*Sugarcane*
Bankura	52	1	19	12	2	24	1	22	1	0	0	0
Paschim Medinipur	69	9	19	14	28	39	0	12	0	0	0	0
Purulia	60	2	34	11	0	16	0	34	5	3	2	2
Grand Total	**181**	**12**	**72**	**37**	**30**	**79**	**2**	**68**	**6**	**3**	**2**	**2**

Source: Based on Primary (Field) Survey.

Table 13.16: Districts-wise Percentages of Tanks by Crops in Tank Command Area

Districts	*Aman*	*Boro*	*Wheat*	*Potato*	*Seasmum*	*Mustard*	*Sunflower*	*Veg.*	*Onion*	*Cauliflower*	*Gourd*	*Sugarcane*
Bankura	100	2	37	23	4	46	2	42	2	0	0	0
Paschim Medinipur	100	13	28	20	41	57	1	49	1	0	0	0
Purulia	100	3	57	18	0	27	0	57	8	5	3	3
Grand Total	**100**	**6**	**41**	**20**	**15**	**43**	**1**	**49**	**4**	**2**	**1**	**1**

Source: Based on Primary (Field) Survey.

We have collected data for the 181 tanks about the crops that are grown in the tank command area. Twelve crops are seen to be grown in the tank command area of our sample tanks. Out of the 181 tanks surveyed, crop-wise numbers of tanks are as follows in Table 13.15: Aman—181, Boro—12, Wheat—72, Potato—37, Seasmum—30, Mustard—79, Sunflower—2, Vegetables—68, Onion—3, Cauliflower—3, Gourd —2 and sugarcane—2. So, the major crops in the tank command areas are Aman Paddy, Vegetables, Wheat and Potato.

The percentages of tanks for different crops have been calculated. The crop-wise percentage of tanks are as follows in Table 13.16: Aman—100 per cent, Boro—6 per cent, Wheat—41 per cent, Potato—20 per cent, Seasmum—15 per cent, Mustard—43 per cent, Sunflower—1 per cent, Vegetables—49 per cent, Onion—43, Cauliflower—2 per cent. Gourd —1 per cent and sugarcane–1 per cent. Therefore, Aman is produced in each tank command area, followed by vegetable, wheat, mustard and potato.

We have collected data about the price of irrigated and non-irrigated land. The difference between the two reflects the importance of irrigation. The irrigated land generally costs high compared to non-irrigated land. The percentage difference between the average price of irrigated and non-irrigated land have presented in Table 13.17. The average price of irrigated land for the whole sample is 55.0 thousands per acre, the average price of non-irrigated land is Rs. 32.0 thousands per acre and the percentage difference is 66. The district-wise percentage differences are as follows: Bankura—52 per cent, Paschim Medinipur—55 per cent and Purulia—92 per cent.

Table 13.17: Districts-wise Average of the Price of Lands (Rs. in thousand/ Acre)

Districts	*Price of Irrigated*	*Price of Non-Irrigated*	*Difference of Price*	*Difference in Price Percentage*
Bankura	26.2	17.3	9.0	52
Paschim Medinipur	50.4	32.4	18.0	55
Purulia	87.9	45.7	42.2	92
Grand Total	**55.0**	**32.0**	**23.1**	**66**

Source: Based on Primary (Field) Survey.

Presence of Associations and Name of the Associations

We have collected information about whether there is association or committees for the management of the tanks. Table 18 shows that out of the 181 tanks only 44 tanks are reported to have informal type associations and 137 tanks have no associations. In percentage terms 24 per cent tanks have water users' associations. The names of committees are different in different places. They are mostly informal and they have been created years back. The committees that we have are named as follows in Table 3.18. *Solo Ana,* Club, Gram Panchayat, *Gram Unnayan Committee, Sabar Committee,* and *Ansidar*. Out of the 44 committees, 23 committees are named as *solo ana* committees. As table 3.18 shows, Bankura district has the highest percentage of associations for tanks—46 per cent and Paschim Medinipur district has lowest percentage of association for tanks—only 9 per cent.

Table 13.18: Districts-wise Numbers of Tanks by Name of the Associations

Districts	*Solo Ana*	*Club*	*Gram Panchayat*	*Gram Unnayan Committee*	*Sabar Committee*	*Ansidar*	*Total*
Bankura	19	1	0	0	0	3	23
Paschim Medinipur	0	2	1	2	1	0	6
Purulia	4	0	3	0	0	8	15
Grand Total	**23**	**3**	**4**	**2**	**1**	**11**	**44**

Source: Based on Primary (Field) Survey.

Tank Efficiency

Water resources management reform occupies a prominent place in agricultural policy due to the scarcity of water resources and the associated issue of management efficiency. The objective of this section is to assess the efficiency of the irrigation tanks in our sample. We have used data envelopment analysis (DEA) for judging the efficiency of the tanks. The methodology was developed by Charnes, Cooper and Rhodes based on M.J. Farrel's contribution to productive efficiency. It is linear programming based technique for measuring the performance efficiency of a decision-making unit (DMU).

DEA models vary in the following ways: according to scale conditions these are constant or variable; according to the models orientation these models may be input or output oriented model and to the mathematical form of the objective function may differ like piece-wise linear, log-linear or Cobb-Douglas forms.

DEA models differ in the emphasis of their orientation (input oriented or output oriented) and on the assumption of returns to scale (CRS or VRS). Input-oriented DEA models tries to maximize the proportional decrease in input variables while remaining within the envelopment space (production possibility set), but output-oriented DEA models maximize the proportional increase in the output variables while remaining within the envelopment space. In other words input oriented technical efficiency is based on the question that how much output quantities be proportionally reduced without changing the output quantities produced. On the other hand, ouput oriented DEA is based on the question that how much output quantity be expanded without altering the input quantities used. Thus, the possible improvement of an inefficient DMU could be achieved by either focusing on a proportional input reduction or proportional output augmentation or both simultaneously. Under VRS the envelopment surface presents convexity as a consequence of the constraint ($1\lambda = 1$) in the model. It ensures that the inefficient DMUs are measured in comparison with those efficient DMUs on the efficient frontier operating at the same scale size as themselves, the efficiency measured is "pure technical efficiency" without considering the impact of the operating scale size of each DMU. The input-oriented VRS DEA model adopted in this study for input saving efficiency is an input-oriented VRS model as follows (Gang and Flemingham, 2002).

$$\text{Min } (\theta, \lambda, S^+, S^-)$$

$$TEc = \theta - \varepsilon\,(1s^+ + 1s^-)$$

$$\text{s.t. } Y\lambda - s^+ = Y_o$$

$$\theta X_0 - X\lambda - s^- = 0$$

$$1\lambda = 1$$

$$\lambda, s^+, s^- \geq 0$$

Where TEc is the cost technical efficiency score and the variable θ is the (proportional) reduction applied to all inputs of DMU0 (the DMU being evaluated) to improve efficiency, λ is the value of constructing a composite unit with inputs $Y\lambda$ and outputs $X\lambda$ outperforming DMU_0, ε allows the minimization over θ to preempt the optimization involving the slack variables s^+ and s^-, the variables s^+ and s^- represent the excess inputs and output slacks and are the distance between an inefficient DMU (X_0, Y_0) and its projected point on the envelopment surface of efficiency frontier. As can be seen, an input-oriented BCC model focuses on the maximal movement toward the frontier through a proportional reduction of inputs, given the output level.

Following the DEA methodology for input oriented VRS model we have derived the efficiency score of each tank (Coelli, 1996). Here, the inputs have been taken as the area and depth of the tanks and output of the tanks has been taken as gross actual command area of the tanks. We have first derived the efficiency scores of each tank and then we have calculated the average efficiency score of tanks for the different categories of tanks. In the following Table 13.19 we have shown the efficiency score of the tanks. The efficiency of tanks for different categories of tanks assuming constant returns to scale are as follows: Personal—0.65, Government—0.59 and community—0.56.

Table 13.19: Category-wise Performance of the Tanks by Scale

	N	*Mean*	*Std. Deviation*
Purulia	60	0.5393	0.199109
Bankura	52		0.600980769
Paschim Medinipur	69	0.6551	0.209833
Total	**181**	**0.6012**	**0.209929**

We have observed that efficiency scores of tanks differ widely across tanks. The difference in efficiency scores may arise due to physical characteristics of the region, socio-economic factors or water management differences. We have tried to find the determining factors for efficiency scores of tanks. The F value shows the significance of the overall regression.

Table 13.20: ANOVA

	Sum of Squares	*df*	*Mean Square*	*F*
Between Groups	0.431	2.000	0.216	5.114
Within Groups	7.502	178.000	0.042	
Total	**7.933**	**180.000**		

Note: b Dependent Variable: EFFSCORE.

Conclusion

Our results show that there is variation in terms of different parametres of tank irrigation like tank management, types of tanks, nature of tanks, Average Actual Cultivated Area, Reconstruction/Re-excavation cost, beneficiaries under tank command Area, average number. of beneficiaries per tank, condition of the tanks, average months of water availability, cropping pattern in the tank command area etc. In most cases we have observed no existence of water users association or committees (formal or informal) for managing the affairs relating to tanks. Tanks and groundwater should not be treated in isolation rather than to follow an integrated approach. The recent policy changes in water management have been limited to surface irrigation (canal and tank) and do not include groundwater. The tubewell irrigation should be made complementary to tank irrigation depending upon the groundwater availability. Sustainable development programme like agro-forestry should be practiced in the tank catchments area and tank bund. This will check the soil erosion. The details of all irrigation tanks should be with Panchayat Office. We have observed that in most of the GP offices records of the tanks in regard to exact location (mapping), area, depth, present condition etc. are not kept. The GP should take initiative to prepare the resource maps. The link between the irrigation department and the local people should also be strengthened.

REFERENCES

Agarwal, Anil *et al.*, eds., (2009), "Making Water Everybody's Business", *Centre for Science and Environment*, New Delhi.

Anbumozhi, V., K. Matsumoto and E. Yamaji, (2007), "Sustaining Agriculture through Modernization of Irrigation Tanks: An Opportunity and Challenge for TamilNadu, India". *http://cigr-ejournal.tamu.edu/submissions/volume3/LW%2001%20002.pdf.*

Balasubramanian, K.R. and N. Selvaraj, (2003), "Poverty, Private Property and Common Pool Resource Management:The Case of Irrigation Tanks in South India", Working Paper No. 2-03, SANDEE.

Bardhan, Pranab, (2000), "Irrigation and Cooperation: An Empirical Analysis of 48 Irrigation Communities in South India", *Economic Development and Cultural Change*, Vol. 48, No. 4, July, pp. 847-865.

Chakravorty, K.K. *et al.*, (eds.), (2006), *Traditional Water Management Systems of India*, Aryan Books International, New Delhi.

Chiranjaeevulu, P., (1992), *Tank Irrigation and Agricultural Development*, Kanishka Publishing House, New Delhi.

Dhawan, B.D., (1986), "Irrigation and Water Management in India", *Indian Journal of Agricultural Economics*, Vol. XLI, October-December, pp. 271-281.

Government of West Bengal, (1967), The Bengal Tanks Improvement Act, 1939 (As modified up to the 1st April, 1967).

Government of West Bengal, (2003), *The Statistical Abstract*, Bureau of Applied Economics and Statistics.

Government of West Bengal, *Economic Review*, Various Years.

Joy, K.J., *et al.*, eds., (2007), Water Conflicts in India, Centre for World Solidarity.

Palanasami, K. and K. William, (1984), "Irrigation Tanks of South India: Management Strategies and Investment Alternatives", *Indian Journal of Agricultural Economics*, Vol. XXXIX, April-June, pp. 214-223.

Palanasami, K. and K.W. Easter, (2000), *Tank Irrigation in the 21st Century*, Discovery Publishing House.

Rao, P. Narasimha, (2007), *"Irrigation Development—Issues and Challenges"*, Discovery Publishing House.

Sakhtivadivel, R., *et al.*, (2004), "Rejuvenating Irrigation Tanks through Local Institutions", *Economic and Political Weekly*, July 31.

Sengupta, Nirmal, (1985), "Irrigation-Traditional *Vs.* Modern", *Economic and Political Weekly*, November, pp. 1919-1938.

Shah, Esha, (2003), *Social Designs: Tank Irrigation Technology and Agrarian Transformation in Karnataka, South India*, Oriented Longman Private Limited, New Delhi.

Shah, Mihir, (2009), "Participatory Watershed Development: An Institutional Framework", in Anil Agarwal *et al.* (eds.) (2009), Centre for Science and Environment, New Delhi.

Sivasubramaniyan, K., (1994), "Decline of Tank Irrigation", *Economic and Political Weekly*, February 26.

Sivasubramaniyan, K., (2006), "Sustainable Development of Small Water Bodies in Tamil Nadu", *Economic and Political Weekly*, June 30.

Sreedhar, G., (2007), "Tank Irrigation Management in the Peril—Emerging Issues and Challenges", in Narasimha Rao, P. (ed.) (2007), *Irrigation Development—Issues and Challenges*, Discovery Publishing House

Vaidyanathan, A., (2006), *India's Water Resources, Contemporary Issues of Irrigation*, Oxford India Paperbacks.

14

Agricultural Efficiency and Levels of Development—A Pathway of Food Security for Rural People

A Study on Paschim Medinipore District

Subrata Kundu

Introduction

Today, India has been facing two most vital problems which are directly related to agriculture, the first one is to meet the swelling demand for food and other agricultural products, and the second is enervating the widespread poverty in rural areas by the ever-increasing population. The good performance in agriculture can diminish levels of rural poverty and meet increasing demand of agricultural products (Ahluwalia, 1978).

Agricultural productivity is a measure of the efficiency with which inputs are used in agriculture to produce an output. When a given combination of inputs produces a maximum output, the productivity is said to be at its maximum. The measurement of agricultural productivity enables a comparison of relative performance of farmers between farms, between the types of farming and between geographical regions. The comparison of productivity goes on to the heart of economic performance and can provide the guidance for planning and development decisions (Kravis, 1976). There are various scholars who have contributed different ideas, methods and techniques to measure the agricultural productivity, like Kendall (1939), Shafi (1960), Bhatia (1967), Khusro (1964), Singh (1979) and Sapre and Despanday (1964). The areas which experiences high land productivity may always have been leading agricultural regions, as witnessed by development of irrigation facilities (Dayal, 1984).

Swaminathan (2009) expressed that agriculture is not just a food providing machine but the backbone of the livelihood of sixty per cent of people of India. According to Datt and Sundharam (2009), agricultural growth has a direct impact on poverty eradication, health, nutrition of rural masses, national security and multiplier effect on entire economy. Peter Timmer (1988) argued that the growth in agricultural productivity is central to development. Agriculture is the largest sector of the nation which provides about one-fourth GDP, gives livelihood to more than sixty per cent of population and employs nearly 69 per cent of the total workforce (Ranganathan, 2003). Thus, the development of agriculture sector can serve up as a catalyst for rapid growth of whole economy (Maity and Chatterjee, 2006).

Recently, growing population as well as income enhances the demand for agricultural products and there is no scope for expanding land frontiers and further there is increasing trend of diversion of cultivable land for non-agricultural purposes (Deshpande and Bhende, 2003). It is estimated that about 260 million tonnes of foodgrains are to be produced annually by the year 2030 to meet the food requirements. However, the opening of the agricultural sector for foreign market creates new opportunities to the farmers in the form of enhanced demand and availability of better technologies. Unfortunately, the available evidence suggests that farmers in the developing countries fail to exploit full potential of a technology and/or enhanced market due to their inefficient production structure (Tayler and Shonkwiler, 1986; Ali and Flinn, 1989; Kalirajon and Shand, 1989; Bravo-Ureta and Evenson, 1994; Shanmugam and Palanisami, 1994; Sharma and Dutta, 1997 and Thomas and Sundaresan, 2000).

One of the important measures of overall resource use efficiency is technical efficiency. The ratio between the actual and the potential outputs is defined as a measure of technical efficiency of an economic decision-making unit in the literature and the production environment in which a farm/firm operates (social-economic characteristics) determines the variations in the efficiency levels of the firm household (Kalirajan and Shand, 1994). Improving Technical efficiency is important to reap the potential benefits of the existing technology, rather than searching for new technology (Kalirajan *et al.*, 1996).

This study attempts to measure the farm-specific technical efficiency of paddy cultivation using stochastic frontier methodology. This study also attempts to compare efficiency across different categories of farmers. The arguments advanced in this context, so far, are, however, highly unsatisfactory. Large farmers tend to diversify in order to alleviate risks involved in agrarian production. Small farmers with their limited resource ability concentrate only on a few crops. As such comparison between these types of farmers should involve inter-crop variation.[1] Secondly, while the regional effects are considered, the distinction between the so-called advanced and backward zones is not rigorous (Dyer, 1998). It appears that these distinctions are made on subjective basis with some *a priori* assumptions. However, in statistical sense, such distinctions must be based on the observed sample characteristics and derived from them properly.

The literature indicates that a range of socio-economic and demographic factors determine the technical efficiency of farms (Timmer, 1971; Muller, 1974; Kalirajan and Flinn, 1983). They include land use, credit availability, land tenure and household labour's education (Kalirajan and Flinn, 1983; Lingard *et al.*, 1983; Shapiro and Muller, 1977; Kumbhakar, 1992, 1994). Techniques of cultivation, share tenancy, farm holding size influence the efficiency as well. Some environmental factors and non-physical factors like information experience; supervision might affect the capability of a producer to utilize the available technology efficiently (Parikh *et al.*, 1995; Kumbhakar, 1992, 1994). In this study we attempted to identify the some socio-economic factors which are influence the technical efficiency at the farm level.

This chapter deals with all these issues in the context of some new data sets that is being available from rural India. The chapter proceeds as follows. In section (II), we give a brief description of the data used. Section (III) provides methodological framework. The SFA approach for measuring efficiency is elaborate in this section. Section (IV) provides the empirical results. Finally, in Section (V) the study is concluded.

Data Description

The present study is based mainly on cross-section data. The required information meant for the study was collected from the primary source. The primary data on various aspects relating to the inputs of production of the sample farms were collected through the personal interview method using suitably designed pre-tested schedule/questionnaire for the year 2009-10. These sample households were selected from four blocks (Midnapore Sadar, Garhbeta-1, Jhargram, Sankrail) located in Paschim Medinipore district in West Bengal, India. Selected sample areas are shown in Table 14.1. Blocks were purposively selected since it had varying socio-economic and geographical features. Total 250 sample farms were selected for collecting the required information for the study. The selected farms were stratified into following categories—Category A (below 1 hectare), Category B (1-2 hectares), and Category C (above 2 hectares). The frequency distribution of the sample farms according to the farm size group is given in Table 14.2.

Table 14.1: Selected Study Areas

Sl. No.	*Block*	*No. of Sample Farms Selected*
1	Midnapore Sadar	55
2	Garhbeta-1	70
3	Jhargram	50
4	Sankrail	75
Total		**250**

Table 14.2: Distribution of the Sample Farms by Size Group

Category	*Farm Size*	*Number of Sample Households*	*Percentage*
Category A	Below 1 hectare	150	60
Category B	1-2 hectares	60	24
Category C	Above 2 hectares	40	16
Total		**250**	**100**

This data set supplies information on various inputs like area, human labour, bullock labour, machinery, irrigation, seed, manure, fertilizer, plant protection chemical (PPC), miscellaneous expenditure and output of all the crops cultivated in both value and quantitative terms. The time period is one year. Information is also provided for other items of farm expenditure as well.

All these farmers are mostly paddy cultivators. They cultivate two varieties of paddy—a traditional variety (*aman*) cultivated in the monsoon and a modern variety (*boro*) cultivated in the winter season. This variety of paddy is a new introduction into the cultivation practice of this area. In this respect it is a *new* (or *modern*) variety of the paddy crop. The cultivation of this crop is essentially irrigation intensive. They, however, cultivate some other crops (such as mustard, beetle leaves, potato, wheat, oilseeds etc.) in very insignificant amount. These crops are so numerous and the sample size so small that it is impossible to calculate individual crop specific efficiency for these crops. Thus, we calculate efficiency of both the varieties of paddy.

Methodological Framework

Analytical Methods

The idea of measuring efficiency of firms was first proposed by Farrell (1957). He introduced the concept of frontier production function in measuring efficiency of productive units. A frontier production function refers to the maximum level of output that can be produced from a given set of inputs. Similarly, a frontier cost function provides us with the information about the minimum expenditure required to produce a given level of output at fixed input prices. Following these it is possible to define frontier profit function as a function that shows the maximum profit available at given levels of output prices and input prices. Specifying the frontier functions, Farrell measured efficiency of productive units through comparisons of the actually observed values of a variable and its frontier value, i.e. the value given by the frontier function.

The estimation of production frontiers has proceeded along two general paths: (i) deterministic frontiers—which forces all observations to be on or below the production frontier so that all deviations from the frontier are attributed to inefficiency; and (ii) stochastic frontier—where disturbance term consists of two components, one component representing technical inefficiency and the other representing the usual random noise. The advantage of the stochastic frontier over the deterministic frontier is that farm-specific efficiency and random error effect can be separated.

The stochastic production function of the *i*-th firm can be written in a modified neo-classical framework as follows:

$$Y_i^* = f\left(x_{i1,}x_{i2,}.....,x_{im}\right)\exp\left(v_i - u_i\right) \tag{1}$$

where, u_i represents the combined effects of various non-price and organizational factors which constrain the firm form obtaining its maximum possible output Y_i^*. In other words, exp (u_i) which is firm-specific, reflect the *i*-th firm's ability to produce at its present level, which is otherwise called the *i*-th firms technical efficiency. The values taken by *u* depend on the real situation that the firm faces. Nevertheless, an upper limit can be set for the value of *u*. When there are no socio-economic and organizational constraints affecting the firm, *u* takes the value zero. When the firm faces constraints, *u* takes the value greater than zero. The actual value of *u* depends on the extent to which the firm is affected by the constraints. The term v_i is, on the other hand, a pure random term varying $-\infty$ to $+\infty$. The presence of this term makes the production function (1) "stochastic".

One advantage of the above model is that it is possible to find out whether the deviation of a firm's actual output from its potential output is mainly because it did not use the best practice technique or is due to external random factors. Thus, one can say whether the difference between the actual output obtained and the potential frontier output, if any, occurred accidentally or not. If both the error terms are not distinguished in the estimation process, then OLS estimation can be carried out and it will give some sort of an average production function.

It is possible to estimate the stochastic frontier production function using the maximum-likelihood method.[2] Through maximum-likelihood estimator (MLE) approach, the source of the difference between the farmer's yield and that estimated by the frontier production was examined by calculating the variance ratio parametre (γ).

Now, let σ_u^2 and σ_v^2 to be the variances of the parametres one-sided (u) and symmetric (v). Therefore,

$$\sigma^2 = \sigma_u^2 + \sigma_v^2 \tag{2}$$

and the ratio of the two standard errors is

$$\lambda = \sigma_u / \sigma_v \tag{3}$$

Then variance ratio parametre (γ), which related the variability of σ_u^2 to the total variability, σ^2 is

$$\lambda = \sigma_u^2 / \sigma^2 \tag{4}$$

γ is defined as the total variation of output from frontier and can be attributed to technical efficiency. Hence, on the assumption that u_i and v_i are independent, the variance ratio from frontier (γ) has two important characteristics: (i) when σ_v tends to zero, then u is the predominant error in equation (1) and γ tends to one. This indicates the differences in the technical efficiency; and (ii) when σ_u tends to zero, then the symmetric error is the predominant error in equation (1), so tends to zero.

Thus, based on the value γ, it is possible to identify whether the differences between a firm's output and efficient output is principally due to statistical errors or firm's less efficient use of technology. The u_i

and v_i parametres of the production frontier equation were estimated using maximum-likelihood method. Further, given a multiplicative production frontier for which, the Cobb-Douglas production frontier was specified, the technical efficiency of the individual firm was estimated by using expectations of u_i conditional on the random variable E_i.

$$TE_i = \exp(-u_i);\ 0 < TE_i > 1 \tag{5}$$

Empirical Model

Various functional forms may be specified for the stochastic frontier production function, *viz*, Cobb-Douglas (C-D), Constant Elasticity of Substitution (CES), Translog etc. However, the C-D functional form is generally preferred in most published papers on technical efficiency because of its well-known advantages. Indeed, its purpose is to show what output of a given product will be achieved by different combinations of factors. As for example, we generally find the difference in net value product per unit of land associated with a difference in the amount of labour used per unit of labour. This may happen when we move from one farm to another (Brown, 1957). In principle, confining the analysis to this functional form can be somewhat restrictive. However, studies done by Kopp and Smith (1980) and Krishna and Sahota (1991) suggest that functional specification had a very small impact on measuring technical efficiency. Therefore, the following stochastic frontier production function of the Cobb-Douglas type was specified to estimate the technical efficiencies for individual farms and crops.

$$\ln Y_i = \alpha + \sum_{i=1}^{10} \beta_i \ln x_i + v_i - u_i \tag{6}$$

where, Y_i is the output of the *i*-th farm (in Rs.), α is constant term, β_1, β_2, ...β_{10} are parametres to be estimated and x_1, x_2, ...x_{10} are inputs area (in acre), human labour (in Rs.), bullock labour (in Rs.), machine (in Rs.), irrigation (in Rs.), seed (in Rs.), organic manure (in Rs.), chemical fertilizer (in Rs.), PPC (in Rs.) and miscellaneous expenditure (in Rs.) respectively. v_i is symmetric component of the error term and u_i is one-sided inefficiency component.

'*u*' takes the value of zero when the farmer is efficient and assumes the value greater than zero when the farmer is inefficient. Negative value of u varies depending on the level of inefficiency. The Maximum Likelihood Estimation (MLE) method enables us to obtain the maximum possible output function. It is assumed that u and v are independent and u follows a half normal distribution with variance σ_u^2 and v follows a normal distribution $N \sim (0, \sigma_v^2)$. The computer programme FRONTIER 4.1 was used to estimate the frontier and firm-specific technical efficiencies.

Determinants of Technical Efficiency

An attempt was made to identify the socio-economic factors influencing the technical efficiency at the farm level. MLE estimates of technical efficiency were regressed on a set of variables. As the technical efficiency variables varies between 0 and 1, the variable was transformed into ln [TE/1–TE], so that the latter transformed variable now varies between $-\infty$ and $+\infty$, which facilitates estimation of the parametres by using the OLS technique.

The following linear regression model was used to identify the socio-economic factors that condition technical efficiencies of sample farmers.

$$\ln[TE_{ij}/(1-TE_{ij})] = \alpha + \beta_1 X_{1ij} + \beta_2 X_{2ij} + \beta_3 X_{3ij} + \beta_4 X_{4ij} + \beta_5 X_{5ij} + \mu_i \quad (7)$$

where, TE_{ij} is the technical efficiency for i-th crop on j-th farm, α is constant term, β_1, β_2, ...β_5 are regression coefficients, x_1, x_2,...x_5 are farm size, rental value per acre of cropped area, proportion of family labour in total agricultural labour, caste dummy, ownership dummy respectively and μ is Error term.

Result and Discussion

Table 14.3 shows the Maximum Likelihood Estimates (MLE) results. In this study we have used area, human labour, bullock labour, machinery, irrigation, seed, manures, fertilizer, PPC and miscellaneous expenditure as input variables in the estimation of parametres. The Maximum Likelihood Estimates (MLE) is comparable to that of OLS results. The OLS function could narrate the responses of the average farms while the frontier function reflects the responses of the best and efficiently managed farm. From this table[3] it is observed that in case of traditional variety all independent variables considered have positive coefficients except seed, plant protection chemical. The variables area, human labour, bullock labour, machinery, manures and fertilizer were positively significant. These positive and significant values indicate that there is scope for increasing production of traditional variety by increasing the level of these inputs. Coefficient value of seed was –0.139, which was significant at 5 per cent level. This gives an indication that farmers are using excess seed in traditional variety production.

In case of modern variety the explanatory variables area, seed, miscellaneous expenditure had a positive and significant influence on the production. These positive and significant values indicate that there

Table 14.3: Parametre Estimates of Stochastic Frontier Function

Variables	*Maximum Likelihood Estimates*	
	Traditional variety	*Modern variety*
Intercept	6.16 (8.16)*	8.59 (10.44)*
Area	0.603 (5.69)*	0.935 (9.60)*
Human Labour	.0383 (4.76)*	0.041 (0.469)
Bullock Labour	0.019 (1.82)**	–0.062 (–3.52)*
Machine Charge	0.018 (1.49)	–0.017 (1.08)
Irrigation Charge	0.016 (1.24)	0.023 (0.798)
Seed	–0.107 (–1.55)	0.139 (4.68)*
Manures	0.023 (2.19)**	–0.002 (–0.114)
Fertilizer	0.068 (4.43)*	–0.052 (–0.716)
PPC	–0.023 (–2.21)**	–0.022 (–1.14)
Misc. Charge	0.003 (0.213)	0.002 (2.88)*
$\sum \beta_i$	1.023	0.995
Sigma Squared (σ^2)	0.078 (4.48)*	0.116 (3.04)*
σ_u^2	0.061	0.092
σ_v^2	0.018	0.024
$\lambda = \sigma_u/\sigma_v$	1.84	1.95
Gamma $(\gamma = \sigma_u^2/\sigma^2)$	0.776 (6.70)*	0.795 (4.19)*
Log Likelihood Function	26.56	2.58

Source: Author's Estimation.

is scope for increasing production of modern variety by increasing the level of these inputs. Again the negativity of the animal labour signifies its diminishing importance in furthering efficiency. Coefficient value of bullock labour was –0.062, which was significant at 1 per cent level. This gives an indication that farmers are using excess bullock labour in modern variety production. However, this might only imply substitution of animal. Similarly, one can contrast the negativity of the variable "seed" in traditional varieties while its positivity in the modern variety. Similarly is the positive nature of fertilizer, machine, labour and irrigation in the traditional variety. Their insignificance in modern variety merely reflects that they are almost necessary ingredient for this variety resulting in negligible sample variances in its use.

The regression coefficients in the Cobb-Douglas production function are the production elasticity and their sum ($\Sigma\beta_i$) indicates the return to scale. When ($\Sigma\beta_i$) = 1 there is constant returns to scale, when ($\Sigma\beta_i$) >1 there is increasing returns to scale and when ($\Sigma\beta_i$) < 1 there is decreasing returns to scale. The sum of the regression coefficients for traditional variety and modern variety were 1.023 and 0.995 respectively. For statistical reliability of the results we test the *F*—statistics and we see that in case of traditional variety farms are operated at increasing returns to scale and in case of modern variety farms are operated at constant returns to scale.

The estimated values of σ_u^2 is higher than the estimated values of σ_u^2 for both traditional variety and modern variety. The higher magnitude of σ_u^2 indicated that the difference between the realized output and the frontier output was more due to inefficiency use of resources at the disposal of the farmer. Here, 'λ' is the ratio of variance of the farm-specific production behaviour σ_u^2 to the variance of the statistical noise σ_v^2. The values of 'λ' for all the crops under indicating that one-sided error component had dominated relatively to symmetric error component.

The variance ratio 'λ' showed that firm specific variability contributed more to the variation in production among firms, which means that the total variation in output from the frontier is attributable to the technical efficiency. The estimate 'γ' which is the ratio of the variance of the firm specific performance of economic efficiency to total variance of output was 0.78 for traditional variety, indicates the presence of significant inefficiency in the production of the crop. In other words, about 78 per cent of the difference between the observed and the frontier output was mainly due to the inefficiency use of resources, which are under the control of the sample farmers. Similarly, in case of modern variety about 79 per cent of the difference between the observed and the frontier output was mainly due to the inefficiency use of resources, which are under the control of the sample farmers.

Technical Efficiency of Paddy

Traditional Variety

Table 14.4 shows the frequency distribution of estimated technical efficiency and Table 14.5 shows the summary statistics of the efficiency measures for the sample households by firm size class as well as for the sample as a whole. From these tables it was observed that technical efficiency of sample farms ranged between 45 and 96 per cent with an average of 72 per cent. This analysis indicates that the output can be raised by 28 per cent by following efficient crop management practices without having to increase the level of application of input.

Table 14.4: Technical Efficiency by Firm Size Group—Traditional Variety (households in %)

Levels of T.E. (%)	*Farm Size Group*			
	Category A (below 1 hectare)	*Category B (1-2 hectares)*	*Category C (above 2 hectares)*	*All*
< 50	11	12	16	14
50-70	25	24	30	25
70-90	42	39	36	39
> 90	22	25	18	22
Sample Size	150	60	40	250

Table 14.5: Summary Statistics of the Efficiency Measures—Traditional Variety

Variable	*Farm Size Group*			
	Category A (below 1 hectare)	*Category B (1-2 hectare)*	*Category C (above 2 hectare)*	*All*
Mean	0.82	0.75	0.71	0.72
Standard Deviation	0.09	0.094	0.058	0.086
Sample Variance	0.007	0.008	0.005	0.007
Kurtosis	6.03	3.34	–0.24	4.17
Skewness	–1.97	–1.36	–1.07	–1.65
Minimum	0.45	0.51	0.58	0.45
Maximum	0.96	0.92	0.87	0.96

It was also observed that about 14 per cent of the farmers were harvesting less than 50 per cent of the frontier output whereas, about 22 per cent were harvesting more than 90 per cent of the frontier output. It was also observed that most of the farmers (64%) operated at the efficiency levels between 50 and 90 per cent. Mean technical efficiency ranged from 0.71 on Category C to 0.82 on Category A farms. In average Category A farms are more efficient than the other categories.

Modern Variety

Table 14.6 shows the frequency distribution of estimated technical efficiency and Table 14.7 shows the summary statistics of the efficiency measures for the sample households by firm size class as well as for the sample as a whole. From these tables it was observed that technical efficiency of sample farms ranged between 42 and 98 per cent with an average of 76 per cent. This analysis indicates the scope to increase

Table 14.6: Technical Efficiency by Firm Size Group—Moderen Variety (Households in %)

Levels of T.E. (%)	*Farm Size Group*			
	Category A (below 1 hectare)	*Category B (1-2 hectares)*	*Category C (above 2hectares)*	*All*
< 50	14	13	15	17
50-70	26	28	32	24
70-90	45	45	28	45
> 90	15	14	25	14
Sample Size	150	60	40	250

Table 14.7: Summary Statistics of the Efficiency Measures—Moderen Variety

Variable	*Farm Size Group*			
	Category A (below 1 hectare)	*Category B (1-2 hectares)*	*Category C (above 2 hectares)*	*All*
Mean	0.72	0.77	0.86	0.76
Standard Deviation	0.12	0.08	0.07	0.104
Sample Variance	0.013	0.005	0.003	0.012
Kurtosis	2.74	–0.68	0.003	2.86
Skewness	–1.41	–0.38	–0.64	–1.34
Minimum	0.42	0.45	0.58	0.42
Maximum	0.89	0.98	0.82	0.98

physical production of modern variety by 24 per cent with the judicious use of existing resources and technology.

It was also observed that the highest number of farms (45%) was found in 70-90 per cent class followed by 50-70 per cent class (24%). The lowest number of farms (14%) was found in more than 90 per cent class. The highest mean technical efficiency was found in Category C (86%) followed by Category B (77%).

Determinants of Technical Efficiency

The effect of each factor on technical efficiency is given in Table 4.8. From this table we observed that the model explained the variation in technical efficiency on sample farms (in terms of R^2) ranging from 51 per cent for modern variety to 58 per cent for traditional variety. The results provide farm size was negatively related with the technical efficiency and coefficient was statistically significant for traditional variety. Rental value per acre of gross cropped area was positively related with the technical efficiency and coefficient was statistically significant. It can be inferred that technical efficiency was influenced by the quality of land as rental value was assumed to reflect the land/soil quality (better land commands higher rent). The contribution of family labour to technical

Table 14.8: Socio-economic Determinants of Technical Efficiency

Variables	*Crops*	
	Traditional variety	*Modern variety*
Intercept	1.31 (5.76)*	1.45 (4.92)*
Farm Size	–0.056 (–1.68)**	–0.008 (–0.098)
Rental value of land	0.001 (11.28)*	0.001 (9.03)*
Percentage of family labour in total labour	–0.004 (–2.54)*	–0.002 (–0.987)
Caste dummy	0.052 (0.66)	–0.052 (–0.472)
Ownership dummy	–1.03 (–4.87)*	–1.11 (–4.12)*
R^2	0.50	0.51

Note: Figure in parentheses are't' values.

* Significant at 1 per cent level.

** Significant at 5 per cent level.

efficiency was negative and statistically significant in case of traditional variety. This indicates that there exists disguised unemployment. From this result we also observed that there exists negative and statistically significant relationship between ownership and technical efficiency for all the crops under study. However, the sociological factors (caste) have no influence on technical efficiency.

Conclusion

This chapter deals with the estimation of farm-specific technical efficiency for traditional variety and modern variety of paddy using Stochastic Frontier Production Function approach. The study reveals that, most of the inputs influence the output and most of the farmers fail to exploit full potential of technology. We also observed that quality of land represented in terms of rental value influences the level of efficiency whereas increase in the farm size and ownership tends to reduce the efficiency level for both traditional variety and modern variety. Thus, the analysis of technical efficiency indicated that there is a considerable scope to improve the productivity levels of paddy with the existing level of input use and the available technology in Indian agriculture.

NOTES

1. Two issues are important here. Firstly, large farmers take their decision on the perspective of cultivating a whole gamut of crops while the small farmers concentrate on the cultivation of a single or a few crops. In a *multi-crop* set-up, input used and efficiency achieved for a particular crop has its spill-over effect over input decisions of other crops (Pal and Sengupta, 1999). Hence, it would be wrong to treat them identically as is usually done. Secondly, large farmers generally prefer highly remunerative crops that may require substantial cost and use of modern inputs. Small farmers are more cautious. They normally prefer traditional crops with low risk that are essential for their survival. Thus, multi-crop comparison is essential in the case of size-productivity relationship.
2. This is because under the assumption of the stochastic frontier model, inference about the parametres of the model can be based on the maximum likelihood estimators because the standard regularity conditions hold.
3. The standard tests of multi-collinearity did not reveal any correlation between the dependent variables. Possibly this is because almost each of the variables incorporate quality components that are not correlated. For example, it is not necessary that better quality seeds will be cultivated in

the best quality land always. Or, most efficient labourers will always operate with the best machines or best animals.

REFERENCES

Ahluwalia, M.A., (1978), "Rural Poverty and Agricultural Performance in India", *Journal of Development Studies*, Vol. 14, pp. 705-722.

Aigner, Lovell and Schmidt, (1977), "Formulation and Estimation of Frontier Production Models", *Journal of Econometrics*, Vol. 6(4), (July).

Ali, M. and J.C. Flinn, (1989), "Profit Efficiency among Basmati Rice Producers in Pakistan's Punjab", *American Journal of Agricultural Economics*, Vol. 71, No. 2, pp. 303-310.

Banerjee, A.V., P.J. Gertler and M. Ghatak, (2002), "Empowerment and Efficiency: Tenancy Reform in West Bengal", *Journal of Political Economy*, Vol. 110(2).

Bhatia, S.S., (1967), "A New Measure of Agricultural Efficiency in Uttar Pradesh India", *Economic Geography*, Vol. 43, pp. 244-260.

Bravo-Ureta, B.E. and R.E. Evenson, (1994), "Efficiency in Agricultural Production: The Case of Peasant Farmers in Eastern Paraguay", *Agricultural Economics*, Vol. 10, No. 1, pp. 27-37.

Brown, Phelps E.H., (1957), "The Meaning of the Fitted Cobb-Douglas Function", *The Quarterly Journal of Economics*, Vol. 71, pp. 546-560.

Coelli, T.J., (1994), *A Guide to FRONTIER Version 4.1: A Computer Programme for Stochastic Frontier Production and Cost Function Estimations*, Working Paper 96/08, Centre for Efficiency and Productivity Analysis, Department of Econometrics, University of New England, Armidale, NSW, 2351, Australuia.

Dayal, E., (1984), "Agricultural Productivity in India: A Spatial Analysis, *Annals of the Association of American Geographers*, Vol. 74, No. 1, p. 106.

Deshpande, R.S. and M.J. Bhende, (2003), *Land Resources and Policy in Karnatak*, Working paper132, Institute for Social and Economic Change, Nagarbhavi, Bangalore.

Dutta, R. and K.P.M. Sundharam, (2009), *Indian Economy*, S. Chand & Company Ltd., New Delhi, p.486.

Dyer, G., (1998), "Farm Size and Productivity: A New Look at the Old Debate Revised", *Economic and Political Weekly*, Vol. 33, No. 26, June 27.

Farrell, M.J., (1957), "The Measurement of Productive Efficiency", *Journal of the Royal Statistical Society*, Series A, 120(3).

Kalirajan, K. and J.C. Flinn, (1983), "The Measurement of Farm-specific Technical Efficiency", *Pakistan Journal of Applied Economics*, 2, pp.167-180.

Kalirajan, K.P. and R.T. Shand, (1989), "A Generalized Measure of Technical Efficiency", *Applied Economics*, Vol. 21, pp. 25-34.

Kalirajan, K.P. and R.T. Shand, (1994), *Economics in Disequilibrium: An Approach from the Frontier*, MacMillan India Limited, New Delhi.

Kalirajan, K.P., M.M. Obwona and S. Zhao, (1996), "A Decomposition of Total Factor Productivity Growth: The Case of Chinese Agricultural Growth Before and After Reforms", *American Journal of Agricultural Economics*, Vol. 78, pp. 331-338.

Kendall, M.G., (1939), The Geographical Distribution of Crop Productivity in England, *Journal of the Royal Society*, Vol. 52, pp. 21-48.

Khusro, A.M., (1964), "Returns to Scale in Indian Agriculture", *Indian Journal of Agricultural Economics*, Vol.19, pp. 52-53.

Kopp, R.J. and V.K. Smith, (1980), "Frontier Production Function Estimates for Steam Electric Generation: A Comparative Analysis", *Southern Economic Journal*, Vol. 46, No. 4, pp. 1049-1059.

Kravis, I.B., (1976), "A Survey of International Comparison of Productivity", *Economic Journal*, Vol. 86, pp. 1-43.

Krishna, K.L. and S. Sahota Gian, (1991), "Technical Efficiency in Bangladesh Manufacturing Industries", *Bangladesh Development Studies*, Vol. 19, Nos. 1 and 2, pp. 89-105.

Kumbhakar, S.C. and A. Bhattarcharya, (1992), "Price Distortion and Resource Use Efficiency in Indian Agriculture: A Restricted Profit Function Approach", *Review of Economic and Statistics*, 74, pp. 221-239.

Kumbhakar, S.C., (1994), "Efficiency Estimation in a Profit Maximizing Model Using Flexible Production Function", *Agricultural Economics*, Vol. 10, pp.143-152.

Lingard, J., L. Castillo and S. Jayasuriay, (1983), "Comparative Efficiency of Rice Farms in Central Luzon in the Philippines", *Journal of Agricultural Economy*, Vol. 34, pp. 163-173.

Maity, B. and B. Chatterjee, (2006), "Impact of Modern Technology on Foodgrain Production in West Bengal: A Econometric Analysis", *Indian Journal of Regional Science*, Vol. 38, No. 2, p.96.

Muller, J., (1974), "On Sources of Measures Technical Efficiency: The Impact of Information, *American Journal of Agricultural Economics*, Vol. 56, pp. 730-738.

Pal, M. and A. Sengupta, (1999), "A Model of FPF with Correlated Error Components: An Application to Indian Agriculture", *Sankhya*, Series B, Vol. 61(2), pp. 337-350.

Parikh, A., A. Farman and M.K. Shah, (1995), Measurement of Economic Efficiency in Pakistan Agriculture, *American Journal of Agricultural Economics*, Vol. 77, pp. 675-685.

Peter, Timmer, (1988), The Agricultural Transformation, in H. Chenery and T. N. Srinivasan, (eds.), *Handbook of Development Economics*, Vol. 1, Elseveir, Amsterdam, pp. 275-331.

Ranganathan, V., (2003). "World Bank and India's Economic Development", *Economic and Political Weekly*, Vol. 38, No. 3, pp. 236-241.

Sapre, S.G. and V.D. Deshpande, (1964), "Inter-district Variations in Agricultural Efficiency in Maharashtra State", *Indian Journal of Agricultural Economics*, Vol. 19, pp. 242-252.

Shafi, M., (1960), "Measurement of Agricultural Efficiency in Uttar Pradesh", *Economic Geography*, Vol. 36, pp. 296-305.

Shanmugam, T.R. and K. Palanisami, (1994), "Measurement of Economic Efficiency–Frontier Function Approach", *Journal of Indian Society of Agricultural Statistics*, Vol. 45, No. 2, pp. 235-242.

Shapiro, K.H. and J. Muller, (1977), "Sources of Technical Efficiency: The Role of Modernization and Information", *Economic Development and Cultural Change*, Vol. 25, pp. 293-310.

Sharma, V.P. and K.K. Dutta, (1997), "Technical Efficiency in Wheat Production on Reclaimed Alkali Soils", *Productivity*, Vol. 38, No. 2, p. 334.

Singh, J., (1979), "A New Technique of Delimiting Agricultural Production Typology in Food-Crop Dominated Economy: Haryana a Case Study, *Geographia Polonica*, Vol. 40, p. 21.

Swaminathan, M.S., (2009), "Drought Management for Rural Livelihood Security, *The Hindu*, 17th August, p.12.

Taylor, G.T. and J.S. Shonkwiler, (1986), "Alternative Stochastic Specifications of the Frontier Production Function in the Analysis of Agricultural Credit Programmes and Technical Efficiency", *Journal of Development Economics*, Vol. 21, pp. 149-160.

Thomas, K. and R. Sundaresan, (2000), "Economic Efficiency of Rice Production in Kerala", *The Behar Journal of Agricultural Marketing*, Vol. 8, No. 3, pp. 310-315.

Timmer, P., (1971), "Using a Probabilistic Frontier Production Function to Measure Technical Efficiency, *Journal of Political Economy*, Vol. 79, pp. 776 794.

15

Issuses of Own Resources Mobilization of Panchayats

A District Level Study in West Bengal

Suman Chakraborty

Introduction

Own revenue of panchayats comes from tax and non-tax resources including voluntary contributions. Panchayats' tax receipt as well as voluntary contributions depend on rural people's willingness and capacity to pay, which in turn depends on people's saving and investment. The structure of own sources revenue in most of the districts of West Bengal changed in the favour of non-tax revenue or against own tax revenue. The compound annual growth rates of per capita own sources revenue of all districts of West Bengal is not significant. The tax, non-tax, and total own sources revenue vary across the districts and also over years for particular district. The variation of per capita own sources revenue across districts of West Bengal significantly explained by Literacy Rate, Income Index, Gender Development Index, Human Development Index. Per capita own sources revenue of panchayats (all tiers) of few districts of West Bengal belonged to a decent PCOR group in the recent year whereas initially that was not observed in any district of West Bengal.

According to the district-wise Broad Pattern of Land Utilization (in hectares) report, the district South 24th Pargana and Midnapore West possesses Largest area (9,53,368 hect., 9,28,581 hect.) again the district Howrah possesses the smallest area (1,38,676 hect.) apart from Kolkata. The district Midnapore West possesses the largest (5,94,155 hect.) and the district Howrah possesses smallest (91,609 hect.) cultivable land area. According to largest forest area the district South 24-parganas takes the first position on the other hand the district Nadia possesses the lowest

Table 15. 1: Broad Pattern of Land Utilization in West Bengal 2004-05

State/District	Reporting Area	Classification of reported area (Area in Hectares)		
		Cultivable area	Area not available for cultivation excluding forest	Forest area
	(In Hectares)	(In Hectares)	(In Hectares)	(In Hectares)
West Bengal*	8687450	5812686 (66.91)	1699993	1174771 (13.52)
Burdwan	698762	479749 (68.65)	196747 (28.16)	22266 (3.19)
Birbhum	451118	343112 (79.06)	92153 (20.43)	15853 (3.15)
Bankura	687995	391025	148040 (21.52)	148930 (21.65)
Midnapore East	396594	303406 (76.50)	92289 (23.27)	899 (0.23)
Midnapore West	928581	594155 (63.98)	162491 (17.50)	171935 (18.52)
Howrah	138676	91609 (66.06)	47067 (33.94)	NA
Hooghly	312224	226435 (72.52)	85259 (27.31)	530 (0.17)
North 24-Parganas	386524	272055 (70.39)	114469 (29.61)	NA
South 24-Parganas	953368	397309 (41.67)	129759 (13.61)	426300 (44.72)
Nadia	390656	308845 (79.06)	80595 (20.63)	12.16 (0.31)
Murshidabad	532499	409077 (79.82)	122651 (23.03)	771 (0.15)
Uttar Dinajpur	312466	279709 (89.52)	32177 (10.30)	580 (0.18)
Dakshin Dinajpur	221907	192584 (86.79)	28391 (12.79)	932 (0.42)
Malda	370862	285603 (77.01)	83580 (22.54)	1679 (0.45)
Jalpaiguri	622700	363041 (58.30)	80659 (12.95)	179000
Darjeeling	325469	165463 (50.84)	35430 (10.89)	124576 (38.27)
Cooch Behar	331566	264984 (79.92)	62326 (18.80)	42.56 (1.28)
Purulia	625483	444525 (71.07)	105910 (16.93)	75048 (12.00)

Notes: 1.* Excluding Kolkata

2. Figures in parentheses are percentage to total area.
3. Cultivable area includes Permanent Pastures and other grazing land, land under misc. tree groves not included.

forest area. From the table 15.1 we can state the districts Burdwan and Darjeeling having the largest and smallest area respectively which are not available for cultivation excluding forest area (Table 15.1).

The districts Burdwan, Murshidabad, Coochbehar have the highest number of regulated principal markets (4) and the districts South Dinajpur, South 24th Pargana, Howrah have the lowest number of regulated principal markets (1). On the other hand in the case of sub-market the district Coochbehar has the highest numbers of sub-markets (108) and the district Howrah has the lowest numbers (6) of sub-markets. Apart from Howrah and Nadia all other districts consist of double digit number of sub-markets (Table 15.2).

Table 15.2: Regulated Markets in West Bengal by Category and District (as on 31st October, 2007)

Districts	*Principal market*	*Sub-market*
Coochbehar	4	108
Jalpaiguri	3	57
Darjeeling	2	37
Dinajpur (N)	2	26
Dinajpur (S)	1	16
Malda	2	17
Murshidabad	4	27
Nadia	3	9
N-24th Pargana	1	53
S-24th Pargana	nil	45
Howrah	1	6
Hooghly	3	85
Midnapore (E)	2	23
Midnapore (W)	3	31
Bankura	3	21
Purulia	2	10
Burdwan	4	41
Birbhum	3	29

Source: Directorate of Agricultural Marketing Government of West Bengal.

The performances of panchayats in respect of own resource mobilization has, however, not been encouraging. Many government studies, e.g. Government of India (2001), Report of the Eleventh Finance Commission, reports of the State Finance Commission, Status Reports prepared by Department of Rural Development reveal that the performance of most of the states in India regarding own resources mobilization is poor. In this background a few questions that arise are: What is the trend and pattern of own resources mobilization in West Bengal

Table 15.3: Own Sources Revenue Pattern of Panchayats' Revenue Collection of Districts During 2006-07 to 2008-09

(Amount in Rs. Lakhs)

Name of the Districts	Population	Tax Collection			Non-Tax Collection			Total		
		2006-07	2007-08	2008-09	2006-07	2007-08	2008-09	2006-07	2007-08	2008-09
Coochbehar	22.54	49.71	41.76	72.84	97.32	112.18	61.06	147.03	153.94	133.9
Jalpaiguri	27.94	159.16	119.53	123.28	115.58	138.4	144.77	274.74	257.93	268.05
Darjeeling	10.89	68.4	131.81	94.24	34.08	81.25	68.12	102.48	213.06	162.36
N. Dinajpur	21.47	54.83	24.18	68.31	48.56	54.26	71.14	103.39	78.44	139.45
S. Dinajpur	13.06	33.27	33.63	45.69	50.3	63.95	88.8	83.57	97.58	134.49
Malda	30.5	74.52	49.41	101.23	90	117.04	108.76	164.52	166.45	209.99
Murshidabad	51.34	115.5	109.88	145.88	100.58	161.17	167.26	216.08	271.05	313.14
Nadia	36.25	202.62	214.32	221.16	135.69	174.08	222.95	338.31	388.4	444.11
N. 24 Pargans	40.83	215.45	245.17	244.37	261.52	352.65	370.47	476.97	597.82	614.84
S. 24 Pargans	58.2	157.07	95.21	190.94	209.3	169.29	296.8	366.37	264.5	487.74
Howrah	21.21	154.6	173.68	220	169.24	195.06	238.03	323.84	368.74	458.03
Hooghly	33.54	231.27	225.3	232.05	392.17	408.72	442.66	623.44	634.02	674.71
E. Medinipur	39.57	116.15	128.43	150.33	252.38	289.66	326.15	368.54	418.09	476.48
W. Medinipur	46.7	188.7	215.49	262.5	361.4	457.29	508.89	550.1	672.78	771.39
Bankura	29.57	62.59	67.83	55.94	282.58	390.49	342.71	345.17	458.32	398.65
Purulia	22.81	6.27	4.85	11.86	18.28	21.52	38.96	24.55	26.37	50.82
Burdwan	43.48	262.65	254.58	328.49	434.88	553.53	616.36	697.53	808.11	944.85
Birbhum	27.57	127.08	125.15	165.65	131.75	160.63	206.07	258.83	285.78	371.72

Sources: Annual Report of WB from WBPRD website.

and her districts during the recent years? Is their any significant variation of own resource mobilization across districts of West Bengal? What are the factors that accounted for the variation of own resource mobilization across districts of West Bengal? The present study seeks to address these and allied questions.

Data Base and Methodology

The entire study based on secondary data, which are collected from official website of dprd web West Bengal Government, Finance Commission and Census Report. We have taken major districts of West Bengal. PCOR data have been taken 2002-03 to 2008-09. These data have been analysed by using simple statistical techniques, (*viz.*, ratio, correlation–regression, compound annual growth rate, coefficient variation etc.). All the calculations have done by using statistical software SPSS and computer software MS excel.

The Objectives of the Study

(i) To examine the pattern of growth and structural changes of own revenue of panchayats in West Bengal across the districts.
(ii) To examine the factors that affects own revenue differential across the districts.

The entire study approaches by the following way. The section 2nd describes total own sources revenue, tax and non-tax revenue of Panchayats and also Per Capita Own Sources Revenue (all tiers) during 2002-03 to 2008-09 in the districts of West Bengal. The section 3rd explains pattern of growth Per Capita own sources revenue and structural changes of own sources revenue. The section 4th reveals the variation of own sources revenue. The section 5th analyses the determinants of own sources revenue and correlation with per capita own sources revenue. The section 6th makes the concluding remarks.

Own Sources Revenue

Table 15.3 shows the tax, non-tax, and total own sources revenue collected by the panchayats of different districts of West Bengal during 2006-07 to 2008-09. In the year of 2006-07 the district Burdwan had the highest own sources revenue (697.53) to be followed by the districts Hooghly

(623.44), and West Midnapore (550.10). The district Purulia had the lowest own source revenue (24.55) followed by the district South Dinajpur (83.57). In the year of 2008-09 again the district Burdwan was on the top position (944.85) and to be followed by Midnapore West (771.39), Hooghly (674.71) and North 24 Pargana (614.84) on the contrary The district Purulia again had the lowest own source revenue (50.82). The district Purulia continued to remain having lowest own source revenue during 2006-07 to 2008-09. The district Burdwan continued to remain having highest own source revenue during 2006-07 to 2008-09.

Per Capita Own Sources Revenue: Table 15.4 Per capita own source revenue of panchayats varies widely across the districts of West Bengal in our study. In the year of 2002-03 Hoogly (Rs. 13.48) and Burdwan (13.33) had the highest PCOR (all tier) to be followed by Midnapore (Rs. 11.03) and Howrah (Rs. 10.29). The district Purulia (Rs. 2) had the lowest Per Capita own source revenue. In the year of 2005-06 the highest per capita own source revenue collector was Burdwan (Rs. 26.84) and to be followed by Hooghly (Rs. 22.18), Howrah (Rs. 17.9) and West Midnapore (Rs. 14.35). The district Purulia was the lowest Per capita own source revenue (Rs. 1.91) collector. In the year of 2008-09 again we have got the highest Per capita own source revenue collector Burdwan

Table 15.4: Per capita Own Sources Revenue of Different Districts of West Bengal During 2002-03 to 2008-09 (*Amount in Rs.*)

Districts	*2002-03*	*2003-04*	*2004-05*	*2005-06*	*2006-07*	*2007-08*	*2008-09*
Coochbehar	4.74	6.09	8.44	11.13	12.45	12.34	15.72
Jalpaiguri	6.2	9.12	8.77	11.93	23.49	15.74	20.14
Darjeeling	4.84	6.06	10.17	14.46	18.26	22.78	20.98
U-Dinajpur	3.48	4.37	5.26	5.2	8.36	6.0	8.98
D-Dinajpur	7.66	6.17	12.49	13.75	11.44	14.99	15.93
Malda	6.23	5.64	13.52	9.71	17.06	12.64	11.81
Murshidabad	5.2	4.67	6.52	8.11	7.63	8.81	9.04
Nadia	6.65	6.49	8.2	9.43	12.77	13.85	16.3
N-24th Pargana	7.23	6.59	9.78	12.06	16.91	23.23	34.74
S-24th Pargana	4.71	5.03	8.27	8.16	11.64	22.03	22.73
Howrah	10.29	12.02	13.75	17.9	28.22	16.13	31.05
Hooghly	13.48	16.96	21.83	22.18	25.85	21.63	27.95
E-Midnapore	11.03	9.65	7.27	10.6	14.62	19.09	18.8
W-Midnapore	4.89	6.38	11.43	14.35	24.64	23.72	30.68
Bankura	3.17	8.73	11.05	14.12	22.4	34.06	17.68
Purulia	2	1.54	6.07	1.91	4.65	3.87	5.97
Burdwan	13.34	19.34	23.25	26.84	32.42	28.16	34.74
Birbhum	7.67	10.62	13.25	14.08	18.46	22.88	20.23
West Bengal	7.13	8.4	11.11	12.61	17.36	18.65	21.64

Source: Annual Report of WB from WBPRD website.

and North 24-Pargana (34.74) to be followed by Howrah (31.05), West Midnapore (30.68) and the result of Purulia remain unchanged (i.e. lowest position) or consistently bad.

Frequency Distribution of Districts of West Bengal by Per Capita Own Sources Revenue of Panchayats (All Tiers): Table 15.5 describes the frequency distribution of per capita own source revenue of the districts of West Bengal (all tiers). It reveals that in 2002-03 eight districts, namely Coochbehar, Darjeeling, Uttar Dinajpur, South Dinajpur, West Midnapore, Bankura, Purulia belonged to the PCOR group below Rs. 6. Only two districts, namely Hooghly and Burdwan belonged to the PCOR group above Rs. 15. Not any district of West Bengal belonged to the PCOR group above Rs. 18. In the year of 2005-06 only two districts, namely uttar Dinajpur and Purulia belonged to the PCOR group below Rs. 6. And seven districts having more than Rs. 15, but less than Rs. 18 and only one district belonged to the PCOR group above Rs. 24, namely Burdwan. In the year 2008-09 only one district of West Bengal namely Purulia belonged to the group below Rs. 6. and six districts belonged to the PCOR group above Rs. 24 those are as follows Burdwan, Birbhum, North 24-Pargana, Howrah, Hooghly, Midnapore West. The district Purulia continued to remain in the lowest PCOR group of below Rs. 6, during 2002-03 to 2008-09 on the contrary the district Burdwan continued to remain in the highest PCOR group of more than Rs. 24 during 2005-06 to 2008-09.

Pattern of Growth of Own Sources Revenue of Panchayats

Table 15.6 shows the districts of the State of West Bengal registered differential growth rate of per capita own source revenue of panchayats during 2002-03 to 2008-09. Most of the districts are statistically significant for their compound annual growth rate in the level of significance at 5 per cent and 1 per cent level of t-statistic, apart from three districts of West Bengal, namely North Dinajpur, Murshidabad and Purulia.

Structural Changes in Own Sources Revenue of Panchayats: Table 15.7 shows the facts that the structure of own source revenue of panchayats of most of districts apart from Coochbehar, Malda, Howrah of West Bengal changed in favour of non-tax revenue, but in the case of the districts Midnapore (East and West) change of share of tax and non-tax revenue is negligible.

Table 15.5: Frequency distribution of districts of West Bengal by per capita own sources revenue of panchayats (All Tiers)

Range	*2002-03*	*2003-04*	*2004-05*	*2005-06*	*2006-07*	*2007-08*	*2008-09*
0-5.99	8 (cb, dj, ud, mur, s24p, wm, ban, puru)	5 (ud, mld, mur, s24p, puru)	1 (ud)	2 (ud, puru)	1 (puru)	1 (puru)	1 (puru)
6-11.99	8 (jpg, dd, mld, nd, n24p, hwh, em, brvm)	10 (cb, jpg, dj, dd, nd, n24p, em, wm, ban, brvm)	11 (cb, jpg, dj, mur, nda, n24p, s24p, em, wm, ban, puru)	7 (cb, jpg, mld, mur, nda, s24p, em)	4 (ud, dd, mur, s24p)	2 (ud, mur)	3 (ud, mld, mur,)
12-17.99	2 (hgly, brdmn)	3 (hwh, hgly, brdmn)	4 (dd, mld, hwh, brvm)	7 (dj, dd, n24p, hwh, wm, ban, brvm)	5 (cb, mld, nda, n24p, em)	6 (cb, jpg, dd, mld, nda, hwh)	4 (cb, dd, nda, ban)
18-23.99	NA	NA	2 (hgly, brdmn)	1 (hgly)	4 (jpg, dj, ban, brvm)	7 (dj, n24p, s24p, hgly, em, wm, brvm)	4 (jpg, dj, s24p, em)
24 and Above	NA	NA	NA	1 (brdmn)	4 (brdmn, wm, hwh, hgly)	2 (ban, brdmn)	6 (n24p, hwh, hgly, wm, brdmn, brvm)
Total	**18**	**18**	**18**	**18**	**18**	**18**	**18**

Source: As above.

Table 15.6: Pattern of Growth of Own Sources Revenue of Panchayats

Remarks	*Name of the Districts*	*Level of Significant***
Statistically Significant	Coochbehar*, Darjeeling**, Jalpaiguri**, S. Dinajpur**, E. Midnapore**, W. Midnapore**, Malda*, Bankura*, Birbhum**, Howrah**, Hooghly**, N-24 Pargana**, S-24 Pargana**, Nadia*, Burdwan**, Jalpaiguri**	*1%,*5%*
Statistically Insignificant	N. Dinajpur Murshidabad Purulia	Nil

Source: As above.

Table 15.7: Structural Changes in Own Sources Revenue of Panchayats

Name of the District	*% Share of Own tax revenue to total OR*			*% Share of Non-tax revenue to total OR*		
	2006-07	*2007-08*	*2008-09*	*2006-07*	*2007-08*	*2008-09*
Coochbehar	33.81	27.13	54.40	66.19	72.87	45.60
Jalpaiguri	57.93	46.34	45.99	42.07	53.66	54.01
Darjeeling	66.75	61.87	58.04	33.26	38.13	41.96
N. Dinajpur	53.03	30.83	48.99	46.97	69.17	51.01
S. Dinajpur	39.81	34.46	33.97	60.19	65.54	66.03
Malda	45.30	29.68	48.21	54.70	70.32	51.79
Murshidabad	53.45	40.54	46.59	46.55	59.46	53.41
Nadia	59.89	55.18	49.80	40.11	44.82	50.20
N. 24 Pargana	45.17	41.01	39.75	54.83	58.99	60.25
S. 24 Pargana	42.87	36.00	39.15	57.13	64.00	60.85
Howrah	47.74	47.10	48.03	52.26	52.90	51.97
Hooghly	37.10	35.54	34.39	62.90	64.46	65.61
E. Medinipur	31.52	30.72	31.55	68.48	69.28	68.45
W. Medinipur	34.30	32.03	34.03	65.70	67.97	65.97
Bankura	18.13	14.80	14.03	81.87	85.20	85.97
Purulia	25.54	18.39	23.34	74.46	81.61	76.66
Burdwan	37.65	31.50	34.77	62.35	68.50	65.23
Birbhum	49.10	43.79	44.56	50.90	56.21	55.44

Source: As above

Variation of Own Sources Revenue of Panchayats Across Districts and Over Years

Table 15.8 explains Panchayats tax, non-tax and total own revenue vary across the districts and also over years for particular districts. The coefficient variation over years for individual districts varied widely. The highest being in the Purulia (48%) for own tax revenue, as well as non-tax revenue (42%) and for total own source revenue (43%). The district Hooghly recorded the lowest coefficient variation for tax (6.21%) and non-tax revenue (4.20%). The district Jalpaiguri recorded the lowest coefficient variation for total own source revenue (3.17%).

Table 15.8: CV (%) of Tax, Own Sources Revenue, Non-Tax of WB, 2006-07 to 2008-09

Name of the Districts	*CV*		
	TAX	*Non-Tax*	*OSR*
Coochbehar	29.48	29.16	7.02
Jalpaiguri	16.33	11.55	3.17
Darjeeling	32.49	39.81	34.75
N. Dinajpur	46.05	20.25	28.64
S. Dinajpur	18.84	28.84	25.00
Malda	34.53	13.16	14.26
Murshidabad	15.65	25.78	18.25
Nadia	4.41	24.63	13.56
N. 24 Pargana	7.21	17.81	13.35
S. 24 Pargana	32.86	28.97	29.97
Howrah	18.40	17.31	17.81
Hooghly	1.61	6.21	4.20
E. Medinipur	13.15	12.75	12.83
W. Medinipur	16.81	16.91	16.68
Bankura	9.59	15.97	14.13
Purulia	48.38	42.37	43.26
Burdwan	14.38	17.23	15.17
Birbhum	16.40	22.55	19.30

Source: As above.

Determinants of Per Capita Own Sources Revenue

Table 15.9 shows the PCOR and its determinants. The PCOR across districts of West Bengal is shown in relation to Literacy Rate (LTR), Human Development Index (HDI), Income Index (II) and Reg: Small Scale and Cottage Industries. The variation of PCOR of different districts of the State West Bengal explained in terms of these factors (LTR, HDI, II Reg: Small Scale and Cottage Industries).

The correlation matrix regarding Panchayat's PCOR is shown in below Table 15.10. It is represented that PCOR is significantly correlated

Table 15.9: Determinants of Per Capita Own Sources Revenue

Districts/Items	*PCOR*	*LTR*	*HDI*	*Income Index*	*Reg: Small Scale and Cottage Industries*
Coochbehar	15.72	66	0.52	0.41	332
Jalpaiguri	20.14	62.85	0.53	0.38	292
Darjeeling	20.98	71.79	0.65	0.49	142
Dinajpur	24.91	57.8	0.51	0.39	189
Malda	11.81	50.28	0.44	0.36	315
Murshidabad	9.04	54.35	0.46	0.29	861
Nadia	16.3	66.14	0.57	0.41	541
N. 24 Pargana	34.74	78.07	0.66	0.49	1002
S. 24 Pargana	22.73	69.45	0.6	0.4	551
Howrah	31.05	77.01	0.68	0.53	1140
Hooghly	27.95	75.11	0.63	0.46	343
Midnapore	49.48	74.9	0.62	0.45	1471
Bankura	17.68	63.44	0.52	0.26	322
Purulia	5.97	55.57	0.45	0.18	289
Burdwan	34.74	70.18	0.64	0.47	941
Birbhum	26.23	61.48	0.47	0.27	309

Source: Annual Report of WB from WBPRD website.

Table 15.10: Correlation Matrix Regarding Per capita Own Sources Revenue of Panchayats

Pearson Correlation					
Districts/Items	*PCOR*	*LTR*	*HDI*	*Income Index*	*Reg: Small Scale and Cottage Industries*
PCOR	1				
LTR	.748**	1			
HDI	.707**	.948**	1		
Income Index	.642**	.773**	.868**	1	
Reg:Small Scale and Cottage Industries	.669**	.512*	.501*	0.428	1

Note: *. Correlation is significant at the 0.05 level (2-tailed).
**. Correlation is significant at the 0.01 level (2-tailed).

Source: As above.

with Literacy Rate (LTR), Human Development Index (HDI), Income Index (II) and Reg: Small Scale and Cottage Industries. The factors Ltr, HDI, II, Reg: Small Scale and Cottage Industries are significantly correlated.

Table 15.11: Regression Equation Concerning Per Capita own Revenue

Idependent Variable	*Constant*	*Coefficient*	*R Square*	*F*
LTR	–40.849 (–2.679)	.970 (4.220)	56%	17.81
HDI	–30.297 (–2.1)	95.435 (3.738)	50%	13.97
Income Index	–5.324 (–.570)	72.862 (3.130)	41%	9.79
Reg:Small Scale and Cottage Industries	12.519 (3.299)	.019 (3.363)	45%	11.3

Note: Figures within Parentheses represent T-Ratio.

The regression equations concerning PCOR of Panchayats are shown in the above Table 15.11. It is revealed that variation in PCOR is explained by Literacy Rate (Ltr), Human Development Index (HDI), Income Index (II) and Reg: Small scale and Cottage Industries to the extent of 56 per cent, 50 per cent, 41 per cent and 45 per cent respectively. All the models are statistically significant.

Concluding Remarks

On the basis of the above findings of the existing study we can draw the concluding remarks by the following way: The level of own sources revenue and its structure of panchayats vary widely across the districts of West Bengal. There is also differential growth rate of per capita own source revenue across the districts of the State. The variation is clearly explained by literacy rate, human development index, registered Small Scale and Cottage Industries and income index which is statistically significant at 5 per cent and 1 per cent level. The present study exhibits that the percentage share of non-tax revenue is greater than percentage share of tax revenue to the total revenue. It proves that the share of tax revenue declines over the years on the contrary the non-tax revenue plays a significant role to boost up the economy. Another challenge of any developing economy as well as Panchayat is high rate of population which leads to disguised unemployment and low rate of per capita income which may pull the economy towards under development or backwardness. The District having significant growth rate have maximum number of prime markets and sub-markets. The process of utilization of land can play a vital role to improve own revenue structure *vis-à-vis* economic condition of gram panchayats.

The policy suggestions may be on enhancing the values of the development indices such as literacy rate, human development index, income index and Reg: Small Scale and Cottage Industries for the districts. The State can adopt strict population control policy to reduce the high growth rate of population to improve per capita revenue structure. The State can enjoy the fiscal autonomy by using the non-tax revenue from its productive resources and to improve the tax structure. The percentage of unused land is not too small. So, that if the panchayats use it in commercial purpose, viz. aqua agriculture, they use the unused land as a park and charge a fee from the visitors etc. The tax structure should be changed according to recent time purchasing power or standard of living index and price index. The policy may reduce the dependency on external grant which leads to a stable economic condition of panchayats of the districts *vis-à-vis* the State.

REFERENCES

Amatya, S.L., (1996), "Decentralization and Local Self-governments in Nepal: An Overview", in Aziz, A. and D.D. Arnold (eds.), *Decentralized Governance in Asian Countries,* New Delhi: Sage Publications.

Bandyopadhyay, D., (2003), "Twelfth Finance Commission and Panchayat Finances", *Economic and Political Weekly*, July 7.

Barnabas, A.P. and O.P. Bohra, (1995), "Finances of Panchayati Raj Institutions—A Case Study", *National Institute of Public Finance and Policy*, New Delhi.

Bhattacharyya, Sib Nath, (1997), "Finances of Panchayats in North Bengal", *Economic and Political Weekly*, November 9.

Chauhan, D.S., (1977), "Democratic Decentralization and Local Government Administration" in Sharma, S.K. (ed.), *Dynamics of Development: An International Perspectives*, Concept Publishing Company, New Delhi.

Dhaka, Rajvir S., (2002), "Panchayati Raj Institutions in Haryana—A field study", *Kurukshetra*, January.

Fernandes, Aureliano, (2003), "Aggrandiser Government and Local Governance", *Economic and Political Weekly*, July 5.

Ghatak, M. and M. Ghatak, (2000), "Recent Reforms in the Panchayat System in West Bengal—Towards Greater Participatory Governance?" *Economic and Political Weekly*, August 3.

Ghorpade, M.Y., (2002), "Strengthening Gram Panchayat", *Economic and Political Weekly*, September 21.

Ghosh, Arun, (1988), "Decentralized Planning: West Bengal Experience", *Economic and Political Weekly*, March 25.

Girglani, J.M., (1994), "Financial Resources of PRIs" in Amitava Mukherjee (ed.) *Decentralization: Panchayats in the Nineties*, Vikas Publishing House Pvt. Ltd., New Delhi.

Helm, D. and J. Smith, (1987), "The Assessment: Decentralization and Economics of Local Government", *Oxford Review of Economic Policy*, Vol. 3, No. 2.

Jana, Anil Kumar, (2005), "People's Participation and Decentralization Perspectives and Issues" in S.N. Sau (ed.), *Decentralization, Planning and Participatory Development*, Firma KLM Pvt. Ltd., Kolkata.

Jena, A.C., (1999), *"Panchayati Raj Finances in West Bengal—A Status Study"*, National Institute of Rural Development, Hyderabad.

Jha, Sikha, (2002), "Strengthening Local Governments: Rural Fiscal Decentralization in India", *Economic and Political Weekly*, June, 29.

Khasnobic, Ratan, (2005), "Financing the Urban and Rural Local Bodies in India" in S.N. Sau (ed.) *Decentralization, Planning and Participatory Development: Essays with Reference to India*, Firma KLM Pvt. Limited, Kolkata.

Maity, Sirsendu and S. Ray, (2004), "Pattern of Growth and Structural Changes in Own Receipts of Panchayats: A Study of Twelve Gram Panchayats in Purba and Paschim Medinipur in West Bengal" in S.N. Sau (ed.), *Participatory Decentralized Planning in India: Issues of Finance and Statistical Information*, Firma KLM Pvt. Limited, Kolkata.

Maity, Sirsendu, (2004), "Some Issues of Finance-Related Functions of Decentralized Planning—A Study of Some Panchayat Samitis and Gram Panchayats in Purba Medinipur and Paschim Medinipur districts of West Bengal" in S. Sau (ed.), *Participatory Decentralized Planning in India: Issues of Finance and Statistical Information*, Firma KLM Pvt. Limited, Kolkata.

Mishra, Suresh and Rajbir S. Dhaka, (2003), "Institutionalising Panchayati Raj", *Kurukshetra*, September.

Navlakha, Goutam, (2004), "Achieving Fiscal Autonomy", *Economic and Political Weekly*, January, 10.

Oommen, M.A., (1995), "Devolution of resources from the State to the Panchayati Raj Institutions: Search for Normative Approach", *ISS Occasional Paper Series 18*, ISS, New Delhi.

Oommen, M.A., (2006), "Fiscal Decentralization to the Sub-State Level Governments", *Economic and Political Weekly*, March 11.

Palharya, Shakun, (2003), "Decentralized Governance Hampered by Financial Constraint", *Economic and Political Weekly*, March 15.

Rajaraman, Indira, (2003), *A Fiscal Domain for Panchayats*, Oxford University Press.

Rao, M. Govinda and U.A. Vasanta Rao, (2008), "Expanding the Resource Base of Panchayats—Augmenting Own Revenues", *Economic and Political Weekly*, January 26.

Reddy, M. Gopinath, (2003), "Status of Decentralized Local Bodies—Post-73rd Amendment Scenario", *Economic and Political Weekly*, March, 22.

Sau, S.N., (2003), "Report of the DRS Workshop on Issues of Decentralized Planning in West Bengal", DRS (SAP), UGC, Department of Economics with Rural Development, Vidyasagar University, West Bengal.

Sau, S.N., (2004), "Prologue", in S. Sau (ed.), *Participatory Decentralized Planning in India: Issues of Finance and Statistical Information*, Firma KLM Pvt. Limited, Kolkata.

Sau, S.N., Sirsendu Maity, (2004), "Own Resource Mobilization of Panchayats: A Study with Special Reference to West Bengal", Vidyasagar University, *Journal of Economics*, Vol. IX.

Subramaniyam, K.S., (2003), "Dynamics of Devolution on Panchayats", *Indian Social Science Review*, Vol. 5, (2).

16

An Integrated Approach towards Rural Development

Tagore's Philosophy

Debashis Mazumdar and *Santanu Bisai*

Introduction

Rural development has emerged as a separate discipline in the event of non-percolation of benefits of economic growth to the unprivileged sections of the society and persistence of poverty, hunger, malnutrition and inequality in the rural areas. It is one of the principal objectives of the rural local institutions like panchayats. While formulating the schemes for rural development, the panchayat has as its main objective the improvement in the quality of life of the people. The scheme relates to eradication of poverty, spread of literacy, enhancement of skill and health-care. Traditional approaches to rural development have focused on improving agricultural productivity, relying on agricultural growth as the engine of rural development and poverty alleviation.

The economic history of India clearly shows that at the time of her Independence, the condition of the rural economy was almost stagnant and stationary. The development scenario of rural India was riddled with the problems of low agricultural productivity, traditional mode of cultivation, inadequate security of tenancy rights under the Zamindari System of land tenure, poor social infrastructure in the fields of education and health, poor economic infrastructure in terms of inadequate transport and communication facilities, rural indebtedness and inadequate supply of rural credit from institutional sources, usurious practices of intermediaries at different levels etc.

The constructive rural development strategy or initiative was completely absent in India during the pre-Independence period. However, this is not true altogether and this chapter is a modest attempt to explore the approach of Rabindranath Tagore towards rural development or more specifically, rural transformation, that evolved during late nineteenth century. We want to show that his approach was appropriate for a complete transformation of a rural economy from its backward state in many less developed countries including India. His philosophy relating to rural upliftment was broad-based and developed countries including India. His philosophy relating to rural upliftment was broad-based and multi-dimensional in nature. His approach is still relevant for analyzing the problems of rural development in many less developed and developing countries of the world in the midst of economic globalization.

Tagore's international experiences over a period of years opened his eyes to comprehend the significance of accentuating an intellectual union of world cultures and challenging all sorts of obstacles through cultural integration.

Approaches to Rural Development

Economic growth and top down diffusion of development impulses received primary importance in the traditional approach towards economic progress of a society. The growth in GDP (Gross Domestic Product) of a country, as an indicator of economic growth, was treated as the function of investment, and the benefits of development were expected to automatically trickle down to different income classes of the society. It was identified, particularly by the end of 1960s, that growth was not necessarily correlated with other development objectives such as rapid employment creation, reduction of poverty and inequality and provision of basic human needs (Sau, 2008).

A close introspection to different approaches towards rural development clearly reveals the following routes particularly in the context of less developed and developing economies including India:

1. The Gandhian approach towards rural development,
2. The Integrated Rural Development Approach (IRDP),
3. The Neo-Classical Approach,
4. The Structural Approach,
5. The Target Group Approach,
6. The participatory development approach, and
7. The Micro-finance/Self-Help Group approach.

The basic tenets of Gandhian approach to rural development are: a non-materialistic view, egalitarian approach and a value-driven perspective. He emphasized sustainable development of villages and establishment of *Gram Swaraj*. Limiting the greed of human being was one of the important goals of development as per Gandhian ideology. The Gandhi model of development has potentialities for offering remarkable opportunities for social reconstruction and perennial social and human progress locally, nationally and globally (Unnithan, 1997:220). Village self-sufficiency serves as a basis of economic development in this approach.

The IRDP approach emphasizes on the need for people's cooperation and the appropriate application of science and technology so that there would be optimum utilization of available resources. The positive aspects of this approach are that it takes into account the sectoral, sectional, environmental, technological and political development in the rural areas leading to the overall development of the rural society. However, efficacy of this approach was challenged on the questions of efficiency and equity which did not receive adequate attention in this approach.

Neo-classical economists argue that a properly functioning market system will stimulate both economic efficiency and economic growth. This approach emphasizes the question of efficiency in the internal micro-economic framework. It emphasizes that in perfect competition there shall be efficient allocation of resources and increase in investment will lead to rapid economic growth whose benefit should percolate even to the lowest rank of the society. However, this approach has some limitations: (1) In a large subsistence sector of a rural society this approach is hardly applicable; (2) This approach faces the problem of market failure which ought to be corrected through institutional mechanisms which are completely ignored in this approach; and (3) The pattern of relationship of the individual with the society is not brought here.

The Structural Approach is concerned with the relationship of people in the process of production. It places the ownership and control of resources at the centre of relationships. Institutional reforms including land reforms and credit reforms emanate from this approach. However, there are serious logical and theoretical objections to this way of conceptualizing the relationship; and it should be seen rather in terms of processes of struggle between conflicting classes. Further, the process of commoditization and the development of capitalism, or the linking up of rural household producers with capitalist production in various ways is perhaps the dominant process of change in contemporary agrarian societies.

The 'Target Group Approach' in this field has been developed on recognition of the fact that the general economic development may bypass the poor, and the benefits of economic growth may not percolate to the poverty stricken people. The great merit of this approach is that it involves a direct attack on poverty. However, failure on the part of the government in framing and implementing the poverty alleviation programmes in an efficient manner often led to a net outflow of government fund without any perceptible impact on the 'target group'.

People's participation in the rural development programmes forms the basis of the 'Participatory Development Approach' towards rural development. It gives special emphasis on decentralized planning and proper functioning of Panchayati Raj Institutions. However, this approach is not also free from some limitations. There may be a failure on the part of the community (viz., the local self-government institutions) in taking appropriate procedure in respect of the selection of beneficiaries. In fact, sustaining the tempo of participation is much more difficult than mobilizing people for the participatory development.

The Micro-finance/Self-Help Group (SHG) approach gives special emphasis on self-development and empowerment of families, particularly the poor families, for poverty alleviation. In recent times, micro-finance, through SHGs, for the poor and women has received an extensive recognition as a strategy for poverty alleviation and economic development. In this approach, the government, the local self-government (panchayat) and the non-governmental organizations play the role of facilitators and thus the notion that the state should only play the pertinent role in poverty alleviation is altered.

Rural Reconstruction: Tagore's View

A close introspection of the principal features of the rural development strategy as viewed by Tagore during late nineteenth and early twentieth century, clearly reveals that his vision was far ahead of the traditional approach towards economic development. Further, his approach towards rural reconstruction in an agrarian and less developed economy like India was much more scientific and broad-based compared to many other approaches stated above. More interestingly, his views were based upon some real life experiences of rural economy during his tenure as a manager of the family estate (Zamindari) at Shilaidaha (Kustia), Shajadpur (Pabna) and Patisar (Rajshahi) estates in East Pakistan (now Bangladesh). Tagore's philosophy regarding rural transformation becomes clear from his writings such as '*Palli Prakriti*' (Nature of the Village), '*Atma Shakti*' (Self Empowerment), '*Samabay Niti*' (Co-operative Policy), '*Rasiar Chithi*' (Letters from Russia), etc. as well as from his speeches in some conferences [say, Provincial Conference at Nator (1897), Provincial Conference of Pabna Congress (1908)], and from '*Pitrismriti*' (Memoires of my Father) written by his son Rathindranath.

His close association and empathy with the poverty-stricken people of rural Bengal left such an indelible mark on his psyche that spurred him to myriads of activities for the rest of his life for rural reconstruction. If we review the Population Census Report (1891), we find that during that period about 58 per cent of the population of Nadia district (Kustia was then within the Nadia District) belonged to Islam by religion, 37.8 per cent belonged to Hindu and the rest 4.2 per cent belonged to other religions. However, within the 'Muslim' community, only 1.6 per cent people were literate; and this portion was only about 7.6 per cent within the 'Hindu' people. Moreover, in both these groups of people, the majority was economically poor (Mazumdar, 2006). This gives us an idea regarding the demographic structure of the tenants in the family Estate (at Shilaidaha) of Rabindranath.

Both subjective and objective factors became prominent in his strategy for rural reconstruction. The unveiling of the enormous potential in every human being particularly in rural areas and an expansion of cooperative spirit among them are supposed to be the important subjective factors, while improved and scientific cultivation, improvement in agricultural research, improvement in rural health and educational facilities, development of cottage industries, expansion of institutional sources of rural credit through the establishment cooperative banks and cooperative societies etc. are the objective factors.

Based on Tagore's philosophy, the first and the most important step towards rural reconstruction, was to create self-respect and self-confidence among the rural people. According to him, "*if the people of a poor country can have a sincere belief and hope to become rich, then that conviction is an asset for that nation.... In fact, our country lacks such belief.... We cannot even think that solution lies in our own hands.*" He believed that proper education and a mind free from any superstition are the preconditions for developing self-respect and self-confidence. But there was a lack of both these factors in rural India.

According to him, the lack of basic education is the fundamental cause of various social and economic maladies in India. He emphasized on the expansion of such education that would help in reducing the gap between the local and global fields of knowledge. He put special emphasis not only upon the formal education but also upon the vocational education for the efficient utilization of the local resources. During his visit to Russia in 1930, he was much impressed by its development efforts and by what he saw as a real commitment to eliminate poverty and economic inequality. But what impressed him most was the expansion of basic education across the Old Russian Empire.

In modern development economics, three core components of economic development have been identified by Dennis Goulet (Todaro and Smith, 2003). These are: (1) Life sustenance (basic necessities of life such as housing, clothing, and food), (2) Self-esteem (i.e., a sense of self-respect), and (3) Freedom (freedom from three evils, viz., from want, ignorance and squalor). Amartya Sen has also explained economic development in terms of the expansion of entitlements and capabilities. The entitlement to adequate income-generating assets, food, shelter, basic education, health-care and other necessities of life determines the capability of a person. Thus, economic development should be thought in terms of an expansion in such entitlements and capabilities in any society. However, long before the evolution of such modern views towards economic development, the core ingredients of those perceptions were already present in Tagore's approach.

While enquiring about the origin of poverty, he particularly pointed out the poverty of our mind. To him, a narrow and self-centred mind is much worse than social injustice and economic poverty. Therefore, it is important to build a broad and positive mindset that can easily incorporate new ideas and values. So, he felt the necessity of organizing and uniting the poor and inculcating new ideas in their minds through the expansion of education. Stray scuffle with poverty is not enough. Occasional help from outside will not alleviate our poverty and privation. It must be eradicated from within. It requires two basic ingredients, viz. expansion of education among the common people so that they can communicate with other people of the world, and the development of a cooperative attitude so that the common people are organized in their quest for livelihood and their work should have a close linkage with the advanced knowledge prevailing in the developed countries.

Emphasis on Cooperative Movement

That cooperative movement could be an effective instrument for overcoming the oppression of zamindars over the poor tenant farmers was realized by Tagore long before the emergence of cooperative movement through government initiatives in India. He believed that people should be united, and also be aware of their own rights. However, Tagore preferred modernity against the tradition. His essay '*Swadeshi Samaj*' envisaged a self-administered and self-reliant society.

One of the principal problems of the Co-operative movement in our country is that they are not at all self-sufficient in term of mobilization of resources. They are almost totally dependent on the fund provided by the Central Co-operative Bank. They lack the will, incentive and initiative to tap the local fund for promoting local production or deposit mobilization.

Since 1980s, several attempts have been made to solve the economic crises of less developed and developing countries of the world through the financial support from the World Bank, International Monetary Fund and other international financial organizations, but most of these helps had lots of conditionality and strings attached with them and they failed to solve the perennial problems of poverty and unemployment in the less developed countries.

In one of his important essays, viz. '*Samabay Niti*' (1928), he stated that "*today, economic power has been captured by a small minority. But it has acquired this power only by accumulating the productive power of others. Their capital is simply the accumulated labour of a millions of working people, in a monetized form. It is this productive power that is the real capital, and it is this power that latently resides in every worker...*" (Tagore, Vol. 13, 1990). He was aware of the economies of large-scale farming. He also felt the need for technological reform along with the institutional reforms in Indian agriculture much before these reform programmes were undertaken by the government in Independent India.

He further stated that, "*the all-embracing poverty, which has overwhelmed our country, cannot be removed by working with our hands to the neglect of science*". And he goes on to declare, "*if we are will fully blind to the grand vision of whirling forces which science has revealed, the charka will cease to have any message for us*" for the spinning wheel "*will no longer talk to us of progress*" (Tagore, Vol. 13, 1990). Tagore was very keen to improve the traditional mode of cultivation by introducing modern technology and equipments in farming. He also introduced crop rotation and crop diversification in agricultural production, and took a positive initiative to import mechanized ploughs and improved seeds to enhance the agricultural productivity thereby raising the income earning capabilities of poor peasants. He brought seven mechanized ploughs from Kolkata and improved seeds of maize from the USA, and fine paddy from Madras for their application at Patisar.

He also arranged training for the peasants since they were ignorant about modern methods of farming. He believed that being an agrarian economy, Indian people should acquire knowledge to become a 'developed peasant' rather than a 'developed gentleman'. After returning home, Rathindranath devoted himself in popularizing modern farming at Patisar.

He believed that the root cause of poverty in countries like India is not population growth, rather the principal cause is inadequate capability of the common people to purchase food items. We find the reflection of this idea in Amartya Sen's work on "*Poverty and Famines—An Essay on Entitlement and Deprivation*" in 1969. In fact, Sen has indicated that poverty can arise due to capability failure, i.e. if the people fails to earn enough in exchange of their labour and other endowments then they become incapable of purchasing the required food items from the market. Sen has indicated that if through better education and health facilities, an individual can raise his income opportunities and acquire the power to convert the characteristics of commodities into their functioning (say, utility derived from a good book only after being literate) then that would imply an improvement in 'capability'. It actually implies the freedom that a person has in terms of the choice of functioning, given his personal features and his command over commodities. Though Tagore did not use these terminologies, his views regarding expansion of human possibilities through proper education, training, and health facilities to common people actually imply this 'capability' formation and a feature that modern economists now call as the formation of 'human capital'.

While working as the manager in different zamindari estates in East Bengal, Tagore also got a clear glimpse of the plight of the poor and marginalized farmers who had been burdened with loan from rural money lenders. He could realize that the arable land of the region was relatively infertile and there was only one harvest in a year; even there were instances of crop failures due to natural calamities in some years. Therefore, farmers were compelled to take loans from money lenders at a very high interest rate to meet their emergency needs. They also struggled to pay land revenues to the zamindars.

Tagore believed that adequate access to credit facilities is a right of the poor. He took initiative to establish a 'Krishi Bank' at Shilaidaha in 1894. The main objective was to free the poor farmers from the grip of money, lenders. Initially, Tagore arranged necessary fund for this bank from his friends and relatives. This enhanced the capacity of the bank to facilitate more credit to the peasants at lower interest rates. Thus, much before the Indian planners' emphasis on rural cooperatives as an escape route for low productivity in India agriculture, Tagore could visualize its importance and took positive steps to implement the same. Tagore also started microcredit programmes to finance rural development activities on cooperative basis (through the formation of cooperative societies) even before establishing the bank. He inspired the poor farmers to build up the habit of small savings. Farmers of neighbouring villages were required to subscribe to the cooperative credit society. The funds so raised were given back to the needy farmers as loan at low interest rates. Tagore introduced such small cooperative initiatives both in Shilaidaha and Patisar. Apart from this, microcredit was also provided for the development of various cottage industries. Such micro-credit programmes have been quite successful in our neighbouring country Bangladesh in recent past (Rahman, 2010).

At present, it is widely accepted throughout the world that if the emancipated small peasants can organize cooperatives, then popular perception regarding farm size and productivity (viz., large farms are more productive than small-sized farms) would be proved to be wrong. Even today, we observe some sad instances of farmers' suicide in some regions of India. Researchers are of the opinion that in many cases, this happens mainly because of inadequate spread of cooperative credit institutions in rural areas. Thus, the lesson that we should learn from Tagore's philosophy of rural reconstruction is that our planning should not be mere 'paper works', rather these plans are to be implemented efficiently through people's participation with particular emphasis upon local needs and resources.

Thus, the programme of rural community development, a conceptualized by Tagore, was based on the twin principles of self-help and enlightenment. He wanted to develop a comprehensive rural governance structure called '*Palli Samaj*' (Rural Society) which encompassed multi-dimensional elements of societal upliftment. In 1908, he finally prepared the roadmap for an ideal Rural Society where the main activities would involve: equity and good relation among different religious beliefs; solving disputes and differences by arbitration ('Salishi'); introduction of home grown or indigenous products, improvement of local industries; establishment of night schools and recruitment of competent teachers; providing facilities for games and sports; maintaining ethical standard, unity and patriotism; establishment of hospital and dispensary in every village; providing free medical treatment and medicine to the poor; ensuring availability of safe drinking water; expanding river transport and road-transport facilities; establishment of agricultural farm; facilitating training and education to young generation on agriculture and animal husbandry; establishment of Grain Banks; expansion of cottage industries; development of woman entrepreneurs; prohibition of alcohol in the locality etc. Sometimes, it seems amazing how does a poet like him could prepare such a comprehensive rural development programme which our modern planners can seldom prepare even after attending dozens of round table conferences and after wasting substantial amount of government funds. Hence, this philosophy deserves an in-depth and a renewed analysis for its relevance in contemporary crisis-ridden world, particularly in less developed and developing countries.

The main intention of the poet was to develop an alternative earning source for the common people since the arable land became tiny with increased population pressure in rural areas. Training centres were set-up to restore local industries and crafts such as leather work, tailoring, carpentry etc.

Conclusion

The foregoing discussion clearly indicates that unlike any zamindar, Tagore was keen on improving the self-confidence of his subjects through an all-round development of the rural environment. He believed that if one or two ideal villages could be reconstructed then that would be a model for the entire India. In his own words, "*I cannot change the entire country alone. I shall conquer only one or two small villages.... If I can ensure a release from the bondage of ignorance and helplessness to only two or three villages, a small prototype of India will be constructed there.*" It is now widely felt that even though traditionalism can 'hinder' development (as some would claim), there are strengths in tradition as well, especially in dynamic tradition. The society which can absorb shocks of change and can organize people in groups for better living cannot be looked down as 'traditional'. There is a growing awareness of the need to reconcile the values of 'universal' knowledge and 'diversity', a conviction that Tagore pioneered not only in his thought process but also in his life of action. He was never indifferent to the changing needs of the society, and tried hard to make a difference with whatever constructive work possible for him for the rural development through the prudent assimilation of local and global knowledge. From that context, Tagore stands relevant even today and his philosophy of rural reconstruction can definitely be treated as a source of inspiration for all those people and planners of the less developed and developing countries who aspire for a change with a humane face.

REFERENCES

Basu, Madhusudan, (1984), "*Rabindra Sahitye Palli O Sahar*" (Bengali Version), Published by Rathindranarayan Saha, Coochbehar.

Das Gupta, Uma, (1977), "Santiniketan and Sriniketan: A Historical Introduction", a *Visva-Bharati Quarterly Booklet*, Visva-Bharati University, Santiniketan.

Das Gupta, Uma, (1977), "Rabindranath Tagore on Rural Reconstruction: The Sriniketan Experiment", 1921-1941, *The Indian Historical Review*, New Delhi, 1977(a), Vol. IV, No.2.

Elmhirst, L.K., (2004), "*The Diary of Sriniketan*", (Bengali translation by Malina Roy), Published by Chetan Dastidar, Santiniketan.

Kripalani, Krishna, (1971), "*Tagore: A Life*", Orient Longman, New Delhi, 1961, 2nd edition.

Mallick, Sukumar, (1989), "*Rabindranather Pallichinta*" (Bengali version), Nabapatra, Kolkata.

Mazumdar, Debashis, (2006), "Bharater Gramin Unnayan: Rabindra Darshan" (Bengali Version), *Bangabasi Academic Journal* (ISSN: 2249-0655), Vol.3, Published by Bangabasi College, Kolkata, pp. 61-71.

Mukhopadhyay, Arunkumar, (1996), "*Palli Punargathan*" (Bengali Version), Dey's, Kolkata.

Rahman, Atiur, (2010), "Tagore's Thoughts on Rural Credit and Development", Bangladesh Bank, *website*.

Sau, S., (2008), "Approaches to Development: A Critique and Relevance", *Vidyasagar University Journal of Economics*, Vol. XIII.

Sen, Amartya, (1997), *"Tagore and His India"*, New York Review of Books, June, 1997.

Tagore, Rabindranath, (1990), '*Palli Prakriti*', in *Rabindra Rachanabali*, Vol. 13, Government of West Bengal, Kolkata.

Tagore, Rabindranath, (1990), '*Atma Shakti*', in *Rabindra Rachanabali*, Vol. 13, Government of West Bengal, Kolkata.

Tagore, Rabindranath, (1990), '*Samabay Niti*', in *Rabindra Rachanabali*, Vol. 13, Government of West Bengal, Kolkata.

Tagore, Rabindranath, (1928), '*Sriniketan—The Institute of Rural Reconstruction*', Santiniketan: Visva-Bharati.

Thompson, E.P., (1991), '*Introduction, to Tagore's Nationalism*', MacMillan, London.

Todaro, Michael, P. and Stephen. C. Smith, (2003), '*Economic Development*' (8th Edition), Pearson Education, Delhi.

Unnithan, T.K.N. (1997), A Gandhian Approach to environmental, human ecological and developmental chanlenges in Sing, R. (ed.), *op. cit.*

Young, Michael, (1982), "The Elmhirsts of Dartington: The Creation of an Utopian Community", Routledge. 07314739100.

17
Development of Rabindrasangeet Industry
A Sociological Study

Susmita Bhattacharyya

Introduction

Music is the artistic representation of human emotion. In the language of sociology, it can be said that music is sum total of different symbols. These symbols are related with meanings. So, music is meaningful interplay of various signs and symbols. These meanings are interpreted by listeners in different ways and perspectives. According to that debunking of meanings, various combinations of listeners are getting involved in music. Rabindrasangeet is full of literary as well as spiritual resource. Hence there are several possibilities of subjective interpretations in the sphere of Rabindrasangeet. Thus this particular genre becomes the area of interest for not only cultural world, but for the academic field also. This overwhelming interest in Rabindrasangeet ultimately takes the shape of Rabindrasangeet industry. The aim of this chapter is to highlight the process of development of Rabindrasangeet industry in Bengal with respect to the reasons and major consequences.

Objectives

There are several objectives of this study. These are—

(a) to determine the potential of Rabindrasangeet as an industry,
(b) to analyse the reasons behind this,
(c) to define the process of dispersion,

(d) to describe the features of this process,
(e) to infer the logic of this process, and
(f) to summarize the consequences of this process.

Methodology

The study has done in Kolkata among the listeners of Rabindrasangeet from various age group. Questionnaire is used for gathering data and opinion of the listeners. For some special cases method of interview is used. Purposive sampling is the most appropriate method in this study because only the listeners associated with Rabindrasangeet are selected as samples. Explanatory research design is used for the purpose of causal interpretation.

Music Industry

Indian music industry is the oldest and the most reputed entertainment sector. Music is the bridge of interaction between two inseparable groups —the creators of music (Singer, instrument player, persons who are associated with production of music) and the receivers of the music. The interaction between two groups can be direct (live performance) and indirect (recorded performance). The role of music industry is important in the sphere of indirect interaction, i.e. recorded performance. In today's world of music cultural marketing as an idea predominates. As a specific genre Rabindrasangeet plays the most important role in the process of marketing.

Music industry depends on listeners' choice of music. The act of listening is a response to a particular pattern of music. This trend is prevalent in listeners of Rabindrasangeet also. Act of listening is somewhat related to pyramid of communication. It can help to analyse the ways of spreading music from individual to societal level. (Intrapersonal →Interpersonal→ intra group→ Inter group→ institution/organization→ society wide). Whole society is involved in the process of spreading music. At an echelon under that of whole society, there are several kinds of musical network. One type involves the larger society at the regional level, city or town another is presented by the organizational level. It should be related with multiple areas of operation. But those factors should be integrated within their own organizational boundaries. Another variety is represented by institution. Following this level there are varied types of communication level. This level is based on some shared features of daily life. Here, the key questions concerned are attachment and identity, co-operation and norm formation. At the inter- group and inter-personal levels, attention is emphasized on forms. As Rabindrasangeet crosses the national boundary, the members of listening group increases day-by-day in cross-national periphery. The listeners are product of different conversation, pattern of interaction, influence, affiliation (i.e. degree of attachment) and normative control. At the inter-personal level, processing information deserves attention. The process of globalization makes communication easily accessible. So, music as an object of communication is not limited to a specific region. The impact of globalization on local culture and the changing role of the nation-state can be examined by observing the particularities of the social and cultural patterns and their local, national and transnational manifestations in India. Rabindrasangeet is no longer confined to West Bengal and Bangladesh today, it swam across the oceans, across-borders and is now at the rudder at western countries too. Anyone can have access to Rabindrasangeet in this era of global communication, i.e. an extension of cultural globalization.

Music is undoubtedly a form of art. Milton C. Albrecht examined art as an institution. According to him art serves basic human need. Sociologists are divided into two groups in terms of the role of art in human life. Some sociologists define art as a major institution, but some others give it secondary importance. Music is accepted by most of the sociologists as an institution. Some features are specifically indicated as the institutional character of music. Those features are associated with music as an object of industry. Technicality or technical system is such a feature. Songs, musical instruments, voice, singing skill and similar factors can be treated as components of technicality. This kind of technicality is prominently present in the sphere of Rabindrasangeet. The role of technology is very important in this part. Actually modern music is revolutionized by technology. World of music revolves around new musical instruments. Rabindrasangeet is no exception. Modern instrumentation becomes part and parcel of Rabindrasangeet of new era. Skill of singing should be coordinated to the instrumentation. Rabindrasangeet singers must be technically sound enough to persist in music trade. In Rabindrasangeet the content is constant but the forms change depending upon the stylization. Sometimes, it is said that the stylization depends upon institutional training. Hence, institutional differentiation can be taken as a causative factor here. Production of music and reward system involves organizers, patrons, concert promoters and agents with their associates. Music critics and reviewers are inseparable parts of industry. They convey their as well as other listeners' view-point to the singers. In Rabindrasangeet all these features are present. In case of Rabindrasangeet it is observed that people are very much sensitive as well as interested in this genre. So huge mass concentration becomes a basic feature of Rabindrasangeet. Media now play a constructive role in spreading music to the listeners. In Kolkata, by and large, musical programmes and performances are associated with Rabindrasangeet. Thus, the spread effect of Rabindrasangeet is highly dispersed in Bengal in specific and Kolkata in particular. The all encompassing impact of Rabindrasangeet helps to develop this genre as an object of industry.

Market statistics shows that Rabindrasangeet has a stable market during last thirty years. Several times downfall takes place in filmy songs and modern Bengali songs, but the situation is completely different in this case. The industry of Rabindrasangeet is subject to least demand—fluctuation, i.e. minimal ups and downs. Normally, it is accepted that the choice of music varies depending upon age, sex and class positions. Surprisingly, this factor is relatively weak in case of Rabindrasangeet. In spite of differential age, sex, education and family background most of the people of Bengal are keen receivers of Rabindrasangeet. As a consequence Rabindrasangeet becomes the most popular as well as marketable product of Bengali music industry.

Process of Operation

Industry has certain features. Etzioni explained the characteristics of organization as sum total of division of labour, power and communication responsibilities with realization of specific goals. One or more power centres are present in the organization for the performance and re-patterning of structure. The third feature is the substitution of personnel if necessary. The division of work is perfectly done in Rabindrasangeet industry with clear cut division of desk job, marketing and sales department. There is a selection committee for the purpose of maintaining quality of production. Production of music is entirely goal oriented. Cassettes and CDs of Rabindrasangeet are mainly released during April to May season (this period is popularly known as *Kabipakhkha*). This proves the inherent commerciality of Rabindrasangeet industry. The very existence of departmentalization indicates that there is the presence of multiple power centres to control. The structure of modern music has undergone a thorough change now-a-days. Hence, a constant need of re patterning is there. Rabindrasangeet industry is concentrating on appointing professionals for the specialized jobs.

In case of Rabindrasangeet the singers have to reach to the consumers, i.e. listeners through the music companies. Here, the companies play the role of agents. The companies also play the actions as distributors. Rabindrasangeet singers are very much anxious in using instruments though new kind of musical arrangements and orchestration are commonplace in Rabindrasangeet today. Companies are taking necessary steps for the job of recording. Promotional activities are associated with distributional system.

Normally, music industry is comprised three main segments—artist, agents and distributing component. Various sub-components are there to perform the function properly.

Producing, reproducing and distributing music become cheaper day-by-day. As a consequence many small and independent record companies can enter in the music market. Music Companies Act normally as organization here, they mediate between consumers and producers. According to Ryan and Peterson a model of decision chain in the popular music industry can be represented by six separate links—(1) from song writing to publishing, (2) from demo tape to recording (where producer and artists are selected), (3) and (4) from recording to manufacturing and marketing, (5) and (6) from there to consumption *via* radio, live performance or direct sales. All these play part in promoting the product in several markets. In the sphere of Rabindrasangeet the question of writing songs did not arise. So, the process of decision sequence of Rabindrasangeet should start from recording. Then the steps of diagram should be followed.

Hierarchy

Industrial workers are organized on a hierarchical basis. In Bengali music industry an occupational pyramid can emerge in present day situation. The situation will look like following structure:

MD
↓
Middle Management
↓
Supervisor
↓
Desk Job Workers
↓
Office Workers

In Bengali music industry as well as in the sphere of Rabindrasangeet the Managing Director takes all the major decisions. Management here plays the contributory role through departmentalization of entire industry. Written papers are maintained by office workers. Physical function of manufacturing and distributing musical products are performed by blue collar workers. This part is related to manual labour.

Causes

Technological development creates a complete transformation in music. It brings economic environment in music industry. Rabindrasangeet is not an exception. Information technology and internet allow musicians to offer their music directly to the consumers. Thus, new intermediaries get opportunity to enter in the music market. People can buy music conveniently with the help of this system. Now increasing use of IT is found in the sphere of music. In case of Rabindrasangeet geographical boundaries start to get dissolved. Technological change has another great impact. New technology is imposed upon the old uses of music. As a result, the old music changes due to different treatments. At the same time new streams of music begin to develop. Rabindrasangeet as a genre is a perfect reflection of this scenario. Another change has been the rapid development of new ways of recording, storage and retrieval of sound. It is fact that new technology attracts new generation. Rabindrasangeet by Pankaj Kumar Mallick was completely rejected by the young generation but the same song by Kishor Kumar was accepted as hit song. The innovation of CD players shifts the control of reception time from senders to receivers. As a result, homogeneity of the listeners declines because of individualization in behaviour and personalization of choice. Interactive use of various media changes the domain of listening. One way system of listening to music now becomes two or multiple network oriented. The significant interconnectedness of new techniques underlies the logic of growth of the act of listening. There is internationalization of transmission and reception. Listeners are no longer confined to one place or within one set of cultural boundaries. In this age of cultural globalization the listeners have access to their favourite Rabindrasangeet from most of the major corners of the world.

Initially music is qualitative factor but marketability of the music makes it quantitative. There are many reasons of this transformation. Western contact is the first cause of change within music industry. The first reaction of European listeners to Indian music was that it was monotonous and melancholic. According to their thought process Indian music seemed repetitive. It was difficult to understand when it started and when it ended. The picture is completely transformed now-a-days. The singers of Rabindrasangeet are now frequently going to western part of the world for the performances on Rabindrasangeet. Rabindranath Tagore very much influenced by western music and melodies. Rabindrasangeet with Western influence has a stable demand in the west. Bango sanskriti sammelon put great emphasis on Rabindrasangeet. The treatment of Rabindrasangeet there is totally different. The listeners are highly affected there by western instrumentation. Hence Rabindrasangeet has to go parallel with that trend. So, it can be said that this kind of contact with listeners from different background encourages singers of Rabindrasangeet to change their traditional form of representation.

The emergence of new educated middle class is related with the revival of interest in Rabindrasangeet. Different organizations of music were founded. Music colleges, Rabindrabharati University and Vishwabharati University were and are associated with the promotion of Rabindrasangeet. The academic aspects of Rabindrasangeet are taught there professionally. In fact the upper, upper-middle and middle class graduates, government officials, lawyers, teachers, doctors, engineers, young industrialists and media personalitics started to take special interest in Rabindrasangeet. There are various uses of Rabindrasangeet in sophisticated films that increased its popularity among common men. There are several examples like *je rate mor duar guli (meghe dhaka tara), aami chini go chini (charulata), bhalobasi bhalobasi (shwet pathorer thala), charono dhorite deogo aamare (dadar kirti).*

There are different musical schools in urban centres mainly. In recent years people have began to learn music in this type of schools. There are many established schools with active cultural orientation. Interested people can attain the status of singer in colleges, neighbourhood and family. They can earn their livelihood by using music as their profession. This helps to increase people's interest in Music. In the sphere of Rabindrasangeet this trend of institutional training is very popular.

Today's world of Rabindrasangeet is related with the upcoming concept of professionalism. Rational and calculable attitudes are two inseparable features of professionalism. Professionalism occurs in the career prospect of Rabindrasangeet singer. A typical trend in modern Rabindrasangeet singers is marked by listeners. Previously Rabindrasangeet was treated as a specific and specialized genre by the singers. So a group of conventional Rabindrasangeet singers were associated with this. Hence, the singers who sang Rabindrasangeet are not related to other genre normally. Hemanta Mukherjee was an exception. Today's Rabindrasangeet has lost this kind of specificity, i.e. particularism. Now, it is completely commercialized. Hence, by and large Bengali singers are related to it. In modern media age music industry is connected with monetary factor. Musicians earn their livelihood in different ways through music industry. Rabindrasangeet is the most important object in the music market of Bengal. Many people are employed in universities and schools as music teachers. Actually financial upward mobility is the cause of the change of social status of the musicians.

A variety of organizations in large urban areas sponsor musical events. Success in concert tours abroad by eminent artists has encouraged many people related to music to freelance in Western world. The return with the abroad marking has become a notable symbol of success and matter of prestige. Few musicians survive on musical performances, while majority of them have to seek some other form of livelihood. TV programmes and reality shows are the popular kind of representation. These kinds of programmes can add additional glamour to their status. As for example a special music competition was arranged by Tara music on Rabindrasangeet.

Listeners are the products of social context which includes the nature of socialization and interaction. The act of listening is a response to a particular pattern of music. Rabindrasangeet represents 'high culture'[1] of Bengal. The specific listeners of Rabindrasangeet generally come from a specific class background. Most of them are the members of middle, upper middle and upper classes. Normally they are very conscious of their tastes, preferences and inclination, but there are various kinds of combinations among the listeners. Listening to music can be direct as well as indirect. Direct listening to music involves live performances on musical shows. Indirect listening to music means the listening to music through technical devices like tape recorder, CD player etc. There are some remarkable differences between these two forms of response of listeners. Direct listening is not only related to the performance, but with the presentation of the performer in the stage (Dress Code, Behaviour), interaction of Artist with the listeners.

It is difficult to trace all the members of the listening group. Actually group of listeners are aggregates of consumers. Apparently, they are unrelated to each other. They do not have any kind of shared identity. Sometimes, they form a group, but the formation of the group is completely temporary. The concept of selectivity is related to choice of the object of listening. This character can be distinguished between ritualized and instrumental pattern of use. Ritualized listening refers to habitual and frequent listening with a strong affinity with media. This kind of listeners are habituated with all kinds of music. Instrumental listening, on the other hand, is purposeful and intentional. Thus, there are some music lovers who are only associated with Rabindrasangeet. They are not at all interested in other genre of Bengali songs.

Personal tastes and preferences attract the listeners for selecting specific music depending upon the genres, format and specific items of content. Economic condition of the listeners also determines the choice of listening to music. Listeners can be able to pay the price of CD on the basis of his/her strength of pocket. So, economic availability refers to the economic potential to be a listener. Awareness of choices available, the amount and kind of information possessed play a part in the formation of group of listeners. Active listeners can be expected to plan their use of music accordingly. Rabindrasangeet lovers must know their favourite sub-genre of songs. There should be specific content of using music as a listening object. The use of music varies from one situation to another. It is related with the location of the act of listening to music. The place of listening to music (at home, at workplace, travelling etc.) can influence the character of the experience as well as the process of choice making. In situation of formal settings like office music makes the work attractive. It destroys the monotony of work. It plays the role of motivating factor. Sometimes, people love to listen to music during the period of driving. Young students like to solve mathematical problems with the rhythm of music. It will increase their level of concentration. In informal settings like home music plays the role of relaxing factor.

There is a clear trend of change in the composition of the group of listeners. Listeners can listen to music from various sources now-a-days. FM radio, specific music channels, availability of CDs are the associated factors. Commercialization in the field of music is the core element of this trend. Rabindrasangeet is popularized among the young generation when it is used in films. The consequence of this is the abundance of supply in response to the demands. Supply in considerable amount increases the choice option of individuals. Adding to this factor there is a gradual increase in reception possibilities as apparatus becomes cheaper. Decrease in cost of CD Players, P.C. and mobile set with music players are the proof. Another change has been the rapid development of new ways of recording, storage and retrieval of sound.

A thorough change takes place in the sphere of music. Art of listening to music is no exception. Considerable increase in listening objects, kinds of music, more musical channels—all are the indicators of complete transformation of the world of music. The explanation for growth lies in increasing demand of listening object. New distribution and production technologies are compiled with low cost. Technological change is the sole responsible factor for the leap of demand. New mode of electronic recording, storing, transmitting of sounds make music more attractive to listeners. As a result diverse groups are now involved in the act of listening to music.

Since, Second World War, commerce and industry have become globalized. TNCs play important role in global economy. National issues may be influenced by international scenario. In this era of internationalization, the field of music is going through various changes. Hence, the responding part of music, i.e. listeners have to be transformed in quality. Informatization is a new trend of today's world. Information society is the consequence of growth of information based occupations. This kind of society revolutionizes the act of listening to music. Intervention of other medium also revitalizes the music like Rabindrasangeet. With the popularization of VCDs of Rabindrasangeet, new listeners become keen receivers of it.

Listeners of music are isolated individuals in this atomized society. It is true that the rise of mass media increased the possibility for solitary attention. It also reduces the dependency of individuals on other people for human contacts. But as a social act listening to music is typically very sociable. Listeners to a particular genre like Rabindrasangeet can make a group of their own. They are discussing about the listening object with each other. The sociability of their behaviour has several aspects. Some people become attentive listeners to Rabindrasangeet in order to maintain peer relationships. Sometimes, listening to music turns into a basis for conversational exchange and thus informal relations and social contacts increase day-by-day. So, listening to music has two opposite aspects. It creates collectivity of like minded listeners. Simultaneously, it dissociates individuals from one another as a solitary receipient of music.

Music can be considered as an institution because here the main activity is the production and distribution of symbolic context. The participation of senders, i.e. creators of music and receivers, i.e. listeners are voluntary. Organization of music is professional and bureaucratic in form. Differentiating forms of listening to music involves certain factors—place (inside or outside home), experience (individual or shared), purpose (public or private use) and interaction (interactive or not).

Music Industry = Direct Listeners + Indirect listeners

Direct listeners are associated with live stage performances. Indirect listeners listen to music through technological devices. Music industry is mainly concerned with indirect listeners. They are the consumers of music market. Recording companies are very much interested about the choice of indirect listeners.

Listening to music can have collective response in a wider sense. But it is also individualized or privatized. So, the socio-cultural background of the individual plays an important role in the act of listening to music. But it can be said undoubtedly that the meanings and contents of the listening objects differ on the basis of the situation. The famous Rabindrasangeet "*pravu aamar priyo aamar paramo dhano he*" can be taken as an example of it. If listeners are collectively listening to the song, then it becomes a tribute to the Supreme God. So, at that time this is a devotional song. But when a listener is listening to this song alone, then it appears to be a song of love—which is dedicated to the 'loved' one. Hence, in the former situation the word '*pravu*' is more important than '*priyo*'. But the reverse is true for the latter.

Self-interested listeners are seeking utility when they are listening to music. The idea of utility varies according to different age structure. In the old age religious utility can be served by music. Rabindrasangeet lovers of old age like "*Jibono Jakhon shukaye jay*" whereas young children like "*aamra sabai raja*" as a medium of serving their utility. Actually, listeners are getting involved with the listening object. Here involvement means affective arousal through music. Sometimes the involvement occurs within the individual. "*Hridoy aamar prokash holo*" of Rabindranath Tagore is an excellent example of such kind of bonding of individual with one's self, i.e. the core of heart. "*Ak sutre badhiachi sahosroti mon*" signifies the collective involvement of the listeners. Collective involvement can easily make a group of listeners. They are talking back to the listening to music. They are talking about the listening object to other listeners. The pattern of listening to music to some extent depends on the background of the listeners. Social background mainly indicates the influence of family. Socialization orients the individual to his/her musical tastes. Love for Rabindrasangeet primarily comes from family. But sometimes peer pressure also plays a negative role in this contest. An individual can for example, dissociate himself/herself from the family due to peer-influence. Age factor also is an important variable for the determination of listening pattern. Rabindrasangeet is not accepted by the children and even the young adults in most of the cases. Up to age 18 people like high power oriented songs. So, during this period they are not attached to listening to Rabindrasangeet but gradually with the increase of age, listeners become attracted to Rabindrasangeet. (On the basis of a survey of '200' college students of Kolkata in the year 2010-2011) 80 per cent of them told the present researcher that after attaining maturity, they are getting interest in Rabindrasangeet.

The act of listening to music depends on different genre. Genre can be defined by any category of content. It has a specific category. The identity of genre is accepted and recognized by the listeners to music of that particular genre more or less equally. This identity should be related to the purpose of listeners. Genre can be determined by the structure and pattern of the listening object. Genre tends to preserve a specific cultural form. Rabindrasangeet represents a typical genre of Bengali music. There can be various additions and alterations within a particular genre. Rabindrasangeet exemplifies an excellent proof of it. A particular structure is followed by genre. But there can be multiform of change. Traditional Rabindrasangeet was presented in a specific way. The role of background music was least important in Rabindrasangeet until 80s. But after that application of technology has revolutionized Rabindrasangeet. Conservative listeners are not accustomed with these new versions. Yet the new form gains popularity among flexible listeners.

Individualism is regarded as a major factor in this age of commercialization. Class system is said to be weaker. Now democratic cultural and political arrangement emerges with service based economy. There are tendencies of decreasing social solidarity, more privatization and weaker collective ties. Family and religious institutions are said to be in decline. As a consequence, individualism becomes the most dominating idea of today. Listening to music as a social act depends mainly on individual's choice. Though the content of listening music is social, but listening to music is a privatized activity. It may cause clear compartmentalization within family members. Old people like to listen to Rabindrasangeet. But young group finds it melancholic and monotonous. So in case of likings of Rabindrasangeet a generation gap takes place prominently. A midway of liking and disliking is represented by fusion Rabindrasangeet. This kind of genre is a new entry in the field of Rabindrasangeet. "*Pagla haowar badal dine*" is an example of fusion Rabindrasangeet. The new version is not accepted by the older people and conservative listeners to Rabindrasangeet. But younger generation is keenly interested in this sub-genre. Some kind of acceptance is established in case of Rabindrasangeet of Bangla Band. A fusion of different sub-genre takes place in this trend.

In as much as "the new global" culture owes its existence to powerful media empires and transnational companies promoting a culture of consumption that announces the arrival of the era of "boundarylessness," (Rao, 1996) as a global cultural signifier. In other words, global culture seen through a desire for the dissolution of boundaries in order that personal freedom and free trade be facilitated and at the very same moment articulates distinct cultural characteristics that are "innate markers of difference" (Rao,1996).

Consequences

Social transformation in Rabindrasangeet has positive as well as negative effects. Positive effects are more than one in number. Now, most of the singers of Bengali music industry are interested in singing Rabindrasangeet due to extension of market. National level singers are taking part there. Another striking feature is involvement of Bangla band in this genre. The demand for this genre is increasing day-by-day. This encourages big corporate houses to invest on Rabindrasangeet. Initially older people were related with this. Young generation thinks this genre melancholic and monotonous. But this situation has changed thoroughly with the introduction of fusion music and new kinds of instrumentation. So, the traditional age barrier breaks down. Hence, Rabindrasangeet cannot be treated as property of older generation. The myth of generation gap centring Rabindrasangeet has disappeared now. Previously, this genre is related with upper and upper-middle class educated people. This class based distinction is totally obsolete today. People of all spheres of life are now listeners of Rabindrasangeet. Now, Rabindrasangeet is used in films and serials in a considerable amount. This effort helps to popularize Rabindrasangeet in a great manner. The market statistics show that Rabindrasangeet faces least ups and downs in comparison to other musical products of Bengali music industry. Now, the industry of Rabindrasangeet involves a lot of common people in its fold. There is only one negative effect of this transformation. Sometimes, the use of Rabindrasangeet becomes unnecessary and forced. Actually the directors think that their product will be the indicator of 'high culture' with the use of Rabindrasangeet. But this attempt is not always fruitful.

There can be many perspectives for understanding the situation. In most of the cases one perspective dominates over others. Industrial logic plays significant role in large media industries. These include production process, content selection, formation of listeners and technological innovations. This is related to media market. These components can be represented through broader institutional aspects. An organizational logic operates within specific circumscribed limits on the basis of different goals. The running of media organization, co-operative work process and the achievement of goal are parts of the whole complex. Technological logic is related to capacities and qualities of a particular technology for collecting, processing, producing and transmitting media content. Sometimes, technological logic is embedded within organizational logic. Cultural logic is more complex factor. It signifies the culture of mass media. Cultural logic includes advertisement, limited set of aims, changing modes and styles.

Theoretical Background

This transformation in the world of Rabindrasangeet theoretically stands well interpreted by the Social structural approach (McQail, 1994: 9). It gives attention to media system and organization and their relationship to society. Like other genre of music Rabindrasangeet has its own structure. It helps to maintain a stable self-regulating balance between demand and supply. The Behavioural Approach (McQuail, 1994: 9) focuses on the behaviour of the individual in the context of listening. Individuals can be classified according to relevant variables like social positions and behaviour. The cause of preference of music of listeners can be determined by this model. Socio-cultural approach deals with the particular social context of the listeners. According to this the musical preferences of the listeners depend upon the pattern of family and the process of socialization. In case of Rabindrasangeet family helps to grow the musical tastes of the listeners. As a theory, functionalism explains social institutions in terms of the society and of individuals. In case of music the needs are mainly associated with continuity, order, integration, motivation and so on. Music as a form of entertainment provides individual reward, relaxation and reduction of tension. It helps people to cope with the problem of life. In this context Parsonian concept of latency and pattern maintenance of AGIL model (Turner,1995: 69) can be applied here. Self-interested listeners are seeking utility when they are listening to music. The idea of utility varies according to different age structure.

Music is a part of cultural industry 2. The Frankfurt School [Turner, 1995 : 184] 3 in its extensive study of cultural industry found that cultural industry implies the entertainment oriented industry. They argue that the spread of culture industry undermines the capacity of individual for critical and independent thought. They opined that art disappears in this age of commercialization. Market becomes the determining force in the sphere of art. Post-modernism undermines the traditional concept of culture. Traditional notion of culture emphasizes on fixity. Post-modern culture opposes this kind of fixation. In Rabindrasangeet there are various signs of post-modernism. '*Koto kalo robe bolo bharoto re*' or '*kali kali bolo re aaj*' can be remembered as examples of post-modern culture of Rabindrasangeet. Actually post-modernism refers to social, economic and technological development through the proliferation of media. Habermas analyses the importance of public sphere in this context. In public sphere various issues emerge. It is the birth place of different debates and a place where individuals come together as equals. They form a forum of discussion. It can be said that the existence of public sphere is marked in Rabindrasangeet. 'Bishwo bidya tirtho prangano' is an example of this. Baudrillard related the spreading of media with the new reality. This is known as hyper reality (Ritzer, 2007: 482) Hyper reality is created and composed by the interaction of people and media image. '*Basanti he bhubano mohini*' is such a composition of Tagore. This is a splendid description of spring nature and the listeners feel a complete detachment from the reality whenever they are listening this type of song. Thus, hyper reality is created by Rabindrasangeet. Walter Benjamin in his classic essay "The Work of art in the Age of Mechanical Reproduction" draws a theory about the revolutionary qualities of media technologies. Rabindrasangeet is no longer tied to the ritual of the concert hall—where tickets are costly. There is a transition from ritual to exhibition value. This is a transition from original use value to reproducible exhibition value. Raymond Williams argued that the history of communications follows the same pattern in different societies. He told that there emerge forms of information and entertainment communications caused by social and cultural demand. In case of Rabindrasangeet this is highly prevalent and it is able to create market and consumer demand so this genre is now related to the entertainment industry.

Transformation in the sphere of Rabindrasangeet is not a new phenomenon. The process has started from the period of contact with the Western world. In terms of sociology it can be said that the process of westernization is the stepping stone of commercial voyage of Rabindrasangeet. Bango Sanskriti Sammelan plays an important role as the initiator of cultural communication across-national boundary. Adoption of proper technology is an added factor today because technology transforms the area of music. Rabindrasangeet is equipped with modern technical devices. Modern technical instruments are utilized in Rabindrasangeet as accompaniment. Presence of music players in cell phones, FM radio, CD facilities in car and the availability of various music channels create a quantitative leap among the listeners of Rabindrasangeet. Now, the listeners are accustomed with on going musical wave. The bureaucratic structure of Rabindrasangeet is concentrated in rational application. Due to its industrial set-up rationality is viewed in business strategy also. There is a constant debate over the quantitative *versus* qualitative aspects of Rabindrasangeet. Quantitative aspects deal with number of cd released in a particular period of time, amount of investment, profit, loss and so on. Qualitative aspect deals with the impact of Rabindrasangeet among the listeners. The debate is never ending.

The present researcher has undertaken a small survey with the listeners of Rabindrasangeet. An interview schedule was used for data collection. The age group starts from 18 years. Because the impact of Rabindrasangeet cannot be studied properly before 18 years. Up to age 18 people like more or less high power oriented song they are not the target listeners of industry of Rabindrasangeet also. Table 17.1 depicts the age groups with respect to their opinion about listening to Rabindrasangeet.

Table 17.1: Age Distribution of the Respondent on the Basis of Traditionaland Fusion Rabindrasangeet

Age Group	*Traditional Rabindrasangeet*	*Fusion Rabindrasangeet*	*Total*
18-25 (Young)	8	32	40
25-35 (Young Adult)	24	16	40
35-50 (Adult)	28	12	40
50-60 (Mature Adult)	36	4	40
60 and Above	40	0	40
Total	**136**	**64**	**200**

Source: Primary Survey.

The data in Table 17.1 show that 80 per cent young listeners (Table 17.1 shows that 32 among 40) are attracted by fusion Rabindrasangeet. They find the traditional pattern of Rabindrasangeet very monotonous. 60 per cent of the total respondents say that children are not interested in this genre. Rabindrasangeet is too serious for their adaptation. 80 per cent of the total respondents say that transformation has taken place in this type of music. They regarded that the existence of new technology along with its application has changed the world of music. Rabindrasangeet is also associated with that change. In case of this genre, instrumentation and new arrangements are causative factors for this entire transformation. They agreed about the marketability of Rabindrasangeet in music market. This is crystal clear from the survey that age factor acts as an important variable here for the determination of listening pattern. Generally, people are non-interested listeners of Rabindrasangeet in earlier age. But the situation changes gradually. In fact, with the increase of age the interest on Rabindrasangeet comes to the surface. Table 17.1 shows that attraction towards fusion Rabindrasangeet decreases with increase of age. Modern technical adoption and fusion Rabindrasangeet have indicated a clear change in the response pattern of this genre. This change of cultural environment has a positive impact on the spreading effect of this genre.

Commercialization helps to maintain this on going wave of music for the listeners. It can be said that man is a social animal. Therefore, the act of listening starts from the individual—but it has the ultimate expression through collective response. Various social attributes are associated with this act. Hence, listening to music entirely depends on social milieu for its creation as well as its execution. Rabindrasangeet is mainly treated as a qualitative resource of Bengal. Commercialization as a process has transformed the world of music. Rabindrasangeet is now compared with an industrial product. An aesthetic debate takes place here. The debate is concerned not the aesthetic aspect of Rabindrasangeet only, but the marketability of this genre also. In fine it can be said that the eternal worth of Rabindrasangeet cannot be ignored by anyone.

NOTES

1. For Bourdieu taste in cultural goods functions as a marker of class and in Distinction (1984) he seeks to map out the social field of the different tastes in legitimated high cultural practices (museum visits, concert going, reading) as well as taste in life styles and consumption preferences (Bourdieu, 1984:128-29).
2. Culture industry is the rationalized, bureaucratized structures that control modern culture. The culture industry, producing what is conventionally called 'mass culture', is defined as the administered non-spontaneous, reified, phony, culture rather than the real thing.
3. The Frankfurt School is a complex phenomenon, and the style of social thought, which has come to be principally associated with critical theory.

REFERENCES

Baker, T.L., (1994), *Doing Social Research*, McGraw Hill, Inc.

Bourdieu, P., (1984), *Distinction: A Social Critique of the Judgement of Taste*, Harvard University Press.

Corbetta, P., (2003), *Social Research*, Sage Publications.

Das Gupta, A. (ed.), (2007), *Music and Modernity*, Thema.

Giddens, A., (2004), *Sociology, Polity.*

McQuail, D., (1994), (3rd ed.) *Mass Communication Theory—An Introduction*, Sage Publications.

Rao, Sangeeta, (1996), Otherwise? The Selling of Global Cultural Difference; *Sanskriti* [a bimonthly publication].

Rao, Subarnalata, (2002), Indian art, music and changing audience world wide; Sangeet Research Academy Proceedings of the seminar on '*Globalization and Indian Music*' (Ed.) Rao, S.; ITC Sangeet Research Academy NCPA and Music Forum, Mumbai.

Ritzer, G., (2007), *Sociological Theory*, McGraw Hill, Inc.

Turner, J.H., (1995), *The Structure of Sociological Theory,* Rawat Publications.

Turner, J.H., (2003), *The Structure of Sociological Theory,* Thomson Wadsworth.

Weber, M., (1958), *The Rational and Social Foundation of Music*, Harvard University Press.

Index

Academic culture, 30, 46, 49
Academic support system, 57–58
Achievement Index (AI), 62, 64–66, 90–92, 94, 158
Achievement parameters, 95–96
Active listeners, 334
Actual class room transactions, 46
Agriculture
 activities, 3, 103
 neglect of, 1, 10
 productivity, 282–283, 320
Agro-forestry, 280
Albrecht, Milton C., 328
Alcoholism, 115
Allocative Efficiency (AE), 152
Alma-Ata, 98
Anaemia, 85–86, 98
Anderson, Michael, 115
Anti-people Impacts of Current Economic Reforms Policies, 3
Anxiety, 12
Arable land, 321, 323
Auto-correlation, 194, 225, 236–239, 242–243
Auto-regressive (AR), 194, 225
Average Actual Cultivated Area, 280

Behavioural pattern, 44, 49
Bengali music industry, 329–331, 338
Benjamin, Walter, 340
Best-practised firms, 128
Bilingual Method (BM), 36
Bi-lingual, 39, 47, 52
Black money holders, 5–6
Breusch-Godfrey test, 194
Bullock Labour (BL), 231, 233, 235–238, 240, 242–243, 245–247, 285, 288–289, 291

Capital
 inflow, 188, 195, 198
 -output ratio, 168–169
 stock, 155–156
Capitalism, 316
 neo-liberal, 2–3
Cash crops, 4, 226–227, 229–231, 246, 264
Caste-dominated region, 42
Central Statistical Organization, 155
Centralized storage arrangements, 264
Charnes, Cooper and Rhodes (CCR), 128, 277
Chemical fertilizers, 236–237, 247, 288
Child
 education, 120
 health, 61–62, 64, 76, 88
 immunization, 98
 labour, 56, 101–105, 107–109, 113, 117–122, 257
 mortalities, 97, 99
 workers, 102–103
Circle Project Coordinator (CPC), 45
Civil practices, 28
Clamouring, 3

Classroom-student ratio, 138
Classroom transactions, 26–30, 34, 39, 44, 48–50, 53–54
Clerk, Collin, 8
Climatic change, 228
Cluster analysis, 67, 92–94
Cluster resource centre, 17
Cobb-Douglas (CD), 152, 157–158, 288, 334, 341
Co-centric education model, 39
Coefficient variation, 21–24, 42, 303, 307
Coelli, Tim, 153–154, 158, 279
Co-integration, 190, 192, 196
Colonial rule, 266
Colonialism, 186
Commercial crops, 251
Commercialization, 334, 337, 340, 342
Community Based Organizations (CBOs), 229
Community Health Centre (CHC), 98
Community ownership, 269
Constant Elasticity of Substitution (CES), 288
Constant Returns to Scale (CRS), 128, 203, 278–279, 291
Constitution of India, 2, 6, 126
Construction activities, 179
Contract farming, 3–4, 10
Contract manufacturing, 151
Co-operative
  movements, 319–320
  policy, 318
Corporate
  led activities, 10
  sectors, 3, 166
Cultivable land, 283
Cultivation
  brinjal, 261
  cabbage, 259
  flower, 252, 257, 259
  groundnut, 261
  mustard, 259, 261
  potato, 259
  practice, 285
Cultural
  industries, 339
  logic, 339
Curricular activities, 35
CWSN, 14, 16, 20

Data Envelopment Approach (DEA), 126–128, 138, 142, 277
Decision-Making Unit (DMU), 128, 277–278
Deforestation of upper catchments, 264
Delivery mechanism, 125–126
Demographic
  factors, 284
  outcome, 60
Dependent variable, 192, 219, 236–239, 241–243
Deprivation, 68, 94, 108, 130, 137, 321
Deprivation Index (DI), 62–63, 66, 91–92, 94
Deprivation parametres, 91, 95–97, 137
Deprived states, 98
Deterministic frontier, 286
Dickey-Fuller (DF), 189
Directive Principle of State Policy, 126
Disabilities, 14
Disabled children, 14
Disadvantaged groups, 14, 56
Distance matrix, 68
District Agricultural Development Office (DADO), 233
District Resource Persons (DRPs), 39, 45–46, 52, 54–55
Domestic
  capital, 203
  duties, 116–117
Drug manufacturing, 150

Economic
  activities, 12, 103
  efficiency, 127, 291, 316
  growth, 4, 11, 15, 60–61, 164, 184, 186–188, 195–196, 198–199, 314–317
  policies, 1–3
  reforms, 1–7, 9, 11, 167, 181, 199
  reform policies, 3, 151

transaction, 230
variables, 190–191
Educational qualification, 30
Efficiency
indicators, 127, 138, 140
measures, 292–293
scores, 127, 151–152, 157, 279
Elementary school education, 12–13, 43, 45, 56–57
Employment
elasticity of output, 173, 181
farm, 177–178
growth, 164, 167–169, 172, 178, 181
non-farm, 167, 177–178, 181
rate, 170–171
ratio, 170
subsidy, 201–203, 211
Encroachment, 264
English language learning, 33, 46
English Language Teaching (ELT), 36, 45
English teaching-learning, 35
Enrolment percentages, 19
Environmental laws, 6
Error Correcting Model (ECM), 191–192, 196
Error correction mechanism, 191
Error correction model, 192, 196, 198
Error Correction Term (ECT), 192, 197
Essential oils, 229–230
Explanatory variables, 153, 156, 218–219, 222–224, 233, 237–239, 241–243, 247
Exportable commodities, 203
Extra-curricular activities, 48–49
External agencies, 1–2, 18, 57
Extremism, 4–5, 10

Factors Explaining Learning Achievement, 26
Farm families, 233, 256, 259
Farming, 228, 230, 282, 320–321
Feedback, 37, 51
Female
employment, 175–176, 179, 181
life expectancy, 71
self-employment, 178, 181
teachers, 127, 129, 141
workers, 176, 178–179, 181
Fertilizer, 285, 289–291
Financial integration variables, 193, 195, 198
Fixed Coefficients (FC), 168
Flow irrigation types, 269
Flower growers, 252, 257, 259
Food security, 10, 227, 282
Foreign capital, 3, 12, 201–203
Foreign Direct Investment (FDI), 12, 184–186, 188
Foreign enclave, 202–203
Foreign exchange, 226, 231, 246
Frontier production function, 286
Functional form of production, 151–152

Gandhian approach, 315–316
Gender discrimination, 71
Gender Parity Index (GPI), 18
Ginger farming, 227, 229–232, 236–237, 242–243, 247
Globalization era, 13, 43
Globalization on Economic Growth, 184
Goulet, Dennis, 319
Government-aided schools, 35
Government-managed schools, 13, 29
Gram Unnayan Committee, 277
Grammar teaching, 35
Granger Causality Test, 189, 191–192
Gross Attendance Ratio (GAR), 219
Gross Domestic Product (GDP), 3–4, 6, 9, 11, 165–166, 168, 171–172, 187–188, 197–198, 226, 231, 315
Gross Enrolment Ratio (GER), 18, 127, 129, 138, 218
Groundnut, 259, 261
Groundwater, 280
Group learning methods, 47

Hazare, Anna, 10
Health facilities, 64, 95, 98, 321
Health for all, 98
Health indicators, 71, 73–74, 86

Hierarchical procedure, 68
HIV, 73, 77, 82
Human capital, 60, 115, 186, 217, 321
Human Development Index (HDI), 125, 299, 308, 310–311
Human resource development, 188, 195, 198
Hyper reality, 340

ICDS centres, 41
Income Index (II), 284, 299, 308, 310–311
Incremental contribution, 222
Indian Economic Reforms, 1–2
Indian Pharmaceutical Industry (IPI), 150–153, 155, 157–158, 160–161
Individualism, 54, 337
Individualization of education, 30
Industrial activity, 108
Industrial policy, 185
Industrialization, 4, 10
Industry classification, 167
Inequality Measurement, 69, 94, 96–98
Infant Mortality Rate (IMR), 63, 69, 71, 75–76, 87
Infant Survival Rate, 71–72
Influence quality education, 48
Information society, 335
Information technology, 12, 166, 331
Information-based learning, 44
In-service teachers training, 43
Integrated Education for Disabled Children, 14
Integrated Water Resources Management (IWRM), 267
Inter-district variation, 131, 134, 136, 140
Internal efficiency, 126
International Institute of Population Science (IIPS), 63
International Labour Organization (ILO), 102
Internet Service Providers (ISPs), 185
Inter-state
 analysis, 88
 variation, 89, 161
 disparity, 131, 134, 136, 140
Irrigation development, 263
Irrigation tanks, 277, 280

Jobless growth, 4, 10–11, 164, 173, 181
Joyful learning, 26–27, 33

Krishi Prajukti Sahayak (KPS), 252
Kuhn, Thomas, 105
Kwiatkowski-Phillips-Schmidt-Shin (KPSS), 189, 195

Labour Productivity (LP), 61, 168–171, 181
 growth of, 172, 181
Land distributions, 272
Land revenue, 321
Land tenure, 284, 314
Landlocked country, 231
Language
 activities, 39
 learning, 28, 31, 35, 52
 skills, 33, 35, 37, 41, 47
 teaching methods, 36
Learning achievement of children, 13, 48–49
Liberalization, 2, 5, 12, 201–202
Life expectancy, 63, 69–71, 73–75, 86
Likelihood Ratio (LR), 152, 157, 196
Linear relation, 219
Listeners
 conservative, 337
 group of, 333–334, 336
 indirect, 336
Listening object, 333–337
Listening Reading Writing and Speaking (LRWS), 27
Literacy, 73, 314
 rate, 125, 127, 219, 299, 308, 310–311

Marginal Physical Productivity (MPPs), 231, 246
Marginal productivities, 203, 256
Marigold, 251, 253, 257, 259, 261
Market economy, 1, 58

Marketability, 331, 342
Marketable product, 329
Material
consumption, 155–156
inputs, 256
Maternal and Child Health in India, 88
Maternal Mortality Rate (MMR), 75
Maximum Likelihood Estimation (MLE), 154, 287, 289
Mega-biodiversity region, 6
MGNREGA, 8–9
Micro-finance, 315, 317
Ministry of Human Resource Development (MHRD), 218
Minority Concentrated Blocks (MCBs), 19
Morbidity Prevalence, 79, 81–82
Mortality rate, 76
Mother tongue, 22, 32, 36–39
MRTP Acts, 150
Mulching, 230, 236–237, 247
Multicollinearity, 156, 222–225
Multi-faculty teachers, 29
Multiple correlation coefficients, 222–223
Music Companies Act, 330
Music industry, 327, 330–331, 333, 336
Muysken, Joan, 60

National Child Labour Policy, 103
National Curriculum Framework (NCF), 26, 32, 41, 44, 46–50, 52–53, 56
National Family Health Survey (NFHS), 63
National Health Policy, 98
National Pharmaceuticals Policy, 150
National Sample Survey Organization (NSSO), 63, 167, 177, 218
Natural logarithms, 157, 187
Natural resources, 11, 267
Negative effects, 186, 338
Neo-classical model, 60
Nepal Agriculture Research Council (NARC), 233
Net Attendance Ratio (NAR), 219
Net Enrolment Ratio (NER), 18–19, 127, 129, 138, 218–219
Non-Economic Factors, 104, 107
Non-English Medium (NEM), 36
Non-farm sector, 167, 177–178, 181
Non-governmental organizations, 101, 317
Non-irrigated land, 276
Non-stationary variables, 190
Non-tax revenue, 299, 303, 305, 308, 310–311
Notional-Functional Syllabus (NFS), 31–32
NPEGEL, 17–18
NREGS, 269–270
Null hypothesis, 189–191, 194–195, 223, 235, 237–240, 242–243

Objective factors, 318
Ordinary Least Squares (OLS), 140, 189, 193–195, 233, 289
Organizational logic, 339
Orientation programme, 45, 51, 53

Pain redresser, 106
Parental income, 115
Parent-teacher workshops, 15
Paschim Banga Sarva Shiksha Mission (PBSSM), 15–17
Patent Act, 150
Peasants, 321–322
Perspective of Indian Economic Reforms, 2
Pesticides, 236–237, 247
Pharmaceutical Industry, 151
Plant Protection Chemical (PPC), 285, 288–289
Policy indicators, 126, 134, 136–137
Policy reforms, 185–186
Political economy, 184
Poor quality of schooling, 104
Post-modernism, 340
Post-reform periods, 179
Poverty alleviation, 314, 317
Pre-reform period, 178–179, 182
Pre-schooling learning, 41

Primary education, 22, 34–35, 49, 108, 125–127, 129
Primary health centre, 98
Privatization, 2–3, 5, 45, 185, 337
Production technologies, 128, 335
Professionalism, 332
Profitability, 252–253
Prostitution, 101–103, 108
Pucca building, 129–131
Pupil-teacher ratio, 127, 129

Qualitative
  analysis, 104–106
  improvement of education, 13
  information, 109
Quality education, 13–14, 26, 30, 41, 44–45, 48–49, 51–52, 55–56, 117
Quality improvement, 33, 48, 51–52
Quality of education, 12, 15, 26, 47–48
Quality of land, 294–295
Quality teachers, 51–52
Quantitative expansion, 13

Rabindrasangeet, 326–338, 340–342
  fusion, 337, 341–342
  generation gap centring, 338
  industry, 326, 329, 338, 341
  listeners of, 327, 333, 338, 341
  singers, 328, 330, 332
  sphere of, 326, 328, 330–332, 340
  traditional and fusion, 341
Rank correlation coefficient, 91–92
RCH Achievement Index, 64–65, 89–90
Recorded performance, 327
Reform
  policies, 3, 5
  process, 2, 7–8
Regional
  diversity, 86
  variation, 63
Regression, 193–194, 252, 279
  coefficients, 219, 222, 235, 239–241, 243, 245, 289, 291
  constant, 235, 237–243
Regressors, 192, 194, 224
Rehabilitation Area (RA), 156, 158, 160
Relative Distance Methodology, 62, 64–65
Reproductive and Child Health (RCH), 62–65, 88–89, 92, 97
Resource mobilization, 301, 303, 320
Retention rate of children, 20
Rhizomes, 226, 229–230
Rote learning, 32, 35
RTE Act, 42
Rural development activities, 322
Rural economy, 314–315, 317
Rural upliftment, 315

Sabar Committee, 277
Sample Registration System (SRS), 63, 70–71, 89
Sampling fraction, 233
Sarva Shiksha Abhiyan (SSA), 14–15, 108
Sarva Shiksha Mission (SSM), 13–16, 18, 26, 40–41, 45, 54, 56
School management, 47
Second green revolution, 4
Self-confidence, 318, 323
Self-esteem, 319
Self-Help Group (SHG), 317
Selfishness, 118
Self-respect, 318–319
Serial correlation, 193–194
Simple English grammar learning, 52
Single teacher schools, 130–131, 140
Smith, Adam, 105
Social acceptance, 7
Social act listening, 335
Social category gap, 14
Social contacts, 335
Social exclusion, 56, 108
Social inclusion, 14–15, 18
Social welfare, 56, 63, 69, 202–203
Socio-cultural environment, 28, 32–34
Soktim Tea Estate (STE), 233
Specialization of teachers, 53
State interventions, 13, 17
State-sponsored tank rehabilitation programmes, 266

Statistical Package for Social Sciences (SPSS), 233
Stochastic Frontier Production Function (SFPF), 150, 152, 156, 158, 287–288, 295
Structural
  approach, 315–316
  changes, 305, 307
Student-classroom ratio, 127, 129
Stylization, 328
Subtropical regions, 226
Summary Statistics, 292–293

Tank Efficiency, 277, 279
Tank Improvement Act, 263
Tank irrigation, 10, 263–264, 266, 268, 272, 280
Target Group Approach, 315, 317
Tax revenue, 299, 307, 310
Tax structure, 311
Tax-to-GDP ratio, 166–167
Tea plantations, 185
Teacher
  awards, 29
  education, 57
  quality, 51
  trainees, 39, 45–46, 51–52, 54–55
  -pupil ratio, 138
Teaching Learning Materials (TLMs), 44, 50, 53–55
Teaching-learning
  participatory, 53
  process, 37, 47, 50
Technical Efficiency (TE), 128, 138–139, 150–155, 157–161, 278, 283–284, 286–289, 291–295
Technical inefficiency, 153–154, 156, 158, 161, 286
Technological
  change, 331, 335
  development, 331, 340
  devices, 336
  innovations, 339
  logic, 339
  reforms, 320
  up-gradation, 185
Tertiary sectors, 165, 181
Timmer, Peter, 283
Topography, 71, 231
Trade-commerce, 178–179
Transfer of skills, 37
Translog specification, 157
Tribal dominated states, 10

Unemployment rate, 169
Universalization of Elementary Education (UEE), 14
Urban unemployment, 202

Value Marginal Productivity of Labour (VMPL), 256
Values of Marginal Productivities (VMP), 256
Variance Inflation Function (VIF), 222
Variance ratio, 287, 291
Village Development Committees (VDCs), 232–233
Vincent, David, 115

Wage subsidies, 202
Wealth inequality, 9
West, Michael, 32
Western practice, 7
Williams, Raymond, 340
Wodon, Quentin, 104
World Development Report (WDR), 9, 71
World Trade Organization (WTO), 9, 201
Writing skills, 29, 35, 37, 39, 52

Zamindars, 319, 321, 323
Zamindari estates, 321
Zonal classifications, 129
Zone, dry, 263, 268